THE THEATER OF PLAUTUS

THE THEATER
OF PLAUTUS

PLAYING TO THE AUDIENCE

TIMOTHY J. MOORE

University of Texas Press
Austin

Frontispiece. Detail of Dioscurides of Samos. Actors preparing for a performance. Mosaic from the House of the Tragic Poet, Pompeii. Late 1st c. C.E. Museo Archeologico Nazionale, Naples, Italy. Courtesy of Alinari/Art Resource, NY.

The publication of this book was assisted by a University Cooperative Society Subvention Grant awarded by The University of Texas at Austin.

Library of Congress Cataloging-in-Publication Data
Moore, Timothy J., 1959–
    The theater of Plautus : playing to the audience / Timothy J. Moore.
        p.   cm.
    Includes bibliographical references and indexes.
        ISBN 0-292-75208-3 (alk. paper). — ISBN 0-292-75217-2 (pbk. : alk. paper)
        1. Plautus, Titus Maccius—Criticism and interpretation.   2. Latin drama (Comedy)—History and criticism.   3. Theater audiences—Rome—History.
    I. Title.
PA6585.M66   1988
872'.01—dc21   98-13014

TO THE MEMORY OF MY GRANDMOTHER

TABLE OF CONTENTS

PREFACE

SOME of my first experiences with the plays of Plautus were as an actor, performing in *Aulularia* and *Mostellaria* while an undergraduate at Millersville University. As a result, when I began to study Plautus more formally, I found the performance-centered work of critics such as Gianna Petrone and Niall Slater most congenial. Inspired by such performance critics and my own experience onstage, I have sought to describe more fully how Plautus's plays may have worked in performance, with particular attention paid to Plautus's actors and their relationship with their audience. In addition to a more thorough view of the roles of actors and spectators, I hope to give readers of Plautus a greater appreciation of the significance of Plautine performance within its social and historical milieu. The book has, I think, much to say to specialists in ancient drama and to classicists in general. At the same time, I would like this book to help bridge a most unfortunate gap: that between classics and theater history, where Plautus—and Roman drama in general—is too often neglected.

I began this work at Harvard University on a Mellon Faculty Fellowship and continued it with a Summer Research Award from the University of Texas at Austin. The Department of Classics at the University of Texas and its two chairs, Michael Gagarin and Thomas Palaima, have been very supportive. David Armstrong, Charlotte Canning, Erwin Cook, Karl Galinsky, Mary Womble Gerdes, Kelvin Gregory, Judith Hallett, Frances Hickson, Jerzy Linderski, and Douglass Parker read parts of the manuscript in earlier versions. Thomas Hubbard, Dan McGowan, Gwyn Morgan, Kenneth Reckford, and Andrew Riggsby were kind enough to read the entire work. The suggestions and critiques of all these readers have been invaluable, as have those of William Anderson, Elaine Fantham, and Sander Goldberg, the readers for the University of Texas Press. Whatever inadequacies remain result from my own stubbornness or negligence. I received help in preparing the manuscript from John Erler, Jesse Harvey, and Chris Williams, and from Jim Burr, Sherry Wert, and the editorial staff at the University of Texas Press. Krista M. Osmundson created the indices. Earlier versions of portions of Chapters 6 and 7 appeared in the online publication *Didaskalia* and *American Journal of Philology* (1991), respectively. A University Cooperative Society Subvention Grant awarded by the University of Texas at Austin helped cover the costs of publication. Many friends, especially Joe and Nancy Golsan, Carol Speer, and Bill Sheldon, provided advice and encouragement when it was most needed. Finally, this book could not have been written without the support of my family, especially Michael Whisenhunt, Wilma Moore, and Richard and Janet Moore.

Unless otherwise stated, citations from Menander, Plautus, and Terence are from the following editions:

Menander, *Aspis* through *Perinthia*: W. G. Arnott (Cambridge, Mass.: Harvard University Press, 1979–).
Menander, other plays: F. H. Sandbach (Oxford: Clarendon, 1990).
Plautus: Friedrich Leo, 2 vols. (Berlin: Weidmann, 1895–96).
Terence: Robert Kauer, Wallace M. Lindsay, and Otto Skutsch (Oxford: Clarendon, 1958).

All translations are my own unless otherwise stated.

THE THEATER OF PLAUTUS

INTRODUCTION

The forms of drama all flow from the confrontation that takes place between any actor and his audience; plays are best understood as ways of intensifying that confrontation and charging it with meaning.

—Michael Goldman

AT the core of any theatrical performance lies the relationship between its two essential components, performer and audience. The first step toward an understanding of any play as a work to be performed, therefore, is an appreciation of the nature of that relationship. This fact presents a great challenge to the student of Plautus, whose plays belong to a performance tradition that vanished some two thousand years ago, leaving almost no evidence of its nature. Plautus's plays were first performed in temporary wooden theaters of which no trace remains. Virtually all the visual evidence used to reconstruct performance—vase paintings from southern Italy, mosaics and wall paintings from Pompeii and other cities, medieval manuscripts of Terence, and remains of later Roman theaters—are the subjects of intense controversy; and Roman writers who describe performances, all of whom lived long after Plautus, are notoriously unreliable. Almost all aspects of performance, therefore, including stages, costumes, and acting styles, remain uncertain.[1] Most distressing of all, though we can, to my mind, be reasonably certain that Plautus's actors wore masks, that question also is controversial.[2]

We do, however, have the texts of twenty of Plautus's plays.[3] As theorists of theater repeatedly remind us, texts are woefully inadequate as substitutes for performance.[4] They represent only a small portion of the complex sign-system at work in the production of a play, and the clues they give as to performance are often open to conflicting interpretations. Texts can nevertheless reveal a good deal about the relationship between actors and audience; for much in the content, style, and structure of a play's script favors certain types of communication between stage and audience over others.

The text is particularly useful in helping us determine how playwright and actors encourage their audience to respond to the psychic paradox involved in watching a play. As any playgoer is aware, spectators at a play simultaneously forget and remember that they are in a theater. They believe, on one level, that the action occurring onstage is "real"; yet at the same time they are aware that what they see is a performance.[5] At any moment of performance, actors can encourage the spectators' forgetful belief by ignoring the audience and maintaining the pretense that their words and actions are "real" rather than part of a performance; or they can encourage awareness of the fact of performance by addressing the audience directly or referring explicitly or implicitly to their own status as performers. This distinguishing factor has been explained in many ways. Plato (*Republic* 3.392d–398b) and Aristotle (*Poetics* 1448a) differentiate between mimetic and diegetic performance.[6] Ingarden offers a distinction between "open" and "closed" theater; Beckerman, between presentation and imitation.[7] The most common way of making the distinction has been to talk about dramatic illusion and the violation or breaking of that illusion.[8] Building on the concept of dramatic illusion, Bertolt Brecht made a distinction between "dramatic" theater, in which performers ignore the fact of performance and communicate with the audience only indirectly, and "epic" theater, where performers strive to keep the audience aware that they are in a theater and that what they observe is a performance.[9]

Whichever theoretical construct we choose, several conclusions become evident. First, all theatrical performances include some aspects that remind the audience that they are in a theater, and others that encourage the audience to forget that they are watching a play. There is, however, a continuum of theatrical traditions from extreme forms of Naturalism, which discourage direct communication with the audience and reminders of the theater, to genres like vaudeville, where such elements are commonplace. Second, the way in which the two modes of communication blend and interact is the central defining characteristic in the relationship between actors and audience, for it determines the extent to which and the manner in which the former acknowledge the existence of the latter. Third, although some reminders of performance—those associated with gesture, posture, inflection, and improvisation, for example—can be appreciated only when a performance is witnessed or described, many, such as explicit audience address and theatrical allusion, will be evident in the text. Thus, though the exact nature of the relationship between actors and audience is in the hands of directors and actors, playwrights can do much to mold that relationship, primarily through their choice of textual elements that encourage direct communication or remind the audience that they are watching a performance. Finally, since all communication between playwright and audience is accomplished through the actors, the way in which playwrights mold the relationship between actors and audience determines to a great extent the meaning and effect of their plays.

Bearing these principles in mind, I offer in the following pages an evaluation of how Plautus molded his actors' relationship with their audience. My primary focus will be on the elements that most affect that relationship: theatrical reminders and direct communication from stage to audience.

The importance of such elements has been acknowledged in the practice, theory, and criticism of theater for some time. Brecht and many other twentieth-century playwrights have made the relationship between actors and audience their central concern, and they have employed many of the effects Brecht would call "epic" to modify that relationship. Brecht himself and others have noted that precedents for modern "epic" theater pervaded earlier drama, especially comedy.[10] Meanwhile, performance critics, evaluating dramatic texts with a sense of performance in mind, have emphasized the importance of what they call "nonillusory" techniques in all theater before the late nineteenth century. Until the rise of Naturalism, they have shown, most drama valued the direct relationship between actors and audience over what later came to be called dramatic illusion.[11] Other critics and theorists have gone still further. A good deal of drama since the Renaissance, they have argued, not only is self-consciously theatrical, but has as one of its main interests the nature of theater itself: it is, to use Lionel Abel's expression, metatheater.[12]

Nor have the nonillusory aspects of Plautus's plays gone unnoticed. To his ancient and modern detractors, Plautus's refusal to maintain the "dramatic illusion" showed that he was a mercenary hack, willing to sacrifice anything for a laugh.[13] Scholars more sympathetic to Plautus have collected many of the relevant passages and proposed connections between audience address, theatrical reminders, and the chronology of Plautus's plays.[14] As all Plautus's plays are almost certainly adaptations of Greek comedies, and it is generally agreed that they are more self-consciously theatrical than their lost Greek sources were, audience address and theatrical reminders have also played an important role in studies seeking to explain how Plautus modified Greek drama.[15] Finally, passages acknowledging the fact of performance, viewed through the perspectives of performance criticism and Abel's theory of metatheater, have inspired one of the most important recent developments in Plautine studies. Analyzing devices such as play-within-the-play, references to characters as actors, and descriptions of disguises as costumes, a number of scholars have demonstrated that Plautus's plays, too, are metatheatrical: that Plautus took great delight in the ambiguous nature of theater; that his plays are filled with continual and conspicuous reminders of the fact of performance; and that portions of many plays are elaborate theatrical metaphors.[16]

Students of Plautine metatheater and other recent critics have thus brought us very far: few would now suggest that Plautus's reminders of performance are unwelcome and inartistic intrusions. In spite of these advances, however, many of the effects of direct address to the audience and theatrical reminders remain unappreciated. A number of questions have not been addressed adequately, among them: Just what does Plautus accomplish through his metatheatrical techniques? How did metatheatrical elements help Plautus's plays to succeed with his audience? What do such elements contribute to the overall effect of individual scenes and of whole plays? How do they relate to the social context of the plays? In short, how did Plautus mold and manipulate the relationship between his actors and their audience, and to what ends? It is to these questions that I dedicate the chapters that follow.

In my first chapter I examine the attitude Plautus encouraged his actors to adopt toward their audience. Plautus's actors, I observe, often appear obsequious: they provide many reminders of their own low social status and their need for the spectators' approval. At the same time, however, they tease, criticize, and even satirize the audience. The license taken by the actors even as they keep the audience aware that they are vulnerable and of low status is an important aspect of the Saturnalian escape that Plautus's plays provided. At the same time, it reveals the readiness of the Roman audience to laugh at themselves, thus opening the door for satire and social commentary.

In Chapter 2 I evaluate the actor-audience relationship from the perspective of the actors as characters. Through monologues, eavesdropping, and other elements, I argue, Plautus created characters who conspicuously desire that the audience sympathize with them and view the action onstage through their eyes. This desire of characters for rapport with the audience contributes much to the humor of Plautus's plays, as characters compete with one another for rapport, and many characters fail to gain that rapport in spite of their efforts. Plautus also creates hierarchies of rapport, as some characters maintain a closer relationship with the audience than others, and variations in rapport, as characters become more or less close to the spectators in the course of a play. In many plays, for example, Plautus's clever slaves attain a high degree of rapport with the audience, but they usually begin with little rapport and become closer to the audience as the play progresses. This delayed rapport makes it easier for the audience to accept the inversion of societal norms inherent in the slaves' successes. As a demonstration of the various ways Plautus manipulates rapport, I conclude the chapter with an examination of Euclio, the miser whose relationship with the audience adds much to the theatrical effectiveness of *Aulularia*.

In Chapter 3 I consider Plautus's allusions to setting. While all of Plautus's plays are set in Greece, they include frequent allusions to things Roman, and actors often remind the audience that the Greek setting is a product of theatrical pretense. After proposing some guidelines for evaluating how different types of geographical allusion would affect an audience, I observe that the allusions contribute significantly to the humor of the plays, to their metatheatrical effect, and to their satire. I conclude the chapter by examining Plautus's use of geographical allusions in connection with his deceptive or pleasure-loving slaves: conspicuous allusions to Greece and Rome, I argue, both distanced Plautus's Roman audience from unacceptable slave behavior and undermined that distance with humorous irony.

Chapter 4 concerns the edifying moral maxims that Romans expected from their theater. Plautus was aware of this expectation, and he frequently fulfilled it: his characters are full of pithy maxims, and Plautus sometimes defends his plays as morally edifying. Yet Plautus's moralistic self-justifications are tinged with irony, and several characters cast doubts on the efficacy of theatrical moralizing. *Miles gloriosus* presents a spectator deceived when he believes that the play-within-the-play offers a moral message, and metatheatrical passages help to undermine the ardent moralizing of Plautus's two most moral-sounding plays, *Rudens* and *Trinummus*.

In the second part of the book I examine six plays that best demonstrate the various ways Plautus molded the actor-audience relationship in response both to the demands of performance and to his social milieu. I begin with two plays where metatheatrical elements play an especially important role in winning over Plautus's audience. In *Pseudolus*, the subject of Chapter 5, Plautus created a tour de force of expected and novel elements and established an unmistakable alliance between the audience and the title character. The result is a play appropriate for the important festival at which *Pseudolus* was first performed. In Chapter 6 I argue that in *Amphitruo*, Plautus used similar techniques in response to the play's generic and religious ambiguities. Plautus averted any discomfort the play's similarities to tragedy might have caused by repeatedly suggesting that he and his actors are making the potentially tragic play a comedy for the sake of the spectators. Another potential source of discomfort was the play's incorporation of the lighter side of Greek mythology. Plautus therefore reminds his audience continually that the mischievous Mercury and Jupiter are not really gods at all, but actors.

Though Plautus's manipulation of the relationship between actors and audience in *Pseudolus* and *Amphitruo* serves primarily to help win over the spectators, in *Curculio* and *Truculentus* the actors' relationship with the audience does much to reinforce satirical messages. I propose in Chapter 7 that well-placed allusions to Rome make clear that the deception in financial matters that pervades *Curculio* is as much a problem in Rome as it is in Greece; this association of the characters' deception with Rome comes to a head in the monologue of the costume manager, who suggests that people like the swindlers who inhabit the stage world are present in the audience itself. In Chapter 8 I argue that the satire of *Truculentus* is directed even more powerfully at the spectators themselves. Roman allusions suggest that the plight of the profligate lovers who inhabit the play is a Roman phenomenon, and monologues, audience addresses, and eavesdropping implicate the spectators in the machinations of the greedy prostitutes who control the plot. Similar techniques discourage the spectators from dismissing the plot as an example merely of the vices of women.

In my final two chapters I examine some more complex and daring connections between the actor-audience relationship and the social and historical surroundings of Plautus's plays. In Chapter 9 I propose that *Casina* represents an undermining of conservative views on contemporary controversies about marriage. By disappointing his audience's expectations and manipulating their rapport with Cleostrata, who overcomes her husband, Plautus encourages his spectators to view questions about the proper role of wives from a new perspective. In my last chapter I examine *Captivi*, where slave characters continually act in ways that an audience accustomed to the stock slaves of Roman comedy would find surprising. By associating the play's disconcerting slave characters both with slaves in the audience and with the actors, many of whom were slaves, Plautus presents a challenge to his audience's preconceptions about both comic slaves and slaves in general.

Finally, I offer some general conclusions about the role of the actor-audience relationship in Plautus. Plautus's manipulation of that relationship contributes significantly to the humor of his plays and reflects not only his own, but also his audience's fascination with the concept of theater itself. The metatheatrical elements through which Plautus molded the actor-audience relationship also played a vital role in winning the goodwill of the audience; and even as they contributed to the escapist and Saturnalian effect of the plays, they helped Plautus both to satirize blatantly persons present in the audience itself and to challenge some of his spectators' preconceptions.

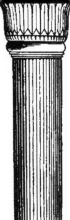

PART

I

1

ACTORS AND SPECTATORS

EVEN in the most naturalistic theater, spectators seldom forget, as they watch characters, that they are also watching actors.[1] The awareness of the character as actor is greater in the nonillusory drama that dominated the stage before the late nineteenth century; and it is still greater in plays as metatheatrical as those of Plautus. Plautus makes many explicit and implicit allusions to the actors as actors, and his plays often mimic nonliterary improvisatory farce, where plays resulted from the spontaneous performance of actors rather than from scripts produced by playwrights.[2]

Plautus's actors not only were conspicuous as actors, but also had a remarkably close relationship with the spectators. One of the first features to strike any reader of Plautus, or any spectator when a Plautine play is performed, is the amount of time actors spend addressing the audience directly. More than one-sixth of Plautus's corpus—and over one-quarter of some plays—is made up of monologues.[3] Though a few monologues include the pretense that characters speak to themselves or think aloud (e.g., *Epid.* 81–84; *Trin.* 1008–27), most must have been addressed explicitly and emphatically to the audience. Through words such as *spectatores* ("spectators") or *vos* (plural "you"), second-person verbs,[4] or pointing words like *ecce* ("look") or demonstrative pronouns, as well as through their general tone, characters/actors make clear that in speaking monologues they are not merely thinking aloud, but wish to provide information to or share their thoughts with the spectators.

Given their conspicuous presence as actors and the amount of time they spend addressing the spectators, the attitude actors adopted toward the audience would have had a profound effect on the impression made by Plautus's plays. An examination of the passages where the actors' status as actors is most conspicuous reveals that Plautus encouraged his actors to approach their audience in a self-contradictory but most effective manner, with a mixture of fawning obsequiousness and brazen arrogance. Plautus's actors make clear that they desire the spectators' attention and need their approval, and they provide repeated reminders of their own vulnerability and low status. Even as they provide such reminders, however, they also manipulate, command, and even mock the audience. Thus, while spectators remain aware of their power over and superiority to the actors, they are also conscious of the license given to the actors by their position onstage.

Stage actors are by nature in a vulnerable position: even in the most favorable of circumstances, they cannot succeed without the approval of the audience. Their vulnerability was still greater on the Plautine stage, where the conditions of performance were far from favorable. The assumption that Plautus's audience was made up of ignoramuses has deservedly fallen from favor.[5] Judging from Plautus's popularity, and the sophistication of his plays with respect to such elements as use of the Greek language, theatrical metaphors, and parody, many in the audience must have been true theatrical connoisseurs. Like the connoisseurs who make up many Italian opera audiences, however, Roman audiences were very demanding, and disturbances in the theater could disrupt performances. Terence reports that the first two attempts to perform his *Hecyra* were undone, first by rumors of a rope walker and boxers (*Hec.* 4–5, 33–36; cf. *Phorm.* 31–32), then by excitement over expectation of gladiators (*Hec.* 39–42). Terence may be exaggerating, or even fabricating, the incident.[6] It is unlikely, however, that the conditions Terence describes were pure fantasy: Terence's audience must have been aware of situations in which performances were brought to a halt by commotion in the theater. In an earlier prologue, Terence suggests the possibility that his plays may be driven from the stage (*An.* 25–27); and in delivering the prologue to the third attempt to perform *Hecyra*, the leader of the theatrical troupe, Lucius Ambivius Turpio, says that in his youth he had similar problems trying to present the early plays of Caecilius:

> in is quas primum Caecili didici novas
> partim sum earum exactu', partim vix steti. (14–15)

> When I first put on new plays of Caecilius, sometimes I was
> driven from the stage, and sometimes I barely held my ground.

There is no evidence that theatrical *ludi* in Rome changed much between the death of Plautus in or near 184 B.C.E. and the first performance of a play by Terence in 166 B.C.E. On at least some occasions, therefore, Plautus's comedies must have been performed in the face of great obstacles. In response to rumors of other entertainment, spectators not only could be distracted from the play at hand, but they, or others entering the theater, could create enough commotion that the play was driven from the stage.[7] References in Terence to spreaders of rumors (*Hec.* 39–40) and in Plautus to claques (*Amph.* 65–85) suggest that there could also be in the audience enemies or competitors who would encourage such commotion.[8]

Even if extreme disasters like those Terence describes were rare, conditions of performance would always have been difficult at best. As plays were performed in temporary outdoor theaters with limited seating, a certain amount of milling around was inevitable.[9] Plautus's own prologues reflect challenging conditions: they refer to heralds whose job was to quiet the audience (*Asin.* 4–5; *Poen.* 11–15), disruptive seating of latecomers (*Poen.* 19–22), passage in and out of the theater (*Mil.* 81–82; *Poen.* 41–43), prostitutes sitting on the stage (*Poen.* 17), and various other potential distractions. Although many of the individual references to disturbances may be jests, they probably present an accurate reflection of the general atmosphere of performance. The actors' position was still more precarious because of their own low status in society: many, if not most, actors were foreigners, slaves, or freedmen, and those who were freeborn lacked many of the rights of citizens.[10] Plautus's actors, more than most, depended upon the goodwill of their audiences.

One way Plautus had his actors respond to these challenges, and encourage the goodwill they needed, was to have them remind the audience repeatedly of their vulnerability, dependence, and low status. The most poignant such reminders are the several passages where Plautus calls attention to the fact that his actors could be punished for unsuccessful performance. The epilogue of *Cistellaria* reminds the spectators that the actors, if they fail to perform adequately, could be beaten:[11]

> ne exspectetis, spectatores, dum illi huc ad vos exeant:
> nemo exibit, omnes intus conficient negotium.
> ubi id erit factum, ornamenta ponent; postidea loci
> qui deliquit vapulabit, qui non deliquit bibet. (782–85)

> Spectators, don't expect them to come out here to you: no one will come out; they will all take care of the business inside. When that has been done, they will put aside their costumes; afterwards the one who has goofed up will get a beating, and the one who has not goofed up will get a drink.

The vulnerability of the actors also contributes to the self-conscious joke that ends *Asinaria*:

> nunc si voltis deprecari huic seni ne vapulet,
> remur impetrari posse, plausum si clarum datis. (946−47)

> Now if you wish to plead for this old man not to be beaten, we think that can be accomplished, if you applaud loudly.

The lines refer not only to the character Demaenetus, in danger of being beaten by his wife (he has been caught trying to have sex with his son's girl-friend). The amount of applause could in reality have determined whether "Demaenetus," and the other actors as well, were to be beaten or rewarded for their performances. A similar double entendre occurs near the end of *Casina*. Lecherous old Lysidamus, also caught by his wife in an attempt at adultery, asks the spectators if anyone will be beaten for him (949−50): he jokes both as the humiliated character and as an actor who could in fact be beaten if he failed to please the audience sufficiently.[12] Humiliated and driven off the stage by Charmides, the Sycophant of *Trinummus* recognizes his opponent as an actor who can be beaten: "vapulabis meo arbitratu et novorum aedilium" ("You will be beaten by my order, and by order of the new aediles," 990; cf. *Amph.* 85).

Supplementing these allusions to the actors' vulnerability are reminders of their low social position. The speaker of the prologue of *Captivi* associ-ates the actors onstage with slaves and other poor spectators who stand in the back of the theater (1−16; see Chapter 10). Before leaving the stage af-ter a scene of dancing and drinking at the end of *Stichus*, the title character says to his fellows: "intro hinc abeamus nunciam: saltatum satis pro vinost" ("Let's go inside now: we have danced enough for our wine," 774). He then addresses the audience with the expected request for applause. The close parallel with the epilogue of *Cistellaria* suggests a double entendre: just as the slave characters are pretending to dance for wine, the actors are slaves, who will be rewarded with wine when the performance is over. The re-quest of Messenio, a slave character in *Menaechmi*, that the audience witness his manumission (1032) gains extra humor if the actor playing Messenio is a slave.

Not all actors were slaves. Two passages where Plautus makes extended allusion to characters as actors suggest that the actors are poor freedmen. The Sycophant of *Trinummus* has been hired by one character to imper-sonate a messenger allegedly sent by another: his status as actor could not be clearer.[13] During the course of his unsuccessful attempt at deception, both the Sycophant and Charmides, whom he tries to deceive, refer repeatedly to the former's status as an actor. Besides his threat that Charmides will be beaten as an actor might be, the Sycophant explains the name of the play in which he performs (it is *Trinummus* because he was hired for three *nummi*, 843–44). Charmides calls attention to the Sycophant's costume (851–52), and the Sycophant elaborates on how the man who hired him instructed him in how to play the role and hired a costume for him from the *choragus*, or costume manager (853–58, 866–67). As an actor, the Sycophant is poor. He enters with a lament that poverty has driven him to perform this role (847–50); he is mightily impressed both with the mere three *nummi* he has earned (843–44, 848–50) and with the money paid for the costume (857); and he threatens to steal the costume (858–60).

Equally conspicuous as actors are the *advocati* ("counselors") who assist in the deception of *Poenulus*.[14] They refer to the kind of character they are playing (522–23), their need to entertain the spectators (550–52; see below), and their use of stage props (597–99; see below). Like the Sycophant, they also call attention to their own low social position. Upon their entrance they tell Agorastocles, the young lover who has hired them, that they are *plebeii et pauperes* (515), and that they have purchased their own freedom (519). They later call themselves *pauperculi* (536). When, after the successful deception, Agorastocles puts off their payment, the counselors exit with a complaint on how the rich treat the poor (809–16).

Even when they are not reminding the audience explicitly of their vulnerability or low social status, Plautus's actors frequently provide more subtle reminders of their dependence on the spectators through their pleas for attention and approval and their obvious eagerness to please. Such reminders are particularly evident in Plautus's prologues. Here the spectators' awareness that they watch an actor would be most acute. Of Plautus's fourteen extant prologues, seven are spoken by an actor in his own person. This actor, whom I will call by his Latin name, *prologus*, is in fact a character: *prologi* have idiosyncrasies of their own, and they sometimes speak as if they belong in the world of the plot. *Prologi* nevertheless spend most of their time speaking explicitly as actors, and they refer to numerous aspects of the production they begin. The same is true to a lesser extent of gods or characters in the play who deliver prologues: while such speakers are undoubtedly characters within the play, they also speak as actors.[15]

Almost all speakers of prologues request the audience's attention and goodwill, sometimes more than once.[16] Several also ask for permission to say the things they say, or sometimes to perform the play at all. According to the *prologus* of *Asinaria*, for example, the play will receive its name only if the spectators are willing (12).[17] The *prologus* of *Poenulus* reveals his dependence on the audience with an elaborate metaphor drawn from the Roman census. Just as censors determined into what class a citizen would be placed based on what property he owned, the spectators are to be *iuratores*—censors' assistants—and are to evaluate the content of the *prologus's argumentum* (55–58).[18] Speakers of prologues also flatter the spectators or wish them well. The god Arcturus, speaking the prologue of *Rudens*, assumes that the spectators are good, pious, and trustworthy (28–29). Other *prologi* remind the audience of their success in war and/or express their wish that that success continue.[19] Finally, *prologi* show their need for the audience's approval through their conspicuous desire to explain. They not only offer extensive explanation, but they repeatedly state how anxious they are that the audience understand who they are and what they say.[20] Two prologue speakers even propose that they owe explanation to their audience, using the metaphor of a debtor paying a debt (*Capt.* 15–16, 23; *Cist.* 188–89).

Conspicuous concern for explanation also occurs outside of the prologues. More explicit explanation occurs in Plautus's monologues than would be necessary even for the densest of spectators, and almost no attempt is made to make the explanation seem "natural."[21] Not only do Plautus's monologue speakers seldom disguise the explanatory purpose of their monologues, but many of them seem to revel in it. The counselors of *Poenulus*, for example, turn and tell the audience that the money used to deceive the pimp is really only *aurum comicum*: stage money (597–99). Spectators hardly need to be told that comic actors are not using real money: the aside serves not to explain, but to remind the spectators that the actors are performing for them and want them to follow all that happens (cf. *Merc.* 851; *Rud.* 293; *Truc.* 463). Actors also remind the audience that they had been explaining things earlier, as when the parasite Gelasimus says, "sed ita ut occepi narrare vobis" ("But just as I began to explain to you . . . ," *Stich.* 579; cf. *Cas.* 788; *Cist.* 366; *Mil.* 1130–31).

In spite of their wish to keep the audience informed, Plautus's actors also acknowledge that they must not bore the spectators by repeating themselves, telling them more than is necessary, or spending too much time on static scenes. It is not surprising that Plautus's second-longest play, *Poenulus*, contains three passages showing such awareness. In one of the three, the counselors, responding to Agorastocles' concern that they be adequately prepared for the deception of the pimp Lycus, spell out the principle explicitly:

> omnia istaec scimus iam nos, si hi spectatores sciant;
> horunc hic nunc causa haec agitur spectatorum fabula:
> hos te satius est docere, ut, quando agas, quid agas sciant. (550–52)

We know all those things already, if the spectators here know
them; this play here is being acted for the sake of these spectators:
it is enough for you to inform them, so that when you act, they
know what you are doing.

It is hard to imagine how Plautus could more emphatically state that the actors are performing for the sake of the spectators.[22] The doctrine of brevity
also appears in other plays. Early in *Mercator*, Charinus and his slave Acanthio banter for nearly fifty lines before the slave reveals what he has run from
the harbor to tell his master. Here Plautus[23] was taking a risk: the long delay is humorous both in its content and because it shows the lovesick Charinus at his most ridiculous; but, if taken too far, it could bore the spectators.
The playwright both acknowledges and averts this danger when he has
Acanthio respond to Charinus's wish to speak *placide* ("calmly"): "dormi-
entis spectatores metuis ne ex somno excites?" ("Are you afraid you'll wake
up the sleeping spectators?" 160). One suspects a similar self-consciousness
in other references to the length of speeches and scenes, even though connections with the length of the performance are not explicitly made.[24] The
logical end of this concern comes in two plays where characters say they will
allow lecherous husbands to escape punishment so that the play does not become too long (*Cas.* 1006; *Merc.* 1007–8).

Perhaps the most important way in which Plautus's actors discuss their
need to serve the audience is through allusions to the spectators' expectations. Plautus's plays belong to a well-defined genre, the *palliata*, or "comedy in Greek dress." As John Wright demonstrated over two decades ago,
the fragments of the plays of Plautus's predecessors, contemporaries, and
successors display remarkable similarities to each other and to the plays of
Plautus himself in language, characterization, humor, plot, and style.[25] Such
similarities suggest that Plautus and other writers of *palliatae* faced an audience with a large and rather rigid set of expectations, an audience that
viewed the job of both the playwright and the actors to be the fulfillment
of those expectations. Plautus's actors often remind the spectators that they
are in fact meeting their expectations, especially those involving stock characters. Toxilus's last words in *Persa*, for example, make clear that his play has
done what a comedy with a pimp should do: "spectatores, bene valete. leno
periit. plaudite" ("Farewell, spectators. The pimp is ruined. Applaud," 858).
Four different characters make sure the audience knows that they are fulfilling the expected role of *servus currens* ("running slave," *Amph.* 986–87;
Capt. 778–79; *Curc.* 280–81; *Epid.* 194; cf. Terence *Phorm.* 848).[26] Not all
reminders of expectations fulfilled involve stock characters: the prologue of

Captivi promises jokingly that all battles will remain offstage, for it would be unjust to perform a tragedy when the audience expects a comedy (58–62; cf. *Amph.* 52–55).

Complementing these reminders of expectations met are efforts to appease the spectators when their expectations are not fulfilled. The handmaid Stephanium, for example, is careful to explain to the audience why she enters from a house other than the one in which she lives (*Stich.* 673–80). Similar uses of such phrases as *ne exspectetis* ("don't expect") and *ne miremini* ("don't be surprised") occur throughout the plays.[27] They remind the audience that the actors want them to follow what is happening, and they reveal an awareness on the part of playwright and performers that they should be meeting the audience's expectations, and that failure to do so requires justification.

Appeasement is not always the way, however, that Plautus has his actors respond to the unexpected. Though Roman audiences liked seeing expected elements performed well, they also, like most theater audiences, enjoyed novelty, and Plautus makes it known that he and his actors are responding to this desire as well. Charinus, for example, begins *Mercator* by saying that he will tell his troubles not to Night, Day, Sun, and Moon, as other lovers do, but to the spectators themselves (3–8). Here the audience is doubly stroked: Charinus the character wants their sympathy and attention, and Charinus the actor will provide them with a novel variation on the expected comic lover's speech.[28]

The obsequiousness of the actors, however, makes up only part of their relationship with the audience. The heavily theatricalized counselors of *Poenulus*, for all their complaints about their low status, are far from subservient to Agorastocles. They refuse to hurry when he wants them to, they respond with indignation when he insults them, and they even tell him proudly, "divitem audacter solemus mactare infortunio" ("We often bring trouble on rich men without flinching," 517). The feistiness of the counselors is indicative of the disposition of actors toward their audience throughout Plautus's plays. Even as they provide reminders of their own lowly position and their dependence on the audience's approval, actors often display an attitude of mock haughtiness toward the spectators, and they exercise remarkable license. Often the haughtiness and license appear together with the apparently subservient messages, so that the actors' attitude becomes a striking paradox.

Actors sometimes deliver even the most deferential messages in such a way that they become ironic jokes at the spectators' expense. This tendency is most clear in the prologues, where flattery, well-wishing, and requests combine to produce humorous attempts at manipulation. The *prologus* of *Captivi*, for example, joins a farewell wish with praise:

> valete, iudices iustissimi
> domi duellique duellatores optumi. (67–68)

> Farewell, most just judges at home, best warriors in war.

By calling the spectators "most just judges," the *prologus* alludes to the fact that their favorable judgment determines the success of the play: the flattery is a blatant tool to gain their approval. Even more flagrant manipulation occurs in *Casina*, where the *prologus* praises the spectators for their trustworthiness (1–2), but then asks for applause to confirm his assertion (3–4).[29] The manipulation, of course, reflects on the speaker himself, but it is also a way of teasing the audience, suggesting that they are susceptible to such manipulation.

Even when they are not manipulating the audience, *prologi* tend to be profoundly and hilariously self-important. The slave Palaestrio, for example, speaking the prologue of *Miles gloriosus* (79–80), asks for the spectators' *benignitas*, and promises them *comitas* in return. Though both *benignitas* and *comitas* mean "kindness," *comitas* implies the kindness shown by someone with greater power or status to someone with less power or status.[30] Mercury, speaking the prologue of *Amphitruo*, equates the *virtus* of actors with that of statesmen and puts the competition between actors on the same level as political competition between *summi viri* (75–78). Given this self-importance, it is not surprising that Plautus's *prologi* can just as easily be imperious authorities as fawning suppliants. A look back at the requests for attention and goodwill cited above reveals that many of them come in the form of imperatives: speakers of prologues pretend that they have the authority to command the audience to be silent. Palaestrio orders anyone who does not wish to hear him to leave the theater (*Mil.* 81–82). Most dictatorial of all is the *prologus* of *Poenulus*.[31] He begins by calling himself *imperator histricus* ("actor-general"), and he continues with a long list of decrees directed at the audience, at various groups of spectators, and even at the magistrates overseeing the production (1–45). When he has finished the commands, he turns to the *argumentum*, and he assigns himself the role of a public official measuring land (48–49).[32] He then promises to give the play's name, and he teasingly reminds the spectators that for all their power, and his own assumption of power, it is the presiding magistrates who actually run the festivals:

> sed nisi molestumst, nomen dare vobis volo
> comoediai; sin odiost, dicam tamen,
> siquidem licebit per illos quibus est in manu. (50–52)

> If you don't mind, I want to give you the name of this comedy:
> if you do mind, I'll give it anyway, if only I have permission from
> those in charge.

Conspicuous explanation also offers excellent opportunities for irony and teasing. There is a fine line between concern that the audience understand and teasing suggestions that the spectators are slow on the pickup. Two *prologi* cross this line conspicuously, as they joke on the need to make sure the audience follows the *argumentum*. The *prologus* of *Captivi* asks, "iam hoc tenetis?" ("Now do you understand this?"), then teases a real or imagined heckler who professes not to follow (10–14). The *prologus* of *Poenulus* asks the same question, then puns on *tenere*, which means both "to hold" and "to understand":

> iamne hoc tenetis? si tenetis, ducite;
> cave dirumpatis, quaeso, sinite transigi. (116–17)

> Have you got it now? If you've got it, pull; please be careful not
> to break it; let it pass through.

The *prologus*'s meaning here is not clear, but he may well be alluding to masturbation at the spectators' expense.[33] Reminders that actors must keep the play moving likewise carry potential for teasing within apparently obsequious messages. Are Acanthio's spectators sleeping because Charinus has been going on too long, or because they are inattentive? Do plays need to be moved along and drawn to a close because they have proper lengths, or because the spectators have inadequate attention spans?

Chrysalus, the clever slave of *Bacchides*, reveals that even anxiety about the spectators' expectations can turn into ironic teasing. Before his final exit, Chrysalus manages to justify his failure to do the expected and to boast that he is doing something novel at the same time:

> sed, spectatores, vos nunc ne miremini
> quod non triumpho: pervolgatum est, nil moror.
> (*Bacch.* 1072–73)

> But, spectators, don't be surprised because I am not holding a
> triumph: they're too common; I don't care for one.

Whether Chrysalus alludes to the plethora of triumphs in contemporary Rome, or the abundance of triumph speeches spoken by comic slaves on-stage, or both,[34] his "I don't care for a triumph, because they are too common" is a hilarious bit of teasing. Earlier in the play he indulged in two of the most lengthy triumph speeches in Plautus, including one that was completely unfounded, as his ruse had been undone: the actor mocks both his character and the expectations of his audience. Plautus and his actors also take advantage of the audience's expectations for more far-reaching effects. They sometimes refuse conspicuously to meet the audience's expectations, without any apology whatsoever; in a theater as predictable as the *palliata*, such refusal to fulfill expectations is an implicit challenge to the audience, far different from the messages of flattery and appeasement usually sent on the surface of the plays. This technique of confounding expectations, which was to become a principal feature of Terence's comedies,[35] is particularly evident in *Casina* and *Captivi*, described below in Chapters 9–10.

The subversion of obsequious messages is perhaps most evident in Plautus's epilogues. Epilogues, with their request for applause, by their very nature suggest actors both dependent on the audience and assuming power of their own; for while they are the clearest possible reminders that the actors need the audience's approval, they are generally expressed as imperatives, as if the actors can in fact command the spectators to applaud.[36] Plautus added to the basic request for applause more powerful reminders of dependence, like the allusions to the actors' status and vulnerability cited above. He also included in his epilogues manipulation and teasing similar to that found in his prologues.

Most of Plautus's longer epilogues, in fact, are transparent attempts at manipulation. Several include ironic suggestions that the spectators have a moral obligation to applaud. At the conclusion of the *Cistellaria* epilogue, the actors tell the spectators:

> nunc quod ad vos, spectatores, relicuom relinquitur,
> more maiorum date plausum postrema in comoedia. (786–87)

> Now, spectators, as to what is left, it is left to you: following ancestral tradition, applaud at the end of the comedy.

The actors propose absurdly that, in applauding, the spectators will be acting in accordance with the revered ways of their ancestors.[37] *Captivi* ends with an explicit connection between morality and applause. This play, the troupe claims, is a rare exception to the typical pattern of lascivious comedies, so that all who approve of chastity should applaud (1034–36). The epilogue of *Amphitruo*, a play in which an actor has played Jupiter, adds religious to moral obligation: the spectators should applaud for Jupiter's sake (1146).

Two epilogues include mock defenses of the plays' amoral plots. Before their request for applause in *Asinaria*, the actors discuss the lecherous Demaenetus:

> hic senex si quid clam uxorem suo animo fecit volup,
> neque novom neque mirum fecit nec secus quam alii solent;
> nec quisquam est tam ingenio duro nec tam firmo pectore
> quin ubi quicque occasionis sit sibi faciat bene. (942–45)

> If this old man got some pleasure he wanted behind his wife's back, he didn't do anything new or strange, or different from what others do; nobody has so strong a mind or so firm a will that he doesn't help himself whenever he gets the chance.

The epilogue of *Bacchides*, which follows a scene in which two old men are seduced by their sons' prostitute girlfriends, is more adamant in its ironic defensiveness: the company produced such a play only because they had themselves seen fathers competing with their sons for prostitutes (1207–10).

Several plays end with bogus promises. Two characters ironically promise the spectators a dinner invitation if they applaud loudly enough (*Pseud.* 1333–35; *Rud.* 1421–22); one promises that she will take care of the spectators' affairs the way she has taken care of her own (*Truc.* 964–66). A variation on the epilogue's promise is the decree of the young man Eutychus that ends *Mercator*, proclaiming that old men must neither pursue prostitutes nor interfere with their sons' love affairs. Eutychus then asks the young men in the audience to applaud extra loudly to overcome the resulting hostility of the old men (1015–26). He thus simultaneously taunts the old men in the audience and manipulates the young. Chalinus, speaking the epilogue of *Casina*, produces Plautus's most effective mixture of manipulation, mock arrogance, and teasing. He manipulates the audience with both a promise and a claim that morality demands their applause, threatens the married male spectators, and teases them with the suggestion that they desire illicit sex:

> nunc vos aequomst manibus meritis meritam mercedem dare:
> qui faxit, clam uxorem ducet semper scortum quod volet;
> verum qui non manibus clare, quantum poterit, plauserit,
> ei pro scorto supponetur hircus unctus nautea. (1015–18)

Now it is right for you to give with your hands the deserved reward to us who deserve it: whoever does this will always win the whore he wants behind his wife's back; whoever does not applaud as loud as he can—instead of a whore, he'll get a goat perfumed with bilge-water.

As the spectators laugh at these blatant attempts at manipulation, they are in part laughing at themselves, for the actors appear to assume that they are open to such manipulation. When they applaud, they extend the joke still further, acting as if they have indeed responded to the manipulation.

In addition to their ironic use and abuse of obsequious messages, actors tease the audience in various ways. Most of this teasing occurs in early scenes, setting the mood for the play that is to follow. *Prologi* insinuate that they could cheat the spectators (*Cas.* 67–78; *Men.* 51–55; *Poen.* 79–82), or that the spectators are miserly (*Truc.* 6–8). Several characters/actors accuse members of the audience of sexual peccadilloes (*Amph.* 284; *Men.* 128; *Pseud.* 203; *Truc.* 105). In *Mostellaria*, audience members are twice mocked for their subjection to wives with large dowries (279–81, 708–9). More general mockery may occur in the first scene of *Curculio*. The lovesick Phaedromus tells his slave Palinurus that he has promised to bring breakfast to Venus's altar. Palinurus mockingly pretends to misunderstand and begins the following exchange:

> *Palinurus:* Quid? tu te pones Veneri ieientaculo?
> *Phaedromus:* Me, te atque hosce omnis.
> *Palin.:*   tum tu Venerem vomere vis.
> (73–74)
>
> *Palinurus:* What? You're going to offer yourself to Venus for breakfast?
> *Phaedromus:* Yup. Me, you, and all of these.
> *Palin.:* So then you want Venus to puke, huh?

While Phaedromus may gesture to his slaves when he says *hosce omnis* ("all of these"), the line is funnier, and more in keeping with the teasing we have seen elsewhere, if Phaedromus gestures to the audience.

We can take for granted that in their quest for the spectators' attention and goodwill, Plautus's actors had an easier time than did their colleagues who performed the works of less popular playwrights, especially late in Plautus's career. Plautus was a very popular and successful playwright, and the prominence of his name in several of his prologues suggests that awareness that a play was by Plautus could in itself have helped to win over an audience (e.g., *Asin.* 11; *Men.* 3; *Truc.* 1). It was the actors, however, not the playwright, who needed to woo the audience, and the actors remained vulnerable, regardless of whose play was being performed. We thus find an equal abundance of messages reminding the audience of their power over the actors in plays known to have been produced early in Plautus's career and those agreed to be late.[38] Also found throughout the corpus, in plays both early and late, is the ironic use of such reminders, and the actors' audacious mocking of the audience. The mixture of blandishment and teasing irony was part of Plautus's formula for success throughout his career.

Neither blandishment nor teasing, of course, is unique to Plautus. Both types of message have appeared throughout dramatic presentations, especially comedy, in many theatrical traditions.[39] All playwrights whose actors acknowledge the presence of the audience, however, choose their own blend of blandishment and teasing, in response to the traditions within which they work, the conditions under which their plays are performed, and their own aims. Significantly, Plautus's blend differs both from those of his Greek predecessors and from that of Terence, his Roman successor.

Aristophanes' actors occasionally remind each other that they must keep things moving for the sake of the spectators (*Eccl.* 581–82), seek support for the play in the competition for prizes (e.g., *Peace* 765–74), let it be known that they need to explain things for the spectators (*Wasps* 54–55; *Knights* 36–37), praise the audience (*Frogs* 675–76, 1109–18), and invite the audience to banquets (*Peace* 1115–16, 1355–57). Many of these flattering comments are ironic, or mixed with mock arrogance; and Aristophanes also inflicts a good deal of direct abuse on the audience.[40] In Aristophanes' plays, however, the playwright himself is seldom far from the surface: the relationship between actors and audience is less important than the satire, teasing, exhortation, and flattery sent from playwright to audience.

In between Aristophanes and the next extant Greek comic playwright, Menander, the playwright stepped into the background; but at the same time, the status of characters as actors became less conspicuous. The epilogue with a request for applause was evidently de rigueur by Menander's day;[41] and the surviving prologues of New Comedy include requests for approval, flattery, and statements of desire to be understood.[42] Each of these elements, however, is more subdued in New Comedy than in Plautus, and all prologues of New Comedy appear to have been spoken by a divinity or by a character within the play rather than by an actor in his own person.[43] Reminders within the bodies of the plays of the actors' desire to please are rare. Monologue speakers of New Comedy sometimes offer extensive explanation, but phrases that suggest emotional outbursts or introverted musing often limit the spectators' awareness of the actor providing necessary information.[44] Teasing is even more restricted. There is some irony, of course, in the pleas of the speakers of prologues and epilogues, but it, too, is subdued, and the extant plays and fragments offer virtually no explicit teasing of the audience.[45]

As we have seen, the conditions under which Terence's comedies were performed were in all likelihood nearly identical to those encountered by Plautus. Terence's response to those conditions, however, was quite different from that of his predecessor. Though Terence's prologues place the spectators in the position of judges and include pleas for the audience's goodwill and attention,[46] their emphasis is on polemic rather than flattery, on the playwright rather than the actor, as Terence responds to the accusations of his opponent, Luscius Lanuvinus, and to other real or alleged obstacles to his success. At least two of Terence's prologues (*Haut.*; *Hec.*, second prologue) were delivered by Ambivius Turpio, the leader of the theatrical troupe performing the plays, so that the potential license of a lowly actor assuming authority was drastically reduced.[47] Terence's epilogues are brief and to the point; and although he includes some monologues that are clearly explanatory,[48] his characters, like those of New Comedy, are more likely to cover their attempts to explain with signs of musing or emotion. Terence's actors never tease the audience. Indeed, in the interest of verisimilitude, Terence appears to have restricted blandishment and teasing, along with other elements, even more than did the writers of New Comedy whose plays he adapted.[49]

Plautus's emphasis on the actor-audience relationship, combined with the actors' mixture of flattering subservience and ironic teasing, would have had several important effects. First, the flattery helped to assure the goodwill of the audience, as the spectators were given a feeling of power: aware that they determined the actors' fate, and that their pleasure was the sole end of the performers' efforts, the audience readily accepted teasing and found the actors' audacious mockery all the more humorous. The mixture of subservience and arrogance also contributed significantly to the Saturnalian element of Plautine performance. Within the plots of Plautus's plays, the lowliest of characters often manage to lord it over their social superiors, bringing to Plautus's audience the pleasure that comes with the removal of everyday restrictions.[50] Outside of the plot, the actors' attitude would have the same effect: Plautus never let his audience forget the actors' low status, but he used repeatedly their license to mock and give orders to the spectators, most of whom were their social superiors. Finally, the license enjoyed by the actors opened up a wider possibility for social commentary. In spite of censorship and the important escapist element of Plautine theater, its spectators were prepared both to laugh at themselves and to receive criticism from the actors they watched. This mixture of modes in the actors' audience address thus lays the foundation for a paradoxical but highly effective union of determined gratification, escape from reality, and social criticism that, as we shall see in the following chapters, pervades Plautine drama.

2

CHARACTERS AND
SPECTATORS

AS much as they keep the spectators aware of their status as performers, Plautus's actors nevertheless present themselves as fictional characters, and these characters, too, have a relationship with the audience. A clear distinction between actor and character, is, of course, impossible; and it will be evident that in many of the passages cited in the previous chapter, it is the character as well as the actor who flatters or teases the audience. An appreciation of the actors as characters is particularly useful when we consider the aspirations of the actors/characters to win over the audience; for these aspirations contribute significantly to Plautine characterization.

The frequency and length of monologues noted in the previous chapter, and the emphasis on the spectators as the intended hearers of monologues, mean not only that the actors develop a close relationship with the audience, but also that the direct relationship between the audience and the characters those actors represent gains in importance. Plautus increased the significance of this relationship still further through the content and style of his monologues. In these monologues, Plautus's characters reveal at every turn that they are remarkably needy: they desperately want the spectators to pay attention to them, to believe what they say, to be on their side in their struggles with their fellow characters, and to sympathize with their situations. In short, they desire rapport with the audience. Upon the foundation of his characters' desire for rapport, Plautus builds a number of comic and dramatic effects. Some of his funniest moments occur when characters fail to win the alliance they desire with the spectators, or when the audience observes characters competing for their attention and goodwill. Plautus also establishes a hierarchy of rapport in each of his plays, arranging monologues so that some characters are more successful than others at allying themselves with the audience; and he often encourages variation in rapport, causing some characters to grow closer to or more distant from the audience as plays progress.

The principal way Plautus shows his characters' desire for rapport is through what I call the rhetorical monologue. Plautus inherited from his Greek predecessors a pattern for beginning monologues, used especially upon a character's entrance. The monologue begins with a generalization (Latin *sententia*), after which the character explains that her/his situation proves the truth of the generalization.[1] In Menander's *Dyscolos*, for example, the young lover, Sostratos, after he has spent the day working in the fields in rural Phyle, enters and reports on his labors:

> ὅστις ἀπορεῖ κακῶν, ἐπὶ Φυλὴν ἐλθέτω
> κυνηγετῶν. ὦ τρισκακοδαίμων, ὡς ἔχω
> ὀσφῦν, μετάφρενον, τὸν τράχηλον, ἐνὶ λόγῳ
> ὅλον τὸ σῶμ'. (522–25)

> If anyone is in need of troubles, let him go hunting in Phyle. Oh poor me! What a state I'm in! My lower back, my whole back, my neck. . . . In short, my whole body!

Sostratos, it will be observed, is only moderately interested in persuading the audience of anything. As in the vast majority of the surviving Greek monologues that begin with *sententiae*, the *sententia* is simply a way to get started, subservient to the statements about the character's particular situation that follow. Sostratos's admonition that Phyle is a source of troubles is not an end in itself, but a means of leading into his description of his aches and pains; and that description forms a new exclamation, not a defense proving a thesis. Occasionally characters of New Comedy come closer to producing a persuasive speech, as in a later monologue by Sostratos:

> οὐδενὸς χρὴ πράγματος
> τὸν εὖ φρονοῦνθ' ὅλως ἀπογνῶναί ποτε·
> ἁλωτὰ γίνετ' ἐπιμελείᾳ καὶ πόνῳ
> ἅπαντ'. ἐγὼ τούτου παράδειγμα νῦν φέρω·
> ἐν ἡμέρᾳ μιᾷ κατείργασμαι γάμον
> ὃν οὐδ' ἂν εἷς ποτ' ᾤετ' ἀνθρώπων ὅλως. (860–65)

The wise man should never despair completely of any project. Everything is attainable through diligence and toil. I now bring an example of this. In one day I have accomplished a marriage that no human ever thought at all possible.

Even here, however, the emphasis is on the παράδειγμα ("example") rather than the maxim: Sostratos has merely introduced the generalization in order to express his joy and pride at his unexpectedly successful courtship.[2]

Plautus developed this pattern of beginning monologues in such a way that many of his monologues became conspicuously aimed at persuasion. First, he added *sententiae* where they had not existed in his Greek originals: Eduard Fraenkel has pointed out a number of monologue-beginning *sententiae* that the linguistic and contextual evidence suggests are Plautine additions.[3] More important, Plautus increased the length and modified the tone of the *sententiae*, so that many of his monologues are blatant and urgent attempts by characters to persuade the audience of the truth of their generalizations.

Plautus expanded his originals' *sententiae* dramatically.[4] Fraenkel argued correctly that this extra attention lavished on the *sententiae* provided Plautus with opportunities for farcical verbal humor.[5] Additional verbal humor, however, is not the only effect of the long *sententiae*. Increased as they are in size, the *sententiae* become means instead of ends. They are not short introductions to characters' accounts of their experiences, but long attempts to prove a thesis; and the characters who speak them are funny not only because of the silly things they say, but also because they are so determined to persuade the audience. A look at two of Plautus's longest monologues makes this rhetorical tendency clear.

Philolaches, the young lover of *Mostellaria*, offers Plautus's most overt attempt to persuade when he proposes in a long monologue that the corruption of a youth like himself is similar to the ruin of a neglected house. After stating his thesis, Philolaches reveals his certainty that he will make the spectators agree:

> atque hoc hau videtur veri simile vobis,
> at ego id faciam esse ita ut credatis.
> profecto ita esse ut praedico vera vincam.[6]
> atque hoc vosmet ipsi, scio, proinde uti nunc
> ego esse autumo, quando dicta audietis
> mea, haud aliter id dicetis.
> auscultate, argumenta dum dico ad hanc rem:
> simul gnaruris vos volo esse hanc rem mecum. (93–100)

And though this seems highly unlikely to you, still I'll make you believe it's so. Really, I will convince you that what I say is true. And you yourselves, I know, when you have heard what I have to say, will say it's just the way I say it is, and not otherwise. Listen, while I give my arguments on this: I want you to be aware of this along with me.

Philolaches then describes how houses fall. When the house section has been completed, he again addresses the audience explicitly:

> haec argumenta ego aedificiis dixi; nunc etiam volo
> dicere, ut homines aedium esse similis arbitremini. (118–19)

> I have stated my arguments regarding houses; now I also want to make you believe that men are similar to houses.

Philolaches' analogy is strained at best, and it tells more about Philolaches' character than about his insights into human nature. His garrulous certainty that he will persuade the audience serves not to make his case stronger, but only to reinforce the humor he produces through the content of the simile as a whole.[7]

Though no other characters are as outspoken about their desire to persuade as is Philolaches, many others are just as earnest in their need to win over the audience. Halfway through *Menaechmi*, for example, one of the brothers after whom the play is named returns from the forum, angry that he is late to lunch because he was drawn unwillingly to the defense of a client. Not content with complaining, he seeks to persuade the audience that the entire patron–client system is corrupt:

> ut hoc utimur maxime more moro
> molestoque multum, atque uti quique sunt
> optumi, maxume morem habent hunc:
> clientes sibi omnes volunt esse multos:
> bonine an mali sint, id haud quaeritant;
> res magis quaeritur quam clientum fides
> cuius modi clueat.
> si est pauper atque haud malus, nequam habetur,
> sin dives malust, is cliens frugi habetur.
> qui neque leges neque aequom bonum usquam colunt,
> sollicitos patronos habent.
> datum denegant quod datum est, litium pleni, rapaces
> viri, fraudulenti,

qui aut faenore aut periuriis habent rem paratam,
mens est in quo *
eis ubi dicitur dies, simul patronis dicitur.
[quippe qui pro illis loquimur quae male fecerunt]
aut ad populum aut in iure aut apud aedilem res est.
sicut me hodie nimis sollicitum cliens quidam habuit, neque
quod volui
agere aut quicum licitumst, ita med attinuit, ita detinuit. (571–89)

What an incredibly stupid custom this is, and really troublesome,
too, and yet all the best people do it most! They all want many
clients: they don't investigate whether they are good or bad; they
care only about how much money their clients have, not about
their reputation for good faith. If a fellow is poor, but good,
he is considered worthless, but if he is rich and bad, he is considered a good client. Those who don't care at all about laws or
justice keep their patrons busy. They deny that they've been
given what they've been given, they're full of lawsuits, they're
greedy and corrupt, and they've made their money through usury
or perjury. They think about . . . [here there is a gap in the text].
When they are called to court, their patrons are, too. There's a
trial, either in front of the people, or in a law court, or before the
aedile. That's what happened to me today: some client kept me
too busy, and I couldn't do what I wanted or be with whom I
wanted: he held me back and detained me.

Menaechmus's diatribe may convey some serious social commentary. Its
principal effect, however, is to make Menaechmus look ridiculous. He
earnestly desires that the audience share his indignation, but his motivation—anger that he has missed lunch with his mistress—undermines all his
authority.

These monologues are just two of the many attempts in Plautus to persuade. Characters of all types—parasites, clever slaves, "good" slaves, misogynists, put-upon matrons, young lovers, old lovers, stern fathers, lenient
fathers—work hard to make the spectators believe that their generalizations
are true.[8]

Even when they do not employ extended generalizations, Plautus's characters are eager to persuade the audience. Sometimes they underline their
desire to persuade by using rhetorical questions. The parasite Ergasilus, for
example, announces upon his first entrance that his nickname is *Scortum*
("Whore"). He explains the nickname with a pun on *invocatus*. A whore is
invocatum ("called by name") at the throw of dice,[9] and he, as a parasite,

comes to dinner *invocatus* ("uninvited"). He interrupts his allusion to the prostitute with a direct plea to be believed: "estne invocatum an non <est? est> planissume" ("Is the whore *invocatum* ['called upon'] or not? Of course she is," *Capt.* 74).[10] Unsuccessful or nervous Plautine lovers are particularly fond of rhetorical questions: they want to make sure the spectators agree that they really are miserable. Alcesimarchus, for example, the lovesick youth of *Cistellaria*, concludes his account of love's tortures with "estne hoc miserum memoratu?" ("Isn't this a terrible thing?" 229).[11] The lovers are already laughable in their histrionic self-pity; they inspire still more laughter when they unsuccessfully try to persuade the audience that their self-pity is justified.

Characters not only want the audience to believe what they say; they also plead for the audience's attention. The most subtle request for attention is the word *ecce* ("look"), found throughout Plautus's monologues. Through it characters reveal their desire for the spectators to turn their attention to what they are pointing out. More explicit are imperatives of *videre* ("see") or similar verbs. Epignomus, for example, one of the two brothers who return home in *Stichus*, finds that his father-in-law, once angry, is mollified when he sees how much money Epignomus and his brother have made in their travels. Impressed, Epignomus addresses the audience: "videte, quaeso, quid potest pecunia" ("I ask you, look at what money accomplishes," *Stich.* 410). Not content to propose a maxim, Epignomus wants to be sure that the spectators take note of it.[12] Sometimes characters go still further in their desire for attention. Preparing to auction off his jokes to the audience, the parasite Gelasimus announces: "adeste sultis, praeda erit praesentium" ("Pay attention, please, there will be a reward for those present," *Stich.* 220). Gelasimus, of course, has every reason to want the audience to pay attention. Elsewhere, however, desire for the audience's attention overcomes what one would expect to motivate a character. Olympio addresses the audience after he has been deceived and beaten by a fellow slave dressed as a woman:

> operam date, dum mea facta itero: est operae pretium auribus
> accipere,
> ita ridicula auditu, iteratu ea sunt quae ego intus turbavi.[13]
> (*Cas.* 879–80)

Pay attention, while I recount what I have done; it will be worth your while to listen to me, for the mess I made inside is so funny both to hear and to tell.

Even though he repeatedly stresses how ashamed he is at what he has to tell (878, 899, 902), Olympio explicitly calls for the spectators' attention. His desire to win over the audience is more powerful than his humiliation.

Plautus achieves a still greater comic effect in those passages where characters not only try to persuade the audience of the truth of their statements or plead for their attention, but even go so far as to make direct requests to the spectators. In *Aulularia* (715–16) and *Cistellaria* (678–79), characters want the audience to help them find lost property, and two characters in *Curculio* ask the spectators to point out someone (301, 590; cf. *Asin.* 910). In *Miles gloriosus* (862) and *Menaechmi* (879–81), characters beg the audience not to tell the other characters in which direction they go when they sneak away from the stage. In *Menaechmi*, when the slave Messenio thinks he has been freed, he coopts the spectators as witnesses of his emancipation (1031–32). Soon after his first entrance in *Stichus*, the parasite Gelasimus proposes to sell himself to whatever spectator will bid highest (171–73, 193–95). He asks for bids from the audience as a whole (222–23), and he assumes that one member of the audience nods to him as if he wants to buy (224).[14] The humor in such passages is twofold. The audience laughs at the pure impossibility of the request: they are reminded, as they liked to be often, of the inherent falsehood of performance. At the same time, the spectators laugh at the characters, who, like the characters who fail in their attempts to persuade, want something from the audience and cannot get it. Two characters even extend such impossible requests from the absurd to the outrageous, asking if anyone in the audience will be beaten or crucified in their place (*Cas.* 949–50; *Mostell.* 354–61).

Speakers of Plautine monologues, then, leave no doubt that they want the spectators to pay attention to them, to sympathize with them, to believe what they say, and to view the action onstage through their eyes. As a result of this desire, characters compete with one another for rapport with the audience. This competition is perhaps most evident in the early scenes of *Mercator*.[15]

Mercator begins with a monologue spoken by Charinus, a young man in love:

> duas res simul nunc agere decretumst mihi:
> et argumentum et meos amores eloquar. (1–2)

> I have now decided to do two things at the same time: I will tell you about both the events leading up to this play and my own love.

Charinus will not, he says, do as he has seen other comic lovers do, telling his troubles to Night, Day, the Sun, or the Moon, who really don't care about humans' problems. Rather, he will share his troubles with the audience ("vobis narrabo potius meas nunc miserias"; "I will tell you my troubles instead," 8). He thus makes clear immediately that he wants the audience's attention and sympathy; and he continues in the same vein throughout the prologue, complaining to them with great verbosity. His solicitation of rapport reaches its peak when he concludes his long history and says of his love for Pasicompsa, the girl he has recently purchased, "vosmet videte quam mihi valde placuerit" ("See for yourselves how much she has pleased me," 103).

After the prologue, Charinus learns from his slave Acanthio that his father, Demipho, has caught sight of Pasicompsa. Acanthio, playing the stock role of the *servus currens* ("running slave"), not only brings the bad news, but competes with Charinus for the audience's favor. After a few lines of talking to himself, Acanthio describes to the spectators his struggle through the crowded streets (116−19). After master and slave meet, they banter for nearly fifty lines before Acanthio reveals his message. The delay is caused primarily by the melodramatic antics of Charinus, in response to which Acanthio assumes an alliance with the audience, accusing his master of putting them to sleep (160). Acanthio himself then delays his message, teasing his master, and when Charinus threatens him, he addresses a sarcastic aside to the audience: "hoc sis vide, ut palpatur. nullust, quando occepit, blandior" ("Just look at how he coaxes me. Once he gets started, nobody's a better flatterer," 169).

As he appears only in this scene, Acanthio presents little threat to the rapport Charinus desires with the audience. A more serious threat comes in the form of Demipho, who enters with a monologue after the departure of Charinus and Acanthio. Whereas Charinus fears that his father will be angry that he has bought the girl, Demipho reveals that in fact he has fallen in love with Pasicompsa himself. He competes with his son not only for the girl, but also for the sympathy and attention of the audience. Changes in meter emphasize the competition. Charinus spoke his prologue in unaccompanied iambic senarii, which changed to accompanied meters with the entrance of Acanthio. Demipho's monologue is once again in iambic senarii: without accompaniment, he, like his son, can address the audience with greater intimacy. After a long description of a dream he has had and of his encounter with Pasicompsa, Demipho points out to the audience the state to which love has brought him, and he echoes the very expression

Charinus used in describing his love for the girl: "vosmet videte ceterum quanti siem" ("Oh well, see for yourselves what I am good for," 267).[16] Like his son, Demipho wants the audience to sympathize with him in his smitten condition.

Just as Charinus, after his long monologue, had to compete for the spectators' attention with Acanthio, so must Demipho compete with his neighbor Lysimachus, who enters at the end of Demipho's monologue. When Demipho reveals to Lysimachus that he is in love, Lysimachus responds with an aside. He tries to bring the audience to his perspective with a variation of the formula used earlier by Demipho and Charinus:

> si umquam vidistis pictum amatorem, em illic est.
> nam meo quidem animo vetulus decrepitus senex
> tantidemst quasi sit signum pictum in pariete. (313–15)

> If you ever saw a painted lover, look: there's one. For to my mind at least, a decrepit old geezer is worth just as much as a picture painted on the wall.

Before he leaves, Lysidamus speaks yet another aside: "hic homo ex amore insanit" ("This guy is crazy from love," 325).

The principal competition for rapport remains that between Charinus and Demipho, as is evident in the next scenes. Demipho, after a brief monologue, remains onstage, and Charinus enters, once again bemoaning his fate in a long monologue. A long series of asides follows, as each lover shares with the audience his fear that the other suspects the truth. The "bidding" scene that follows brings to a climax the competition for rapport. Demipho, more ingenious than his less experienced son, not only makes up an imaginary "buyer" for Pasicompsa, but points to a spectator who allegedly nods to increase the bidding (433–37). Charinus follows Demipho's lead: he also begins "responding" to someone "bidding" (437–40). Finally, Demipho heads off to buy the girl, forbidding Charinus to go with him. Father leaves with another monologue revealing his plans to the audience (466–68), and son returns to his habit of lamenting to the spectators (468–73).

Much of the first half of the play is thus an extended competition for the attention and sympathy of the audience, primarily between Charinus and Demipho, but with Acanthio and Lysimachus competing as well. Both lovers, in closely parallel sequences, emphatically establish their desire for rapport in long monologues, then find their rapport threatened by a second character. When father and son meet, their competition for rapport comes to a head: not only do they seek the audience's sympathy in asides, but they coopt individual spectators to their respective sides of the struggle as well. The competition between Demipho and Charinus continues throughout the play, as each delivers further monologues seeking the audience's sympathy (544–61, 588–600, 830–66, 978). The struggle for rapport adds much to the humor of the play: both Demipho and Charinus inspire laughter as they work so hard to win over an audience that only finds them ridiculous. The rivalry also underlines the struggle between old and young love that is the play's central theme.

Through the number, length, tone, style, and content of their monologues, then, Plautus's characters show to an unusual degree that they desire rapport with the audience, and they earnestly compete for that rapport with other characters. The failure of many characters to win the audience's favor in spite of this desire contributes much to the humor of the plays. Plautus does more with rapport, however, than merely create characters who desire it. As important as characters' desire for rapport is the degree to which they do or do not attain it. Through monologues and other elements, Plautus encourages in his plays a hierarchy of rapport, as some characters are more successful than others in their attempts to form a bond with the spectators.

Even if they fail to win the spectators' sympathy, speakers of monologues form a bond with the audience not shared by those who address only their fellow characters.[17] One way, therefore, that Plautus encourages a hierarchy of rapport is through the amount of time each character spends speaking monologues. *Mercator* is a case in point. Though both Demipho and Charinus appear ridiculous, there can be little doubt that the latter aligns himself with the audience more successfully than the former does: we would certainly expect such a hierarchy, for in the struggle between old and young love, Plautus comes down decidedly on the side of the young. Part of the reason for Charinus's greater rapport is that he speaks about 100 more lines of monologue than Demipho does. Even as he inspires laughter through his ranting and whining, Charinus forms a bond with the audience deeper than that forged by his father. Further contributing to Charinus's greater rapport is the number of times he explicitly acknowledges the audience's presence. Characters like Charinus who pepper their monologues with *vos, spectatores,* and second-person verb forms gain a connection with the audience greater than that of monologue speakers who do not explicitly recognize the audience.

One type of monologue, the aside, plays an especially important role in encouraging a hierarchy of rapport. Characters able to address the audience unheard by an interlocutor onstage make a powerful connection with the spectators. Characters whose asides are overheard, however, lose rapport: they are incapable of forming a connection with the audience not shared by their interlocutor. In terms of asides, Charinus and Demipho are relatively evenly matched. As they discuss Pasicompsa, each concealing his love for her from the other, both manage a number of asides unheard by the other. Charinus gains an advantage, however, when Demipho emphasizes that he cannot understand one of his son's asides (379).

The differential in rapport that comes from one character overhearing another is still more pronounced in Plautus's many scenes of eavesdropping. Eavesdroppers gain a great advantage in the competition for rapport: they share with the audience a sense of power over the character being over-heard, and they encourage the audience to see the actions of others through their eyes.[18] Therefore, whenever one character overhears the words of an-other, the hearer is likely to gain rapport: the longer the eavesdropping goes on, the greater the rapport; and that greater rapport is increased when eaves-droppers comment in asides to the audience on what they hear. A differ-ence in their parallel scenes of eavesdropping thus gives Charinus an advan-tage over his father in attaining rapport. Charinus eavesdrops on Acanthio for twenty-three lines before the slave notices him, and he delivers several asides while he eavesdrops. In the parallel sequence, Demipho eavesdrops on Lysimachus for only twelve lines, which include only one aside. Also important are the various ways in which characters eavesdrop. More often than not in Roman comedy, eavesdropping occurs when a character who has remained onstage overhears the entrance monologue of a new charac-ter, or the dialogue of two characters who enter.[19] This pattern is common enough that it would have been striking when characters onstage failed to notice the arrival of a new character, especially if the new character spoke a long monologue unheard by the others. Thus, for example, Charinus gains extra rapport relative to his father when Demipho, though onstage, is incapable of hearing his son's long monologue (335–64). Perhaps gaining the most rapport are those characters who deliberately allow themselves to be overheard, for they have the power to take what would normally be the inferior position and make it superior.[20]

Asides, monologues, and eavesdropping contribute to variations in dra-matic irony, a factor that plays a significant role in establishing hierarchy of rapport. Characters gain rapport not only when they address the audience, but also when they share knowledge with the spectators not shared by oth-ers. The effect of shared knowledge is greatest in the scenes of deception that pervade Plautus's corpus, and it is here that the hierarchy of rapport becomes most evident. All of Plautus's plays involve at least some element of deception, and most of them revolve around deception.[21] The audience, aware that the deception is occurring, is continually drawn in as an ally of the deceivers. In one play, Plautus makes this alliance quite explicit. The old woman who speaks the first prologue of *Cistellaria*, after telling the audience how she gave an abandoned baby to her friend, says:

> id duae nos solae scimus, ego quae illi dedi
> et illa quae a me accepit, praeter vos quidem. (145–46)

> Only we two know this, I who gave to her and she who took
> from me—except, of course, for all of you.

Throughout his scenes of deception, Plautus uses monologues and eavesdropping to reinforce the rapport attained by the deceiver. At every stage of deception, deceivers share their thoughts with the audience. They inform the spectators of their intent to deceive, their difficulties in devising a plan, and their arrival at a plan.[22] During the deception, they comment aside both when they feel the plan is going well and when they fear disaster. Finally, they celebrate their success with the audience in monologues. They also eavesdrop repeatedly, both on those they deceive and on others.

In *Mercator*, the failure of Demipho and Lysimachus to carry out the deception inherent in their plans for Pasicompsa contributes to their lack of rapport relative to their sons. As deception plays a smaller role than usual in *Mercator*, however, let us turn to another play for an example of the role of deception in creating hierarchy of rapport. In *Bacchides*, the clever slave Chrysalus deceives his master Nicobulus three times. Throughout his deceptions, Chrysalus gives elaborate descriptions to the audience of what he plans to do and what he has done. Upon learning that his young master Mnesilochus needs money to gain his beloved, Chrysalus immediately informs the audience that he plans to play a trick with the money he and Mnesilochus acquired in Ephesus (229–33). He is equally explicit about the victim of his deception, as he sees his old master enter: "extexam ego illum pulchre iam, si di volunt" ("Now I will fleece him beautifully, gods willing," 239). When the old man has fallen for his story, Chrysalus spells out in detail in a monologue what he has accomplished and what he expects to happen (349–67). He returns later with a long song of triumph (640–66). When he learns that another deception is necessary, he explains nothing to those onstage, but when they leave he tells the audience that he will again deceive the old man (761–69). After more asides reporting his deception as it occurs (772–73, 792–93), he celebrates its success with Plautus's longest monody of triumph (925–78); and when he has achieved all his goals, he sums up his accomplishments in another aside (1053–58) and in a final exit monologue (1067–75). Two of Chrysalus's long monologues are spoken while other characters are onstage and apparently do not hear him (640–67,[23] 925–78[24]), and one includes an emphatic *spectatores* (1072). Meanwhile, Chrysalus eavesdrops on Nicobulus (235–38, 770–71), commenting aside as he does,[25] and he stages an entire scene for the benefit of his unwitting master (871–904). In short, Plautus never lets the spectators forget that they are Chrysalus's allies against those he deceives.

Monologues, audience address, eavesdropping, and relative knowledge thus give some characters more rapport with the audience than others. Plautus used the same elements to modulate rapport between single characters and the audience. Depending on when in the play they speak monologues, acknowledge the audience, eavesdrop, deceive, or are victims of eavesdropping and deception, many characters become more or less close to the audience as their play progresses. The best examples of this variation in rapport are Plautus's clever slaves.

No character type enjoys greater rapport with the audience than the *servus callidus*: as the most common plotters of deception, clever slaves always share knowledge with the audience unknown to others; like Chrysalus, they indulge in many long monologues, often acknowledging the spectators explicitly; and they eavesdrop skillfully and frequently. Yet this great rapport is seldom uniform throughout the play: it is almost always limited in the first scenes but increases as the play progresses. Three of Plautus's *servi callidi*—Libanus, Epidicus, and Pseudolus—share the same pattern of increasing rapport: each of them appears first in dialogue with another character, speaks his first lines of monologue to himself, and then addresses the audience. Other deceiving slaves also reach their state of greatest rapport only late in their plays.

Asinaria begins with a dialogue between Libanus and his master, Demaenetus. Libanus interrupts the dialogue with only one short aside (50–51). It is Demaenetus who enjoys greater rapport with the audience here: his allusion to "omnes parentes . . . qui mi auscultabunt" ("all parents who will listen to me," 64–65) implies a recognition that he has an audience beyond his interlocutor. After Libanus leaves, Demaenetus speaks a nine-line monologue that includes several intimacy-creating second-person verbs (118–26) and, perhaps, an allusion to a member of the Scipio family present in the audience itself (124).[26]

When Libanus returns to the stage three scenes later, he first addresses to himself an admonition that he must work hard to devise a deception (249–55). He concludes with the following command, still addressed to himself:

> serva erum, cave tu idem faxis alii quod servi solent,
> qui ad eri fraudationem callidum ingenium gerunt. (256–57)

> Save your master. Make sure you don't do the same as other slaves usually do, who have a nature clever for deceiving their masters.

Libanus's reference to *servi* ("slaves") who have a *callidum ingenium* ("clever nature") recalls the *servi callidi* of comedy.[27] The theatrical reference, an implicit acknowledgment that Libanus is in a theater before an audience, begins to move Libanus from introverted distance to rapport. After a set of deliberative questions that could be addressed either to himself or to the spectators (258), he offers an explanation and a joke to the audience (259–64).[28] He then introduces his fellow slave Leonida to the audience, and he eavesdrops, commenting repeatedly with insulting asides, as Leonida delivers a running-slave monologue. Only now has Libanus established his position as the primary liaison between stage and audience.

The clever slave who gives his name to *Epidicus* experiences a similar increase in rapport. He begins the play in dialogue with his fellow slave Thesprio, during which he speaks no asides. When Thesprio leaves, Epidicus explicitly ignores the presence of the audience, saying, "solus nunc es" ("Now you are alone"), and he continues addressing himself for four lines (81–84). The meter then changes from trochaic septenarii, a meter that often suggests forward motion, to cretics, which with their lilting rhythm contribute to the sense that the forward action has stopped temporarily. At the same time, Epidicus begins describing himself in the first instead of the second person: he appears to shift from self-address to audience address as he explains his predicament (85–93). Yet Epidicus has not yet turned himself completely over to the audience: after several lines of explanation, he debates with himself as if the spectators are not present (94–99).[29] Before he finishes the monologue, however, he announces the entrance of his young master Stratippocles and his friend Chaeribulus to the audience (100–103). He then eavesdrops on the two young men and comments aside in response to what he hears (124–26): his rapport is increasing. When the youths exit, Epidicus addresses himself again, then explains to the audience what he plans to do (161–65).

Epidicus's rapport grows still further at his next entrance (181). In a variation on the usual pattern, Epidicus's entrance monologue is unheard by his master, Periphanes, and his friend Apoecides, who are already present onstage. Epidicus addresses the audience directly (181–82), announces his intention to eavesdrop (184–88), and responds to what he hears with an aside (192–93). When he again addresses himself, he speaks not an introverted monologue, but a self-conscious preparation for the role of *servus currens* that he takes on:

> age nunciam orna te, Epidice, et palliolum in collum conice
> itaque adsimulato quasi per urbem totam hominem quaesiveris.
> (194–95)

> All right, now, get yourself ready, Epidicus. Throw your cloak over your neck and pretend that you've been looking for the man all over the city.

After Epidicus has deceived the two old men, he is again left onstage alone. This time he does not speak to himself, but explains to the audience in a fourteen-line monologue his hopes and fears. Here Plautus offers the play's first extended passage in unaccompanied iambic senarii, underlining Epidicus's tone of confidentiality. He has gradually built his rapport until he and the audience are in close alliance.

No character achieves greater rapport with the audience than Plautus's premier *servus callidus*, the eponymous character of *Pseudolus*. Even in Pseudolus's case, however, the rapport is not immediate: Pseudolus builds his rapport in a way similar to that of Libanus and Epidicus. During his first scenes, Pseudolus foreshadows the great rapport to come through several asides and implied audience addresses (see Chapter 5). He does not, however, address the audience explicitly or speak any long monologues. When Pseudolus and his young master, Calidorus, eavesdrop on the pimp Ballio, it is Ballio who addresses the audience, and for sixty lines he is uninterrupted by the eavesdroppers. When Pseudolus and Calidorus finally do express in words their reactions to Ballio, they speak not to the audience, but to each other.

Only after nearly 400 lines is Pseudolus left onstage alone; and like Epidicus and Libanus, he at first addresses himself rather than the audience (394–400). As was the case with Libanus, a metatheatrical reference draws Pseudolus out of his introversion: he abandons his self-address to tell the audience that he will come up with a plan out of nothing as a poet creates from nothing (401–5).[30] The audience address continues as he explains the need for caution, introduces his old master Simo and his friend Callipho, and announces his intention to eavesdrop (409–14). Now the audience is Pseudolus's confidant, and his rapport with them continues to grow as he comments aside while he eavesdrops. Like Epidicus, he addresses himself one last time as he prepares to accost his master: "itur ad te, Pseudole. / orationem tibi para advorsum senem" ("You're being attacked, Pseudolus. Make up a speech to use against the old man," 453–54). From that point on, however, he repeatedly addresses the audience explicitly and emphatically.

Other clever slaves who do not share this precise pattern of speaking first in dialogue, then to themselves, and then to the audience, nevertheless experience increasing rapport. The first scene of *Mostellaria* is a dialogue between the *servus callidus* Tranio and his enemy, Grumio, and it is Grumio who has greater rapport: he comments aside on his fellow slave's behavior (38) and ends the scene with a monologue complaining that Tranio has ruined his young master (76–83).[31] Alliances change dramatically, however, when Tranio reenters nearly 300 lines later with the news that his master, Theopropides, has returned. Tranio not only addresses his comic lament directly to the audience, unobserved by the four other characters who are onstage, but teasingly asks if any spectator will be crucified in his place (348–62).[32] He maintains this rapport with the audience throughout his deception of his master, Theopropides, continually sharing with them his plans, his anxiety, and his self-satisfaction.

Chalinus, the male deceiving slave of *Casina*, has no monologues or asides during the first three scenes in which he appears. Only after more than 400 lines does he address the audience in a monologue (424–36); and even here, the degree of rapport is limited by a difference in knowledge: the audience knows, as Chalinus does not, the plans of his master, Lysidamus. This situation is soon rectified, and Chalinus's rapport increases as he eavesdrops on Lysidamus and his ally, Olympio, comments frequently and aggressively on their words and actions, and learns the truth. By the end of the scene, he affirms his rapport with the audience with a monologue (504–14). Because of the unique nature of *Casina*, where Chalinus shares the role of deceiver with Pardalisca, Cleostrata, and Myrrhina, the slave does not remain the principal liaison between audience and stage.[33] His rapport, however, is not lost, for he delivers the play's long and humorous epilogue.[34] Pardalisca, the female slave who contributes to the deception in *Casina*, speaks no lines of monologue until line 621, but is closely aligned with the audience thereafter (see Chapter 9).

Milphio, the clever slave of *Poenulus*, has a short monologue (198–205) and several short asides (260, 324, 348, 352) early in the play, but he then speaks no asides for nearly 500 lines. Only late in the play does he establish sustained rapport with the audience, as he eavesdrops on and responds to Syncerastus (817–922). This delayed rapport grows through the scene with Syncerastus, until Milphio acknowledges the audience explicitly at its end, assuring them he will not repeat before them what they have already heard (921).

Chrysalus's increase in rapport is more rapid. He enters with an address to Apollo. When he sees Pistoclerus, he responds with a pro forma aside of recognition (*Bacch.* 181), and he builds rapport with a conspicuous theatrical reference (214–15), a short monologue when Pistoclerus leaves (229–34), and a response aside to the entrance monologue of Nicobulus (239–42). As we have seen, he maintains exceptional rapport from that point on.

Why do slaves gradually build their rapport, rather than enjoying it from the play's beginning? Part of the answer is aesthetic: the slaves' low rapport early on makes their later closeness with the spectators all the more impressive and pleasurable. More important, however, is the same principle of inversion that explains their rapport in the first place. There can be no doubt that Plautus's audience enjoyed watching slaves. Slaves play significant roles in all of Plautus's plays, and in nine of the plays a deception devised by a clever slave provides the core of the plot. Indeed, it has been argued that the expansion of the role of slaves, especially the heroization of the *servus callidus*, is Plautus's most significant modification of the Greek plays he adapted.[35] Erich Segal's explanation of Plautus's fascination with slaves remains the most persuasive: the power and freedom he gives to his slaves is Plautus's most effective way of providing his audience with a joyous release from everyday Roman life.[36]

As much fun as the Saturnalian power of the *servi callidi* and of other slave characters must have been, however, it could only work within the fantasy of the stage world, for the inversion of a master's authority over his slaves undermines one of the basic foundations of a slave society. The presence of slaves both in the audience and as actors, and the vast number of new slaves that followed the Roman conquests of Plautus's lifetime, can only have made most Roman spectators more sensitive to any hints of subversion associated with slaves.[37] Evidence of this sensitivity is the fact that in *fabulae togatae*—plays set in Italy—slaves were not generally portrayed as more clever than their masters (Donat. *ad Eun.* 57). The delay and gradual increase of rapport is in part a response to this situation. Instead of trying to align slaves and spectators immediately, Plautus made the slaves the principal liaison between stage and audience only when the spectators had been seduced into an acceptance of the Saturnalian world onstage; and the gradually increasing rapport that most *servi callidi* experience itself contributes to the seduction.[38]

This effect of delayed rapport is most evident in the case of Tranio. Tranio is surely Plautus's least excusable *servus callidus*. His plots serve no real purpose except to make a fool of his master: it is clear from the beginning that they can only delay, not prevent, Theopropides' discovery of what has been going on in his household while he has been away.[39] Theopropides is a bit on the parsimonious side and not terribly bright, but he is scarcely culpable. Plautus's audience, however much it may have reveled in Saturnalian inversion, was not likely to have found such a character as Tranio palatable, had he merely been thrust upon it. Plautus therefore led his spectators to a state of mind in which they could align themselves more easily with Tranio and his antics. Grumio, rather than Tranio, has more rapport with the audience at play's beginning. Though Grumio is not the most lovable of characters, he expresses views on corruption and profligacy with which many in the audience probably sympathized. Before Tranio returns, the amoral fantasy onstage is gradually made more acceptable to the audience. Tranio's young master, Philolaches, through his long monologue, proves that he is something more than merely a stock corrupted youth, and that he feels remorse for his profligacy. The next scene reveals that Philematium, the primary reason Philolaches is broke, is not only charming, but feels real affection and gratitude toward Philolaches. Finally, the audience is caught up in the party that occurs onstage, and all thoughts of morality are replaced by fascination and fun. Only then does Tranio begin his long series of addresses to the audience.

The exceptions to the pattern of delayed rapport among *servi callidi* further demonstrate the importance of seduction. Chrysalus's increase in rapport is unusually fast, but by the time he enters the plot of *Bacchides*, it is already well advanced. The seduction of the audience has occurred with the conquest of the young man Pistoclerus by the Bacchis sisters, and Pistoclerus's rejection of the stern admonitions of his teacher, Lydus.[40] Palaestrio shares his thoughts with the audience in asides and monologues from his first entrance in *Miles gloriosus*. Palaestrio, however, also serves as the play's *prologus*, so that much of the first rapport he gains is less as a character than as an actor, speaking the prologue. Finally, in *Persa*, no masters appear, and the principal *servus callidus* is also the play's lover. The status of the *servi callidi* as slaves thus becomes less significant, and both of them, Toxilus and Sagaristio, can establish rapport with the audience immediately through monologues (1–15).

Messenio, the slave of Menaechmus of Syracuse in *Menaechmi*, provides a revealing contrast to the *servi callidi*. Messenio transcends the stock characterstics of Plautine slaves. He is not a *servus callidus*, for he does not deceive; but he is considerably more sympathetic than most of the "good slaves" in Plautus. Since he does not challenge the audience's sense of proper authority, Messenio does not require a delay in his rapport, but he maintains rapport with the audience during all his appearances onstage. Indeed, Messenio's status as a slave lies at the heart of his rapport. His first aside is a response to a warning from his master not to speak beyond his station:

>   em
> illoc enim verbo esse me servom scio.
> non potuit paucis plura plane proloqui.
> verum tamen nequeo contineri quin loquar. (250–53)

> Ouch! When he talks like that, I know I'm a slave. He couldn't have said more, more clearly, in so few words. Still, I can't be held back from speaking the truth.

The aside aligns the audience immediately with Messenio: he is looking out for his master's interests but is aware of his subservient position. When Menaechmus enters the house of the prostitute Erotium, Messenio shares his fears for his master with the audience and again reminds them of his own status as slave:

>   periit probe:
> ducit lembum dierectum navis praedatoria.
> sed ego inscitus qui domino me postulem moderarier:
> dicto me emit audientem, haud imperatorem sibi. (441–44)

> He's really done for: the pirate ship is towing our sailboat to its destruction. But how silly I am to expect to control my master: he bought me to obey him, not to give him orders.

Messenio is then absent for a long time, but when he returns, his rapport with the audience is magnified, as he delivers his own variation of the "good-slave" monody, explaining how obedience is preferable to punishment (966–89). Such monodies occur in many of Plautus's plays. Usually, however, they are in some way ironic: the slave is not really a good slave at all, or he is a pompous ass, or he is being duped.[41] The sincerity of Messenio's monody is thus particularly striking: he really is a good slave, he has done as his master ordered, and he is honestly concerned about Menaechmus's welfare.[42] He maintains his close relationship with the audience through two asides as he rescues Epidamnian Menaechmus from the slaves who try to tie him up (1004–6, 1019). When he thinks he has been freed, the same character who throughout the play has shared with the audience the fact of his slavery appropriately addresses the spectators, assuming that they agree to act as witnesses. He turns to them as if to lead them in the requisite formula of emancipation: "cum tu liber es, Messenio, / gaudeo" ("Since you are free, Messenio, I rejoice," 1031–32); and then he adds, "credo hercle vobis" ("By Hercules, I believe you," 1032). It is Messenio who ultimately brings about the recognition of the two brothers, and he shares with the audience his growing realization of the twins' identities (1071–72, 1082–84, 1110). Finally, Messenio speaks a humorous epilogue announcing the auction of Epidamnian Menaechmus's property.

Plautus's portrayal of Euclio, the miser whose pot of gold (*aulula*) gives its name to *Aulularia*, offers an excellent example of all the phenomena discussed in this chapter: desire for rapport, failure to gain rapport, competition for rapport, and hierarchy and variation of rapport. When *Aulularia* begins, Euclio has found the pot of gold in his house. He guards it maniacally, digging it up and burying it again many times a day. Meanwhile, Euclio's daughter has been raped by a young man named Lyconides, and she is pregnant (she gives birth offstage in the course of the play). Unaware of the rape and pregnancy, Euclio agrees to give his daughter in marriage to his neighbor, Megadorus, Lyconides' rich uncle. (Megadorus is also unaware of the rape and pregnancy.) Euclio is convinced that Megadorus has somehow found out about his gold, and when Megadorus sends a troop of slaves to Euclio's house to prepare the wedding feast, the miser panics and decides to remove the gold to the grove of the god Silvanus. Lyconides' slave,[43] who has been sent by his master to find out what is happening at Euclio's house, sees where Euclio hides the gold and steals it. Just after Euclio discovers that his treasure is gone, Lyconides arrives to confess that he raped Euclio's daughter and to ask to marry her. After a hilarious scene of confusion, as Euclio thinks Lyconides has come to confess that he stole the gold,[44] Euclio learns the truth about his daughter. Lyconides' slave then tells his master that he has stolen the treasure (he hopes to buy his freedom with it). Here the text breaks off, but an ancient summary of the play and some remaining fragments suggest that Euclio experienced a conversion and gave some or all of the gold to Lyconides as a dowry.[45]

Euclio's most conspicuous characteristic, after his obsession with the gold, is his alienation.[46] To Megadorus's kindness, he responds with paranoia. His encounters with the other characters in the play—Staphyla (his maid), the cooks sent by Megadorus, Lyconides' slave, and Lyconides himself—are all hostile. He is reluctant to take part in community events (105–12), he tries to avoid greeting his fellow citizens (113), and he is so absorbed with his gold that he has not noticed that his daughter is in the last stages of pregnancy. Patterns of staging underline the miser's isolation. Euclio repeatedly leaves the stage, often in the middle of a dialogue, in order to check on the gold (66, 203, 242, 397, 444, 627, 660); and he spends several scenes carrying his treasure (hidden) with him, a visual reminder that he values the gold over his relationships with his interlocutors (449–586).

Euclio does, however, have one human connection: the audience. He tries to establish rapport with the spectators almost immediately, complaining to them that Staphyla walks too slowly (46–47) and responding with an aside when Staphyla murmurs under her breath (52). He then begins a pattern that he is to repeat throughout much of the play: asides and short monologues expressing his fear for his gold (60–66, 79–80). Such fear is also at the center of his next three soliloquies (105–19, 178–81, 265–67), as well as the suspicious asides with which he responds to the kind words of Megadorus (184–216). At the end of his scene with Megadorus, Euclio leaves to buy food for the wedding. He reenters with his longest monologue yet, explaining that he bought no food, because everything was too expensive (371–87). When he sees that his door is open and overhears a cook talking about a pot, he enters the house in terror, but not before he prays briefly to Apollo for aid (394–96) and again expresses his fears to the audience (391–93, 397).

After a violent encounter with the cooks, Euclio carries the gold from the house himself, explaining his motivations in a monologue (449–71). On seeing Megadorus, he reluctantly acknowledges that he will have to talk to him (473–74), and he responds with several asides to Megadorus's long monologue against dowered wives. In the ensuing dialogue, he continues his skeptical asides in response to Megadorus (547–48, 574–78).

When Megadorus leaves, there is a subtle change in Euclio's relationship with the audience; for he now addresses not them, but his pot of gold, and then the goddess Fides ("Good Faith"), in whose shrine he plans to hide the treasure (580–86). This distancing of Euclio from the audience prepares them for the entrance of his antagonist, Lyconides' slave, who arrives onstage as Euclio enters the shrine. The slave speaks a variation of the "good-slave" speech (587–607), the longest monologue since the prologue that is not spoken or observed by Euclio. The monologue helps bring the slave the rapport he needs to win over the audience: he is, after all, both a tricky slave and a thief. At the same time, it provides the play's first significant threat to Euclio's position as principal liaison between stage and audience.

When Euclio emerges from the shrine, he again addresses Fides rather than the audience, and he is overheard by the eavesdropping slave (608−15). After Euclio goes back into the house, the slave addresses the audience again (as well as the gods and Fides), and he enters the shrine to steal the gold (616−23). Euclio reenters with a brief monologue (624−27), and after he catches the slave in the shrine, he shares with the audience his exasperation and his uncertainty as to what to do (656−58). The slave, however, is now winning the battle for rapport: he also has an aside (642), and when Euclio goes back into the shrine, the slave informs the audience of his determination to get the gold (661−66). Euclio reenters with another monologue: this time his chattiness with the audience does him in, for he reveals to the eavesdropping slave where he will hide the treasure now (667−76). The series of alternating short monologues ends with the slave telling the audience that he will hide and watch Euclio conceal the gold (677−81). Since his entrance, Lyconides' slave has spoken more lines to the audience than Euclio has. He has also twice eavesdropped on Euclio without himself being observed. This pattern, in which a character enters and exits without ever being aware that an eavesdropper is present, occurs only three other times in Roman comedy.[47] Lyconides' slave has usurped Euclio's position as the major confider in the audience.

When the slave returns, he has stolen the pot of gold, and he rejoices with another monologue (701−12). In sharp contrast to the slave's joy, Euclio enters in complete confusion, and he delivers his last monologue of the extant portion of the play:

> perii interii occidi. quo curram? quo non curram? tene, tene.
> quem? quis?
> nescio, nil video, caecus eo atque equidem quo eam aut ubi sim
> aut qui sim
> nequeo cum animo certum investigare. obsecro vos ego,
> mi auxilio,
> oro obtestor, sitis et hominem demonstretis, quis eam abstulerit.
> quid est? quid ridetis? novi omnes, scio fures esse hic
> complures, 717
> qui vestitu et creta occultant sese atque sedent quasi sint
> frugi. 718
> quid ais tu? tibi credere certum est, nam esse bonum ex voltu
> cognosco.[48] 719
> hem, nemo habet horum? occidisti. dic igitur, quis habet? nescis?

heu me miserum, misere perii,
male perditus, pessime ornatus eo:
tantum gemiti et mali maestitiaeque
hic dies mi optulit, famem et pauperiem.
perditissimus ego sum omnium in terra;
nam quid mi opust vita, qui tantum auri
perdidi, quod concustodivi
sedulo? egomet me defraudavi
animumque meum geniumque meum;
nunc eo alii laetificantur
meo malo et damno. pati nequeo. (713–26)

I'm finished! Dead! Ruined! Where should I run? Where should
I not run? Grab him! Grab him! Grab who? Who is it? I don't
know! I can't see anything! I'm blind, and I can't even tell for sure
where I'm going or where I am or who I am! Please, you folks,
I beg you, I beseech you, help me, and show me the guy who
stole it. What is it? What are you all laughing at? I know the
whole lot of you! I know there are a plenty of thieves here, hiding themselves in their nice white clothing and sitting there as if
they were decent people. [*He addresses a member of the audience*:]
What do you say? I have decided to trust you, for I can tell from
your face that you are good. Hey! Doesn't one of these have it?
You've killed me. Tell me, then, who has it? You don't know?
Oh, poor me! I've perished miserably, I'm completely ruined,
utterly destroyed: this day has brought me so much misery
and evil and sadness, hunger and poverty. I'm the most miserable person in the whole world; for what's the point of living,
when I have lost all that gold, which I guarded so carefully? I've
cheated myself of everything I might desire or enjoy, and now
other people are rejoicing in this, in my suffering and loss. I
can't bear it.

In his despair, Euclio seeks his bearings where he has found them throughout the play: with the audience, whom he addresses explicitly for the first
time (715–16). He has discussed the gold with them and with them only
since the play's beginning, so he naturally expects that they will help him
recover it. Euclio's special relationship with the audience, however, has
eroded since the entrance of Lyconides' slave, and now it fails him completely. When his plea inspires only laughter, Euclio realizes that his bond
with the audience as a whole is gone. He accuses them of being thieves: the
thieves "hiding themselves in their nice white clothing and sitting there as
if they were decent people" are the more respectable members of the audi-

ence, who wear togas whitened with chalk and who sit in the available seats in the theater.[49]

Despairing of help from the audience as a whole, Euclio appeals to an individual spectator. With the failure of this attempt to find at least one ally in the audience, Euclio's mood changes from hysteria to despondency, and he begins to recognize that his obsession with the gold caused him to deprive himself to no avail. Euclio has slowly begun the progression that will lead to his awareness in the play's last scenes that the gold brought him only trouble (frags. 3–4). This recognition of his own failure is directly connected with Euclio's alienation from the audience. At the same time that he acknowledges that he cheated himself, he says that others (*alii*, 725) gain pleasure in his situation. Those others are the spectators.[50] Euclio refers to them in the third person, for his rapport with them is gone.

In *Aulularia*, then, Plautus uses Euclio's rapport with the audience to reinforce his association between the miser's gold and his alienation. He establishes through staging that Euclio is completely alienated from all other characters onstage, but he arranges his monologues and asides so that Euclio has one human connection, the audience. That connection revolves around Euclio's obsession with his gold, for in almost all his monologues and asides he talks about his fears for the gold or his miserliness. When the gold is threatened, Euclio's relationship with the audience also begins to fade; and when the gold disappears, so does Euclio's rapport with the spectators. The audience can thus appreciate Euclio's alienation, and they can feel personally involved in his conversion.[51]

Rapport between characters and audience, then, is a central feature of Plautine dramaturgy, and hierarchy and variation of rapport are key elements in Plautus's method of characterization. Not only do characters desire rapport with the audience and compete to win over the spectators, but often the effect of entire plays depends upon which characters most succeed in winning them over, and when. As was the case with blandishment and teasing, the techniques used to manipulate rapport are not unique to Plautus. They appear throughout drama, especially comedy, in all ages. One thinks, for example, of the importance of monologues in molding Hamlet's relationship with his audience.[52] Even in a much more naturalistic tradition, rapport can play an important role, as when monologues and asides align Algernon with the audience early in Wilde's *The Importance of Being Earnest*. Manipulation of rapport, however, plays a uniquely important role in the plays of Plautus, where the relationship between actors and audience is so close and open, and where characters spend such an unusually large amount of time making their case to the audience. Again, a comparison with the other ancient comic playwrights is revealing.

Characters in Aristophanes seek the audience's goodwill (e.g., *Knights* 36–39, 1209–10; *Clouds* 1437–39; *Birds* 30), and sometimes they even ask the spectators for help (e.g., *Ach.* 206–7; *Peace* 20–21, 150–53). Monologues such as Strepsiades' at the beginning of *Clouds* help to mold spectators' responses to characters, as do the occasional eavesdropping scenes, like the scene in which Trygaeus observes War preparing to grind up the Greek cities (*Peace* 236–88). Both eavesdropping scenes and extended monologues by characters other than the chorus, however, are rare in Aristophanes. In the whirlwind experience of Old Comedy, where a chorus is present during most of the play, and the playwright himself is never far from the audience's minds, rapport between characters and the audience is severely restricted.

In New Comedy, rapport plays a much larger role. The characters of New Comedy spend a great amount of time speaking monologues, and Menander's plays offer several excellent examples of manipulation of rapport. Demea and his son Moschion, for example, each strive to win the audience's sympathy through long monologues in *Samia*; and monologues and scenes of eavesdropping encourage drastic readjustment of the audience's alignment with characters during the course of *Epitrepontes*. Rapport does not, however, appear to have had the same importance in New Comedy that it has in Plautus. As we have seen, the extant monologues of New Comedy tend to be less rhetorical than those of Plautus. Deception appears to have played a smaller role in New Comedy, and, at least in the extant plays, deceivers make much less of an effort to coopt the spectators as allies. It appears, for example, that Plautus added a third deception when he transformed Menander's *Dis exapaton* ("The Double Deceiver") into his *Bacchides*; and Menander's most extensive deception scenes, those of *Aspis*, show little attempt to align the deceiver with the audience through monologues or eavesdropping.[53] Menander also has considerably fewer scenes of eavesdropping than Plautus does, and his eavesdroppers are much less likely to tell the audience that they will eavesdrop or to respond in detail to what they hear.

Terence offers a similar contrast. His plays, too, feature monologues, eavesdropping, asides, deception, and the other features that contribute to rapport. In each of Terence's plays, hierarchy and variation in rapport play a role, sometimes a vital one. The long, intimate, and unexpected monologue of the *adulescens* Pamphilus, for example, has a powerful effect on the alignment between characters and spectators in *Hecyra* (361–414); and the distribution of monologues reverses the relative rapport of the competing *senes* Micio and Demea between the beginning and the end of *Adelphoe*. Nevertheless, manipulation of rapport is less central to Terence's dramaturgy than it is to Plautus's. A greater percentage of Plautus's corpus than of Terence's is dedicated to monologues,[54] and Terence's monologue speakers usually place less emphasis on their desire to persuade or win over the spectators. Deception also plays a smaller role in Terence, and both deceivers and eavesdroppers spend far less time sharing their plans and reactions with the audience. Rapport is important both to the writers of New Comedy and to Terence, and deserves further study; but Plautus relies on and manipulates rapport to an unusual degree.

I have concentrated in this chapter on the status of the character/actor as character. Again, however, we will do well to remember that Plautus seldom lets his audience forget the position of the actor as actor. The characters who so desire rapport with the spectators are also actors who want their performances to be noticed and appreciated. The same mixture of actors' attitudes evident in the previous chapter therefore applies to the phenomena described in this chapter as well. The characters' desire for rapport is an extreme example of the performers' dependence on the spectators, and the major examples of variation in rapport, namely the clever slaves, show Plautus adjusting his portrayal of characters to assure that his performers win over the audience. Even within the context of characters' desire for rapport, however, teasing of the audience is occasionally evident. The characters' requests for attention, for belief, for sympathy, and even for impossibilities, reveal the same kind of teasing manipulation found in the prologues and epilogues. The element of teasing becomes more blatant—and funnier—when the characters ask spectators to do things detrimental to their own interests: act as witnesses to an illegal emancipation, bid for a worthless parasite, and even be beaten or crucified. The actor playing Euclio teases the spectators more directly, accusing them of being thieves. Once again, then, Plautus emphasizes two realities and two attitudes: the spectators are encouraged to respond simultaneously to both actors and characters, and to appreciate both the subservience and the license of the actors/characters.

3

GREECE OR ROME?

PLAUTUS not only emphasized that his performers were both actors and characters; he also kept his audience continually aware that the actors/ characters were both Greek and Roman. All of Plautus's plays are set ostensibly in the Greek world, and characters repeatedly call attention to the Greek locale. Yet the way in which characters emphasize their "Greekness" often only serves to remind the spectators that they are not really Greek at all; and characters also make frequent allusions to Italy and Rome that are incongruous coming from Greeks. This mixture of self-conscious geographical allusions is of profound importance for the history of Rome. Set in Greece but acutely and conspicuously aware of their Roman origins, Plautus's plays are, in the words of Erich Gruen, "our chief document for the cultural convergence of Hellas and Rome," the earliest and one of the most wide-ranging literary sources for the reaction to the Greek world that was to be a defining feature of Roman culture.[1] For the history of European theater, Plautine geography is equally significant. Plautus's self-conscious response to setting was not completely without precedent. Aristophanes' Olympus (*Peace*) and Cloudcuckooland (*Birds*) are decidedly theatrical locations; and Pan, speaking the prologue of Menander's *Dyscolos*, asks for the help of the spectators' imagination in establishing the play's setting in Phyle (1–4).[2] Naevius, Plautus's older Roman contemporary, had his Greek characters make allusions to cities near Rome (*CRF* 21).[3] As the first extant author of plays derived from and set in a foreign culture, however, Plautus set the precedent for the play with place that has continued to pervade European and American drama, especially comedy, through the twentieth century. Shakespeare's Italians, Beaumarchais's

French nobles disguised as Spaniards, and the very British Japanese of Gilbert and Sullivan's *Mikado* all derive ultimately from Plautus's partially Romanized Greeks.[4]

It is therefore no surprise that Plautus's use of geography has received a good deal of scholarly attention. In placing his plays in Greece, critics have noted, Plautus protected himself from the charge that he ridiculed Romans, and he provided his audience with the exoticism and prestige of Greek culture. On the other hand, some scholars, noting the irony of characters' insistence that they are in Greece, have argued that Plautus's "Greece" is most important not as a real location, but as an escape from the constraints of Roman morality. Whereas some have emphasized the Hellenophobic implications of Plautus's portrayal of Greeks, for others the mixture of Greek and Roman elements allows Plautus to mock both Greek and Roman life. Specific allusions to Greece and to Rome have also played an important role in Plautine studies. Scholars have made lists of Plautus's geographical allusions and have used them as evidence for Plautine originality, the chronology of the plays, and Plautus's metatheatrical tendencies.[5]

There is nevertheless more to be said both about how allusions to Greece and Rome would have affected a Roman audience, and about what Plautus accomplished with the allusions. In this chapter, I will first argue that in evaluating Plautus's allusions to things Roman, we must always consider whether or not most members of Plautus's audience would have recognized that the institution alluded to is incongruous in a Greek milieu, and that allusions to Greece can, depending on their intensity and context, either reinforce or undermine the Greek setting. Next I will consider how Plautus arranged his geographical allusions in order to intensify their comic, metatheatrical, and satiric effects. Finally, I will evaluate the role of geography in scenes describing illicit behavior of slaves, where Plautus uses Greek and Roman allusions both to distance the events onstage from his audience and to subvert that distance through irony.

In order to appreciate the variable effect Plautus's geographical references had on his audience, it will be useful to begin with some allusions of one of his modern descendants, Cole Porter. In his *Kiss Me, Kate*, based on *The Taming of the Shrew*, Porter created one of his most audacious list songs. Taking his cue from a line of Shakespeare, Porter has his Petruchio sing, "Where Is the Life That Late I Led," in which he laments his marriage to Katherine and recalls his previous romances. Among the lyrics are:

Where is Fedora, the wild virago?
It's lucky I missed her gangster sister from Chicago

> And sweet Lucretia, so young and gay-ee?
> What scandalous doin's in the ruins of Pompeii!

Both sets of lyrics are anachronisms. The two anachronisms, however, would have different effects on most members of the audience. Almost all in the audience would be struck immediately by the fact that "Petruchio" could have heard of neither Chicago nor gangsters. Only the more scholarly members of the audience, however, would be aware that Pompeii was not excavated until the eighteenth century, and even most of those scholars would not notice the anachronism unless given the opportunity to reflect on it. For most members of the audience, therefore, the "Chicago" line would produce an immediate laugh, and a conspicuous reminder that they are watching an American actor in contemporary United States. The "ruins of Pompeii" line, however, would seem to most members of the audience perfectly in place within the Renaissance Italian setting of the scene. Allusions that look similar to a scholar, therefore, would have quite different effects on most spectators. It is important to keep this fact in mind when evaluating the allusions to Rome within Plautus's plays set in Greece.

Confronted with many of Plautus's Roman allusions, the audience could not have helped but be reminded that they were watching not real events in Greece but a play in Rome. Such a reminder occurs, for example, near the end of *Rudens*. Labrax the pimp uses as one of his several excuses for getting out of an oath the absurd assertion that he is under twenty-five (*Rudens* 1380–82). He refers to the *lex Plaetoria*, recently enacted at Rome, which removed those under twenty-five from responsibility for their debts.[6] This excuse most, if not all, members of the audience would recognize as Roman and not Greek: the line is funny for its absurdity with respect to both Labrax's age and his geographical position.

Few spectators, however, would have noticed more than a fraction of the Roman allusions that scholars point out after studying Plautus in the library. Most spectators probably had at least a superficial knowledge of Greek life and institutions.[7] Plautus's own sophisticated use of the Greek language suggests that many of his spectators knew at least some Greek. Veterans in the audience would have served in Greek lands. Many Greeks visited or lived in Rome, as slaves, diplomats, teachers, and merchants; and affluent Romans taught their children Greek literature and history. Nevertheless, few could have had the thorough knowledge of Greek culture necessary to recognize that many of the items peculiar to Roman life mentioned by Plautus's characters could not be found in Greece. Furthermore, it is doubtful that any spectators would have been on the lookout for geographical incongruities in their afternoon's entertainment. Consider, for example, references to crucifixion. Crucifixion of slaves was far more common among the Romans than in the Greek world.[8] Still, it would be unwise to assume that Plautus's audience would have recognized his slaves as Roman rather than Greek when they fret about being crucified, or when their masters threaten them with crucifixion (e.g., *Asin.* 548; *Aul.* 59; *Mil.* 310, 372; *Rud.* 1070).[9] Most in the Roman audience would have taken crucifixion for granted, unaware that it was not generally practiced as a punishment of slaves in Greece. More sophisticated or well-traveled spectators may have been able, upon reflection, to recall that they had seen no crucifixions in their own experiences with Greeks, but the fast pace of performance hardly encouraged such reflection. Allusions like those to crucifixion are certainly important: they show Plautus making changes in his Greek originals, and they would make the plots and characters more familiar and understandable. Their effect on the spectators, however, would be limited, as they would not appear out of place in the Greek milieu.[10]

It is impossible to distinguish for certain which Roman allusions would and would not have been recognized as incongruous by Plautus's audience. Indeed, each individual spectator would have had a different experience, recognizing some incongruities not acknowledged by other spectators and missing some that others saw. In evaluating Plautus's use of Roman allusions, therefore, it is wisest to concentrate on those which are almost certain to have caught the attention of most in the audience: references to specific locations in Rome or Italy, or to institutions that most Romans would recognize as exclusively Roman.

As virtually everyone in the audience would have been familiar with Roman life and culture,[11] allusions to Greek institutions not found in Rome would seldom have gone unnoticed. Here, too, however, a distinction must be made. Many allusions to things Greek would, of course, reinforce the Greek setting. Others, however, are presented with such intensity that they would in fact remind the audience that the characters are not really Greek at all. Petruchio's song again provides a useful tool for comparison. By itself, his reference to Pompeii would reinforce the Italian setting for all spectators except those very few who recognize the anachronism. The allusion to Pompeii, however, comes in the midst of a vast number of allusions to Italian places: Mona was in Verona, Alice in the Pitti Palace, Lisa at the Leaning Tower of Pisa, and so forth. Together the allusions to Italian geography make the song *too* Italian for any approximation of verisimilitude. The audience is reminded that they are watching a play, and that Petruchio (or rather Porter) is taking extra pains to be as Italian as possible. Similarly, when Plautus gratuitously piles up his allusions to things Greek or otherwise causes his characters to be too Greek, they call attention to the fact that they are not really Greek at all. Such exaggerated allusions have been aptly called "hyper-Hellenization." [12] In *Menaechmi*, for example, the Syracusan Menaechmus and his slave Messenio have recently arrived in Epidamnus. Menaechmus insists that Messenio give him the purse with their travel funds. When Messenio asks why, the master responds, "ne mihi damnum in Epidamno duis" ("So that you don't damn my money in Epidamnus," 267). The Latin pun does more to undermine than to reinforce the Greek setting.

The sophistication with which Plautus employs hyper-Hellenization is most evident when he has his characters use the term *barbarus*. The Greek word βάρβαρος refers to anyone who does not speak Greek. Not surprisingly, given the ethnocentricity of the Greeks, the word also carried connotations of contempt: hence the English word "barbarian." [13] These two implications—non-Greek, and uncivilized—remain in Plautus's Latin use of the word, but Plautus almost always uses *barbarus* to mean not just non-Greek, but specifically "Roman" or "Italian." Thus, for example, he uses it of his own adaptation of Greek plays ("Maccus vortit barbare," *Asin.* 11; "Plautus vertit barbare," *Trin.* 19) and of Roman auctions (*Stich.* 193). The result is exquisite. On the one hand, by describing Italians as *barbari*, characters would intensify their own Greekness, expressing the contempt for non-Greeks that the Romans knew Greeks felt. Yet at the same time, the audience is reminded that these are in fact actors in Rome feigning disdain for things Roman. [14] The effect of such hyper-Hellenization is clearest in a passage of *Captivi*. Unable to get anyone to invite him to dinner, the parasite Ergasilus says he will resort to desperate measures:

> nunc barbarica lege certumst ius meum omne persequi:
> qui consilium iniere, quo nos victu et vita prohibeant,
> is diem dicam, irrogabo multam, ut mihi cenas decem
> meo arbitratu dent, cum cara annona sit. (492–95)

> Now I have decided to exercise all my legal rights according to barbarian law: those who have conspired to keep me away from food and livelihood I will bring to court, and I will demand a fine of ten dinners given at my discretion, when food is expensive.

Ergasilus emphasizes that he is in Greece, where the Roman way of bringing suit against conspirators in business can be called "barbarian law." [15] But the irony of *barbaricus* and his own familiarity with Roman legal practice and legal language turn Ergasilus's Greekness on its head.

Ergasilus's use of *barbaricus* thus blurs the distinction between hyper-Hellenization and Roman allusion. That distinction is blurred still further when Plautus's characters call themselves Greeks, as if that were something unusual, or use the term *pergraecari* ("act like a Greek") to describe dissolute behavior; for when characters call one another Greeks, they are in fact speaking not as Greeks but as Romans, to whom Greekness is something to be noted. Roman playwrights may occasionally have used such expressions with indifference to the resulting incongruity: Cicero reports that in one of his tragedies, Pacuvius wrote, "id quod nostri caelum memorant, Grai perhibent aethera" ("That which our people call *caelum* ["sky"], and the Greeks call *aether*," *TRF* Pacuvius 89 = Cic. *Nat. D.* 2.91).[16] As we shall see, however, Plautus's uses of *graecus* and *pergraecari* reveal not only that he intended the incongruity, but that he took pains to call attention to it.

The humorous effect of Plautus's play with place is obvious, and it has been observed in many previous studies.[17] The extent to which Plautus arranges Greek and Roman allusions for the maximum comic effect, however, has not been sufficiently appreciated. Throughout his corpus, Plautus introduces conspicuous allusions to things Roman and to things Greek almost simultaneously, thus creating what I call "juxtaposition jokes." These juxtaposition jokes can occur with remarkable efficiency, as in the dialogue between the slave Sagaristio, disguised as a Persian, and the pimp Dordalus in *Persa*. Asked his name, the "Persian" responds, "Vaniloquidorus Virginesvendonides Nugiepiloquides Argentumexterebronides Tedigniloquides Nugides Palponides[18] Quodsemelarripides Numquameripides" (702–5). The name is funny not only because it is so long and pompous—it means something along the lines of "Liarodore Girlsellerson, Nonsensetalkerson Moneyrubbingoutson Sayingwhatyoudeserveson Nonsenseson Strokeson WhatonceIgrabson Neversnatchawayson"—but also because it is made up of Latin words with Greek suffixes: Sagaristio, pretending to be a Persian, actually speaks simultaneously as a Greek and as a Roman.

The first scene of *Mostellaria* shows how juxtaposition jokes can work on a larger scale. The rustic slave Grumio chastises his colleague, Tranio, "dies noctesque bibite, pergraecamini, amicas emite liberate" ("Go ahead, drink night and day, act like Greeks, buy prostitutes and free them," 22–23). Eight lines later, Plautus intensifies the joke inherent in one Athenian slave telling another, "Go ahead and act like Greeks": Grumio says that Tranio's master, Philolaches, used to be the finest youth *ex omni Attica* ("from all of

Attica"). Yes, these are Greeks saying, "Go act like Greeks." Later in the scene, Plautus repeats the same joke. When Grumio again says, "Go ahead, *pergraecamini*," Tranio responds that he is going to Piraeus to buy fish (64–67). The reference to Piraeus probably comes from Plautus's Greek original: to an Athenian, Tranio would have seemed especially profligate because he is willing to travel all the way to the harbor at Piraeus to find the best fish.[19] Plautus's retention of the line, however, does not reflect mindless repetition of a joke meaningless to a Roman audience. Rather, Plautus has used a reference to a Greek locale to help turn much of the scene into a joke based on the fact that these are Romans, pretending to be Greeks, insulting each other for acting like Greeks. The spectators, now in Rome, now in Greece, are left with their heads spinning.

Juxtaposition jokes also remind the spectators that the characters are in fact actors in Rome pretending to be in Greece. This metatheatrical effect of Greek and Roman allusions also has not gone unnoticed, but again, the sustained way in which Plautus intensifies the effect remains insufficiently appreciated. Indeed, the Greek setting in itself encourages awareness of theater. Here, as so often when one considers questions of place, an analogy with English Renaissance drama is most productive. The plays of Shakespeare, Jonson, and their contemporaries set in Italy lent themselves to metatheater: Elizabethan and Jacobean playwrights and audiences viewed Italians as deceitful and therefore like actors, and they associated Italy with various forms of theater and spectacle.[20] Almost the same words could describe the Roman view of Greeks and Greece in Plautus's day. Greeks, it was agreed, were deceitful,[21] and much of the theater Plautus's audience knew, including Plautus's own genre of comedy, derived from Greece. Moreover, in all likelihood some of Plautus's actors were themselves Greeks resident in Rome, or members of Greek guilds of actors stopping in Rome.[22] It is therefore not surprising that Plautus, like Shakespeare and Jonson, took advantage of his setting for metatheatrical effects. Both hyper-Hellenization and incongruous allusions to Rome often occur in scenes where the sense of "play as play" is at its most intense.

The key passage for the theatricality of Plautus's geography is the prologue of *Menaechmi*.[23] After greeting the spectators, seeking their attention and goodwill, and joking that he brings them Plautus, with his tongue, not his hands ("apporto vobis Plautum, lingua non manu"), the *prologus* calls attention to the fact that all *palliatae* are set in the Greek world:

> atque hoc poetae faciunt in comoediis:
> omnis res gestas esse Athenis autumant,
> quo illud vobis graecum videatur magis;

ego nusquam dicam nisi ubi factum dicitur.
atque adeo hoc argumentum graecissat, tamen
non atticissat, verum sicilicissitat. (7–12)

> This is what poets do in comedies: they say that everything
> occurs in Athens, so that it will seem more Greek to you; as for
> me, I will say this story occurred nowhere except where it is said
> to have happened. And though this *argumentum* is "Greekicized,"
> nevertheless it is not "Atticized"; rather it is "Sicilicized."

The setting of plays is Greek because playwrights make it that way; and
this play will be no exception. The *prologus*'s *nusquam* ("nowhere") can
mean either that the play occurred only where the *prologus* heard it did, or
that it occurred nowhere at all.[24] The jingling made-up verbs—inaccurate, since the play and most of the events leading up to the play do not occur in Sicily[25]—reinforce this reminder that the Greek setting is a falsehood. Moreover, Sicily was recognized as an important center of farcical
theater.[26]

The emphasis on the Greek milieu as a theatrical phenomenon continues when, in the middle of the *argumentum*, the location of the events
changes to Epidamnus, and the prologue speaker suggests that he also will
return to Epidamnus:

nunc in Epidamnum pedibus redeundum est mihi,
ut hanc rem vobis examussim disputem.
si quis quid vestrum Epidamnum curari sibi
velit, audacter imperato et dicito,
sed ita ut det unde curari id possit sibi.
nam nisi qui argentum dederit, nugas egerit;
qui dederit, magis maiores nugas egerit.
verum illuc redeo unde abii, atque uno asto in loco. (49–56)

> Now I must return with my feet to Epidamnus, so that I can
> describe this matter to you thoroughly. If any of you wants some-
> thing taken care of in Epidamnus, let him speak right up and tell
> me what he wants, so long as he gives me the resources with
> which it can be taken care of for him. For if anyone does not give
> money, he's wasting his time; anyone who does give money is
> wasting even more. But now I am going back where I came
> from, and yet I am standing in one place.

The prologue speaker can go by foot to Epidamnus: his "Epidamnus" is not
the real Greek city across the Adriatic Sea, but a creation of the physical
stage, and—since *pedes* can also mean the feet of meter—of Plautus's verse.

Anyone who would trust him to take care of business in Epidamnus is a fool, for there is no Epidamnus here, only a pretense, which allows him to go to Epidamnus without moving.

The *argumentum* completed, the *prologus* calls attention yet again to the play's setting:

> haec urbs Epidamnus est dum haec agitur fabula:
> quando alia agetur aliud fiet oppidum;
> sicut familiae quoque solent mutarier:
> modo hic habitat leno, modo adulescens, modo senex,
> pauper, mendicus, rex, parasitus, hariolus. . . .[27] (72–76)

> This city is Epidamnus while this play is being performed: when another play is on, it will be another town; just as the households also tend to change: now a pimp lives here, now a young man, now an old one, a pauper, a beggar, a rich man,[28] a parasite, a soothsayer. . . .

The point could not be clearer: "Epidamnus" is restricted to the stage. Like the characters, it is an arbitrary creation of the playwright and the theatrical company. A large portion of the prologue is thus a discourse on the theatricality of the Greek setting. Though the *Menaechmi* prologue is Plautus's longest such discourse, it is typical of the way he responds to setting throughout his work.

The emphasis on the theatricality of the setting would seem to remove Plautus's geography from reality.[29] Yet because geographical allusions remind the audience that the plays are occurring not in Greece, but in the audience's own Roman world, they also have an effect on what Plautus has to say about that world. When characters undermine or even remove their pretense of being Greek, they encourage the audience to acknowledge that their behavior and that of their fellow characters reflects Roman as well as, or even instead of, Greek reality. It is therefore significant that even when the allusions themselves do not refer to contemporary controversies, they often occur in scenes or plays that have relevance to such controversies. Another reference to the *lex Plaetoria* demonstrates well this effect of Roman allusions. Early in *Pseudolus*, the clever slave Pseudolus and his young master, Calidorus, banter with the pimp Ballio. Ballio wants Calidorus to borrow money in order to buy from him the girl he loves. Pseudolus complains about the ways of bankers (296–98),[30] and Ballio says that Calidorus should be like olive merchants, who use deceptive business practices (301–2). The lines are almost certainly satirical references to Roman bankers and olive merchants, who are also the brunt of characters' remarks elsewhere (e.g., *Capt.* 489; *Cas.* 25–28; *Curc.* 506–11). In order to underline the lines' relevance to Rome, Plautus includes the play's most conspicuous Roman allusion in the next line: Calidorus says that no one will lend to him because of the *lex quinavicenaria* ("the twenty-five-year-old law")—that is, the *lex Plaetoria* (303–4).

Satirical play with place is particularly evident when characters call themselves Greeks. Passages like Grumio's sarcastic *pergraecamini* not only make effective jokes and reminders of theater; as Erich Gruen has pointed out, the disdainful references are also a parody of Roman disparagement of Greeks.[31] They reflect on Rome in other ways as well. When Grumio tells Tranio, "Go ahead, act like Greeks," he is speaking as if both he and Tranio were Romans. By implication, then, the very depravity Grumio criticizes in Tranio and his companions is placed within a Roman as well as a Greek setting. The satirical possibilities of such allusions become still stronger when those who call themselves and others Greek are themselves involved in immoral behavior. In *Mercator*, for example, Lysimachus buys the courtesan Pasicompsa for his friend, the *senex amator* Demipho. The scene in which Lysimachus leads Pasicompsa home is filled with racy double entendres. In the midst of one of them, involving weaving, Lysimachus says that he will bring Pasicompsa a "sheep" sixty years old. The sheep, he says, is *generis graeci* ("of the Greek kind," 525) and thus well suited to being fleeced. The reference to a Greek sheep allows the audience to laugh both at the double entendre and at the incongruity of a Greek referring to a Greek sheep as if that were something special. Even as the reference reinforces the Greekness of Demipho, however, Lysimachus speaks as a Roman might, and the audience is thus encouraged to see both Lysimachus and Demipho as men who could be found in a Roman setting. A similar use of *Graecus* occurs in *Asinaria*. The madam Cleareta tells the young lover Argyrippus that she and her prostitute daughter sell their goods *Graeca fide* ("with Greek credit"; i.e., without giving any credit, 199). Plautus creates a potent mockery of Greeks by having a Greek woman herself speak of their untrustworthiness; but at the same time, Cleareta takes on a Roman perspective, and thus reminds the audience that she and women like her are not only a Greek phenomenon, but occur in Rome as well.[32]

Even as his use of Greek settings distanced his characters from his audience's reality, therefore, Plautus played with the setting in such a way as to bring those characters closer to home. At the same time, geographical allusions contributed significantly to both the humor and the metatheatrical nature of his plays. These various uses of geographical allusions play a significant role in Plautus's portrayal of slaves. As we have seen, Donatus reveals that in *fabulae togatae*, set in Italy, slaves were as a rule not more clever than their masters. The sense that it was not acceptable for slaves to outsmart their masters in an Italian milieu seems to have affected Plautus as well. Plautus's slaves, especially his *servi callidi*, are among his most Greek-sounding characters,[33] and many of his most conspicuously Greek scenes are those in which slaves deceive their masters or other free persons, or indulge in other behavior, such as partying or loving, forbidden to slaves in real life. Plautus nevertheless provides continual reminders that the slaves' Greekness is only a pretense, for the slaves often adapt a Roman perspective even as their Greekness is emphasized.

Besides Hellenizing his *servi callidi* in general, Plautus frequently includes one or more emphatic references to the Greek setting at the climax of a slave's deception. In *Asinaria*, for example, Libanus makes the play's first explicit reference to its Attic setting as he is about to succeed in his deception:

> neque me alter est Athenis hodie quisquam,
> cui credi recte aeque putent. (492−93)

> There is nobody in Athens today they think they can trust as much as me.

He then reinforces his Greekness with a gratuitous reference to a Rhodian (499).

Through most of *Aulularia*, the setting is a vague foreign locale. There are no explicit allusions to the play's setting in Athens until, late in the play, Lyconides' slave enters with Euclio's stolen pot of gold and crows, "quis me Athenis nunc magis quisquam est homo cui di sint propitii?" ("Who is there in Athens now to whom the gods are kinder than they are to me?" 810). When the slave's audacity reaches its height, Plautus underlines the Athenian setting.

Epidicus makes a conspicuous allusion to the Athenian status of his master when he has just succeeded in deceiving him:

> nullum esse opinor ego agrum in agro Attico
> aeque feracem quam hic est noster Periphanes. (*Epid.* 306−7)

> I don't think there is any land in the land of Attica as fertile as this Periphanes of ours.

When Periphanes learns that he has been deceived, he emphasizes his own Athenianness:

fateor me omnium
hominum esse Athenis Atticis minimi preti. (501–2)

I confess, I'm the most worthless of all men in Attic Athens.

Finally, in his triumphant entrance when his deception has led to a success that will bring him his freedom, Epidicus uses the Greek word *apolactizo* ("I shake off," 678). Use of the Greek language would not automatically have made Epidicus seem particularly Greek: already by Plautus's day, many Greek words had been incorporated into Latin, and some residents of Rome peppered their conversation with Greek words.[34] A long and conspicuously Greek word like *apolactizo*, however, would have drawn attention to the Greek milieu.[35]

The conspicuous emphasis on the Greek setting here and in other scenes of deception by slaves suggests that Plautus and his audience were aware of the need to dissociate deceptive slaves from Rome. No one, of course, was fooled into believing the slaves were actually in Greece. Periphanes' redundant *Athenis Atticis* clues us in that the Greek references at crises of slaves' deceptions are examples of hyper-Hellenization. Furthermore, the conspicuous Greek allusions are part of a great juxtaposition joke, for even though they seem so Greek, Plautus's clever slaves are also Plautus's most Roman-sounding characters. Libanus, for example, offers a parody of Roman augural language in the scene before he deceives the merchant (259–64). Epidicus parodies Roman augury (182) and refers to such things as the senate (59, 188)[36] and a Roman-style colony (343). A juxtaposition joke in the play's first scene calls attention to Epidicus's status as both Greek and Roman:

> *Thesprio*: iam tu autem nobis praeturam geris?
> *Epidicus*: quem dices digniorem esse hominem hodie Athenis
> alterum?
> *Th.*: at unum a praetura tua,
> Epidice, abest.
> *Ep.*: quidnam?
> *Th.*: scies:
> lictores duo, duo ulmei
> fasces virgarum. (25–28)

Thesprio: So now you have a praetorship over us?
Epidicus: Who else in Athens would you say deserves the job more?
Th.: But one thing is missing from your praetorship, Epidicus.
Ep.: What?

Th.: I'll tell you: two lictors, and two fasces of elm rods [scil., for whipping Epidicus].

In itself, Thesprio's reference to Epidicus's praetorship may not have seemed incongruous in its Greek setting, for Plautine characters refer to the praetor casually and frequently enough that the word may have been taken as a generic word for a magistrate (e.g., *Aul.* 317; *Capt.* 505; *Merc.* 664; *Poen.* 727).[37] The addition of lictors, however, would let the audience know that Thesprio means the Roman praetor, who was accompanied by lictors bearing fasces. Epidicus's use of *Athenis* thus makes a juxtaposition joke that foreshadows his simultaneous Greekness and Romanness later in the play.

The irony of the Greek allusions that surround slaves' deceptions is evident in several plays where the word *barbarus* occurs as slaves deceive their masters. In *Mostellaria*, the slave Tranio convinces his master that his son has purchased his neighbor's house and convinces the neighbor that his master wants to see the house only for comparison. When this double deception reaches its greatest audacity, and Tranio is showing the house to his master while the neighbor looks on, he boasts: "non enim haec pultiphagus opifex opera fecit barbarus" ("This is not the work of a barbarian porridge-eating [scil. "Roman"] craftsman," 828). Tranio and those he dupes are Greeks, to whom Romans are foreign. Tranio's determined reminder that he is Greek is undone, however, by the irony of *barbarus*, reinforced by the fact that as part of the stage set, the house certainly was the work of craftsmen at Rome.[38]

The many references to Greek locales in *Miles gloriosus* (e.g., 100, 122, 239, 384, 439, 938, 1186, 1193) are partly for clarity, in a play where there is much complicated description of movement from Athens to Ephesus and back. The frequency of such references nevertheless suggests that Plautus has taken pains to emphasize that this play, with its two deceptions plotted by a slave, takes place in Greece. As Palaestrio plans his first deception, however, his fellow character Periplectomenus reminds the audience that all the Greekness is only a pretense. Observing the slave thinking, Periplectomenus compares him to a *poeta barbarus*, a barbarian poet (211). With the word *barbarus*, Periplectomenus simultaneously reinforces the Greekness of Palaestrio and his plot and reminds the audience that the slave is an actor performing in Rome. The fact that the *poeta barbarus* is almost certainly the Roman playwright Naevius makes the Roman reminder even stronger.[39]

Casina includes several passages where reminders of the Greek setting mark places where slaves' actions are most audacious. The first comes in the prologue. Responding to hypothetical queries from the audience about the fact that slaves are to marry in this play, the *prologus* says slave marriages oc-cur in Greece, Apulia, and Carthage: again, slaves can behave in ways un-acceptable in Rome because they are in Greece. As he continues, however, the *prologus* reverses his claim:

> at ego aio id fieri in Graecia et Carthagini,
> et hic in nostra terra † in Apulia;
> maioreque opere ibi serviles nuptiae
> quam liberales etiam curari solent;
> id ni fit, mecum pignus si quis volt dato
> in urnam mulsi, Poenus dum iudex siet
> vel Graecus adeo, vel mea causa Apulus.
> quid nunc? nihil agitis? sentio, nemo sitit. (71–78)

> Well, I say this happens in Greece, in Carthage, and here in our
> own country, in Apulia. There slaves' marriages are performed
> with even greater care than free men's marriages. If anybody
> wants, I'll bet you a jar of honeyed wine that this is true, so
> long as a Carthaginian is judge, or a Greek, or, for all I care, an
> Apulian. Well? No bets? I see, no one is thirsty.

As Carthaginians, Greeks, and Apulians all had reputations for perfidy, the *prologus* acknowledges that he could not win the bet honestly; and he con-cludes by admitting that even with the help of deceitful foreigners, he would lose the bet. The entire geographical explanation is nothing but a joke, and the characters are no more in Greece than they are in Carthage or Apulia.

Later in the play, Pardalisca, who is not only a slave, but a female slave at that, deceives her master. In both of her two scenes of deception, Parda-lisca emphasizes that she is Greek. Persuading her master, Lysidamus, that Casina, the woman he hopes to sleep with, is raging madly within the house, Pardalisca says Casina acts in a way "quod haud Atticam condecet disciplinam" ("which is hardly fitting for Athenian manners," 652). When she enters two scenes later to report that she and her fellow conspirators have been depriving her master of food, she says that the deception is more fun than the Olympian or Nemean games (759–62).

In between the two speeches of Pardalisca is a scene in which the slave Olympio lords it over his master. This scene, too, is heavily Hellenized. Master and slave speak Greek (728–30), and when Olympio orders food, he says, "lepide nitideque volo, nil moror barbarico bliteo" ("I want things nice and elegant, I don't care for barbarian [i.e., Roman] spinach," 747).

Again, the use of *barbaricus*, even as it makes the characters seem more Greek, introduces a reminder that the play is really occurring in Rome. This reminder that things are not really as Greek as they seem is reinforced by a boast by Olympio that he walks *patricie*, that is, like a patrician, one of the upper class at Rome (723).[40]

Pseudolus is one of Plautus's most heavily Hellenized characters. He calls upon the youth of Attica (*iuventus Attica*, 202) to combat Ballio; Ballio addresses him as "serve Athenis pessume" ("the worst slave in Athens," 270), and says that if he (Ballio) died, there would be no one worse than Pseudolus in Athens (339). Calidorus describes Pseudolus as his εὑρετής ("finder," 700),[41] and Pseudolus boasts that he dances an Ionian dance (1275). At the crisis of one of his deceptions, as he acquires from Harpax the letter necessary to acquire Calidorus's girl, he makes a Greek pun (654). At the same time, however, Pseudolus is decidedly Roman. He proclaims an edict in the language of a Roman magistrate (125–28), he boasts of holding a triumph as a Roman general might (586–91, 1051), and Ballio speaks as if Pseudolus has had him convicted in a Roman judicial assembly (1232).

The first confrontation between Pseudolus and his master, Simo, calls attention to this paradox. The scene is the most Greek-sounding in all of Plautus. When he gets excited, Pseudolus cries not, "O Juppiter" ("O Jupiter"), but "Ὦ Ζεῦ" ("O Zeus," 443). Simo describes Pseudolus's haughty appearance as a *status basilicus* ("kingly posture"), using a word closely associated with the Greek word for king, βασιλεύς (458);[42] and he compares Pseudolus to Socrates (465) and Agathocles (532). Pseudolus promises to speak as truthfully as the Delphic oracle (480), and master and slave exchange comments in Greek (483–88). Once again, Greek allusions surround the slave's most audacious moment, for it is in this scene that Pseudolus brazenly informs Simo that he is going to deceive him. Even here, however, Plautus shatters the Greek pretense with a juxtaposition joke. As the scene begins, Simo complains about his spendthrift son:

> si de damnosis aut si de amatoribus
> dictator fiat nunc Athenis Atticis,
> nemo anteveniat filio, credo, meo. (415–17)

> If a dictator should now be created from among the spendthrifts and lovers in Attic Athens, I don't think anyone would be a better candidate than my son.

Dictator suggests not a generic magistrate, but the specific Roman magistrate given absolute power in times of emergency. Combined with the hyper-Hellenized *Athenis Atticis*, the word thus creates a juxtaposition joke that reminds all that the characters in the most Greek-sounding scene in Plautus are not really in Greece at all.

Plautus shows his most self-conscious awareness of the need to keep comic slaves Greek in *Stichus*. Here there is no *servus callidus*, but the title character throws a party for himself and his fellow slaves. When he first announces his plan for a party, Stichus tells the audience:

> atque id ne vos miremini, hominis servolos
> potare, amare atque ad cenam condicere:
> licet haec Athenis nobis. (446–48)

> And don't be surprised that we slaves have drinking parties, girlfriends, and arranged dinners: we're allowed to do these things in Athens.

Indeed, the party of Stichus and his colleagues is another of Plautus's most Greek-sounding scenes.[43] Stichus's friend Sangarinus makes a point of addressing Athens at his entrance (649). Stichus calls the wine "Dionysus," Plautus's only use of the Greek god's name (661), and he encourages his friends to be as Athenian as possible (670). Later in the party Stichus cites, in Greek, a Greek drinking song (707). Just at the point where the scene has become as Greek as it could possibly be, however, Stichus makes clear that this Greekness is a construction of the performance, for he refers to the song as a *cantio Graeca* ("Greek song"). No Athenian slave, of course, would point out that his drinking song is Greek.

Persa features slaves involved in all the principal taboo behavior of Plautine slaves: deceiving, loving, and partying. In the first scene of that play, Toxilus reveals to his fellow slave Sagaristio that he is smitten with a girl belonging to the pimp next door. Sagaristio responds, "iam servi hic amant? ("Are slaves lovers here now?" 25). To his audience, familiar with Plautus's concurrently Hellenized and Romanized slaves, Sagaristio's *hic* would have had a double meaning: the unexpected slave behavior occurs both in the characters' Athens and in the actors'—and spectators'—Rome.

The geographical allusions of Plautus's slaves, therefore, are the equivalent of a sly wink to the audience. Plautus makes the slaves ever so Greek, as if he seeks to ward off through geographical distancing any possible criticism for their outrageous behavior. Yet at the same time, reminders of Rome turn the Greek allusions into a kind of inside joke between actors and audience. The juxtaposition jokes say to the audience: "We all know we're not really in Greece, but we also know that we have to be in Greece for slaves to get away with this kind of thing." The slave scenes thus provide repeated opportunities for humor, and for playful reminders of performance. They also present the paradoxical mixture of escapism and relevance that accompanies so many of Plautus's geographical allusions. Here, it appears, Plautus and his audience not only recognized the need for geographical distance, but Plautus had his characters acknowledge that need. Yet even as Plautus reinforced this distance through Greek allusions, he undermined it through Roman allusions and hyper-Hellenization.

It has been argued that in creating his *servi callidi*, Plautus was inspired by his own familiarity with deceitful slaves in Rome.[44] Whether or not the slaves actually reflect real Roman slaves, Plautus's geographical allusions suggested to his audience that for all their apparent Greekness, tricky and intractable slaves, like many other supposedly Greek features of his plays, were perhaps not such a foreign phenomenon after all.

4

METATHEATER AND MORALITY

PLAUTUS'S actors/characters, then, continually reminded the spectators of their determination to please, yet at the same time they could tease and challenge their audience; and Plautus's use of setting encouraged the spectators to recognize the relevance of what happened onstage to their own milieu, even as it provided an escape from that milieu. This mixture of resolute gratification with irony and even satire is evident as well in Plautus's response to theatrical moralizing.

Although the modern stereotype of Plautus's contemporaries as hopelessly stern moralists is an exaggeration, it is nevertheless undeniable that Rome had a long and honored tradition of moralizing, and that moralizing *sententiae* were a ubiquitous part of Roman life and literature.[1] Roman drama is no exception: both Roman tragedy and Roman comedy offered a great amount of explicit moralizing.[2] Plautus, although he also included many moralizing *sententiae* in his plays, responded to the association between comic theater and moral didacticism with great skepticism. Whenever Plautus implicitly or explicitly draws a connection between theater and moralizing, his message is the same: theater, especially comedy, is inadequate as a purveyor of moral truths, and audiences should expect from it not edification but pleasure. He sends this antididactic message in several ways. First, he includes a great amount of moralizing in his heavily theatricalized scenes of deception. This union of deceptive theater and moralizing suggests that theatrical moralizing is an expected element of drama, ornamental rather than educational, as likely to mislead as to edify. Second, Plautine characters who say they have learned something from the theater are inevitably wrong, or they learn lessons of dubious value, and those who profess to teach the audience are without exception ironic. Finally, in three plays, conspicuously metatheatrical passages help to undermine the moralizing presented within the play: the moralizing epilogue to *Miles gloriosus* is a misreading of the play-within-the-play; the moral tone of *Rudens* is replaced by merriment after a character points out that no one pays attention to the moral advice of comic actors anyway; and allusions to the theater contribute to the irony that pervades Plautus's most moralistic play, *Trinummus*.

Many of Plautus's moralizing *sententiae* occur in scenes of deception, and on several occasions characters suggest that moralization is an expected element of such scenes. Deception scenes are also made to look like performance: they become virtual plays-within-the-play, performed by the deceivers for an audience of the deceived. This recurring combination of theatricalization, moralization, and deception is particularly damaging to the notion of theatrical didacticism. Through it, Plautus suggests that moralizing is a tool for deception and an ornament of performance rather than a source of edification.

In *Captivi*, Philocrates and his slave, Tyndarus, each pretending to be the other, moralize while they deceive Hegio. When Philocrates-as-Tyndarus discourses stoically about his status as a slave (271–73) and says "philosophically" that he does not know whether Philocrates' father is alive or dead (282–83), Tyndarus comments aside, "salva res est, philosophatur quoque iam, non mendax modo est" ("We're safe: now he's not just a liar, he's a philosopher," 284): the moral maxims are tools to help Philocrates deceive Hegio. Tyndarus-as-Philocrates also moralizes, reminding Hegio of the power of fortune (304) and admonishing him to keep his promises with the ardent, "est profecto deus, qui quae nos gerimus auditque et videt" ("There really is a god, who hears and sees what we do," 313). The climax of the moralizing comes as Tyndarus and Philocrates say farewell. Tyndarus-as-Philocrates praises "Tyndarus" for his loyalty (401–13), and Philocrates-as-Tyndarus lauds "Philocrates": "nam quasi servos meus esses, nihilo setius / <tu> mihi obsequiosus semper fuisti" ("For you were always no less obliging to me, than if you had been the slave," 417–18). Hegio is moved to tears by his captives' sentiments (418–21), unaware that Tyndarus and Philocrates are in fact praising themselves, and the whole dialogue is a performance for him. The old man is deceived by the performance he witnesses, in part because he takes the show's moralizing at face value.

Moralizing is also a tool of deception in *Pseudolus*. Simia, disguised as Harpax, moralizes as he deceives Ballio: he reminds the pimp that few people actually know themselves (972–73), and he says twice that his "master" does what a good soldier should do (992, 1004). The former bit of philosophizing inspires a reaction from the eavesdropping Pseudolus similar to Tyndarus's response to Philocrates: "salvos sum, iam philosophatur" ("I'm safe: now he's philosophizing," 974). Here even more than in *Captivi*, Plautus presents the deception as a performance: Simia, in costume, performs for Ballio, who is deceived in part because he accepts the sincerity of the actor's moralizing.

Plautus's most effective deceiving moralizer is the daughter of the parasite Saturio, dressed as a Persian captive and sold to the pimp Dordalus in *Persa*.[3] Asked what she thinks of Athens, the girl responds with a long list of vices: if they are absent, she says, the city is well protected (554–60). Later she philosophizes on slavery (615–16, 621, 641), on friendship (655), and on the human condition (637–38). Like Philocrates and Simia, she moralizes to make her deception more effective; and her ally, Toxilus, like Tyndarus and Pseudolus, acknowledges the effectiveness of her moralizing with an aside: "ita me di bene ament, sapienter" ("Damn, she's clever!" 639). Here Plautus has taken extra pains to portray the deception as a play-within-the-play.[4] He pays much attention to the preparation of actors, including a boast by the girl's fellow performer Sagaristio that he is as well prepared to perform as are "tragici et comici" ("tragic and comic actors," 465–66), and an admonition to Saturio that he is to get his own and his daughter's costumes from the *choragus* ("costume manager," 159–60). The reaction of the girl's "audience," Dordalus, is telling. Impressed by her first moralizing speech (about the vices to be excluded from a city), he says, "verba quidem haud indocte fecit" ("She really knows what she's talking about," 563).[5] He says this in spite of the fact that Toxilus has just reminded him that the girl would wish Dordalus himself exiled, for Dordalus is a *periurus leno* ("perjuring pimp"), and one of the vices she would exclude from the city is perjury. Dordalus is a typical receiver of dramatic *sententiae*: he values the moralizing for how fine it sounds, and it has no effect on his own behavior.[6]

On several occasions, Plautine characters suggest explicitly that the audience will learn from their words or actions, or that they themselves have learned from theater. The irony of these passages confirms Plautus's antididactic bias.

Plautus's most obvious claims to didacticism are the prologue and epilogue of *Captivi*. The *prologus* boasts that the audience will benefit from the play at hand:

> profecto expediet fabulae huic operam dare.
> non pertractate facta est neque item ut ceterae:

neque spurcidici insunt versus, immemorabiles;
hic neque periurus leno est nec meretrix mala
neque miles gloriosus. (54–58)

> It will certainly profit you to pay attention to this play. It is not
> hackneyed, nor is it the same as other plays: there are no dirty
> lines in it that should not be repeated; here there is no lying
> pimp, no bad prostitute, no braggart soldier.

The prologue speaker not only boasts of the play's novelty, but he claims
that it will profit the audience because it lacks immoral elements. Yet the
list of items allegedly missing from the play is misleading at best. The first
character to enter at prologue's end is Ergasilus the parasite, as much an
unedifying stock character as any of those listed by the prologue speaker.
Ergasilus's very first words provide not only the first of several off-color
jokes that will dot the play (cf. 888–89, 955–56, 966), but also a substitute
for the *meretrix* ("high-class prostitute") excluded above: "Iuventus nomen
indidit Scorto mihi" ("The youths have given me the name Whore," 69).[7]
Soon thereafter the audience learns that though the play may not have a
miles gloriosus, it does have a character with a braggart soldier's name: Hegio's son Philopolemus ("battle lover," 95).

Captivi's epilogue claims that the play should be applauded as an induce-
ment to *pudicitia* ("chastity"):

> spectatores, ad pudicos mores facta haec fabula est,
> neque in hac subigitationes sunt neque ulla amatio
> nec pueri suppositio nec argenti circumductio,
> neque ubi amans adulescens scortum liberet clam suom patrem.
> huius modi paucas poetae reperiunt comoedias,
> ubi boni meliores fiant. nunc vos, si vobis placet
> et si placuimus neque odio fuimus, signum hoc mittite:
> qui pudicitiae esse voltis praemium, plausum date. (1029–36)

> Spectators, this play was made in accordance with chaste morals.
> In it there is nothing erotic, no love affair, no false placing of a
> boy,[8] no stealing of money, nor does a young lover free a prosti-
> tute behind his father's back. Poets find few comedies of this type,
> where the good become better. Now it is your turn: if you like
> this and we have pleased you rather than bored you, send this
> sign: applaud, if you want chastity to be rewarded.

Again, the boast to provide moral edification is ironic. As Erich Segal has
pointed out, the play's homosexual allusions are erotic, the loss and return

of Tyndarus is similar to a *pueri suppositio* (false placing of a boy), and Tyndarus is freed *clam suom patrem* ("behind his father's back").[9] The epilogue is not a serious claim to moral didacticism, but an ironic variation on the request for applause, as the actors jokingly suggest that morality requires that the spectators show their appreciation enthusiastically.

Another ironic claim to edify comes in *Casina*. When Olympio is reluctant to tell how he was beaten by Chalinus, disguised as Casina, Pardalisca responds, "cavebunt qui audierint faciant" ("Those who hear will be careful not to do the same thing," 902).[10] "Those who hear" are the audience: the only other listeners are Pardalisca's fellow conspirators. Yet Pardalisca scarcely can be serious when she implies that the spectators, uninformed by Olympio, might fall in with an aggressive slave in drag. The line is another ironic response to the didactic tradition with which Plautus's audience would be familiar. The humor of Pardalisca's words becomes still more apparent when one contrasts them with Olympio's own speech to the audience slightly earlier:

> operam date, dum mea facta itero: est operae pretium auribus
> accipere,
> ita ridicula auditu, iteratu ea sunt quae ego intus turbavi.
> (*Cas.* 879–80)

> Pay attention, while I recount what I have done; it will be worth your while to listen to me, for the mess I made inside is so funny both to hear and to tell.

Olympio recognizes that the audience will benefit from his tale, but the benefit will be pleasure rather than moral edification or knowledge.

Two Plautine characters claim that they themselves have learned from the theater. Phronesium, the *meretrix* of *Truculentus*, says to one of her exasperated suitors:

> venitne in mentem tibi quod verbum in cavea dixit histrio:
> omnes homines ad suom quaestum callent et fastidiunt.
> (*Truc.* 931–32)

> Do you remember what an actor said in the theater? "All people are indifferent or squeamish in keeping with their own profit."

Phronesium's maxim is similar to cynical statements elsewhere in Plautus (*Cist.* 194; *Stich.* 520). Indeed, it echoes her own words earlier in the play: "ad suom quemque aequom est quaestum esse callidum" ("It is right for everyone to be clever for his own profit," 416); her quotation of it proves that one is just as likely to learn selfishness as virtue from the theater.

Though Plautus usually emphasizes his own genre of comedy when he casts doubts on the efficacy of theatrical moralizing, in *Curculio* he cites tragedy also as the source of a misleading moral generalization. Curculio, escaping from Planesium when she tries to get his ring from his finger, says:

> antiquom poetam audivi scripsisse in tragoedia,
> mulieres duas peiores esse quam unam. res itast. (591–92)

> I heard that an ancient poet wrote in a tragedy that two women are worse than one. It's true.

He goes on to claim that Planesium is the worst of all. Curculio's citation is in keeping with the misogynistic tendencies of the *palliata* (see Chapters 8 and 9), but it is peculiarly inappropriate. It is not at all relevant to the situation, as only one woman is involved here, and Curculio is decidedly mistaken about Planesium: she is a sympathetic character throughout, and she is justified in trying to see Curculio's ring, the only token left of her lost family. Curculio's maxim, derived from a theatrical source, is inaccurate and useless.[11]

MILES GLORIOSUS

In *Miles gloriosus*, Plautus discredits theater as a moral teacher by presenting a moralistic misreading of a play-within-the-play. When the play begins, Pyrgopolynices, the braggart soldier, has kidnapped Philocomasium, and he has also purchased Palaestrio, the slave of Philocomasium's lover, Pleusicles. Pleusicles, upon learning where his lover and slave are, has become the guest of Periplectomenus, Pyrgopolynices' next-door neighbor, and Philocomasium visits him through a hole dug in the wall between the two houses. Sceledrus, another of Pyrgopolynices' slaves, has spied Philocomasium embracing Pleusicles in Periplectomenus's house. Two deceptions make up the bulk of the play. First, Philocomasium, by running back and forth between houses, convinces Sceledrus that Pleusicles embraced not herself, but her twin sister. Then the conspirators add to their number the *meretrix* Acroteleutium, who, assisted by her handmaid, Milphidippa, persuades Pyrgopolynices that she is Periplectomenus's wife and loves the soldier madly. Pyrgopolynices sends Philocomasium and Palaestrio away and rushes into Periplectomenus's house for a tryst with Acroteleutium, only to be beaten and threatened with castration. Both deceptions, especially the second, are highly metatheatrical: the conspirators not only deceive the soldier, but they also perform. In the process, they get a great amount of pleasure, emphasizing throughout their enjoyment. Their principal spectator, Pyrgopolynices, however, finds not pleasure but what he thinks is edification in the performance. He wrongly draws an irrelevant moral, assuming that what he has experienced teaches a lesson against adultery.

The prologue of *Miles*, spoken by Palaestrio after the first scene, would encourage the audience to think of the play as a play. Being delayed, it does not provide an introduction after which the pretense of reality can remain intact for the rest of the play, nor does it allow the audience to dissociate the rest of the play from the prologue, as is the case when the prologue is spoken by a god or goddess, an unnamed actor, or a character who plays little or no further role in the play.[12] Plautus may have inherited the position and speaker of his prologue from his original,[13] but Plautine additions exploit its metatheatrical potential to the fullest. Palaestrio—or, more precisely, the actor playing Palaestrio—barges into the imaginary world created by the play's first scene and indulges in the same kind of bantering with the audience typical of actors identified only as *prologi*. He expresses his pleasure at explaining the *argumentum*, orders the audience to pay attention, and gives the Latin and Greek names of the play (79–87, 98). Later he tells what will happen in the first third of the play: he and his colleagues will make Sceledrus not see what he sees, for one woman will be two (147–52). Palaestrio the *prologus* thus reveals a plan that Palaestrio the character does not come up with for another ninety lines (237–41): he is simultaneously a character with limited knowledge and an omniscient actor.[14] Palaestrio's reference to Philocomasium's *imago* ("appearance" or "mask," 151) adds still more theatrical imagery.[15]

Having thus emphatically established the notion of "play as play" in the prologue, Plautus constructs an elaborate image of the play's two deceptions as plays-within-the-play, and of Palaestrio and his comrades as a troupe of comic actors performing those plays. Soon after the prologue, the audience learns that Palaestrio is not only more than a character; he is, in fact, like so many of Plautus's clever slaves, a playwright.[16] As Palaestrio plans the deception of Sceledrus, Periplectomenus, in a long address to the audience, describes in detail the slave's gestures. He concludes with a direct reference to a contemporary poet, almost certainly Plautus's fellow playwright Naevius:

> columnam mento suffigit suo.
> apage, non placet profecto mi illaec aedificatio;
> nam os columnatum poetae esse indaudivi barbaro,

cui bini custodes semper totis horis occubant.
euge, euscheme hercle astitit et dulice et comoedice.
(*Mil.* 209–13)

He is putting a column under his chin. Whoa! I really don't like that construction; for I happened to hear that the face of a barbarian poet, the one whom two guards watch at all times, was put on a column. Wow! I tell you, he is standing beautifully, like a slave in a comedy.[17]

What follows is the first of the play's two plays-within-the-play, as Palaestrio, Periplectomenus, and Philocomasium play the roles necessary for the deception of Sceledrus. The nature of the deception as a play is brought to the fore as Palaestrio puns on the verb *ludo* ("play" or "perform," 324–25), gives advice to Philocomasium on how to play her part (354–55), and responds with an aside to Philocomasium's alleged dream: "Palaestrionis somnium narratur" ("Palaestrio's dream is being told," 386). Palaestrio even refers to what Sceledrus has seen as a *fabula* (293), a word that Plautus almost always uses explicitly to refer to dramatic performances.[18] Periplectomenus concludes the Sceledrus section with a double theatrical double entendre:

usque adhuc actum est probe;
nimium festivam mulier operam praehibuit. (590–91)

So far we've acted well: that woman really did a job fitting for a festival.

The deception of Sceledrus is a kind of dry run. After its success, the image of a troupe of actors becomes more explicit as more performers are added and the conspirators prepare for their major performance, the deception of the soldier. Before the planning begins, Periplectomenus indulges in a long description of his own unusual personality, and it becomes clear that much of what he prides himself on is his ability as an actor.[19] He boasts of various roles he can play (642, 663–68), and of his ability as a dancer (668), and he says that he remembers when to say his lines, and when to remain silent (645–46). After Periplectomenus leaves to fetch two more performers, Palaestrio admonishes Pleusicles as he would an actor:

interea tace,
ut nunc etiam hic agat ac tu tum partis defendas tuas. (810–11)

Meanwhile, be silent, so that he, too, can act now, and you can sustain your part later.

With the entrance of Acroteleutium and Milphidippa, the image of a performance becomes still clearer. Periplectomenus enters coaching the women for their parts, and he boasts of their costumes (899). Palaestrio takes over Periplectomenus's role of coach, and when the old man shows impatience with the repeated instructions, Acroteleutium responds with a metaphor from shipbuilding (915–21): Palaestrio is *architectus* ("designer"), and the other characters are *fabri* ("craftsmen"). The metaphor recalls not only earlier descriptions of Palaestrio as a builder (209, 901; cf. *Poen.* 1110), but also an image common in ancient poetry: the poet as an architect or builder.[20] Acroteleutium was unwilling to hear repeated instructions from Periplectomenus, but she accepts them from Palaestrio, because he is the playwright for their play. Acroteleutium also establishes more precisely Periplectomenus's role:

> si non nos materiarius remoratur, quod opus qui det
> . . . cito erit parata navis. (920–21)

> If our supplier, who can give us what we need, does not delay us . . . the ship will be ready in no time.

It has generally been assumed that the *materiarius* ("supplier") is Pyrgopolynices.[21] Although Pyrgopolynices is the material upon which the conspirators work, however, he does not take an active role in providing any material himself. A more likely explanation, and more consistent with Acroteleutium's gentle teasing of Periplectomenus, is that the *materiarius* is Periplectomenus himself, who provides the costumes, much of the "set" (his home), and two of the actors for the play-within-the-play. Periplectomenus is thus not only an actor, but also the *choragus* (supplier of costumes and props).[22] Here and in later scenes, Palaestrio repeats and refines his instructions to his comrades almost to the point of tedium (904–13, 1025–29, 1143–97). Such repetition of instructions, like the shipbuilding metaphor, increases the perception that a troupe of actors is carefully preparing for a performance.[23]

Milphidippa announces that her scene with the soldier is to begin a play-within-the-play, presented, like all Roman plays, as part of *ludi* ("games"): "iam est ante aedis circus ubi sunt ludi faciundi mihi" ("Here in front of the house is the circus where I must hold my games," 991).[24] As she and Palaestrio deceive the soldier, they each ask the other how their acting is going: ("ut ludo?" "How am I performing?" 1066, 1073). In the final coaching scene, Palaestrio, after further admonishing Acroteleutium and Milphidippa, tells Pleusicles to take on the costume of a ship's captain

(1177). He describes the costume in great detail and makes clear that it will come from Periplectomenus's house, that is, from the *choragus* (1178–82).[25] After the women's performance, Pleusicles enters, referring again to his costume (1286), and self-consciously musing on his role as an actor who must speak in a way proper for his part: "oratio alio mihi demutandast mea" ("I must change my delivery," 1291). Philocomasium performs a tour de force as she leaves Pyrgopolynices, and when Palaestrio's attempt to outdo her almost inspires Pyrgopolynices to keep him, he is forced to improvise (1368–72).[26]

In the last scene of the play and of the play-within-the-play, Plautus adds one final metatheatrical touch. Though Pyrgopolynices is spared, his tormentors make a point of saying that his tunic, cloak, and sword will not be returned from Periplectomenus's house (1423): the play is over, and the costumes go back to the *choragus*. The staging further contributes to the audience's sense that the deception of the soldier has been a play: everyone leaves the stage except Pyrgopolynices and his servants, who, as the spectators, remain to go home (1437) after the actors have made their exits.[27]

Miles gloriosus, then, is unique among Plautus's plays in the consistency and the intensity of its imagery of performance. Plautus here makes an extra effort to establish his *servus callidus* as a playwright, includes an unusual amount of direct references to acting and instruction of actors, and provides Palaestrio with a troupe of actors that even includes a *choragus*. The play is also unique in the size of the cast of the deception plays and in the quantity of deception through performance. *Miles* is thus the closest Plautus—or any ancient playwright, for that matter—comes to producing an outright play-within-the-play similar to those which have encouraged audiences to ponder the nature of theater in countless pieces since the Renaissance.[28]

Plautus offers two different perspectives on the nature of his theater. The spectator of the primary play-within-the-play, Pyrgopolynices, finds a moral message in the play he witnesses. Humiliated, beaten, stripped of his armor, and made aware that he has been duped by his slave and the others, Pyrgopolynices concludes:

> iure factum iudico;
> si sic aliis moechis fiat, minus hic moechorum siet,
> magis metuant, minus has res studeant. (1435–37)

> I conclude that this has been done justly. If this happened to other adulterers, there would be fewer adulterers here, they would be more afraid, and they would be less eager for such things.

The trite moral is in itself unobjectionable, but it results from a misunderstanding of what Pyrgopolynices has experienced. There is no lesson about adultery here, as Acroteleutium and Periplectomenus's marriage was all part of the ruse. Because the deception of which he was a victim has been so emphatically portrayed as a theatrical performance, Pyrgopolynices' conclusion is a misreading of the play he has witnessed. His moralizing epilogue reveals that he is not only a profoundly stupid person, but also a failed spectator.

Just as in *Casina* Plautus counters Pardalisca's ironic claim to didacticism with Olympio's more accurate boast that he will bring amusement, in *Miles* Plautus opposes references to fun to Pyrgopolynices' misplaced moral lesson. Unlike their audiences—Sceledrus, who is hopelessly miserable, and Pyrgopolynices, who takes himself far too seriously—the conspirators all have a wonderful time as they perform. The performers repeatedly describe their plays-within-the-play as *lepidus* ("pleasant," "charming," or "fun"), and one of their number even has a name that means "lover of revels" (Philocomasium).[29] In contrast to their onstage audience, the performers, toward whom Plautus directs his own and the spectators' sympathy, value theater not because it offers moral edification, but because it is a source of pleasure.

RUDENS

Only the foolish Pyrgopolynices sees a moral message in *Miles gloriosus*. Several of Plautus's other plays, however, appear in their first scenes to have a decidedly moral intent. Yet even the most earnest Plautine morality has a habit of collapsing in mid-play, so that the audience realizes by the end that it has been seduced into a play that is anything but edifying. *Bacchides* begins with lofty thoughts about friendship and resistance of temptation and ends with almost everyone except the deceptive slave seduced by the prostitutes. *Curculio*'s first scenes offer much talk about sexual propriety, all of it forgotten in the deception scenes that make up most of the rest of the play. *Stichus* starts with a dialogue between two Penelope-like wives and ends with wild revelry.[30]

In *Rudens*, a similar seduction of the audience is accompanied by explicit skepticism about the value of comic moralizing. The play's central plot is one of virtue rewarded and evil punished.[31] Daemones is reunited with his long-lost daughter, Palaestra, after he helps her escape from the pimp Labrax, who has been shipwrecked while trying to steal Palaestra from her beloved, Plesidippus. Explicit and heavy moralizing reinforces the moral message throughout the play. The god Arcturus, who delivers the prologue, informs the audience that Jupiter sends him to observe the deeds of mortals: with this knowledge Jupiter punishes the evil and rewards the good (9–30). As he delivers the *argumentum*, Arcturus establishes clearly the virtue of Daemones (35–38) and the vice of Labrax and his companion in crime, Charmides (40, 47–50), and he reveals how he, Arcturus, caused a storm in order to punish Labrax and reward Palaestra (67–71). Throughout the first two-thirds of the play, various characters expostulate on the themes established by Arcturus: the extent to which Labrax and men like him deserve punishment (158, 318–19, 346, 505–6, 617–21, 643–46, 651–56), the kindness and justice of the gods (261–62), and the value of virtues such as hospitality (286–89, 406–11), honesty (338), and industry (914–25).

Plautus nevertheless provides several hints that the world is not as morally simple as his play might suggest. Palaestra argues against Arcturus's worldview, complaining after her shipwreck that the treatment she has received from the gods is not in keeping with her virtuous life (185–219); true, the audience knows that things will eventually be set right, but her powerful rhetoric nevertheless complicates the play's easy view of morality. The fishermen, who call attention to their poverty with a direct address to the audience (293), also clash with the assumption that virtue is automatically rewarded. As they make clear, they are poor, and their lives are hard: their moral states have no bearing on their economic conditions. When Plesidippus's slave, Trachalio, tries to reassure Palaestra's companion, Ampelisca, she reminds him that many mortals are deceived in their hopes (401).

When Trachalio and Gripus, Daemones' slave, begin their altercation over who is to have possession of the trunk Gripus has fished from the sea (the trunk contains tokens that will prove Palaestra's birth), both misuse moral maxims in a way reminiscent of the deception scenes of other plays. Trachalio pretends that he grabs hold of the rope connected to the trunk only in order to help Grumio carry it: "at pol ego te adiuvo nam bonis quod bene fit haud perit" ("But I am helping you, for good things done for good people are hardly done in vain," 939). After much legalistic wrangling, the two decide on an arbitrator, and it is Gripus's turn to moralize disingenuously. Pretending that he has not met the potential arbitrator, Gripus says:

> quamquam ad ignotum arbitrum me appellis, si adhibebit fidem,
> etsist ignotus, notus: si non, notus ignotissimust. (1043–44)

> Although you call me to an unknown arbitrator, if he is honest, I know him, even though he is a stranger: if he is not honest, he is a complete stranger, even if I know him.

The arbitrator Trachalio has chosen, however, is hardly unknown, but is Daemones himself, Gripus's master.

These hints of skepticism toward and misuse of morality are relatively slight, and the play easily survives them to maintain its high moral tone through the melodramatic recognition of Palaestra by Daemones. Indeed, after the recognition scene, Daemones provides a summary of the central message in a monologue:

> satin si cui homini dei esse bene factum volunt,
> aliquo illud pacto optingit optatum piis? (1193–94)

> Is it not the case that if the gods want to help someone, somehow it turns out that the pious get what they pray for?

Soon thereafter, however, a particularly scathing indictment of onstage didacticism brings the play's moral facade crashing down. Exasperated that Daemones refuses to keep for himself the valuable trunk, Gripus says that his master is poor because he is "nimis sancte pius" ("too righteous and honest"), and Daemones responds:

> o Gripe, Gripe, in aetate hominum plurimae
> fiunt trasennae, ubi decipiuntur dolis.
> atque edepol in eas plerumque esca imponitur:
> quam si quis avidus poscit escam avariter,
> decipitur in trasenna avaritia sua.
> ille qui consulte, docte atque astute cavet,
> diutine uti bene licet partum bene.
> mihi istaec videtur praeda praedatum irier,
> ut cum maiore dote abeat quam advenerit.
> egone ut quod ad me allatum esse alienum sciam,
> celem? minime istuc faciet noster Daemones.
> semper cavere hoc sapientis aequissimumst
> ne conscii sint ipsi malefici suis.
> ego mihi cum lusi[32] nil moror ullum lucrum. (1235–48)

> Oh, Gripus! Gripus! In the lives of men are many traps, where they are deceived by tricks. And often, by Pollux, bait is put in those traps: the rapacious man who greedily goes after this bait is caught in the trap because of his own greed. The man who is careful to use his reason, his learning, and his brains can enjoy wealth earned honestly for a long time. It seems to me that plunder like that will itself be plundered, so that, like a divorced wife, it will carry away more dowry than it brought. Would I conceal

what has been brought to me and I know is someone else's? Never will our Daemones do that. It is always best by far for the wise to be careful that they themselves do not become wrong-doers in collusion with their slaves. When I have acted in a play, I do not care at all for any profit for myself.

Daemones' speech is among the most ardently moralistic in Plautus. It is also one of the most conspicuously metatheatrical. Daemones begins with tragic parody in the repetition of *Gripe*,[33] and he concludes by jumping out of character completely. Not only the character Daemones, but the actor playing Daemones wishes to relay the play's central message: virtue is more profitable than vice.

Gripus is not impressed:

> spectavi ego pridem comicos ad istunc modum
> sapienter dicta dicere atque eis plaudier,
> cum illos sapientis mores monstrabant poplo:
> sed cum inde suam quisque ibant divorsi domum,
> nullus erat illo pacto ut illi iusserant. (1249–53)

> I have often before seen comic actors speak wise sayings in this way, and they were applauded, when they showed those wise ways to the people. But when the spectators left and went home to their own houses, not a one of them acted the way the actors had told them to.

Daemones provides Gripus with a nice summation of the moral message that has run throughout the play, only to have it undermined by Gripus's all-too-perspicacious observation. Regardless of what Daemones might say as character or as actor, even a play as moralistic as *Rudens* is not likely to improve its audience's morals.[34]

Gripus's cynicism not only bursts the bubble of Demea's moralizing speech, but also introduces a change in the moral tone of the play as a whole. Daemones himself dismisses Gripus perfunctorily and continues with more moralizing typical of comedy, telling the audience that Gripus is an example of how slaves can get into trouble (1258–62). The plot of the play, however, does not recover. There is no more heavy moralizing, and Labrax, who continues to perjure himself with reckless glee (1355, 1374), finds himself not punished but rewarded with dinner and the return of half his money, which he thought he had lost in its entirety. It is as if Plautus says with Gripus's speech, "Enough moralizing; let us return to what comedy is really about."

TRINUMMUS

Trinummus offers far more moralizing than any other Plautine play, even *Rudens*. When the play begins, Charmides has been traveling on business for some time. Only his friend Callicles knows that before he left, Charmides had hidden treasure in his house. Charmides' profligate son, Lesbonicus, has since been forced to put the house up for sale, and Callicles has bought the house in order to save the treasure. In the early scenes, Lesbonicus's friend Lysiteles offers to marry Lesbonicus's sister without a dowry. Unwilling to let Charmides' daughter be dowryless, or to permit Lesbonicus to sell his land, his last remaining possession, for the dowry, or to allow the spendthrift Lesbonicus to find out about the treasure, Callicles plots with his friend Megaronides to hire a shyster (the Sycophant), who will claim to bring a dowry from the absent Charmides. Charmides himself, however, arrives home and intercepts the Sycophant, and comic confusion ensues until Callicles reveals what he has done and the play ends happily for all. Several characters supplement this moral plot with seemingly endless discourses on morality. Yet irony undermines all the moralizing, and the high moral tone almost disappears before play's end; two scenes with conspicuous allusions to acting help send the message that even a play as full of moralizing as this one is more valuable as a source of pleasure than of edification.

The goddess Luxuria ("Extravagance") opens the play with a moral allegory. She commands her daughter, Inopia ("Destitution"), to enter the home of Lesbonicus, and then explains to the audience that because Lesbonicus spent all his money with her (Luxuria's) assistance, he will now dwell with Inopia.[35] Luxuria is unrelievedly stern: she offers none of the bantering typical of Plautine prologues. Even as the prologue establishes the play's moral tone, however, it undermines that tone, for Luxuria, the epitome of frivolity, is a profoundly ironic source of severity, especially as she describes herself in language reminiscent of a comic prostitute ("is rem paternam me adiutrice perdidit"; "He has destroyed his patrimony with me as helper," 13; cf. *Truc.* 107–11, 209–17).[36]

The first mortal character to appear, Megaronides, is another stern moralizer. Believing that in buying Charmides' house, Callicles has taken advantage of Lesbonicus, he delivers a long monologue on moral decline:

> amicum castigare ob meritam noxiam
> immoene est facinus, verum in aetate utile
> et conducibile. nam ego amicum hodie meum
> concastigabo pro commerita noxia,

invitus, ni id me invitet ut faciam fides.
nam hic nimium morbus mores invasit bonos;
ita plerique omnes iam sunt intermortui.
sed dum illi aegrotant, interim mores mali
quasi herba inrigua succrevere uberrime:
eorum licet iam metere messem maxumam,
neque quicquam hic nunc est vile nisi mores mali.
nimioque hic pluris pauciorum gratiam
faciunt pars hominum quam id quod prosint pluribus.
ita vincunt illud conducibile gratiae,
quae in rebus multis opstant odiosaeque sunt
remoramque faciunt rei privatae et publicae. (23–38)

It is not a pleasant task to chastise a friend, even when his offense
deserves it, but it is sometimes useful and to the common good.
Today I am going to chastise my friend, for his offense deserves
it; I don't want to, but my loyalty beckons me to do it. For too
much has sickness attacked our good morals here; so much so
that most of them are dead by now. But while the good morals
suffer, the bad ways have grown lushly, like irrigated grass: now
you can harvest a big crop of them, and there is nothing cheap
here except bad ways. And a lot of the people here care a lot
more about winning the favor of the few than about what would
benefit the majority. Therefore favoritism overcomes what is
to the common good; it gets in the way of all sorts of things,
and it is burdensome, and it interferes with private and public
matters.

Megaronides is very earnest: indeed, in his mistrust of the new and his
antagonism toward aristocratic cliques, he is reminiscent of the most conspicuous moralist of Plautus's day, Cato the Elder.[37] In several ways Plautus
reinforces the association between Megaronides and Roman conservatism. Megaronides' repeated use of the word *hic* ("here") in the monologue
helps drive home the point that his words are what one might hear in the
place where the play is being performed: Rome. During the ensuing dialogue, Megaronides argues that Callicles should have avoided all suspicion
of blame:

> . . . omnis bonos bonasque adcurare addecet,
> suspicionem et culpam ut ab se segregent. (78–79)

> . . . All good men and women should see to it that they separate
> themselves from both suspicion and blame.

Megaronides is a practitioner of extreme Roman *severitas* ("severity"), especially as he takes the unusual step of specifying that his words apply to both men and women: the Roman notion that one must avoid even the suspicion of wrongdoing applied particularly to women.[38] In case anyone has missed the fact that Megaronides is spouting Roman ideals, Callicles includes in his response a detailed and explicit allusion to the largest temple in the city of Rome, the temple of Jupiter on the Capitoline:

> ne admittam culpam, ego meo sum promus pectori:
> suspicio est in pectore alieno sita.
> nam nunc ego si te surrupuisse suspicer
> Iovi coronam de capite ex Capitolio,
> qui in columine astat summo: si id non feceris
> atque id tamen mihi lubeat suspicarier,
> qui tu id prohibere me potes ne suspicer? (81–87)

> As steward of my own thoughts, I can control whether or not I do wrong: suspicion lies in someone else's thoughts. For suppose I should suspect right now that you have stolen the crown from the head of the statue of Jupiter on the Capitoline Hill, the one that stands on the top of the temple. Even if you didn't do it, if I want to suspect that you did it, how can you keep me from suspecting it?

Depending on where the play was performed, the actor playing Callicles may have been able to gesture directly toward the Capitoline itself, visible to the audience, as he spoke the lines.[39]

However Roman it may have sounded, however, Megaronides' moralizing would surely have had a humorous rather than a serious effect on most of his audience; for Megaronides rambles hopelessly. He begins his monologue with what we have seen is the typical monologue opening of New and Roman comedy: a generalizing *sententia*, followed by its application to his own situation. With his second *nam* ("for"), however, he returns to the general, unable to restrain himself from eleven more lines of moralizing. Most of his remarks are entirely irrelevant: whatever Callicles' actions may have been, they have nothing to do with the rise of cliques at the expense of the majority. Furthermore, Megaronides is completely mistaken about Callicles, who has rescued rather than abused Lesbonicus. The sentiments themselves may be admirable, but Megaronides is an old fool.

After he has learned the truth from Callicles, Megaronides continues his obsession with morality. Before he exits, Callicles speaks the standard formula of parting: "numquid vis?" ("Is there anything else you want?"). This formula, like the English "How do you do?" does not require an answer, and it usually remains unanswered unless a character wants to make a joke.[40] Megaronides, however, cannot resist the chance to moralize, so he responds, "cures tuam fidem" ("I want you to remain faithful to your charge," 192). Megaronides does, to his credit, acknowledge in another long monologue that he was foolish to believe the rumormongers; but his moment of self-awareness is lost in another sea of rambling moralizing about the vices of gossip (199–222). Again, Megaronides is not content to follow the normal monologue pattern. He produces a generalization about gossiping loiterers, says how he was a victim of their slander, discourses further on the bad habits of the loiterers, returns to his own situation, then comes back yet again to the general, proposing punishment for repeaters of scandal.[41]

The next scene offers another long moralizing monologue: a "debate" between profit and love offered by Lysiteles. Lysiteles says that he is trying to make up his own mind whether to follow *amor* ("love") or *res* ("business," 223–33). He will therefore make a trial of the matter, acting as both judge and defendant (233–34). His "trial," however, turns out to be a tirade against *amor*. After a long list of pejorative adjectives describing love (239a–41), he explains how a lover loses all his money, adding another long list of specialized servants in the household of a *meretrix* (241a–54). This train of thought leads him to a vehement apostrophe of *Amor* ("apage te, Amor, non places nil te utor"; "Get away, Love, I don't like you, and I have no use for you," 257), to more description of love's horrors (258–70), and finally to a resounding conclusion:

> certumst ad frugem adplicare animum,
> quamquam ibi labos grandis capitur.
> boni sibi haec expetunt, rem, fidem, honorem,
> gloriam et gratiam: hoc probis pretiumst.
> eo mihi magis lubet cum probis potius
> quam cum improbis vivere vanidicis. (271–75a)

> I have made up my mind to dedicate myself to what's worthwhile, even though that means lots of hard work. Good people seek these things: profit, good faith, respect, glory, and goodwill; this is the reward for the virtuous. For that reason I prefer to live among good people rather than depraved chatterboxes.

Lysiteles should have called himself advocate rather than judge and defendant. He has already made up his mind, and he seeks to persuade his audience, not himself. Like Megaronides, Lysiteles is a figure of fun, as he gets carried away in his earnest desire to persuade the audience of his moralistic views.[42]

The next character to enter is Lysiteles' father, Philto. Like Megaronides, Philto sees the world in terms of declining morality. His greeting to his son accelerates rapidly and apparently inevitably into a discourse on the evils of contemporary morals (280–300), as verbose and irrelevant as Megaronides' first monologue. Philto is more passionate than Megaronides. He delivers in a mixture of accompanied meters a diatribe twice as long as Megaronides' first speech, using a powerful rhetorical style;[43] and he tells of his own personal grief at living in such an age (291–93). The passion only makes the speech more humorous: like Megaronides and Lysiteles before him, Philto is completely carried away with himself, and the audience is far more likely to be amused than moved by his harangue. In the next scenes, Philto reveals that he just cannot stop moralizing, even in the least likely places. He fills with maxims his conversation with Lysiteles (305–12, 318–23, 339–43, 345, 353–54, 363–64, 367–68), moralizes aside as he eavesdrops on the dialogue between Lesbonicus and his slave Stasimus (416–17, 422–24), and offers various bits of moral advice to Lesbonicus (447, 461–62, 466–73, 485–87). Philto even finds an opportunity to talk about bad morals when Stasimus tries to convince him that the land that Lesbonicus wants to give as his sister's dowry is worthless. If, says Philto, anything sown in the land perishes, *mores mali* ("bad morals") should be sown there (531–32); and if the land wears out the slaves who work it, bad slaves should be sent to it (547–52).

Like Megaronides, Philto is associated with Rome. Trying to convince Philto not to accept Lesbonicus's land as a dowry, Stasimus says that even Syrian slaves, "genus quod patientissumumst hominum" ("the most long-suffering race of men"), cannot survive six months working the hard soil (542–44). Philto responds, "Campans genus / multo Surorum iam antidit patientia" ("Now the Campanian race far surpasses the Syrians in endurance"). Philto refers to the fate of the people of Capua, enslaved because they had gone over to Hannibal during the Second Punic War.[44] In the next scene, Stasimus, describing the dialogue with Philto, makes a joking reference to the Italian city of Praeneste (609).

The first half of *Trinummus*, then, offers three characters—Megaronides, Lysiteles, and Philto—whose obsession with moralizing makes them look silly. Shortly after Philto's exit, Plautus offers a dialogue full of moralizing that is not silly, but that its onstage audience hears through self-interested ears. Lysiteles and Lesbonicus debate whether or not Lesbonicus should give

Lysiteles a dowry in what is arguably the most serious dialogue in all of Plautus. Its seventy-eight lines, as the two young men vehemently accuse each other of acting immorally, are unbroken by any comical interruptions, and the arguments are severe, even brutal. The entire scene, however, is overheard by Stasimus, who frames it with theatrical metaphors. As the young men enter, Stasimus says that they stand "haud ineuscheme" ("quite elegantly," 625). *Ineuscheme* is evidently a word with connotations of performance: *euscheme* is used elsewhere of Palaestrio preparing his "play" in *Miles gloriosus* (213). Stasimus then eavesdrops, without interrupting, until the debate reaches its most intense point, and Lysiteles claims that Lesbonicus, after selling his last remaining property to provide a dowry for his sister, will go into exile as a mercenary and leave Lysiteles himself looking greedy and responsible for his friend's ruin. Stasimus then comes out from hiding and proclaims:

> non enim possum quin exclamem euge. euge, Lysiteles, πάλιν.
> facile palmam habes: hic victust, vicit tua comoedia.
> hic agit magis ex argumento et versus melioris facit.
> etiam ob stultitiam tuam te † curis multabo mina. (705–8)

> Really, I can't keep from shouting, "Bravo! Bravo, Lysiteles! Encore!" You easily win the prize. Lesbonicus here has been defeated; your comedy has won. Lysiteles here performs more in keeping with the plot, and he makes better verses. But you, Lesbonicus, I will fine a mina because of your stupidity.

In describing the debaters as actors, Stasimus places himself in the position of a spectator, as well as a judge of actors.[45] As for his judgment, it is certainly debatable that Lysiteles' arguments are superior to those of Lesbonicus: indeed, Lysiteles' self-satisfaction at the favor he is doing is less sympathetic than the remorse and concern of Lesbonicus.[46] Stasimus does not interrupt with his praise until Lysiteles talks about his fear that Lesbonicus will become a mercenary, for it is this fear, and its relevance to his own situation, that most concerns him (cf. 595–99, 718–26). The implications for didacticism are similar to those provided by Gripus's speech in *Rudens*. Gripus's spectators liked the sound of actors' *sententiae* but failed to respond to their content. Here the spectator, Stasimus, hears what he wants to hear; he approves of the *sententiae* that suit his own interests, and he gives the prize to the actor whose plot, if successful, would save him from becoming the slave of a mercenary.

Another parallel with Gripus's speech is that here as well, the moral tone of the play diminishes considerably after the theatrical reference. In the next scene, Callicles and the great moralizer Megaronides find themselves in the incongruous position of plotting a deception. The idea is Megaronides', and his language is reminiscent of clever slaves and characters like them who plan and watch deceptions elsewhere in Plautus.[47] Callicles, at least, is aware of the incongruity:

> satis scite et probe;
> quamquam hoc me aetatis sycophantari pudet. (786–87)

That's a great idea! Still, I'm ashamed to plot tricks at my age.

Megaronides' plot is doomed to failure before it begins, for no sooner have the two old plotters left the stage than Charmides himself enters, and he promptly encounters the Sycophant. What follows is, as we saw in Chapter 1, one of the most conspicuously theatrical scenes in all of Plautus: the status of the Sycophant as an actor could hardly be emphasized more. Charmides' mockery of that actor is a source of great comic amusement, and it erases the moral earnestness from this previously all-too-serious play. Charmides, who enjoys the Sycophant's failure immensely, is the opposite of the stern moralists who have preceded him onstage.[48] By contrasting the pure fun of this scene with the failed attempts at moral seriousness elsewhere, Plautus once again makes his point that the proper end of comedy is pleasure, not edification. Furthermore, the audience is aware that the most severe moralist of the play, Megaronides, lies behind the Sycophant's failed attempt at deception. The Sycophant reminds them of Megaronides' role with several references to his *conductor* ("employer," 853, 856, 866), and a claim that he will himself deceive Megaronides if he can:

> ipse ornamenta a chorago haec sumpsit suo periculo.
> nunc ego si potero ornamentis hominem circumducere,
> dabo operam, ut me esse ipsum plane sycophantam sentiat.
> (858–60)

He himself rented the costume from the *choragus* at his own risk. Now if I can trick the fellow out of the costume, I'll see to it that he learns that I really am a trickster myself.

Poor Megaronides fails both as a moralist and as a Machiavellian: his severity only causes him to look a fool, and his attempt at deception is a disaster.[49]

The moralists nevertheless make one last attempt to dominate the play. When the Sycophant has left in disgrace, Stasimus enters with a strangely moralistic variation on the running-slave motif. After his initial admonition to himself to hurry, Stasimus realizes that he has lost a ring, and he fears that one of his good-for-nothing friends has stolen it. Then, even more unexpectedly than Philto and Megaronides before him, he turns suddenly to a lament for the loss of *veteres mores* ("old ways," 1028–29). He indulges in a long discourse on *mali mores* ("bad ways") ranging through the topoi of conservative complaints: decline in *parsimonia* ("thrift"), *ambitio* ("unfair election practices"), soldiers throwing away shields in battle, *flagitium* ("crime"), failure to reward the *strenui* ("the virtuous and brave"), the inadequacy of laws, perfidy (1032–54). His thoughts on *fides* ("trustworthiness") lead him to another sudden change of topic: he himself made a loan of a talent to a friend, and it was not returned. Finally, Stasimus restrains himself, in an implicit acknowledgment that such matters as public morality are not the proper domain of theater:

> sed ego sum insipientior, qui rebus curem publicis
> potius quam, id quod proxumumst, meo tergo tutelam geram.
> (1057–58)

> But it's silly of me to worry about public matters rather than protect my own back, which is closest to me.[50]

Stasimus's tirade brings the crowning touch to the mockery of obsessive nostalgia for old morals begun by Plautus's portrayals of Megaronides and Philto. Stasimus echoes much of the earlier moralizers' vocabulary,[51] and his pattern of thought—from disappointment in friends to *mos* and back to friends—is the same as that of Megaronides. The audience has learned enough about Stasimus from earlier scenes to know that he is a most incongruous proponent of such morality. His concluding words about the loan of a talent reinforce the incongruity: what is he doing with such a large amount of money when his master is broke?[52]

One way in which Stasimus's speech differs from those of his predecessors is that he is overheard by Charmides. Charmides' asides have been interpreted as words of agreement from a more reliable source, who reveals that however untrustworthy and humorous Stasimus is, his words should be taken seriously.[53] In fact, Charmides' words are the kind of derisive response typical of one eavesdropping on a *servus currens* (cf. *Asin.* 272–95; *Capt.* 793–833). Charmides first makes humorous comments on Stasimus's haste (1015–16)[54] and the thief who stole Stasimus's ring (1024). When Stasimus turns to *mores*, Charmides' first reaction is:

di immortales, basilica hic quidem facinora inceptat loqui.
vetera quaerit, vetera amare hunc more maiorum scias. (1030–31)

Immortal gods! This guy is starting to speak royally! He longs
for the old ways; you can tell that he loves them, just as our
ancestors did.

Basilicus ("kinglike") is used elsewhere of slaves and parasites speaking or
acting pompously, beyond their station (*Capt.* 811; *Persa* 29, 31, 462, 806;
Poen. 577; *Pseud.* 458). Given this context, Charmides' assertion that Stasimus loves old ways is surely sarcastic.[55] Charmides' later words of approval
are also playful: he recognizes that Stasimus is reciting clichés, and he enjoys them (1041–42). Such playful asides are in keeping with Charmides'
character: he made similar jokes as he listened to the Sycophant (851–69).
Just as he earlier enjoyed the performance of the Sycophant, Charmides
now gets pleasure, not edification, from the moralizing performance of
Stasimus.

What follows is largely pro forma: Callicles explains all to Charmides,
Lysiteles wins Charmides' daughter for himself and pardon for Lesbonicus,
and Lesbonicus promises to reform and to marry Callicles' daughter. It cannot be denied that the most important moral example in the play, Callicles'
loyalty to Charmides, remains intact in spite of all the irony and ridicule of
moralizing.[56] Nevertheless, metatheatrical elements reinforce a pervasive
undermining of the heavy moralizing that dominates most of the play.
Rather than any of the lessons proposed by its ardently moralizing characters, *Trinummus* provides satire of those very moralists, and a clear signal that
comedy is for pleasure, not for moral instruction.[57]

It is not surprising, of course, that Plautus should make fun of pompous
moralists: from Aristophanes' *alazones* ("braggarts") through Shakespeare's
Malvolio to the prigs and busybodies of modern sitcoms, the self-righteous
have always been an irresistible target of comic dramatists. What is striking
is the extent to which Plautus connects awareness of performance with
deflation of moralizing, and the number of passages in which he explicitly
debunks dramatic *sententiae*. Taken together, the passages and plays discussed here suggest not only that Plautus was keenly aware of the usefulness
of moralizing and moralists as targets for comedy, but also that he presented
a programmatic dismissal of comic moralizing as a source of edification.

This is not to say that Plautus sought to subvert the moral views of his
more upright characters or of his audience. With the exception of the shad-

ows cast upon the comfortable moral universe of *Rudens*, Plautus seldom suggests that the high moral principles sometimes espoused in his plays are wrong: it is moralizing rather than morality that Plautus mocks. Nevertheless, the repeated undermining of theatrical moralizing has repercussions beyond the comic stage. As I noted above, moralizing was a pervasive part of Roman life both on and off the stage. Much of Plautus's ironic moralizing, especially in *Trinummus*, is reminiscent of the kind of moralizing spectators would have heard in contemporary political and cultural debates. The persistent antididacticism, therefore, carries with it yet another layer of irony: even as he rejects the use of comedy to send moral messages, Plautus himself sends a message of his own with distinct relevance to the moral and political discourse of his day.

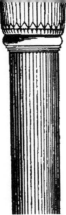

PART

II

5

AUDIENCE AND OCCASION: *PSEUDOLUS*

FOR Plautus, then, the aim of theater was pleasure; and one of the primary features of the relationship between his actors and their audience was the former's conspicuous determination to provide the greatest possible pleasure to the latter. This determination is especially prominent in two plays: *Pseudolus* and *Amphitruo*. In *Pseudolus*, Plautus uses the close relationship between actors and audience to reinforce the play's effectiveness as a tour de force, appropriate for the extraordinary occasion at which the play was first produced. In *Amphitruo*, blandishment of the audience and theatrical awareness help remove potentially disquieting elements of the unusual plot.

A number of critics have noted the success of *Pseudolus* as a piece of meta-theater, observing that Plautus repeatedly describes the action onstage in theatrical terms, and that he has created in the play's title character both an actor accomplishing ever more dazzling theatrical feats and a metaphor for the playwright himself.[1] The success of a play, however, depends ultimately not on its playwright or actors, but on the reaction of its audience; and *Pseudolus* shows a remarkable degree of self-consciousness about this third element of dramatic performance as well. In *Pseudolus*, Plautus not only offers a tour de force, but also repeatedly reminds the audience that the play's unique qualities have been designed for their pleasure; and he involves the spectators in the action onstage in unparalleled ways.

The plot of *Pseudolus* revolves around the very typical acquisition of a *meretrix* by a clever slave. Calidorus is in love with Phoenicium, who is owned by the pimp Ballio. Learning that Ballio has sold Phoenicium to a soldier, and waits merely for the remaining five minae of her twenty minae price to hand her over, Calidorus's slave, Pseudolus, contrives to get the girl through trickery. He intercepts a letter from the soldier and gets another clever slave, Simia, to impersonate the soldier's servant, bring the owed five minae, and take the girl. To this typical plot, Plautus added a menagerie of motifs possible in the *palliata* tradition, fulfilling almost every possible expectation of his audience. At the same time, he extended these familiar elements, offering novelty, surprise, and pure virtuosity; and he never let his audience forget that they were being treated to something special. It is hardly unusual for Plautus to include and elaborate elements not necessary to the accomplishment of a play's central plot. The number of such elements in *Pseudolus*, however, is without parallel in Plautus's corpus.

First, Plautus added to the plot a pair of bets. Early in the play, Calidorus's father, Simo, bets Pseudolus twenty minae that he will not be able to obtain Phoenicium. Later, Ballio promises Simo both the girl and twenty minae if Pseudolus succeeds in his quest. Either Simo's promise of the twenty minae or Ballio's promise of the girl alone would have been sufficient to explain, for anyone who cared to consider the matter, why at play's end Calidorus could legally keep Phoenicium. Not content with such a simple solution, Plautus has Pseudolus end the play with both Simo's money and Ballio's girl. Though most *servi callidi* overcome either their elder master or a pimp, Pseudolus accomplishes both tasks, and in spectacular ways. The spectators not only see Ballio triply undone—he loses the girl, the money he bet Simo, and the money he now owes the soldier—but they are treated to an extra scene of Simo forced to give money to Pseudolus and then begging Pseudolus for half the money back.[2]

The superfluous but delightful bets are indicative of how Plautus approached the play as a whole. Through the play's structure, Plautus reveals his determination to include as many expected and novel elements as possible. Pseudolus promises after only 100 lines that he will come up with a plan to get Phoenicium for Calidorus; yet nearly 500 lines later, he still does not have a plan. After calling attention to this apparent lack of progress through a verbal echo (106–7, 566–68),[3] Pseudolus leaves the stage with a promise that while he devises a plan offstage, the *tibia* player will entertain the audience (573a). Pseudolus's reference to the *tibicen* has often been used as evidence that Roman playwrights regularly interrupted their plays with instrumental interludes.[4] Yet it is just as likely that Pseudolus announces a novelty in naming the *tibia* player, and there is no good evidence that Roman comedies regularly included such interludes.[5] There is evidence, however, that *tibicines* played overtures before performances of Roman plays: Cicero claims that connoisseurs could recognize the title of a tragedy merely by hearing the music played before the play began.[6] The interlude by the *tibia* player, then, would probably appear to the audience not like an entr'acte, but like an overture: Plautus has offered them an entire play just for fun, and now he will start all over again with, as it were, a completely new play. Indeed, the portion of the play before Pseudolus's exit (Act 1 in the manuscripts) is only about 156 lines shorter than Plautus's shortest play, *Curculio*.

Even after this new beginning, Plautus delays before he gets the central plot under way. Pseudolus returns with a song of triumph, exulting in the plan he has devised; but the audience never even learns that plan, for Pseudolus abandons it when he discovers the slave Harpax bringing a letter from the soldier. For the first 600 lines of the play, then, almost nothing happens that is necessary for what is ostensibly the central aim of the plot, the winning of Phoenicium. Plautus has stuffed the first half of the play with monologues and comic scenes purely for the fun they provide the audience. The second half of the play is almost as conspicuously filled with extra elements. The scenes that contribute to the acquisition of Phoenicium— Pseudolus's deception of Harpax, the arrangement with Charinus to attain the necessary money and slave, and the actual deception of Ballio—make up only about 240 of the remaining 741 lines of the play. The rest is extra entertainment: monologues by Pseudolus, Ballio, Simo, Harpax, and the *puer* ("boy slave"); a cook scene; the humorous "preparation" of Simia for his deceptive performance; the humiliation of Ballio and Simo at the return of Harpax; and Pseudolus's final celebration.

A look at the list of dramatis personae reveals even more clearly the extent to which Plautus has "pulled out all the stops" in *Pseudolus*. The eponymous character fulfills and then exceeds all the possible expectations of the stock *servus callidus*. He is one of Plautus's most audacious deceivers. He delivers stellar examples of all the monologues that might be expected of a *servus callidus*: two "I don't know what to do" monologues (394–405, 562–73a), two "I do know what to do" monologues (574–91, 759–66), a philosophizing monologue (667–87), a monologue of anxiety (1017–36), and a song of triumph (1246–84).[7] He excels in teasing his lovesick master and insulting the greedy pimp, and he even treats the audience to some drunken dancing at play's end. In this play, however, one clever slave, even such an outstanding one, is not enough. Simia, Pseudolus's helper, far exceeds the expectations of the typical helper in a slave's deception, outdoing even his instructor in wiliness and braggadocio.

The slaves' antagonist, Ballio, is, as one critic aptly put it, a "super-pimp."[8] He steals the show as he fulfills and exceeds every expectation of a stock comic pimp. His first entrance, as he threatens his slaves and prosti-tutes with hyperbolic punishments, is a verbal masterpiece; and it must also have been one of Plautus's most impressive scenes visually, for it includes an unusually large number of mute extras, all subservient to the bigger-than-life pimp.[9] Ballio remains magnificent through the ensuing bantering with Calidorus and Pseudolus, so that his humiliation at play's end is all the more impressive. It is no wonder that Roscius, the great actor of Cicero's day, chose to play the part of Ballio.[10] Just as Pseudolus is outdone by Simia, however, the verbal genius of Ballio meets its match in the cook. The meet-ing between Ballio and the cook, the longest cook scene in extant ancient comedy, is completely unnecessary for the acquisition of Phoenicium: it is designed to show off yet another stock character, as the cook carries the boastfulness and threats of thievery expected in a comic cook as far as they can go.[11]

The other characters also reveal a desire to fulfill and exceed all the au-dience's expectations. Harpax, the soldier's slave who unwittingly provides the sealed letter used to deceive Ballio, manages to bring two stock charac-ters into the play. With his military costume and his boasts about his prowess (655, 1170–71), he is, along with his absent master, a stock braggart soldier; but he also delivers an elaborate "good slave" speech (1103–23). The "good slave" speech brings extra humor because even as he boasts of how well he serves his master, Harpax has unknowingly helped cause the loss of his master's prostitute. Calidorus is the quintessential Plautine lover, pining hopelessly and ridiculously. Simo, Calidorus's father, goes beyond the audi-ence's expectations of the *senex durus* ("harsh old man"). Callipho, Simo's friend, contributes no more to the central deception than does the cook; he does, however, give Plautus the opportunity to present a stock *senex le-nis* ("mild old man") to counter Simo.[12] Charinus, the friend of Calidorus, is more important to the plot: he lends Pseudolus the five minae and the slave, Simia, necessary to complete the deception. The close parallels be-tween the scene featuring Callipho and Simo and that featuring Charinus and Calidorus, however, suggest that Charinus is equally important as an-other addition to the list of expected stock characters: he is the helpful friend of the young master, a parallel to the friend of the old master.[13] Finally, the *puer* adds as a kind of lagniappe an obscene monologue in the center of the play.[14]

In its plot, its structure, and its characters, then, *Pseudolus* is extraordinary. Nor was Plautus content merely to write a remarkable play: throughout, he has his characters call attention to the play's extraordinary qualities and remind the audience that those qualities are designed to fulfill and exceed their expectations, thus bringing them as much pleasure as possible. First, he has the actors refer repeatedly to their skill at playing the stock characters they portray. Admonished by Pseudolus to act more sensibly, Calidorus responds: "nugae istaec sunt: non iucundumst nisi amans facit stulte" ("Nonsense, it's no fun unless a lover is an idiot," 238). The audience's expectations require that he, the stock young man in love, act foolishly. Ballio, told that he could never be expected to give good advice, replies, "non lenoniumst" ("That's not what a pimp is supposed to do," 289); and he later promises that if given the chance, he will break his oath to the soldier: "hoc meum est officium" ("That's my duty," 377). When he overhears Simia saying that he seeks a man with all the qualities of the stock pimp ("hominem ego hic quaero malum, / legirupam, impurum, peiurum atque impium"; "I'm looking for a man here who is bad, lawbreaking, foul, perjuring, and impious," 974–75), Ballio responds that those adjectives are his *cognomina*: he is the stock pimp to a tee. Simia also refers to the *officium* ("duty") inherent in his stock role (913); and he insists that he must be haughty in order to fulfill the expectations of his role (917–18; cf. 1048). He is indignant that Pseudolus should question his ability to carry out even the most difficult deception (931), and he boasts that he will outdo Pseudolus himself in lies and deceit (932–33).[15] Even the old man Simo emphasizes to the audience that he is determined to fulfill and exceed their expectations. As he prepares for his last encounter with Pseudolus, he says:

> nunc mihi certum est alio pacto Pseudolo insidias dare,
> quam in aliis comoediis fit, ubi cum stimulis aut flagris
> insidiantur: at ego iam intus promam viginti minas,
> quas promisi si effecisset; obviam ei ultro deferam. (1239–42)

> Now I've decided to ambush Pseudolus in a different way from other comedies, when masters ambush their slaves with goads or whips: I will go inside now and bring out the twenty *minae* I promised him, if he succeeded in this, and I'll bring it to him of my own accord.

Simo will ambush Pseudolus as old men often do tricky slaves near the end of comedies,[16] but not in the same way: he will ambush his slave with the money he owes him. The passage epitomizes the message Plautus's characters have been sending throughout the play: they are providing the audience with everything they might expect from their roles, and more.

The most salient reminders of this determination to provide the audience with everything it might want and more come from the title character. Early in the play, Pseudolus misquotes a proverb. Taken to task by Calidorus for the error, Pseudolus responds, "at hoc pervolgatumst minus" ("But my way is less hackneyed," 124): Pseudolus is determined to provide something new. Responding to Calidorus's claim that a young lover should be silly, Pseudolus makes clear that for him, simply fulfilling expectations is not enough:

> *Pseudolus*:   pergin?
> *Calidorus*: o Pseudole mi, sine sim nihili,
>   mitte me sis.
> *Ps.*:   sino, modo ego abeam.
> *Cali.*:   mane, mane, iam ut voles med esse ita ero.
> *Ps.*:   nunc tu sapis.
>   (238–40)

> *Pseudolus*: Are you through?
> *Calidorus*: Oh, Pseudolus, let me be worthless, please! Let me go!
> *Ps.*: All right, but then I'm outta here.
> *Cali.*: Wait! Wait! I'll act just the way you want me to now.
> *Ps.*: Now you're talking sense.

Pseudolus later assures Simo and Callipho that he will produce something to be marveled at (522); and after he has provided a disquisition on Fortune of a type clearly beloved by Roman audiences,[17] he concludes, "sed iam satis est philosophatum. nimis diu et longum loquor" ("Okay, that's enough philosophizing, I'm talking too long now," 687). He has completed the requisite "philosophical" monologue. Not content to show off with the most outrageous tragic parody as he accosts Charinus and Calidorus, Pseudolus tells the audience that he is going to act *magnufice* ("magnificently," 702), using a word often associated in Plautus with outstanding performance.[18]

Reinforcing the characters' allusions to their own accomplishments are other characters' praise for the performances of Ballio, Simia, and Pseudolus. Observing Ballio's tirade against his slaves and prostitutes, Calidorus asks Pseudolus, "satin magnificus tibi videtur?" ("Doesn't he seem magnificent to you?"). Pseudolus responds, "pol iste, atque etiam malificus" ("He sure does, and maleficent, too," 194–95). Calidorus is impressed with Ballio's performance; and Pseudolus's pun, rather than undermining Calidorus's praise, reinforces it, for *malificus* is just the way one would want a comic pimp to be. Later in the same scene, Calidorus becomes impatient with Pseudolus for making long asides: he does not want to miss any of Ballio's performance (208–9). Simia receives praise for his ability as an actor before he even enters (724–50), and Pseudolus provides repeated reminders that his colleague excels in the qualities expected in a *servus callidus* (905–7, 931, 934, 938, 942, 944, 974, 1017–18). Pseudolus himself is praised by Simo for his ability to strut pompously (458, 1288), and by Charinus for his tragic parody (707).

The most telling praise of performance surrounds one of the play's greatest moments, its parody of a *flagitatio* or *occentatio*, an Italian custom whereby a citizen could shower his debtor or enemy with insults on the street.[19] Calidorus and Pseudolus take turns insulting Ballio, but the pimp responds to their revilement with delight rather than shame. This scene is presented in theatrical terms that emphasize that all three characters are fulfilling the expectations of their roles. Ballio calls his insulters *cantores probi* ("excellent chanters"), implying that they are doing their duty as performers well (366);[20] and when asked later about the incident, he calls the insults

> nugas theatri, verba quae in comoediis
> solent lenoni dici, quae pueri sciunt.[21] (1081–82)

> theatrical nonsense, words that are usually said to pimps in comedies, that boys know.

In two of Pseudolus's planning monologues, Plautus extends this emphasis on the fulfilling and exceeding of expectations from actors to playwright. In the first, Pseudolus has promised Calidorus that he will get Phoenicium, but when Calidorus leaves, the slave admits to himself that he has no idea how he will carry out his promise:

> sed quasi poeta, tabulas cum cepit sibi,
> quaerit quod nusquamst gentium, reperit tamen,
> facit illud veri simile, quod mendacium est,
> nunc ego poeta fiam: viginti minas,
> quae nusquam nunc sunt gentium, inveniam tamen. (401–5)

But just as a poet, when he has taken up his tablets, seeks what is nowhere in the world, and still finds it, and makes a lie like the truth, so I will now become a poet. The twenty minae, which are nowhere in the world now, I will find nevertheless.

Comparing himself to a poet, Pseudolus becomes a metaphor for Plautus, the playwright.[22] As he does so, he promises novelty. Plautus, like Pseudolus, is creating something new for the audience.

Later, after he has made promises to Simo as extravagant as those he made to Calidorus, Pseudolus delivers a second planning monologue:

> suspicio est mihi nunc vos suspicarier,
> me idcirco haec tanta facinora promittere,
> quo vos oblectem, hanc fabulam dum transigam,
> neque sim facturus quod facturum dixeram.
> non demutabo. atque etiam certum, quod sciam,
> quo id sim facturus pacto nil etiam scio,
> nisi quia futurumst. nam qui in scaenam provenit,
> novo modo novom aliquid inventum adferre addecet;
> si id facere nequeat, det locum illi qui queat.
> concedere aliquantisper hinc mi intro lubet,
> dum concenturio in corde sycophantias.
> \<sed mox\> exibo, non ero vobis morae;
> tibicen vos interibi hic delectaverit. (562–73a)

I suspect that you suspect that I only promise such great deeds in order to amuse you, while I keep this play going, and that I am not going to do what I said I would do. I will not renege. Still, so far as I know, I know nothing for sure, as to how I am going to do it, except that it is going to happen. For whoever comes onto the stage ought to bring something new done in a new way; if he can't do that, he should make room for the one who can. Now I want to go off here awhile and muster up some trickery in my mind. But soon, I'll come back out: I won't hold you up. Meanwhile the *tibia* player here will entertain you.

What Pseudolus thinks the audience suspects is in fact true: he is making promises only in order to delight them. Given the earlier identification of Pseudolus and a playwright, the slave means also that Plautus the playwright is going through the possible variations of a clever slave's planning in order to give extra fun to the audience. Plautus then assures the spectators that the fun-filled delay is only the prelude: he has in fact taken extra trouble to provide them with something novel, as well as everything they might expect, in what follows. Like the *tibia* player, Pseudolus the actor and the character, and Plautus the playwright, all aim to delight the audience.

Pseudolus's "non ero vobis morae" ("I won't hold you up") calls attention to another of the play's leitmotifs: time. Throughout the play, characters present a continual struggle between their desire to offer additional words or action and their need to hasten. Pseudolus's first words are a reluctant acknowledgment that he and Calidorus must take the time for questioning and response, if he is to learn what is troubling his master (3–8). Pseudolus later tells Ballio that he and Calidorus don't want to take the time to hear the pimp describe himself (275), and Ballio has no time to listen to Pseudolus's requests (278). Pseudolus warns Calidorus that his words delay him (389, 393). Both the real Harpax and Simia dressed as Harpax are impatient as they get ready to carry out their exchanges (638, 951, 997, 1016, 1157–58, 1166, 1174). Simia's pace during the second exchange is a concern to Pseudolus as well (958), and both before and after that exchange, each *servus callidus* accuses the other of delay (920–22, 940, 942, 1044–48). Both Calidorus and Pseudolus are anxious that Charinus produce the money, costume, and slave necessary for the deception quickly (756–58); and Ballio is exasperated that the cook talks so long (889). Much of this concern with time is implicitly connected with the performance of the play. Pseudolus's words about the need for him to question Calidorus are an implicit allusion to the need for exposition at the beginning of a play. When Pseudolus tells Ballio not to describe himself, he seeks to end Ballio's performance, with which he has stolen the show for nearly 150 lines. The references to time surrounding Charinus and Simia are about the play's most theatricalized scene, Simia's performance for Ballio. All this concern with time thus provides another reminder to the audience that Plautus and the actors are serving their interests.

Elsewhere, the connection between pacing and the audience's pleasure is made explicit. As we have seen, Pseudolus assures the audience that he won't be offstage too long while he devises a plan (573), and he acknowledges that he has spoken long enough in his "philosophizing" speech (687). Lest the spectators be in any doubt that they are the reason for the actors' concern about time, Plautus twice has Pseudolus say so categorically. First, he refuses to tell Calidorus his plan:

> *Calidorus*: cedo mihi, quid es facturus?
> *Pseudolus*:   temperi ego faxo scies.

nolo bis iterari, sat sic longae fiunt fabulae.
Cali.: optumum atque aequissimum oras. (387–89)

Calidorus: Tell me, what are you going to do?
Pseudolus: I'll let you know when the time is right. I don't want
to repeat myself; plays are long enough already.
Cali.: That's a very excellent and fair request.

As a character, Pseudolus's real reason for reticence is that he does not yet
have a plan. As an actor, however, Pseudolus is concerned that the audience
not be subjected to unnecessary repetition; and Calidorus the actor agrees.
In a similar joke later, Plautus states the principle still more explicitly. Calidorus asks Pseudolus how he deceived Harpax, and Pseudolus responds:

horum causa haec agitur spectatorum fabula:
hi sciunt, qui hic adfuerunt; vobis post narravero. (720–21)

This play is being performed for the sake of these spectators: they
know [scil., how I deceived Harpax], since they were here. I'll tell
you later.

All this concern with time in general, and with the pace of performance
in particular, is both sincere and tongue-in-cheek, and in both respects it is
flattering to the audience. The actors state sincerely that no matter how
much fun material playwright and performers add, they must keep the play
moving to keep the audience entertained. In this play, however, where so
many extra characters, scenes, and monologues have been added with such
self-consciousness, the characters' obsession with time is gloriously ironic.
They pretend to be concerned to keep the play moving, all the time
aware—and aware that the audience is aware—that they and their playwright have in fact worked in just the opposite direction, drawing the play
out to provide the spectators as much pleasure as possible.

Besides keeping the spectators aware that they are the end of his own and
his actors' extraordinary efforts, Plautus also involved them in the action in
unparalleled ways. The play's two major characters, Ballio and Pseudolus,
show in the extreme both hierarchy of rapport and the desire of characters
for rapport. Each seeks to make the spectators his allies: Ballio fails miserably, Pseudolus succeeds spectacularly.

Ballio first enters addressing his slaves; but after a few lines, he speaks of
the slaves in the third person: he has begun to address the audience, seeking to persuade them that the slaves, though they look innocent enough, are
actually lazy thieves (136–42). He then shouts to the slaves once more, but

he soon addresses the spectators again, striving to make them see the slaves through his eyes: "hoc sis vide, ut alias res agunt" ("Just look at how they do everything but what they're supposed to do!" 152). Later in the play, Ballio renews his attempts to gain rapport with the spectators. Monologues frame his scene with the cook (790–97, 892–904; the latter includes another *sis vide*), and Ballio offers his own version of the stock "triumph monologue" when he thinks he has avoided Pseudolus's trickery (1052–62). The spectators thus get the distinct pleasure of denying their sympathy to the dastardly Ballio; the failed attempts of Ballio the character to win rapport with them give them a great sense of power, even as they delight in the antics of Ballio the actor.

Plautus reinforces this sense of power through the context and staging of Ballio's asides and monologues. Both his asides about the slaves and his first monologue about the cook are overheard by other characters. His next monologue, as he associates the cook and Pseudolus, reminds the audience that both characters are destined to outwit him; and his "triumph monologue" is spoken only moments after he has been deceived. When he learns that Pseudolus has in fact tricked him out of Phronesium, Ballio addresses the audience one last time before he leaves in humiliation:

> nunc ne expectetis, dum hac domum redeam via;
> ita res gestast: angiporta haec certum est consectarier. (1234–35)

> Don't wait now for me to return home on this street [scil., the street represented by the stage]; the way things have turned out, I have decided to follow these alleyways.

His words amount to nothing less than, "You won't have Ballio to kick around any more." The spectators can personally share responsibility for the villain's discomfiture.

In splendid contrast to Ballio's failure is Pseudolus's success in coopting the spectators as allies. From early in the play, Pseudolus makes clear that the spectators are to be on his side. As soon as he decides that he will use deception to get Phronesium, he announces:

> nunc, ne quis dictum sibi neget, dico omnibus
> pube praesenti in contione: omni poplo,
> omnibus amicis notisque edico meis,
> in hunc diem a me ut caveant, ne credant mihi. (125–28)

> Now, so that no one will say he was not warned, I say to everybody, while the adults are present in a public meeting: I make

a proclamation to all my friends and those who know me: watch out for me for this day; don't trust me.

Even as he ironically suggests that they themselves might be the victims of his plots, Pseudolus includes the spectators among his friends. During his ensuing scenes with Ballio and Calidorus, he addresses to the audience insulting words about Ballio (335)[23] and a promise that he will succeed in deceiving the pimp (380–81). He then begins his series of monologues. The first two, quoted above, are explicit promises to the audience. In between them, Pseudolus eavesdrops on Simo and Callipho, commenting to the audience on what he hears. In case any spectators miss the implied alliance, Pseudolus makes it still clearer in the middle of his third monologue, the exuberant triumph speech after he has come up with a plan:

> nunc inimicum ego hunc communem meum atque vostrorum
> omnium,
> Ballionem, exballistabo lepide: date operam modo. (584–85)

> Now I will very nicely exballiate Ballio,[24] this common enemy of me and all of you: just pay attention.

More eavesdropping ensues, as Pseudolus overhears the entrance monologue of Harpax. When he prepares to eavesdrop now, Pseudolus addresses members of the audience as if they were a fellow character, eavesdropping along with him: "st, tace, tace, meus hic est homo, ni omnes di atque homines deserunt" ("Sh! Quiet! Quiet! This guy is *mine*, unless all gods and men desert me," 600).[25] In the rest of the play, in addition to the remaining four monologues, Pseudolus eavesdrops with more asides on Calidorus and Charinus (692–702), and he shares with the audience his enthusiasm and fears as he watches Simia deceive Ballio (970, 974, 984–85).

Crowning this alliance between Pseudolus and the spectators at the expense of Ballio is the implicit identification of the audience with a political or judicial assembly. In his first address to the audience, Pseudolus uses the language of a Roman magistrate, addressing the people as if they were an assembly, a *contio* (126).[26] Near the end of the play, Ballio, in his final exit monologue, just before he admonishes the spectators not to expect to see him again, says: "Pseudolus mihi centuriata habuit capitis comitia" ("Pseudolus today had me convicted of a capital charge in the *comitia centuriata*," 1232). The *comitia centuriata*, like the *contio* earlier, is the audience, whom Pseudolus has led in judgment against the pimp. Their status has now changed from that of a *contio*—a public meeting at which no voting occurred—to that of an assembly that could vote to convict defendants.[27] Led by Pseudolus, they have themselves condemned Ballio.

In the play's last scenes, a third character, Simo, also seeks rapport with the spectators. He begins with the monologue quoted above, promising the audience that he will treat them to an unusual variation of the stock ambush scene (1238–45). When he returns, Simo points out to the spectators Pseudolus's drunken state (1285–86, 1288–89), and tells them what he plans to do (1290). Faced with Pseudolus's arrogance, he asks the audience what he should do (1315–16). Finally Simo goes so far as to ask Pseudolus to invite the spectators to join in the party at play's end.

Through Simo's request in the epilogue, and Pseudolus's response to it, Plautus shows an ironic awareness of the determination to please and involve the audience that pervades the play. Pseudolus invites Simo to join him and Calidorus in celebrating:

> *Pseudolus*: i hac. te sequor.
> *Simo*:   quin vocas
>   spectatores simul?
> *Ps.*:   hercle me isti hau solent
>   vocare, neque ergo ego istos;
>   verum sei voltis adplaudere atque adprobare hunc
>   gregem et fabulam in crastinum vos vocabo.[28]
>   (1331–34)

> *Pseudolus*: Go on in. I'm following you.
> *Simo*: Why don't you call the spectators in, too?
> *Ps.*: Well, they never invite me, so I won't invite them. But if you all want to applaud and approve of this theatrical troupe and play, I will invite you for tomorrow.

When Simo proposes that they invite the spectators, Pseudolus seems to say, "Even in this play we can't go that far." Yet in continuing, he suggests that perhaps they can. The flattering messages sent from the stage have become so effective that they appear even to be able to bridge the impassable gulf between fantasy and reality.[29]

Why such conspicuous determination to please in *Pseudolus*? Plautus need not, of course, have had any special reason: mature in his dramatic skills and confident of his popularity, he may simply have produced a tour de force and then taken pains to announce that fact. It is likely, however, that at least in part, *Pseudolus*'s uniqueness, and the reminders of that uniqueness, were a response to the circumstances under which the play was first performed. *Pseudolus* is one of only two Plautine plays whose first performance we can date with certainty: it was presented at the games surrounding the dedication of the temple of the Magna Mater in 192 B.C.E. by the urban praetor, Marcus Iunius Brutus.[30] Within a short time of this dedication, two other sets of games were given: Scipio Nasica, consul this year, held games that lasted a full ten days to fulfill a vow he had made two years before while leading an army in Spain; and Gaius Licinius Lucullus gave games to accompany his dedication of a temple of Juventas (Livy 36.36). So many festival days in a short period was still a rare phenomenon in the early second century: Plautus and the theatrical company that produced *Pseudolus* must have been aware that something special was needed if they were to stand out in the midst of so much other entertainment.

Those who sponsored the games, Iunius Brutus and the Roman senate, may have had similar concerns. The importance of dramatic *ludi* in the politics of the mid-Republic has probably been overestimated. In Plautus's day, the state rather than the sponsoring magistrates themselves provided most of the funds for the great public *ludi*, the events at which most plays appear to have been performed; and there is little evidence that elaborate games brought political success at this date.[31] Nevertheless, magistrates would have received credit for the games they sponsored,[32] as spectators would have been aware of who was responsible for the festival. Thus, even if the *ludi* did not have a direct effect on elections for the highest offices in the *cursus honorum*, they nevertheless would have won much goodwill for political leaders.[33]

In several passages, Plautus encourages this goodwill by reminding his audiences of the role of the magistrates in sponsoring his plays. Toxilus is confident that the authority of the aediles will make the costume manager provide costumes (*Persa* 160), and the Sycophant counts on the aediles to punish Charmides (*Trin.* 990). Mercury equates *ambitio* (illicit methods of acquiring votes) in theatrical competition with *ambitio* in political elections, jokingly warning even the aediles to avoid any foul play in assigning prizes (*Amph.* 72, 80). The speaker of the *Poenulus* prologue reminds the spectators that performance of the play depends on the will of the magistrates in charge (50–52). The *prologus* of *Asinaria* makes a wish for a wide range of people:

> hoc agite sultis, spectatores, nunciam,
> quae quidem mihi atque vobis res vertat bene
> gregique huic et dominis atque conductoribus. (1–3)

Please pay attention now, spectators, and may this turn out well for me and for you and for this company and its leaders and those who hired us.

The *conductores*, "employers," are the magistrates responsible for the festival.[34]

The political possibilities of Plautine performance, moreover, go beyond winning favor for specific magistrates. The audience certainly would have been aware that funds for the public festivals came from the state treasury, and that the senate was responsible for distributing those funds. Plays performed at state-sponsored *ludi* would thus also be a source of goodwill between the people and the ruling class of Rome as a whole.[35]

At nearly the same time as the games at which *Pseudolus* was performed, Scipio Nasica would have won a great deal of such goodwill through the long games he funded himself. Roman politics were highly competitive, and the first decades of the second century B.C.E. present a pattern of opposition by the aristocracy as a group to overly successful individuals.[36] The circumstances surrounding Scipio's games and Iunius's dedication of the temple of the Magna Mater appear to fit this pattern, for they suggest senatorial concern that the influence of the popular Scipio Nasica be kept within bounds. First, the funding of Scipio's games: Scipio had requested public funding from the senate, and it was refused. Second, the choice of dedicator: Scipio had been chosen over a decade before to lead the Magna Mater to Rome; he would himself therefore be a logical candidate to dedicate her temple.[37] Iunius and other members of the senate, observing or anticipating the success of Scipio's games and hoping to match it, may themselves have encouraged Plautus and the company who presented *Pseudolus* to come up with something unique and special. Their encouragement may thus have provided part of Plautus's inspiration for producing a tour de force, and making sure his audience knew it was a tour de force.[38] This is not to suggest that Plautus was taking sides in a political struggle, or that he was dependent on the leaders of one political faction: in spite of the efforts of various scholars, there is no evidence to suggest that Plautus was dependent on any "patrons" in the Roman leadership.[39] It is, however, quite possible that Plautus found in the desires of the festival's sponsors extra incentive to make *Pseudolus* conspicuously special.

Even if the political desires of his sponsors had no effect on Plautus as he wrote *Pseudolus*, he most certainly created a play appropriate for the circumstances under which it was to be performed. The Magna Mater was not just any goddess: she had been brought to Rome in response to an oracle saying that her arrival would lead to the expulsion of Hannibal (Livy

29.10.4−8); indeed, soon after she had reached Rome, Hannibal had been defeated. Her temple, in front of which *Pseudolus* most likely was performed, would become one of the central landmarks of the Palatine Hill.[40] The dedication of a temple to such an important new goddess was a remarkable event, and it called for a remarkable play. *Pseudolus* is such a play, not least because Plautus so effectively aligns the audience with its title character, and because he never lets the spectators forget that he and his actors have worked especially hard to please them.

6

GODS AND MORTALS: *AMPHITRUO*

μεγίστην δέ μοι δοκεῖ διαφορὰν ἔχειν τὸ Ῥωμαίων πολίτευμα πρὸς βέλτιον ἐν τῇ περὶ θεῶν διαλήψει.

But the quality in which the Roman commonwealth is most distinctly superior is in my opinion the nature of their religious convictions.

—Polybius 6.56.6 (Paton's translation)

AMPHITRUO, like *Pseudolus*, is a tour de force. It does not, however, offer a typical plot upon which Plautus builds an edifice of expected and unexpected elements. Rather, its plot is the most unusual in the entire Plautine corpus. When the play begins, Jupiter, disguised as Amphitruo, has impregnated Amphitruo's wife, Alcumena, while Amphitruo is away at war. Assisted by Mercury, who is disguised as Amphitruo's slave, Sosia, Jupiter inflicts a series of ruthless and hilarious deceptions on the mortal characters. After the misunderstandings nearly lead Amphitruo and Alcumena to disaster, Alcumena gives birth to children of both her husband and Jupiter, and Jupiter appears in his own person and explains all.

Plautus's source for this unusual plot remains a mystery. Some have proposed that Plautus drew on Middle Comedy; others, that he was inspired by South Italian farce, or that he himself adapted a tragedy.[1] Whatever its source, the play must have seemed quite strange to most of its original audience. Mercury states in the prologue of the play that kings and gods belong in tragedy rather than comedy (61), implying that mythological burlesque was unfamiliar to his audience. Neither extant Roman comedy nor the surviving titles of *palliatae* known in Plautus's day give any hint of plays involving gods in the way *Amphitruo* does.[2] The surviving titles of the literary Atellan Farce, another popular comic genre in Republican Rome, do include some mythological names.[3] Our fragments of written *Atellanae*, however, all date from the late Republic, and Höttemann has made a strong case that mythological subjects were first introduced by Pomponius in the first century B.C.E.[4] Even if the earlier nonliterary *Atellanae* did deal with the same subjects as the later literary *Atellanae*, the limited range of stock characters in *Atellanae* makes it unlikely that gods played important roles in any Atellan mythological plays.

This novelty is surely a large part of the reason Plautus chose to present *Amphitruo*: it would give the play a special appeal. Yet that same novelty brought some serious challenges. First, the unique and complicated plot would have been more difficult to follow than most other Roman comic plots. Second, there was great potential for generic confusion: a Roman audience naturally would have associated a mythological tale involving gods and generals with tragedy rather than comedy, and the situation of Alcumena, accused of adultery, is not without serious implications.[5]

Finally, there was the question of religious propriety. The difference between modern and ancient notions of piety, blasphemy, and reverence must never be underestimated.[6] Plautus's plays themselves demonstrate that difference. Though the performances were part of religious festivals, they included such features as a parasite, a lecherous old man, and a pimp who call themselves Jupiter (*Capt.* 863; *Cas.* 331–37; *Pseud.* 326–35), a young lover who says Jupiter fears him (*Poen.* 1191), a slave who says he would not yield to Jupiter (*Cas.* 323–24), and repeated parodies of religious ritual (e.g., *Asin.* 259–66; *Epid.* 182).[7]

It would nevertheless be most unwise to assume for Plautine Rome the same attitude toward divinity found in the theater of fifth-century Athens, where Aristophanes could present laughable gods with impunity. Although Greek mythology had begun to influence Roman religious thought at a very early date, Plautus's characters offer explanations of myths that suggest that much of Greek mythology was still relatively novel in Rome.[8] Many members of Plautus's audience would not yet have grown accustomed to the cavalier approach to divinity found in much Greek literature. The only other gods to appear on the Plautine stage in person are the divine speakers of the prologues of *Aulularia, Cistellaria, Rudens,* and *Trinummus.* Though these divinities are presented with a light touch,[9] they are scarcely the victims of burlesque, and their words and actions are of impeccable morality.

Plautus must therefore have recognized an element of daring in portraying on the comic stage a shady romantic interlude of the greatest Roman god.[10]

Plautus responded to these challenges with techniques familiar from the previous chapters: an emphatic hierarchy of rapport; flattery of the audience; reminders of novelty and expectations fulfilled; and the explicit desire to please, persuade, and inform the spectators. He also turned each of the play's potential difficulties to his advantage. Aware of the challenges to understanding presented by the plot, Plautus made much of the play a puzzle for the audience to solve: in figuring out the puzzle, spectators could feel both superiority over the characters who do not know the truth, and satisfaction at their own cleverness. Plautus used the play's generic uncertainty to remind the spectators of their power, as his characters suggest that the play has become a tragicomedy in response to the audience's wishes. Finally, theatricalization saves Plautus from any charge of blasphemy: at every turn he makes clear that "Jupiter" and "Mercury" are not really gods at all, but are actors striving to please the audience.[11] In short, *Amphitruo* was a daring experiment, and manipulation of rapport and flattering reminders of the performers' determination to please the audience helped assure that the experiment succeeded.

The play begins with a puzzle. The actor playing Mercury enters, wearing a slave's costume ("cum servili schema"; "with a slave's outfit," 117). He also wears a slave's mask, identical to that which will be worn by the actor playing Sosia: Mercury and Sosia will both say later that the god has taken the slave's *imago* ("appearance" or "mask," 124, 141, 265, 458), and Sosia will marvel that Mercury has the same facial features as himself (444–45).[12] Indeed, Mercury will later state that only the feathers in his hat will allow the audience to distinguish him from Sosia (142–43). Given this costume and mask, the first words of the prologue would be completely bewildering: in a remarkably long and convoluted sentence, Mercury admonishes the spectators that if they want him to bring them profit and good messages, they should listen to the play in silence (1–16). "What," spectators must have asked, "has this slave to do with profit or messages?" Near the end of the sentence, Mercury pauses for a parenthesis:

> (nam vos quidem id iam scitis concessum et datum
> mi esse ab dis aliis, nuntiis praesim et lucro). (11–12)

> (For certainly you already know that it has been bestowed upon and granted to me by the other gods, that I be in charge of messages and profit).

He thus begins to solve the puzzle, establishing that he is not a slave but a divine prologue speaker. His "you already know" praises the audience for figuring out the puzzle even as he explains it to them.

For those whose heads are still spinning from his first sentence, Mercury next states plainly just who he is: his name is Mercury, and he has been sent by Jupiter as a pleader to the spectators, even though Jupiter knows that he could get what he wants from the audience *pro imperio* ("by command"), because the spectators fear and revere him (20–23). Mercury thus implies that the spectators themselves have power over these gods even as he praises them for their pious obedience to divine will. The reason such a paradox is possible, of course, is because Jupiter and Mercury are really not gods at all, but actors, as Mercury reveals in his next lines:

> etenim ille, cuius huc iussu venio, Iuppiter
> non minus quam vostrum quivis formidat malum:
> humana matre natus, humano patre,
> mirari non est aequom, sibi si praetimet;
> atque ego quoque etiam, qui Iovis sum filius,
> contagione mei patris metuo malum. (26–31)

> For you see, the guy who ordered me to come here, Jupiter, fears trouble no less than any of you; as he is descended from a human mother, and a human father, it is no wonder that he fears for himself; and I, who am Jupiter's son, also fear trouble along with my father.

"Jupiter" is no god at all, but a human; and the fact that he gives orders to "Mercury," the actor who delivers the prologue, suggests that he is the lead actor of the company performing the play, and the trouble (*malum*) he fears is failure of the production. Mercury also fears *malum*, a word often used of punishments given to slaves.[13] The actor playing Mercury, probably a slave, fears that he will be beaten if the performance is not successful. The layering of ambiguity is exquisite: "Mercury" is a slave, pretending to be a god, pretending to be a slave.[14] The audience has the pleasure of figuring out this verbal and visual puzzle, and they remember their power over the fate of the actors, even when those actors are "gods."

Mercury continues with some tongue-twisting moralizing, in which his implicit flattery of the spectators becomes explicit:

> iustam rem et facilem esse oratam a vobis volo,
> nam iusta ab iustis iustus sum orator datus.
> nam iniusta ab iustis impetrari non decet,

iusta autem ab iniustis petere insipientia est;
quippe illi iniqui ius ignorant neque tenent. (33–37)

I wish to request from you something fair and easy, for I have
been assigned to be a just requester of just requests from just
people. For it is not right to seek unjust things from just people,
and it is foolish to seek just things from unjust people, since the
unjust neither know nor care for justice.

He then turns from the spectators' justice to his own and Jupiter's worthiness:

nunc iam huc animum omnes quae loquar advortite.
debetis velle quae velimus: meruimus
et ego et pater de vobis et re publica;
nam quid ego memorem (ut alios in tragoediis
vidi, Neptunum Virtutem Victoriam
Martem Bellonam, commemorare quae bona
vobis fecissent) quis bene factis meus pater,
deorum regnator * architectus omnibus?
sed mos numquam illi fuit patri meo, †
ut exprobraret quod bonis faceret boni;
gratum arbitratur esse id a vobis sibi
meritoque vobis bona se facere quae facit. (38–49)

Now, then, all of you, pay attention to what I am going to say.
You ought to wish what we wish: both my father and I have
done well by you and the state; for why should I recount what
benefits my father, the king of the gods, the chief builder for
everyone, has brought (as I have seen other gods—Neptune, Virtus, Victory, Mars, Bellona—recount in tragedies the good things
they have done for you)? But it was never my father's way to take
the good to task for the good he has done them; he thinks that
you are grateful to him for what he has done, and that you have
earned the good things he does for you.

On one level, Mercury, in character, reminds the audience of the benefac-
tions they have received from the king of the gods; but given the identifi-
cations Mercury has made, "Jupiter's" kindnesses are also the previous theatrical successes of his company. Mercury reinforces the identification of
Jupiter as chief actor by calling him *architectus*, a word Plautus uses elsewhere
of play-producing clever slaves.[15]

The other gods Mercury mentions here are probably deities who recited
their accomplishments in the prologues of tragedies.[16] His analogy between

himself and these speakers of tragic prologues leads Mercury to examine the
genre of the play at hand:

> nunc quam rem oratum huc veni primum proloquar,
> post argumentum huius eloquar tragoediae.
> quid? contraxistis frontem, quia tragoediam
> dixi futuram hanc? deus sum, commutavero.
> eandem hanc, si voltis, faciam ex tragoedia
> comoedia ut sit omnibus isdem vorsibus.
> utrum sit an non voltis? sed ego stultior,
> quasi nesciam vos velle, qui divos siem.
> teneo quid animi vostri super hac re siet:
> faciam ut commixta sit: <sit> tragicomoedia.[17]
> nam me perpetuo facere ut sit comoedia,
> reges quo veniant et di, non par arbitror.
> quid igitur? quoniam hic servos quoque partes habet,
> faciam sit, proinde ut dixi, tragicomoedia. (50–63)

Now first I'm going to tell you what I have come here to ask;
then I'll give the background of this tragedy. What's that? Are
you frowning, because I said this would be a tragedy? I'm a god,
I'll change it. If you want, I'll turn this tragedy into a comedy,
using the very same verses. Do you want that, or not? Silly me, as
if, being a god, I didn't know that's what you want. I understand
what you think about this: I'll make it mixed: let it be a tragicomedy. For I don't think it would be right for it to be continually a comedy, since there are kings and gods in it. How about
it, then? Since a slave also has a part here, I will make it a tragicomedy, just as I said.

The spectators are as likely to be frowning in perplexity as in discontent.
Mercury has been teasing them both in his appearance and in his words.
They now must ask themselves not only, "What is this god doing in a slave's
costume and mask?" "How can Jupiter be human?" and "What is Jupiter's
request?" but also, "What is this tragedy business?"

Again, Mercury solves the puzzle as he presents it, and at the same time
he reminds the spectators of the playwright and actors' desire to please
them. Mercury's pretense is that he agrees to make the play a comedy rather
than a tragedy in response to real or imagined dissatisfaction in the audience. Only after he has established that the play will in fact be a comedy
does he go on to discuss his proposal that the play be a *tragicomoedia*, and
later in the prologue he twice refers to the play as a *comoedia* (88, 96). This

is the first extant occurrence of the word "tragicomedy" anywhere. Plautus's *tragicomoedia*, however, is far removed from the true mixture of serious and comic elements that tragicomedy has become in its various manifestations since the Renaissance.[18] Mercury's tragicomedy is not, in fact, a separate serio-comic genre, but a kind of one-sided generic battle, in which comedy triumphs over tragedy in response to the desires of the audience, even when the verses themselves are tragic.

When Mercury finally reaches Jupiter's request, he offers the petition not of a god, but of an actor. Jupiter wants investigators to search the audience for claques: those guilty of unfair practices favoring one actor over another in the competition for prizes, even the magistrates in charge of the performance, will be punished (64−74). In spite of Mercury's ironic assumption that he and his boss have power over the spectators and even the magistrates, the request in fact reminds the audience yet again of their power to make or break the performance. It also remains phrased in terms flattering to the spectators:

> virtute dixit vos victores vivere,
> non ambitione neque perfidia: qui minus
> eadem histrioni sit lex quae summo viro? (75−77)

> He [scil. Jupiter] said that you live as victors because of your excellence, not through bribery or deception: why should this law apply any less to an actor than it does to a statesman?

As he had earlier turned from explicit flattery of the audience to a reminder of the actors' service, he now moves from flattery to a reminder of the actors' vulnerability: actors guilty of unfair practices in seeking prizes will be beaten and will lose their costumes (85). Mercury next makes "Jupiter's" real status completely clear: the audience should not marvel that Jupiter cares about actors, for Jupiter himself will perform in this comedy (86−88). As a precedent for his father's performance, Mercury cites Jupiter's response to the prayers of actors in the previous year, probably as *deus ex machina* in a tragedy.[19] The audience begins to see Mercury's principle of tragicomedy at work: comedy has taken over a tragic motif, the appearance of Jupiter (89−92).

When Mercury finally begins the *argumentum* after nearly 100 lines, he shows even more pointedly than most prologue speakers his desire that the audience understand.[20] Among the things he explains are his own and Jupiter's appearance: the audience will distinguish the two gods from their mortal counterparts because Mercury will wear feathers, Jupiter a gold *toru-*

lus, apparently a headband or tassel (141–47).[21] Mercury's feathers and Jupiter's *torulus* serve as visual equivalents to the direct addresses that keep the spectators aware of what is happening throughout the play. Both costumes and words allow the audience to feel superior to the ignorant mortal characters and pleased at their ability to figure out the ongoing puzzle. Mercury also reminds the spectators of the novelty that makes this play so special: "veterem atque antiquam rem novam ad vos proferam" ("I will bring you an old and ancient matter, made new," 118). He concludes with an admonition that it will be worth the audience's while to watch attentively:

> adeste: erit operae pretium hic spectantibus
> Iovem et Mercurium facere histrioniam. (151–52)

> Pay attention: it will be worth your while to watch Jupiter and Mercury perform as actors here.

Plautus's longest prologue thus demonstrates clearly and emphatically to the spectators that regardless of how strange the ensuing play may appear, it is designed to give them the greatest possible pleasure. The prologue also establishes a remarkable degree of rapport between Mercury and the audience that will remain as long as he is onstage. Altogether Mercury speaks more lines of monologue than any other Plautine character; and he repeatedly acknowledges the audience explicitly. He peppers his scenes with asides, spends more time eavesdropping than any other character in Plautus, and speaks Plautus's longest passage in which a character deliberately allows himself to be overheard (301–40). To increase his intimacy with the spectators still further, Plautus has Mercury spend most of his time speaking in unaccompanied iambic senarii, whereas the mortal characters of *Amphitruo* generally use accompanied meters.[22]

Mercury uses his rapport most successfully in the next scene. At prologue's end, Sosia enters, sent home to report Amphitruo's victory, and it soon becomes evident that Sosia and Mercury are two actors competing for the audience's sympathy and attention.[23] Sosia tries to convince the spectators (and perhaps himself as well) of his courage (153–54), complains about the danger of being punished (155–62), and bemoans his lot as slave of a rich man (163–75). The eavesdropping Mercury tries some one-upmanship: he should be the one complaining, for he is now acting as a slave, though he is free, while Sosia was born a slave: "hic qui verna natus est queritur" ("This guy, who was born a house-born slave, is complaining," 179). Sosia is not to be outdone: he echoes Mercury ("sum vero verna verbero"; "I really am a rascal of a house-born slave," 180), showing that even if, as a character, he is not yet aware of Mercury's presence, as an actor he is.[24]

When Sosia describes Amphitruo's victory to the audience in a long speech, the competition between slave and god becomes also a struggle between comedy and tragedy. Almost every word of Sosia's battle report would be at home in a tragedy. Its subject, war, Plautus explicitly associates with tragedy elsewhere (*Capt.* 61–62); and its patriotic and eulogistic content, serious tone, and numerous religious and legal formulas are suitable for a tragedy in the style of Plautus's contemporaries Ennius and Naevius.[25] This "tragic messenger speech," however, is made comic by its context. First, however he may speak, Sosia establishes himself as a typical deceitful comic slave: "si dixero mendacium, solens meo more fecero" ("If I tell a lie, I will do what I usually do," 198). Second, Sosia introduces his battle description by saying that it is all a lie: he hid inside his tent during the battle, and his dignified report is merely hearsay (199–200); he knows the battle lasted all day only because he missed his lunch (254).[26] Mercury reinforces this incongruity when he informs the audience in an aside that he, unlike Sosia, really was present at the battle (248–49). Third, the audience knows that Sosia's battle report is too late: Mercury has told them that Jupiter at this moment is inside telling Alcumena what happened on the battlefield (133–34). Sosia has fulfilled the promise Mercury made in the prologue: tragedy has become comedy in the same verses.

The speech concluded, Mercury reveals that the tragic messenger speech will be further undone, for he will prevent Sosia from delivering it:

> quando imago est huius in me, certum est hominem eludere.
> et enim vero quoniam formam cepi huius in med et statum,
> decet et facta moresque huius habere me similes item.
> itaque me malum esse oportet, callidum, astutum admodum
> atque hunc, telo suo sibi, malitia a foribus pellere. (265–69)

> Because I have this guy's mask, I've decided to make fun of him. And since I've taken his appearance and bearing, it's fitting for me to be like him in what I do and the way I act. So I should be bad, clever, and really tricky, and drive this fellow from the house with his own weapon, trickery.

Because Mercury looks like a comic slave, he will act like one. It has become clear by this point that Mercury's slave costume is a metaphor for the play as a whole. Just as the god Mercury is turned into the comic slave by his costume, the story of Hercules' birth is turned into comedy by the accoutrements, visual and verbal, that accompany the basic plot.

What follows is a long series of asides, as each actor addresses the specta-tors, fighting for their attention. Sosia makes three attempts to impress the audience, each of which is undermined by an aside of Mercury (271–90). When Sosia finally discovers Mercury, he addresses a series of pointing words to the audience (292, 294, 296, 298): he wants the spectators to see his potential opponent through his eyes. Mercury then allows himself to be overheard by Sosia, and he announces that he will perform ("clare advor-sum fabulabor, <ut> hic auscultet quae loquar"; "I will speak out loudly, so that this fellow can hear what I say," 300). Sosia addresses several lines to Mercury, and when he remains unacknowledged, he speaks aside again, re-newing his string of pronouns and adjectives that point out Mercury to the audience (317, 319, 320, 323). It is as if, failing to reach Mercury, Sosia ap-peals to the audience for an ally. The asides end with a summation for the audience by both sides. Mercury, with an emphatic *eccum*, announces his pleasure that Sosia approaches him (335), and Sosia proclaims both his fear and his determination to bluff his way to the door (335–40).

The competition between the actors also continues the lopsided con-test between tragedy and comedy. Observing the length of the night (as Mercury has revealed in the prologue, Jupiter has made the night longer so that he can spend more time with Alcumena), Sosia describes the constel-lations in fine-sounding astronomical language that would certainly have been at home in a tragedy (272–75).[27] His description, however, is pre-sented as an argument for Sosia's own explanation of the long night: the god Nox (Night) must be drunk. To undo the elevated language further, Mercury responds with an address to Nox, encouraging him to keep up the good work, helping out in Jupiter's adultery; and Sosia says that only the night he spent hanging, punished, seemed longer to him (277–81). When Sosia returns to his theory of drunken gods, suggesting that since Sol (Sun) has not risen, he must also be drunk, Mercury responds with an-other aside: "ain vero, verbero? deos esse tui similis putas?" ("What's that, you rascal? Do you think the gods are like you?" 284). The irony, of course, is that in this play, the gods *are* like Sosia, both in appearance and in action. In spite of Mercury's claim in the prologue that gods mean tragedy, gods here fit much better in the comic world represented by Sosia's character and actions than in the tragic milieu suggested by his elevated astronomical dis-course. The next pair of asides undoes the gods' pretensions to tragedy still further:

> *Sosia*: ubi sunt isti scortatores, qui soli inviti cubant?
> haec nox scita est exercendo scorto conducto male.
> *Mercury*: meus pater nunc pro huius verbis recte et sapienter facit,

qui complexus cum Alcumena cubat amans animo obsequens.
(287–90)

Sosia: Where are those whoremongers who hate to be in bed
alone? This night is perfect for using an expensive whore.
Mercury: My father follows that advice well and cleverly; for he is
in bed making love with Alcumena to his heart's delight.

In spite of the fact that Alcumena is hardly a *scortum*, Mercury speaks of
Jupiter as if he were a typical lover of comedy, enjoying the favors of a prostitute (cf. *Merc.* 985, 1018).

The ensuing dialogue between god and slave contains two more abortive
attempts to introduce tragedy. Mercury first addresses Sosia with an over-
blown allusion to the lamp he carries: "quo ambulas tu, qui Volcanum in
cornu conclusum geris?" ("Whither do you walk, you who carry Vulcan
closed up in a container of horn?" 341).[28] The tragic tone collapses when
Mercury asks whether Sosia is free or a slave. Sosia responds that he is
whichever he pleases: as an actor, he can play either role. His response leads
to a typical comic joke about slave beatings (344–45). Soon thereafter, Sosia
makes an attempt at tragedy. Asked his name, he responds, "Sosiam vocant
Thebani, Davo prognatum patre" ("The Thebans call me Sosia, the scion
of Davus," 365).[29] Besides being undermined by its incongruous source, a
slave who by Roman law has no parent,[30] Sosia's tragic tone is instantly destroyed by the long string of puns that follows (366–75).

The battle of identities reaches its climax, and both "Sosias" argue their
cases directly to the audience. Mercury says aside, "hic homo sanus non est"
("This fellow is crazy," 402). Sosia seeks reassurance from the audience that
he is Sosia:

> quid, malum, non sum ego servos Amphitruonis Sosia?
> nonne hac noctu nostra navis <huc> ex portu Persico
> venit, quae me advexit? nonne me huc erus misit meus?
> nonne ego nunc sto ante aedes nostras? non mi est lanterna
> in manu?
> non loquor, non vigilo? nonne hic homo modo me pugnis
> contudit? (403–7)

Well, dammit, am I not Sosia, the slave of Amphitruo? Didn't
our ship come here tonight from the Persian port, carrying me?
Didn't my master send me here? Am I not standing in front of
our house right now? Am I not holding a lamp in my hand? Am
I not talking, and staying awake? Didn't this guy just plaster me
with his fists?

As Sosia becomes increasingly aware of the persuasiveness of Mercury's arguments, he confides his doubts to the audience (416–17, 420, 423–26, 429, 431–32, 441–49); and he announces to the audience that he will make an attempt at playing his own stock role, and will try to deceive Mercury (424). The attempt is a failure, for as he reminds Sosia, Mercury is the character, and the actor, with power: "ubi ego Sosia nolim esse, tu esto sane Sosia" ("When I do not want to be Sosia, then by all means you be Sosia," 439).

When Sosia is finally put to flight, it becomes clear that his entire scene with Mercury was only for fun, for Mercury returns to the *argumentum*. He summarizes the plot of the play, emphasizing his own role as trickster, and he promises the audience a happy ending, thus helping to assure that the scenes that follow will be comic rather than tragic. Almost as an after-thought, he adds what from a mythological standpoint is the most important part of the story, the birth of Hercules. In this "second prologue," Mercury continues his conspicuous concern for the audience's understanding, asking them if they are following (485) and using phrases of a decidedly explanatory nature (479, 491).

Mercury's high level of rapport and his concern for the audience's understanding remain evident as he eavesdrops on the ensuing entrance of Jupiter and Alcumena. Watching Jupiter charm his conquest, Mercury comments to the audience:

> nimis hic scitust sycophanta, qui quidem meus sit pater.
> observatote <eum>, quam blande mulieri palpabitur. (506–7)

> This guy is really a great flatterer. Well, he is *my* father after all. Just watch how sweetly he'll soften the woman.

Mercury continues to make asides throughout the scene, helping the audience to follow the dialogue and, more importantly, promoting a tone appropriate to comedy.

The comic tone is unthreatened in the next scene, as Sosia fails to convince Amphitruo that there are two of him. Like Sosia before him, Amphitruo appeals to the audience when he cannot seem to get through to his interlocutor, seeking their confirmation that Sosia is drunk or insane (574, 576–77, 605–6). He will do the same in the next scene, when he becomes exasperated with Alcumena (769, 818); and near the end of the play, when he has reached the height of anger and confusion, he directs several desperate questions to the spectators (1040–46). Amphitruo's asides, however, only reinforce his position on the bottom of the hierarchy of rapport, for they are repeatedly overheard, first by Sosia (574, 576, 605–6), then by Bromia (1083).

Meanwhile, Alcumena enters and delivers a long monologue (633–53). She, too, desires the attention and sympathy of the audience: she begins with a question, and then tries to persuade the spectators of her own misfortune and the value of *virtus* ("virtue"). Both Alcumena's lament and her patriotic encomium to a general's virtue could in themselves fit well in a tragedy.[31] Like Sosia's battle report, however, Alcumena's monologue is made comic by its context. The audience is aware that Alcumena is being deceived, that it is not Amphitruo but Jupiter who has just left her; and the returning Amphitruo and Sosia, present onstage, underline her error visually. More important, Alcumena is very obviously in the last stages of pregnancy, as Sosia will point out in the next scene (664–67). The appearance of a male actor stuffed to look pregnant would certainly have been humorous, especially to Plautus's predominantly male audience; and Alcumena's pregnant state casts a comic light over her tragic lines about the fleeting nature of human pleasures, since she uses for "pleasure" the word *voluptas*, a word often used to mean sexual delight.[32]

The following scene, which climaxes in Amphitruo's accusation that his wife has been unfaithful, is the closest the play comes to real tragedy. Sosia makes sure the scene remains comic with many humorous comments and asides.[33] In spite of Sosia's comic interjections, however, by the end of the scene the plot may appear to some to be heading toward tragedy. As if in response to this danger, Jupiter enters with a kind of "third prologue":

> ego sum ille Amphitruo, cui est servos Sosia,
> idem Mercurius qui fit, quando commodumst,
> in superiore qui habito cenaculo,
> qui interdum fio Iuppiter, quando lubet;
> huc autem quom extemplo adventum adporto, ilico
> Amphitruo fio et vestitum immuto meum.
> nunc huc honoris vostri venio gratia,
> ne hanc incohatam transigam comoediam. (861–68)

> I am that fellow Amphitruo, who has a slave named Sosia, who becomes Mercury when it is convenient for him; I live in the room up above, and I become Jupiter sometimes, when I want to; but as soon as I make an appearance here, straightaway I become Amphitruo, and I change my costume. Now I come here for your sake, and I will complete this comedy we have begun.[34]

Jupiter's self-description is, of course, backwards: Amphitruo does not become Jupiter, Jupiter becomes Amphitruo; and Sosia does not become Mercury, Mercury becomes Sosia. The inaccuracy provides another puzzle for the audience to figure out. This one will be easy, for they know that Jupiter is the one with the *torulus*. The reversal also calls attention to the fact that what the audience sees onstage is not actually Jupiter or Amphitruo, but an actor, capable of playing both roles: Amphitruo, who lives upstairs in the house, and Jupiter, who lives "upstairs" on Olympus.[35] It is in this capacity as actor, made still clearer by his reference to a change of costume, that Jupiter continues: he enters now for the audience's sake, in order to continue the comedy. Again, genre is a response to the audience's wishes.[36] Jupiter goes on to promise a comic plot: he will bring the greatest possible confusion to the household; and he will make sure everything turns out happily. Like Mercury before him, Jupiter is solicitous of the spectators' understanding: he spells out exactly what is going to happen both here (873–81) and in his later monologues (891–96, 952–53, 974–75, 1039). In the ensuing scene, Plautus reinforces Jupiter's higher position in the hierarchy of rapport by having Alcumena make clear to the audience that she does not hear Jupiter's aside of over four lines ("mirum quid solus secum secreto ille agat"; "I wonder what he is saying to himself in private," 954).

After confusing Alcumena and Sosia still further, Jupiter calls upon Mercury, who enters with an actor's tour de force:

> concedite atque abscedite omnes, de via decedite,
> nec quisquam tam audax fuat homo, qui obviam obsistat mihi.
> nam mihi quidem hercle qui minus liceat deo minitarier
> populo, ni decedat mihi, quam servolo in comoediis?
> ille navem salvam nuntiat aut irati adventum senis:
> ego sum Iovi dicto audiens, eius iussu nunc huc me adfero.
> quam ob rem mihi magis par est via decedere et concedere.
> (984–90)

Get out of my way and scatter, everybody! Get off the road! And don't let anyone be brazen enough to stand in my way. For really, why should I, a god, be any less allowed to threaten people, if they don't get out of my way, than the little slave in comedies? That slave announces that a ship is safe, or that an angry old man is coming: *I* follow the orders of Jupiter, and I bring myself here at his command. For that reason, it is more proper to get out of my way and clear the road for me.

Mercury calls attention to the fact that he is fulfilling the expectations of the stock *servus currens*, or running slave, the most stereotypical of comic characters:[37] he has made his potentially tragic role exceedingly comic in order to please the audience. He even adjusts his meter to suit this role. Up to this point, the two gods have always spoken in unaccompanied iambic senarii when alone onstage: Mercury here uses an accompanied meter (iambic octonarius), as do all of Plautus's other running slaves.[38]

As he continues, Mercury boasts still more of his versatility as an actor:

> pater vocat me, eum sequor, eius dicto imperio sum audiens;
> ut filium bonum patri esse oportet, itidem ego sum patri.
> amanti subparasitor, hortor, adsto, admoneo, gaudeo.
> si quid patri volup est, voluptas ea mi multo maxumast.
> amat: sapit; recte facit, animo quando obsequitur suo,
> quod omnis homines facere oportet, dum id modo fiat bono.
> (991–96)

> My father calls me: I follow him, and I obey his word, his command; I behave toward my father just as a good son should. I help him when he is in love as a parasite would; I encourage him, I stand beside him, I give him advice, and I take pleasure in his success. If anything pleases my father, it really pleases me, too. He loves: he's smart; he does right, when he follows his hankerings; all men[39] should do that, so long as they do it in moderation.

Mercury not only plays simultaneously the roles of god, clever slave, and running slave, but he is also acting the role of a parasite (*subparasitor*);[40] and his speech is a variation of the "good slave" speech, as he is playing a slave and boasts of how obedient he is. Indeed, Mercury's emphasis on the like-mindedness of himself and Jupiter echoes a "good slave" speech delivered by Sosia in the previous scene (960–61). Furthermore, by emphasizing his own position as *filius* ("son") and then praising love, Mercury would remind the audience of the stock comic *adulescens*, though Mercury is a most atypical *adulescens*, as he helps his father's love affair.

Mercury goes unusually far out of his way to call attention to his next action: he describes in detail how he will go onto the roof and, pretending that he is Sosia, drive away Amphitruo. No other Plautine characters appear on the roof, or even suggest that the scene building has a visible roof: the roof seems to have been reserved for divine epiphanies in tragedies.[41] Just as he has turned a tragic character into a comic one, Mercury now converts the ultimate tragic stage appearance into the play's most farcical comic event. His words to the audience associate this conversion with their will and pleasure:

> faxo probe
> iam hic deludetur, spectatores, vobis inspectantibus. (997–98)

I'll see to it that this fellow is finely fooled, spectators, while you watch.

> iam ille hic deludetur probe,
> siquidem vos voltis auscultando operam dare.[42] (1005–6)

Right now that fellow here will be finely fooled, so long as you wish to take the trouble to listen.

Unfortunately, much of the next scene, in which Mercury douses poor Amphitruo with water, has been lost, along with several other scenes.[43] When the text resumes, both "Amphitruos" are onstage. Amphitruo's friend, Blepharo, who has been called upon to decide which is really Amphitruo, gives up in bewilderment, and Jupiter sneaks into the house to help Alcumena give birth (1039). Left alone onstage, Amphitruo makes a determined attempt to turn the play into a tragedy. He threatens to bring the imposter before the king (1042), a figure associated with tragedy in the prologue (61); and when he sees that Jupiter is gone, he makes a drastic decision:

> certumst, intro rumpam in aedis: ubi quemque hominem
> aspexero,
> si ancillam seu servom sive uxorem sive adulterum
> seu patrem sive avom videbo, obtruncabo in aedibus.
> neque me Iuppiter neque di omnes id prohibebunt, si volent,
> quin sic faciam uti constitui. pergam in aedis nunciam. (1048–52)

That's it, then: I will burst into the house, and whoever I see there, whether it's serving girl, slave, wife, adulterer, father, or grandfather, I'll cut them down right in the house. Neither the will of Jupiter nor all the gods will stop me from doing as I have decided. Right now I will go into the house.

Amphitruo's words are classic tragedy, echoing the hubris of Capaneus, who was struck down after he boasted that even Zeus could not stop him from surmounting the walls of Thebes.[44] Fortunately for Amphitruo, he is in a comedy, not a tragedy. His determination is comic irony rather than tragic hubris, since Jupiter is inside as Amphitruo speaks. Jupiter remains true to the principles of genre he and Mercury have established throughout the play: with a thunderbolt, he promptly ends Amphitruo's attempt to produce tragedy, and the hapless mortal is left unconscious on the stage.

Bromia, Alcumena's maid, now enters and delivers the third long monologue that in itself could fit in a tragedy. In emotional and elevated language, she reports her own terror and the supernatural events that surrounded the birth of Hercules (1053–71).[45] The tragic tone of her speech, however, is undermined by the presence onstage of the thunderstruck Amphitruo, especially when she finally notices him and says: "sed quid hoc? quis hic est senex, qui ante aedis nostras sic iacet?" ("But what's this? Who's this old man lying like this in front of our house?" 1072).[46] Amphitruo, who in the traditional myth is still a young man (Apollodorus 2.4.6–8), has become a stock comic *senex* (cf. 1032).

Bromia now tells Amphitruo about the birth and parentage of Hercules. Even as he becomes more aware of what is going on, Amphitruo still wants to be in the world of tragedy. He plans to go and consult the seer Tiresias, a character with stellar tragic credentials (1128–29).[47] Before he has a chance to do so, Jupiter once again uses some stage thunder to make sure the play remains a comedy. This time he not only thunders, but appears as himself. Here is another excellent opportunity for tragedy: a god, this time undisguised, appears on the roof. Jupiter's speech, however, is matter-of-fact and prosaic, with no tragic pretensions. He has accomplished his purpose of amusing the audience with a long string of comic tours de force. Now he simply goes through the motions of providing the necessary ending. Amphitruo finally gets the message. He decides to forget Tiresias, the tragic seer, and go inside to his wife: to the domestic world of comedy. Before he leaves, he asks the audience to applaud "Iovis summi causa" ("for the sake of Jupiter almighty," 1146). Jupiter almighty is a powerful god; but he is also the chief actor. He and his company have flattered and stroked the audience throughout the performance, created an unmistakable hierarchy of rapport with the gods on top and mortals on the bottom, and provided a series of entertaining puzzles. Most important, they have given the spectators what they wanted: a comedy.

Like *Pseudolus*, then, *Amphitruo* shows most clearly how Plautus manipulated the close relationship between his actors and their audience in order to make sure the audience responded warmly to his plays. Whereas in *Pseudolus*, manipulation of rapport and flattery of the audience converted what might have been a typical play into a work appropriate for an extraordinary occasion, in *Amphitruo*, those same elements assured Plautus's success, even though the content of the play was audacious and unusual.

7

BANKERS AND PIMPS: *CURCULIO*

nunc vero a mani ad noctem festo atque profesto
totus item pariterque die populusque patresque
iactare indu foro se omnes, decedere nusquam;
uni se atque eidem studio omnes dedere et arti—
verba dare ut caute possint, pugnare dolose,
blanditia certare, bonum simulare virum se,
insidias facere ut si hostes sint omnibus omnes.

But, as it is, from morning till night, on holiday and workday, the whole commons and the senators too, all alike go bustling about in the Forum and nowhere leave it; all give themselves over to one and the same interest and artifices— namely to be able to swindle with impunity, to fight cunningly, to strive, using soft words as weapons, to act the "fine fellow," to lie in wait, as though all of them were enemies of all men.

—Lucilius 1145–51 Warmington (Warmington's translation)

IN both *Pseudolus* and *Amphitruo*, the dominant mode of interaction between actors and audience is blandishment. The conspicuous metatheatrical elements that pervade those plays flatter the audience and remind them of the performers' desire to serve them. The next two plays to be considered, *Curculio* and *Truculentus*, reveal a very different approach to the relationship between actors and audience. In these plays, the dominant mode is not blandishment, but satire. Monologues provide far more teasing than flattery, and pervasive allusions to Rome suggest that illicit actions onstage have relevance in a Roman milieu.

Curculio, like most Plautine plays, has deception at its center. Phaedromus is in love with Planesium, who belongs to the pimp Cappadox and has been promised to the braggart soldier Therapontigonus. After several comic scenes between Phaedromus, Cappadox, and various other characters, Phaedromus's parasite Curculio enters. He has stolen Therapontigonus's seal ring; with it, he acquires Planesium for Phaedromus by deceiving Cappadox and Lyco, the banker who holds on deposit the money Therapontigonus will pay for Planesium. When Therapontigonus tries to reclaim Planesium, he discovers that she is his long-lost sister, and he willingly gives her to Phaedromus.

The deception in *Curculio* has two distinctive features. First, it is more varied and widespread than that of most Plautine plays. Though neither the intrigues of the parasite nor the pimp's attempts to defraud are unusual, by adding his portrayal of the banker Lyco, Plautus depicts a world with a greater share of deceit than an average comedy requires. Lyco, who is barely necessary to the plot and whose scenes show clear evidence of Plautine reworking of his Greek original,[1] shows continually a willingness to deceive for profit. Plautus elsewhere portrays greedy moneylenders on stage (*Epid.* 620–47; *Mostell.* 532–654) and offers harsh satire of *argentarii* as a class (*Cas.* 25–28; *Persa* 433–36, 442–43; *Pseud.* 296–98), but only in this play does a deceptive banker play a major role. Second, deception in *Curculio* is intimately connected with courts of law. Legal imagery and parody abound in the play, and Cappadox and Lyco both see the praetor's court as a place where they can get out of paying debts. *Curculio* is not the only Plautine play, of course, where law courts play a role. Trips to court or threats of suits occur throughout Plautus's plays.[2] Nowhere else, however, is the leitmotif of law courts as conspicuous as it is in *Curculio*.

Another distinguishing feature of *Curculio* is its Roman allusions. The play has no prologue to establish its setting,[3] and Epidaurus, where the plot occurs, is not named until almost 350 lines into the play. The audience thus is discouraged from associating the action with a specific Greek locale.[4] A number of conspicuous Roman allusions encourage them instead to connect the play's plot with Rome.[5] These three salient features—deception, references to law and the courts, and Roman allusions—turn the play into sharp satire; for through them, Plautus insists that the spectators acknowledge that the play offers not just a parcel of deceitful foreigners, but criticism of deception and legal misconduct in their own Rome.

The themes of deception, law, and Romanness begin in the play's first scenes. Phaedromus and Planesium meet behind the back of Cappadox, with the help of the bibulous old servant Leaena, and to the chagrin of Phaedromus's moralistic slave, Palinurus, who disapproves of *clandestinus amor* ("hidden love," 49). The scenes are peppered with legal language,[6] including Phaedromus's first words, a claim that he will not leave his beloved's door, even if he is called to a lawsuit (3–6). Phaedromus reminds the audience of the falseness of the Greek locale when he asks the bolts on the door of the pimp's house to become *ludii barbari* ("barbarian dancers," 150) and jump open, so that he can see Planesium. The barbarian dancers are entertainers on the Italian stage:[7] Phaedromus speaks as a Greek, but his allusion to performers reinforces the reminder, already inherent in his use of the word *barbarus*, that his Greekness is itself only the imaginary product of performance.

Soon after the entrance of Cappadox, one of the play's primary deceivers, a conspicuous Roman allusion establishes the connection between Rome and deception. When Cappadox reports that he has been trying to cure his illness by spending the night in the temple of Aesculapius (the god of medicine), his interlocutor suggests that since he is a perjurer, the pimp should seek healing instead by sleeping in the temple of Jupiter, who watches over oaths. Cappadox responds:

> siquidem incubare velint qui periuraverint,
> locus non praeberi potis est in Capitolio. (268–69)
>
> If those who perjured wanted to spend the night there, there
> would be no room left on the Capitolium.

He refers to Rome's most important temple, that to Jupiter on the Capitoline Hill.

Curculio furthers the intermingling of Rome and Greece at his first entrance. He plays the running slave, warning anyone in his way to move or else. No one, he says, is powerful enough to escape his wrath:

> nec <homo> quisquamst tam opulentus, qui mi obsistat in via,
> nec strategus nec tyrannus quisquam, nec agoranomus,
> nec demarchus nec comarchus, nec cum tanta gloria,
> quin cadat, quin capite sistat in via de semita. (284–87)
>
> Nor is there anyone so rich—I don't care if he's a *strategos*, a
> tyrant, an *agoranomus*, a demarch, a comarch, or somebody with
> so much glory—that he won't fall and land on his head on the
> side of the road if he gets in my way.

The list of persons threatened is unmistakably Greek, but its length suggests hyper-Hellenization. Furthermore, it is quite possible that Curculio moves through the audience as he speaks.[8] If so, the "Greeks" he threatens are in fact Roman spectators. Whether or not Curculio is among the spectators, he switches to a Roman's perspective with his next words: he complains about *Graeci palliati* (Greeks wearing *pallia*) who walk about with books and baskets, offer their opinions when they are not wanted, and drink too much (288–95). The *Graeci palliati* are evidently "intellectuals," either Greeks or philhellenes, resident in Rome.[9] Whoever they are, Curculio speaks as a Roman when he calls them *Graeci*. Curculio concludes by threatening slaves who play in the street (296–98). The slaves belong to *scurrae* ("men about town"), another type associated with Rome.[10] The play's first long monologue thus joins Greeks, Romans, and in all likelihood the spectators themselves as victims of Curculio's satire.

The next character to enter, Lyco the banker, intensifies the association between Rome, deception, and law courts. Though Lyco himself is generally called by the Greek name *trapezita*, he and the other characters refer to his class by the Latin term *argentarii*, suggesting that his behavior represents that of bankers in Rome.[11] Lyco first enters with a confident claim that he is rich, so long as he does not repay the deposits people have left with him (373). If anyone demands said deposits, he will simply go before the praetor, as most *argentarii* do (375–81).[12] An interchange in the ensuing dialogue between Lyco and Curculio encourages the audience to recognize the praetor to whom Lyco takes his case as the Roman magistrate responsible for many law cases:

> *Curculio*:   quaeso ne me incomities.
> *Lyco*: licetne inforare, si incomitiare non licet?
> *Curc.*: non inforabis me quidem, nec mihi placet
> tuom profecto nec forum nec comitium. (400–403)

> *Curculio*: Please don't pester me.
> *Lyco*: Can I poke you, if I can't pester you?
> *Curc.*: You will not poke me. I really don't like your poking place [lit., your forum] or your pestering place [lit., your comitium].

The double pun depends on the similarities between *comitium* (a meeting place on the north side of the Roman forum) and *incomitio* ("abuse"), and *forum* and *inforare* ("sodomize"). The joke continues the leitmotif of Roman topography begun by Cappadox's allusion to the Capitolium. It also connects the topography with the theme of courts and the fraudulent use of courts; for the court of the *praetor urbanus*, who generally tried cases between Roman citizens, was located in the comitium;[13] and that of the *praetor peregrinus*, who normally dealt with cases involving noncitizens, was in the forum (see below). The close association Romans made between the forum and comitium and law cases is evident from a passage in the Twelve Tables, Rome's oldest recorded laws: "ni pacunt, in comitio aut in foro ante meridiem causam coniciunto" ("If [two parties in a disagreement] do not reach an agreement, let them make a summary statement of their case before noon in the comitium or in the forum," 1.7).[14]

Lyco and Curculio then meet Cappadox, and the three go off to get Planesium. When they return, Curculio indulges in a tirade against both pimps and bankers. He continues the topographical theme with two allusions to the forum. Any association with pimps, he says, brings shame:

> nec vobiscum quisquam in foro frugi consistere audet;
> qui constitit, culpant eum, conspicitur vituperatur,
> eum rem fidemque perdere, tam etsi nil fecit, aiunt. (502−4)

> And no decent person dares stand beside you in the forum. If anyone does, he is censured, eyed, condemned; he is on the road to ruin, they say, even though he has done nothing.[15]

When Lyco congratulates Curculio on his knowledge of pimps, Curculio says that bankers are no different from pimps:

> eodem hercle vos pono et paro: parissimi estis hibus:
> hi saltem in occultis locis prostant, vos in foro ipso;
> vos faenore homines, hi male suadendo et lustris lacerant.
> (506−8)

> By Hercules, I put you both in exactly the same category: you are exactly like them. At least they do business in hidden places; you work in the forum itself; you harm people with interest, they do it with seduction and vice.

Curculio's final words against bankers bring to a climax the connection between Rome and Epidaurus:

> rogitationis plurumas propter vos populus scivit,
> quas vos rogatas rumpitis: aliquam reperitis rimam;
> quasi aquam ferventem frigidam esse, ita vos putatis leges.
> (509−11)

The people have passed countless laws because of you, but you
just break them; you find some loophole; you think laws become
obsolete as fast as boiling water grows cold.

The reference to laws against bankers and the flouting of those laws connects Lyco and his antics to contemporary controversies in Rome over
moneylending. In 193 B.C.E., new laws were passed to prevent moneylenders from avoiding earlier laws against usury by lending in the names of
noncitizens (Livy 35.7.2−5; the earlier laws applied only to citizens).[16] The
allusion to Roman laws and the flaunting of those laws makes clear what
Plautus has implied throughout the play: Lyco is a satirical portrait not so
much of a hypothetical Greek banker as of a Roman *argentarius*.

After such an explicit connection with Rome, the audience will not fail
to recognize that Plautus has Roman courts in mind when he describes several shady or questionable legal dealings in the play's last scenes. Cappadox
complains that only the admonitions of his friends prevented Lyco from
pleading before the praetor to avoid paying the ten minae he owed him; like
Lyco himself earlier, Cappadox considers Lyco's behavior typical of *argentarii* (679−85). The pimp also tries to avoid paying what he owes the soldier by means of a trip to the praetor (721−22). Meanwhile, Phaedromus
threatens to take Therapontigonus to court when the soldier tries to take
back Planesium (621−25), and he pretends to act as praetor in deciding that
Cappadox owes Therapontigonus money (701−17).

Crowning these connections between deception, law courts, and Roman topography is the play's longest monologue, and the longest and most
striking Roman allusion in all of Plautus. When Curculio goes off with
Cappadox and Lyco to arrange the transfer of Planesium, the *choragus* enters and makes the following speech:[17]

> edepol nugatorem lepidum lepide hunc nactust Phaedromus.
> halapantam an sycophantam magis esse dicam nescio.
> ornamenta quae locavi metuo ut possim recipere;
> quamquam cum istoc mihi negoti nihil est: ipsi Phaedromo   465
> credidi; tamen asservabo. sed dum hic egreditur foras,
> commonstrabo, quo in quemque hominem facile inveniatis loco,
> ne nimio opere sumat operam si quem conventum velit,
> vel vitiosum vel sine vitio, vel probum vel improbum.
> qui periurum convenire volt hominem ito in comitium;   470
> qui mendacem et gloriosum, apud Cloacinae sacrum,
> ditis damnosos maritos sub basilica quaerito.
> ibidem erunt scorta exoleta quique stipulari solent,

symbolarum collatores apud forum piscarium.
in foro infimo boni homines atque dites ambulant,   475
in medio propter canalem, ibi ostentatores meri;
confidentes garrulique et malevoli supera lacum,
qui alteri de nihilo audacter dicunt contumeliam
et qui ipsi sat habent quod in se possit vere dicier.
sub veteribus, ibi sunt qui dant quique accipiunt faenore.   480
pone aedem Castoris, ibi sunt subito quibus credas male.
in Tusco vico, ibi sunt homines qui ipsi sese venditant.
in Velabro vel pistorem vel lanium vel haruspicem[18]
vel qui ipsi vorsant vel qui aliis ubi vorsentur praebeant . . .
[ditis damnosos maritos apud Leucadiam Oppiam]   485[19]
sed interim fores crepuere: linguae moderandum est mihi.
(462–86)

By Pollux, Phaedromus has nicely found himself a nice liar here.
I don't know whether I should call him a con man[20] or a shyster.
I'm afraid I won't be able to get back the costumes I rented out;
but I don't have business with him: I entrusted them to Phaedromus himself; still, I'll keep watch. But while he's away, I'll point
out where you can easily find any kind of person, so that nobody
spends too much effort if he wants to meet someone, someone
either with or without vices, someone good or bad. Anyone who
wants to meet a perjuring fellow should go to the comitium; if
he wants to meet someone who lies and boasts, he should go to
the shrine of Venus Cloacina. Let him look for rich profligate
husbands under the walls of the basilica. In the same place will
be male prostitutes, and the ones who get promises of money; the
ones who contribute to group meals are at the fish market. At
the bottom of the forum good and rich men stroll about; but in
the middle, near the gutter, are the pure pretenders. The ones
who are arrogant, talkative, and spiteful, who brazenly speak slander against someone else on no grounds, and who have plenty
that could truly be said against themselves, are just above the
Lacus Curtius. In the shadow of the old shops are those who give
and receive money at interest. Go behind the temple of Castor
and Pollux: right there are those you would be a fool to trust.
In the Vicus Tuscus are the people who sell themselves; on the
Velabrum [you can find] a baker [or miller] or a butcher or a seer,
or those who themselves cheat or offer others a place where they
can cheat. . . . But I hear the door creaking: I need to shut up.

The *choragus*, who not only provided costumes, but sometimes acted as
stage manager (Donat. *ad Eun.* 967), is both a character and part of the ap-

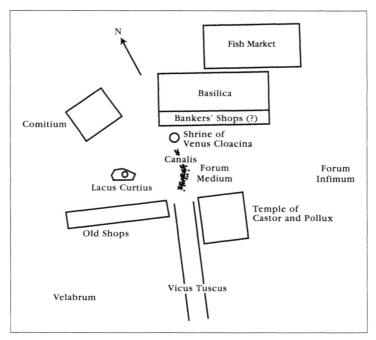

Plautus's Forum

paratus of production; and he is hired by the magistrate responsible for the play from the Roman world outside of the performance (*Per.* 159–60). His appearance is thus a most effective way for Plautus to jumble together the play's Greek setting, the performance, and the Roman surroundings of the performance. In his opening lines, the *choragus* takes advantage of his own ambiguous position to suggest that "Epidaurus" and Rome are one, joined in the production itself. He begins by admiring the good luck of Phaedromus in finding Curculio: he is still in Epidaurus (462–63). He then moves to the production of the play: he is concerned about his costumes, but not too concerned, for his business is with Phaedromus, not Curculio (464–66). The actor playing Phaedromus is the play's chief actor, who rented the costumes from the *choragus*. Finally, the *choragus* steps beyond the production into the world of the audience, saying that he will show them where they can find anyone they are looking for (466–69). The *choragus*'s words encourage the audience to realize that in what follows, the joke will be at least in part on them, for he assumes members of the audience would wish to associate themselves with the shady characters he is going to describe.

The first stop in the ensuing tour sets the tone for what is to follow: spectators can find a *periurus*—a perjurer—in the comitium (470; see fig.). *Periurus* is so closely tied with pimps in Roman comedy that Plautus's audience cannot but have thought of that stock character here.[21] They will be surprised and amused to learn that this *periurus* is someone speaking before the tribunal of the urban praetor in the comitium.[22] The *choragus* has entered the Roman forum, but he has brought the stock characters of comedy with him.

The *choragus*'s next stop is the shrine of Venus Cloacina, where, he says, one can find someone "mendax et gloriosus" ("lying and boastful," 471). Again he suggests a stock comic character, for hearing *gloriosi* without an accompanying noun, the audience would think of the *miles gloriosus*, the braggart soldier.[23] It appears that the shrine of Cloacina was associated with purification after battle.[24] Plautus has soldiers performing such a purification in mind when he refers to the shrine. By calling them *gloriosi*, he produces scathing satire of Roman military men, suggesting that some of them are no different from the stock braggart soldiers of his plays.

Next the *choragus* suggests that in the shadow of the basilica, one can find *dites damnosi mariti*—"rich and profligate husbands" (472). *Damnosi* in a comic setting suggests men squandering money on prostitutes.[25] Here the *damnosi* are married and rich: such a combination—married, rich, and a lover—evokes another stock comic character, the *senex amator*. Again the *choragus* humiliates the Roman victims of his satire—those who hire the prostitutes on the north side of the forum—by equating them with a "Greek" stock character.

Where there are *senes amatores*, one might expect to find another stock character, the prostitute. Plautus does not disappoint, but he does add an unexpected twist, for the *choragus* suggests that one can find in or near the basilica not female but male prostitutes: *scorta exoleta* (473).[26] Also around the basilica with the prostitutes and their potential lovers are *qui stipulari solent*: those who exact a promise of money. Joined as they are to the *scorta*, *qui stipulari solent* appear to be pimps, demanding money for the services of the prostitutes.[27] The satire will be particularly effective when the audience hears Curculio say thirty lines later that anyone even standing near pimps in the forum loses his reputation (502–4; see above). The verb *stipulari*, however, is used of any formal oral agreement, and it was the form of contract used when money was lent at interest.[28] Given, then, that bankers' shops were located here on the north side of the forum, next to the basilica,[29] *qui stipulari solent* could also be the bankers and their customers.[30] The ambiguity is deliberate. Elsewhere Plautus associates prostitutes, pimps, and bankers, as Diniarchus places them all together "circa argentarias" ("around the bankers' shops," *Truc.* 66–73). Here Plautus goes one step further: by using a phrase that could mean pimps or bankers, he suggests that bankers are no better than pimps. He thus prepares the audience for the explicit equation of pimps and bankers to be made by Curculio in the next scene (506–8; see above). He undermines, however, the assertion Curculio will make in the same lines, that pimps work "in occultis locis" ("in hidden places"): the *choragus* proclaims in the open what his victims think is hidden.

When he moves northeast of the basilica to the fish market, the *choragus* remains in the world of comedy; for the market offers not ordinary Romans buying provisions, but *symbolarum collatores*: those who make contributions for a dinner party (474). Preparations for parties and banquets are a topos of Roman comedy.[31] Plautus's only other reference to a dinner for which the guests contribute *symbolae* is the party of Stichus and his fellow slaves (*Stich.* 432, 438), in a passage set emphatically in a Greek milieu (*Stich.* 446–48) that is probably a parody of dinners elsewhere in comedy.[32] Likewise Terence, in conspicuously Greek settings, refers to comic *adulescentes* arranging dinners with *symbolae* (*An.* 88; *Eun.* 540).[33] Again the *choragus* has placed in the heart of Rome behavior elsewhere considered a part of the Greek comic world.

The north side of the forum, then, is crowded with characters like those one might find in the supposedly Greek setting of the *palliata*. As he reaches the easternmost side of the forum, the *forum infimum*,[34] the *choragus* temporarily abandons the characters of comedy and provides the only fulfillment of his promise to speak of the good as well as the bad: here walk "boni homines atque dites" ("good and wealthy men," 475). *Boni homines* for the upper class is very respectful Roman language, as far removed from the seedy world of comedy as the *choragus* will get; yet even here, the verbal echo of *dites* reminds the audience that they are not that far from other rich Romans who are far from good. The next line reveals that the *boni* have been included merely for the sake of contrast with poorer people who put on airs, pretending to be *boni* and *dites*; for the *choragus* continues, "in medio propter canalem, ibi ostentatores meri" ("In the middle near the *canalis* are the pure pretenders," 476). The *canalis* was an open drain that ran south from the shrine of Venus Cloacina through the middle of the forum.[35] The *ostentatores meri* are probably the loiterers called *canalicolae* ("gutter dwellers") because they lounged about near this drain.[36] That such loiterers already abounded in the middle of the forum in Plautus's day is evident from the desire of Cato the Elder to cover the forum with sharp stones in order to discourage such loitering (Pliny. *HN* 19.24).

The *choragus* spends more time on the next group, the arrogant, hostile, talkative speakers of slander, than on anyone else (477–79). The lines have generally been taken to be a reference to gossips loitering in the forum.[37] It is not clear, however, why gossips should be called arrogant or speak brazenly: they seem to be doing nothing particularly daring; and in the five other passages where Plautus uses *contumelia* ("insulting language") of words rather than of general mistreatment or bad reputation, the *contumelia* is an insult or accusation spoken directly from one person to another, not anything spoken behind one's back.[38] Plautus's *supera lacum* provides a clue as to who the *malevoli* might be, for it is almost certain that the tribunal of the praetor peregrinus was located just to the west of the Lacus Curtius.[39] The *confidentes* and *garruli* are those who are brazen enough to accuse others before the praetor even though they are guilty of worse crimes themselves.

Moving to the south side of the forum, the *choragus* first calls attention to the *tabernae veteres* ("old shops"), where, he says, one can find those who give and receive money at interest (480). Having hinted at bankers in the reference to *stipulatio* above, Plautus now makes clear that the third of the play's three main antagonists, like the pimp and the braggart soldier, would feel right at home in the Roman forum.[40]

Nor is the *choragus* through with bankers. His next stop is behind the temple of Castor and Pollux, where he claims to know of those *quibus credas male* ("whom you would trust to your loss," 481). Cicero reveals that the tables of money-changers were near the same temple (*Quinct.* 4.17), and two inscriptions referring to bankers behind the temple confirm this location (*CIL* 6.363, 9177). There is no reason to doubt that in Plautus's day as well, a group of *argentarii* worked *post aedem Castoris*.[41] One begins to get the impression that untrustworthy bankers like Lyco are everywhere around the *choragus*'s forum.

Moving farther south, the *choragus* suggests that on the "vicus Tuscus" ("Etruscan Street"), one can find "homines qui ipsi sese venditant" ("persons who sell themselves," 482): more prostitutes.[42] The masculine pronoun *ipsi* reveals that the prostitutes are once again male (or both male and female), but they are a different class from the *scorta exoleta* above, for they are not the property of pimps, but sell their own services.[43]

The *choragus*'s last stop is the Velabrum (483). Here, he says, are *pistores* ("millers" or "bakers"), *lanii* ("butchers"), and *haruspices* ("seers"). Although all these professions are hardly foreign to Rome,[44] each is also a conspicuous feature in the background of the world of the *palliata*.[45] Also on the Velabrum, one can find "either those who themselves cheat, or those who offer to others a place where they can cheat."[46] Various merchants had businesses on the Velabrum:[47] "those who cheat" are the merchants, deliberately left undefined to give the impression of a general atmosphere of deception on the Velabrum. "Those who offer others a place where they can cheat" are persons who provide stalls to the petty businessmen on the hill. The implication is that anyone who acquires such a stall has swindling in mind.[48]

The effect of this tour of the Roman forum must have been stunning, for it is not merely a reference to things Roman, but the most blatant possible reminder that the production occurs in the city of Rome. All distinction between play, production, and "real life" has been obliterated; and as the physical landscapes of "Epidaurus" and Rome become one, the audience is forced to recognize the applicability of the Epidaurian social landscape to their own city, Rome. The *choragus* takes advantage of this association of places to introduce into the Roman world characters reminiscent of comedy in general and of *Curculio* in particular.

The resulting identification of actors' pretense and audience's reality would have been especially effective if, as is probably the case, the spectators themselves stood and sat in the midst of the places the *choragus* pointed out.[49] Though evidence for the locations of theatrical performances in Plautus's day is meager, what there is suggests that on some occasions, plays were performed in the forum.[50] As has long been observed, the *choragus's* tour is both restricted and orderly.[51] It includes only places in the immediate vicinity of the forum, east of the western end of the comitium. It is most unlikely that, if the play were performed at some other location, Plautus would have discussed only this small area, or that the *choragus* would have been so careful to lead his spectators from the comitium east along the north side of the forum to the fish market, then back through the middle of the forum to the west of the Lacus Curtius, then along the south side of the forum to the temple of Castor and Pollux, and finally south a little to the Velabrum. Given, then, that the *choragus* does not mention such places farther west in the forum as the temples of Saturn or Concordia, there is every indication that he speaks from a stage just south of the comitium, facing east. Almost everything on the tour would be visible to the *choragus* and his audience,[52] and spectators would actually be watching the play from some of the locations cited.

At several points in the speech, the *choragus* takes advantage of the presence of the audience to make jokes at their expense. It appears that the comitium was customarily covered for the *ludi*, probably so that wealthier citizens could watch the gladiatorial games and, presumably, the plays, protected from the elements.[53] If this is in fact the case, the *choragus's* location of the *periurus* in the comitium is a double joke: he satirizes the perjurers who plague the praetor's court daily, and he rather daringly mocks the wealthy, who watch him from the Roman equivalent of box seats. Other spectators, watching from the balconies that lined the north and south sides of the forum, would bear the brunt of Plautus's references to wealthy profligates near the basilica and to lenders and borrowers near the old shops.[54] If spectators watched from the area directly in front of the porticoes, Plautus's references to the shrine of Cloacina is also a double entendre. The *choragus* mocks the very last rows of his audience, standing just to the west of the drain that ran through the middle of the forum, when he refers to the pure pretenders near the gutter. Finally, the *choragus* himself is probably standing on a stage just above the Lacus Curtius. His reference to the loquacious speakers of slander is in part a bit of self-mockery, as he acknowledges that his own speech and those of the actors are often unjustified insults.

In both its context and its content, then, the *choragus*'s speech breaks down the barriers between what the spectators see onstage and their own experience. Plautus chooses for the speech the *choragus*, a character who himself bridges the gaps between pretense, performance, and reality; and by pointing out places visible from the stage, the *choragus* unites Rome and "Epidaurus" physically. Plautus encourages this geographical confusion by refusing to distinguish between characters and actors at the beginning of the speech, and by including in the *choragus*'s list of laughable people many who seem to belong in the supposedly Greek world of the *palliata*. Double entendres, in which the *choragus* refers both to what goes on daily in the places he points out and to the audience or actors currently present, reinforce this lack of distinction. Plautus makes the speech relevant to *Curculio* in particular by including in the forum characters similar to Cappadox, Therapontigonus, and Lyco, and by referring twice to the praetors' courts, which play an important role elsewhere in the play.

As he moves from the imaginary Epidaurus through the current performance to the audience's Rome, the *choragus* takes the theme of deception with him. He begins by praising Curculio's skill as a trickster (462–63). When the *choragus* reveals his own fear that Curculio will walk off with his costume, he extends the idea of deceit from within the imaginary world of the play to the performance, from the character Curculio to the actor playing Curculio. He then reveals that the actor playing Curculio is not the only performer who is unconcerned with ethical business practices, for he implies that he himself does not really care about the costumes, as he can still hold Phaedromus responsible.[55] His own attitude is thus reminiscent of that of Cappadox and Lyco, both of whom are completely unconcerned with the logistics of their transactions with Therapontigonus, so long as each gets his money. Although the *choragus* promises, when he enters the world of the audience, that his tour of the forum and its surroundings will include those who are good as well as those who are bad (469), nearly every stop is filled only with the latter, especially with those who deceive: perjurers, liars, illicit lovers; prostitutes and pimps, always considered dishonest; people who pretend to greater wealth than they have; people who make false accusations; untrustworthy bankers; butchers, known to be cheats (cf. *Pseud.* 197); seers, often accused of being charlatans;[56] and, finally, simply "those who cheat." The audience can draw only one conclusion: deception is as widespread in their own Rome as it is in Curculio's Epidaurus.

Curculio is Plautus's shortest play. The satirical monologues—the *choragus's* speech, Lycus's and Cappadox's descriptions of *argentarii*, and Curculio's running-slave speech—thus stand out all the more conspicuously. Together with the play's other Roman allusions, they make clear that the deceitful practices of men like Lyco and Cappadox can be found in Rome as well as in Greece. Plautus's satire, however, applies not only to bankers and pimps. *Fides*—trustworthiness—was one of the Romans' cardinal virtues, and one of the ways they liked to distinguish themselves from other peoples.[57] By portraying an Epidaurus in which *fides* is nonexistent, and then associating that Epidaurus unmistakably with Rome, and even with the audience itself, Plautus challenges his audience's assumption that even though other peoples (Greeks, for example) might practice deception regularly and willfully, Romans can be trusted. The further association of deception with Roman courts of law and the topographical centers of Roman religious, economic, and civil life would make the satire still more damning. Even as they delighted in the characters' antics, many spectators must have found themselves agreeing with Curculio's rebuke of Lyco early in the play: "I really don't like your forum or your comitium" (403).

8

PROSTITUTES AND LOVERS: *TRUCULENTUS*

*Catone transeunte quidam exiit de fornice; quem, cum fugeret, revocavit et lau-
davit. Postea cum frequentius eum exeuntem de eodem lupanari vidisset, dixisse
fertur: adulescens, ego te laudavi, tamquam huc intervenires, non tamquam hic
habitares.*

*A certain man came out of a brothel while Cato [the Censor] was going by.
When the man started to run away, Cato called him back and praised him
[scil. because he was releasing his libido with prostitutes rather than with virgins
or married women]. Later, when he had seen him coming quite often out of the
same brothel, he said, as the story goes: "Young man, I praised you on the
assumption that you visited here, not that you lived here."*

—Pseudo-Acron on Horace *Sat.* 1.2.31–32

WHEREAS the satire of *Curculio* extends from the specific machinations of
Lyco and Cappadox to deception in general, in *Truculentus* Plautus concen-
trates his satire on one phenomenon: the squandering of wealth on prostitutes.[1] Phronesium, Plautus's most outrageous femme fatale, has three
lovers. The first, Diniarchus, has spent all his money on her and has been
relegated to the position of confidant. The second is the soldier Stratophanes; Phronesium pretends that she has just had his baby in order to get
more money from him, using for the purpose someone else's unwanted infant. Most of the plot is Phronesium's manipulation of these two and a third
lover, Strabax, a young rustic. She is assisted by her handmaid, Astaphium,
who also manages in the course of the play to seduce Truculentus, Strabax's
grim and severe slave. Meanwhile, it becomes known that the baby Phrone-

sium is using for her charade is actually the product of Diniarchus's rape of his former fiancée. Diniarchus agrees to marry the girl he raped; but he is persuaded by Phronesium to let her keep the baby until she has gotten more money from the soldier, and he seems destined to continue his desperate attempts to win her more securely for himself. As the play ends, Strabax and Stratophanes compete for Phronesium with gifts while the prostitute and her handmaid look on in delight.

Phronesium, like most of Plautus's *meretrices*, is almost certainly derived from a prostitute in Plautus's Greek original.[2] Most prostitutes of Greek comedy reflect real-life *hetaerae*, courtesans who played an important role in Greek sexual and social life.[3] Before considering the satirical significance of Phronesium and her lovers, therefore, it is necessary to determine whether Plautus's prostitutes could have appeared at all relevant to his audience, or if they represented an exotic Greek species totally foreign to Rome.

There can be no doubt that prostitutes were a conspicuous feature of Plautus's Rome. The anecdote about Cato cited above dates from during or shortly after Plautus's lifetime. Other evidence suggests that prostitutes were not only present in Rome in the late third and early second century, but that their numbers were increasing: Rome's incessant warfare caused more slaves to be captured and made prostitutes, and more free women became prostitutes for want of any other means of support.[4] Plautus himself, as we have seen, has his *choragus* refer to prostitutes in and around the Roman forum (*Curc.* 473, 482); and one of his *prologi* alludes to male prostitutes in the theater itself (*Poen.* 17–18). The portrayal of *meretrices* at the temple of Venus in *Poenulus* may reflect contemporary Roman religious controversies involving prostitutes.[5] Several plays include jokes about members of the audience or persons known to the actors hiring prostitutes (*Amph.* 287; *Bacch.* 1209–10; *Cas.* 84–86, 1015–18; *Merc.* 1017–24): though the jokes are not to be taken seriously, their comic effect depends upon the audience's familiarity with prostitutes and their customers.

It might be argued that although the members of Plautus's audience would be familiar with low-class *scorta* like those who could be found both in the brothels and on the streets of Rome, they would have found higher-class *meretrices* such as Phronesium strange and exotic.[6] Polybius, after all, writes that it was at the end of the Third Macedonian War, about sixteen years after Plautus's death, that Roman youths gave themselves over to courtesans, boy-lovers, and other such luxuries (31.25.4–7). Polybius, however, is at pains to draw a contrast between the other Roman youths and Scipio Aemilianus, who reached adulthood in the early 160s; and he does not suggest that courtesans or any of the other luxuries were completely absent from Rome before the war with Macedon. Further evidence for the existence of figures like Plautus's *meretrices* in the early second century comes from the historian Livy. His Hispala Faecenia, who helped to bring to light the so-called Bacchanalian Conspiracy in 186 B.C.E., is a prostitute of some refinement, a long-term mistress of her lover, Aebutius, much like Phronesium and many of the other *meretrices* of Roman comedy (39.9.5–7). Though the details of Livy's account may themselves have been influenced by comic motifs, the status of Hispala is probably historical.[7] Thus, although the *hetaera* had not yet become in Rome the kind of institution she was in much of the Greek world, most in Plautus's audience would certainly have known of *meretrices* with much higher pretensions than the average *scortum*. Nor are Phronesium and Astaphium completely removed from the lower-class prostitutes whom Plautus's audience would find most familiar. Plautus makes the house of Phronesium and Astaphium seem like a brothel, where such lower-class prostitutes would live and work: he gives the impression that a large number of lovers passes through Phronesium's door, and Astaphium even says that some of them pilfer from the prostitutes (98–111, 658, 760, 944).[8]

Though the greed and the success of Phronesium are grossly exaggerated, then, both residents of Rome and, presumably, some members of Plautus's audience spent money on *meretrices* like her: the play's satirical treatment of prostitutes and their lovers could have relevance for Romans. Through his arrangement of Roman allusions, addresses to the audience, eavesdropping, and monologues, Plautus made clear that the events of the play were in fact relevant to Rome and to the audience. Conspicuous allusions to Rome and Italy are arranged so as to encourage the spectators to recognize that the play's profligate lovers are Roman as much as Greek phenomena. *Truculentus* also has more lines of monologue relative to its total length than almost any other Plautine play,[9] and characters repeatedly address the audience explicitly: the monologues and direct addresses are arranged in such a way as to implicate the audience in the action onstage. Finally, scenes of eavesdropping cause the lovers themselves to be spectators, parallel with the actual spectators.

The prologue of *Truculentus* begins with joking similar to that of the *Menaechmi* prologue (see Chapter 3):

> perparvam partem postulat Plautus loci
> de vestris magnis atque amoenis moenibus,
> Athenas quo sine architectis conferat.
> quid nunc? daturin estis an non? adnuont.

scio rem quidem urbis me ablaturum sine mora;
quid si de vostro quippiam orem? abnuont.
eu hercle in vobis resident mores pristini,
ad denegandum ut celeri lingua utamini.
sed hoc agamus qua huc ventumst gratia.
Athenis mutabo ita ut hoc est proscaenium
tantisper dum transigimus hanc comoediam. (1−11)

Plautus requests a little spot from your great and pleasant city
where he can introduce Athens without any builders. What do
you say? Will you give a spot or not? They say they will. I see
that I can take public land, at least, with no trouble. What if I ask
for some of your own property? They say they won't. Great! You
still maintain the ancient virtues, for you are quick to refuse to
pay anything. But let's get back to what I came here for. I will
change this stage so that it is in Athens as long as we are performing this comedy.

The basic joke here is the same as that in *Menaechmi*: this is Greece, but it
isn't. There are, however, some important differences. While the *prologus* of
Menaechmi is concerned mainly with the inherent falseness of the theatrical
setting, the *prologus* of *Truculentus* emphasizes that even as Plautus and the
actors create "Athens," they remain within the audience's Rome. The association of the play's action with Rome continues as the *prologus* describes
Phronesium: "haec huius saecli mores in se possidet" ("This woman possesses the ways of this age," 13). The ways of Phronesium are to be found
specifically in contemporary Rome.

Though the prologue thus associates the play's actions with Rome, it
would seem at first sight to separate the spectators from the actions of the
play.[10] The spectators, after all, are praised for their *mores pristini* ("old
ways," 7), whereas Phronesium and prostitutes like her have *huius saecli
mores* ("the ways of this age," 13). The prologue speaker, however, is teasing the audience, suggesting that the thrift on which they and Romans like
them so praised themselves was in fact stinginess. The irony of the praise
undermines as well the distinction between audience and characters it
might seem to imply.

The ensuing lament by Diniarchus sets a pattern of Roman allusion and
involvement of the audience that will continue throughout the play. In a
remarkably long expansion of the monologue-beginning generalization,
Diniarchus delivers a tirade against prostitutes for more than fifty lines. In
the middle of this discourse, he lists items demanded by a prostitute, in-

cluding *armariola Graeca*: Greek jewel boxes (55). As no Athenian would refer to a "Greek jewel box," Diniarchus has entered the Roman world,
where Greekness is something worthy of remark. It is thus from a Roman
perspective that Diniarchus offers the suggestion that follows: if lovers con-
sulted their fathers, there would be fewer pimps, prostitutes, and profligates.
As it is, Diniarchus says, pimps and prostitutes are more common than flies
in the summer, and they sit every day near the *argentariae* ("bankers' tables,"
64–73). By presenting prostitutes who sit outside along with pimps, and by
alluding to a familiar feature of Roman topography, the bankers' tables in
the forum, Diniarchus leaves little doubt that he is talking not about exotic
hetaerae, but about prostitutes in a Roman milieu. He concludes his general
comments by explaining the abundance of pimps and prostitutes in language that makes the connection with Rome still clearer:

> postremo id magno in populo multis[11] hominibus,
> re placida atque otiosa, victis hostibus:
> amare oportet omnis qui quod dent habent. (74–76)

> In short, that is what happens among a great people with a large
> population, when the state is at peace and tranquil, and the ene-
> mies have been defeated: everybody who has the money has to
> play the lover.

Diniarchus's string of ablatives is a parody of Roman official language, and
the reference to peace and victory almost certainly refers to the situation at
Rome when the play was produced, shortly before Plautus's death.[12] When
Diniarchus finally turns from his generalizations to his own situation (77),
he does not abandon his Roman perspective, for he complains that Phronesium wants to *pergraecari* ("Greek it up") with his rival, the soldier (87). Finally, as if to say, "Oops! I'm supposed to be in Athens," Diniarchus ends
his monologue with a reference to his own recent return to Athens from
Lemnos (91). The juxtaposition joke comes too late to remove the strong
connection Diniarchus has established between the events of the play and
the audience's Rome.

At the same time, Diniarchus associates himself and lovers like him with
the spectators themselves. The length of this monologue—at seventy-three
lines, it is one of Plautus's longest—in itself connects Diniarchus and the
spectators to an unusual degree, and intimate modes of address reinforce
the connection. Though he begins with the third person, he uses a second-
person verb early in the speech: "temptat benignusne an bonae frugi sies"
("She tests to see if you are nice to her or a worthwhile person," 34). Al-

though the second person can be interpreted as impersonal, it nevertheless joins speaker and addressee, as does Diniarchus's next second-person verb: "prius quam unum dederis, centum quae poscat parat" ("Before you can give her one thing, she has a hundred other demands," 51). Diniarchus thus joins the spectators with himself and lovers like him, so that they appear to be included as subjects of the first-person plural verbs that follow:

> atque haec celamus nos clam magna industria,
> quom rem fidemque nosque nosmet perdimus,
> ne qui parentes neu cognati sentiant;
> quos cum celamus si faximus conscios,
> qui nostrae aetati tempestivo temperent,
> unde anteparta demus postpartoribus,
> faxim lenonum et scortorum † plus est
> et minus damnosorum hominum quam nunc sunt siet. (57–63)

> And we take great pains to keep these affairs secret, while we destroy our property and our credit and ourselves, so that no parents or relatives find out; if instead of hiding it from them, we told those who could restrain our youth in time, so that we could hand our inheritance on to others, I bet there would be fewer pimps, prostitutes, and bankrupts than there are now.

Later, when speaking of the money the abundant prostitutes keep track of, Diniarchus makes clear that he is taking the spectators into his confidence: "accepta dico, expensa ne qui censeat" ("I mean money that has been received, lest anyone think I mean money paid out," 73). As we have seen, it is hardly unusual for Plautus's characters to draw close to the audience in their monologues. The combination of Diniarchus's general Romanness and the intimacy of his address, however, means that here, not only do the spectators see the action through Diniarchus's eyes, but they themselves become implicated in his attitudes and his behavior.

The association of Diniarchus and lovers like him with the spectators increases as Diniarchus eavesdrops on Astaphium in the next scene. As she enters, Astaphium makes the play's most obvious connection between spectators and lovers. After complaining to her fellow handmaids that prostitutes' customers rob them, she suddenly addresses the spectators:

> fit pol hoc, et pars spectatorum scitis pol haec vos me hau mentiri.
> ibist ibus pugnae et virtuti de praedonibu' praedam capere.
> at ecastor nos rusum lepide referimu' gratiam furibu' nostris:

nam ipsi vident quom eorum abgerimus bona atque etiam ultro
ipsi aggerunt ad nos.[13] (105–11)

> That's what happens, by Pollux, and some of you spectators are
> well aware that I'm not lying. That's where their glorious battle
> is: taking booty from the booty-takers. But we repay our thieves
> nicely, by Castor: for they themselves watch while we carry off
> their possessions, and they even bring them to us of their own
> accord.

The unexpected accusation of "some of you spectators" is made in fun and
could hardly have been taken seriously. Indeed, it is one of a number of
teasing audience addresses that Plautus places early in his plays in order
to help "warm up" the audience (see Chapter 1). Yet the link between the
spectators and lovers that has already been established gives this teasing
audience address extra significance: members of the audience are now explicitly included in the class of men who lose their wealth to prostitutes.
Diniarchus responds to Astaphium's words with an aside:

> me illis quidem haec verberat verbis,
> nam ego huc bona mea degessi. (112–13)

> I'm the one she strikes with those words, for I have brought all
> my possessions here.

As an eavesdropper, Diniarchus is himself a spectator. His application of
Astaphium's audience address to himself demonstrates that the universal
generalities, the specific characters onstage, and the audience are all inter-
twined.

After a dialogue full of quips about the perils of loving prostitutes,
Diniarchus reveals to Astaphium that he is not completely broke, but still
has a house and an estate. Astaphium's attitude therefore changes from hostility to welcome, and she lets him enter the house to wait for Phronesium.
When he has left the stage, Astaphium rejoices:

> hahahae, requievi,
> quia intro abiit odium meum.
> tandem sola sum. nunc quidem meo arbitratu
> loquar libere quae volam et quae lubebit. (209–12)

> Hooray! Now I can rest: my nemesis has gone inside. At last I'm
> alone. Now I will say freely what I wish and what I feel like, at
> my own discretion.

Astaphium, of course, is not really alone. She uses her freedom from Diniarchus not to muse introspectively, but to offer her own perspective to the audience, delivering in an intimate tone a long monologue on the "proper" way for prostitutes to impoverish their lovers. She continues to offer her perspective through the next scene, her first encounter with Truculentus. She twice comments aside on the slave's gruffness and boorishness (265, 269), and when she leaves, she tells the spectators that she hopes to seduce him (315–21).

Diniarchus then reenters, and he continues his close relationship with the audience. He speaks two more monologues (322–25, 335–51), and when he finally sees Phronesium, he presents her to the audience with a second-person verb ("ver vide, ut tota floret, ut olet, ut nitide nitet!" "Look! The Spring! What a sweet smelling, glistening flower she is!" 353–54). He shares with the audience both his suffering (357) and his joy (371) as Phronesium seduces him; and after Phronesium tells him about her plan to deceive the soldier, Diniarchus rejoices in another monologue (434–47).

It is now Phronesium's turn to implicate the audience. She had left the stage before Diniarchus's last monologue. When she returns, she addresses her handmaids (448), then the audience (448–75), then the handmaids again (476–81): the audience is as much a part of the action as those on-stage. Like Diniarchus and Astaphium, Phronesium eagerly discusses her vices with the audience, gloating in her own greed and duplicity. Just as in the previous scene Phronesium had made Diniarchus an accomplice in her conspiracy against Stratophanes, she now does the same to the audience, addressing them explicitly:

> vosmet iam videtis, ut ornata incedo:
> puerperio ego nunc med esse aegram adsimulo. (463–64)

> See for yourselves how properly I'm dressed: I mean to look as though I've just given birth.[14]

Phronesium's next victim, the soldier Stratophanes, enters immediately after Phronesium's monologue with a monologue of his own. Plautus thus offers three monologues in a row, a pattern very rare even in his monologue-filled corpus.[15] Like Diniarchus before him, Stratophanes takes on a Roman perspective; and he addresses the audience even more explicitly than Diniarchus had:

> ne exspectetis, spectatores, meas pugnas dum praedicem:
> manibus duella praedicare soleo, haud in sermonibus.

scio ego multos memoravisse milites mendacium:
et Homeronida et postilla mille memorari pote,
qui et convicti et condemnati falsis de pugnis sient.
non laudandust cui plus credit qui audit quam <ille> qui videt:
[non placet quem illi plus laudant qui audiunt, quam qui vident.]
pluris est oculatus testis unus quam auriti decem;
qui audiunt audita dicunt, qui vident plane sciunt.
non placet quem scurrae laudant, manipularis mussitant,
neque illi quorum lingua gladiorum aciem praestringit domi.
strenui nimio plus prosunt populo quam arguti et cati:
facile sibi facunditatem virtus argutam invenit,
sine virtute argutum civem mihi habeam pro praefica,
quae alios conlaudat, eapse sese vero non potest.
nunc ad amicam decimo mense post Athenas Atticas
viso, quam gravidam hic reliqui meo compressu, quid ea agat.
(482–98)

Spectators, don't expect me to tell you about my battles: I generally announce my wars with deeds, not words. I know that many
soldiers have told lies: I could mention Homeronides and a thousand after him, who have been convicted and condemned for
false battles. The one who persuades a listener more than an eyewitness does not deserve praise: one eyewitness is worth more
than ten listeners. Those who hear just say what they have heard:
those who see really know. I don't care for the one whom the
loiterers praise, while the soldiers are quiet, or those whose
tongues blunt the edges of swords at home. The people benefit
a lot more from the brave than from the talkative and clever:
courage easily finds abundant eloquence for itself; but I consider
the talkative citizen without courage like a professional mourner,
who praises others, but can't honestly praise herself. Now I am
visiting Attic Athens in the tenth month after I left it, to see how
my mistress is doing: she was pregnant from my embrace when
I left.

The monologue is, first of all, a metatheatrical statement. Stratophanes
boasts that he will not act like the stock braggart soldiers of comedy, something the audience would certainly expect seeing the soldier's costume and
the grand procession of slaves and gifts that accompanies him. He thus
makes an even bigger fool of himself when he does act the part of the braggart soldier in the next scene, calling himself Mars (515), and wondering
why his five-day-old son has not yet won any battles (508). The speech is
also topical, however. It responds to the numerous allegations in the years

before the first production of *Truculentus* that Roman generals sought triumphs on false pretenses; Stratophanes may even echo the title of a speech of Cato, "In Q. Minucium Thermum de Falsis Pugnis" ("Against Quintus Minucius Thermus Concerning His False Battles," Gell. 10.3.17; Cato *ORF* 58).[16] Besides introducing some direct satire on contemporary controversies, the topical allusion places Stratophanes, like Diniarchus before him, within a Roman milieu.[17] Like Diniarchus, Stratophanes ends the Roman allusion with a juxtaposition joke—he even uses the tautologous "Attic Athens"—but the satirical damage has already been done.

Stratophanes' long monologue also connects him closely with the spectators: he acknowledges them explicitly, and he appears to address them without being understood by Astaphium and Phronesium, although they are onstage throughout the monologue.[18] The soldier maintains his connection with the spectators through the next scenes: he comments aside when he first sees Phronesium and Astaphium (502, 503), and he shares with the spectators his exasperation when Phronesium refuses to be impressed or pleased with the gifts he brings (535, 538, 542–46). He then eavesdrops while Cyamus, the cook who brings presents from Diniarchus, delivers his own long monologue on the perils of *amor*.

Cyamus, like Phronesium earlier, begins by addressing the slaves who accompany him (551–52), then changes to audience address (553). The subject of his intimate audience address is the same as those of Diniarchus, Astaphium, and Phronesium: the financial perils of loving prostitutes. Like his predecessors, he is remarkably frank about his own vices: he reveals that he regularly pilfers from Diniarchus. Plautus calls attention to the fact that Cyamus shares with the audience things he does not want the other characters to know: when he sees that Phronesium is present, he is afraid that she has overheard his monologue (575). There is no indication, however, that Phronesium, Astaphium, or even the eavesdropping Stratophanes hears what Cyamus says.

When Cyamus observes Stratophanes, the soldier renews his series of asides to the audience, telling them of his anger (603). What must have been a visually hilarious scene follows, as Stratophanes, armed with a sword, and Cyamus, brandishing a kitchen implement, threaten each other. Cyamus then leaves, confessing his cowardice to the audience (630), and Phronesium leaves as well. Left alone, Stratophanes again tells his troubles to the audience, seeking their sympathy with a series of rhetorical questions (635–44).

The next character to enter is Phronesium's third lover, the rustic Strabax. Strabax's entrance monologue is shorter than those of his predecessors, but it is equally self-incriminating. After reporting that he has in his possession twenty minae that he was supposed to use to buy sheep for his father, he says that he intends to impoverish his father, and then his mother, in order to bring money to Phronesium (645–62). The sheep Strabax was to have bought were *oves Tarentinae*: Tarentine sheep (649). Sheep from the region of the Italian city of Tarentum were famous throughout the Greek and Roman world, and they may have been exported to cities on the Greek mainland like Athens.[19] Tarentum itself was a Greek colony. Nevertheless, the allusion to an Italian city associates Strabax with rural Italy, and hence with the Roman world: the rustic, like the soldier and the effete urbanite, is a kind of character both present and seduced in Rome.[20]

All three suitors, then, take on a Roman, or at least Italian, perspective as they enter, and not only the suitors, but the seducing *meretrices* and the observing cook as well, have aligned themselves closely with the audience. The one exception to these patterns has been the play's eponymous character, Truculentus. When he first encountered Astaphium, Truculentus exemplified in many ways the virtues traditionally expected in Romans: he opposed vehemently the corruption of his young master Strabax; he praised Strabax's father for his *parsimonia* ("thrift," 310)[21] and his *duritia* ("endurance," 311); and even Astaphium admitted that he was dedicated to his master (316). There was nevertheless no allusion in that first scene that placed Truculentus in Rome, and he did not speak any lines of monologue. After Astaphium has led Strabax into Phronesium's house, however, Plautus presents the play's biggest surprise. Truculentus enters, and it looks as if the earlier hostile encounter between Truculentus and Astaphium will be repeated. Truculentus wonders if Strabax has gone into Phronesium's house, which he calls Strabax's *corruptela* (the source of his corruption). Astaphium comments aside that she expects Truculentus to shout at her again (672). Then, without any warning, Truculentus reveals that he, too, has been seduced. He tells Astaphium that he is no longer *truculentus* ("ferocious"), and that he will do whatever she wishes. After some weak attempts at wit and one last burst of indignation at Strabax's behavior (694–95), Truculentus joins his master in Phronesium's house. Here, after he has been seduced, Truculentus suggests that he, too, is a Roman. He describes himself as exchanging *veteres mores* ("old ways"), for *novi mores* ("new ways," 677), echoing the language of Roman debate over changing morals; and he indulges in a joke at the expense of the Praenestine dialect that no Athenian could have understood (690–91).[22] He also addresses five lines to the audience, including two in which, like Diniarchus and Strabax before him, he acknowledges his depravity (669–71, 697–98).

Now that each of the seduced men has been associated both with Rome and with the audience, Plautus returns to his first and most important profligate: Diniarchus enters with yet another monologue. This time he tells the spectators how happy he is at Cyamus's report that Phronesium preferred his gifts to Stratophanes', and he continues to confess to them his own worthlessness (699–710). After the monologue, he again becomes a spectator himself, eavesdropping on the entering Astaphium. Astaphium promptly disabuses him of his happiness, informing him that Strabax is inside with Phronesium. Refused entry and left alone by Astaphium, Diniarchus again complains to the audience (758). He then shouts into the house:

> iam hercle ego tibi, inlecebra, ludos faciam clamore in via,
> quae adversum legem accepisti a plurimis pecuniam;
> iam hercle apud novos omnis magistratus faxo erit nomen tuom.
> (759–61)

> Now, by Hercules, I'll have some fun, shouting out your crimes in the street, you enchantress, you who have taken money from lots of people against the law; now, by Hercules, I'll bring your name before all the new magistrates.

While *magistratus* could be the magistrates of any state, Diniarchus's *novos* suggests magistrates in Rome, who took office shortly before the performance of the play.[23] He is once more in a Roman milieu. He also remains joined with the audience, whom he addresses again when he realizes that his threats are futile (766–69).

Diniarchus then eavesdrops yet again, in a scene that brings to a climax the pattern of eavesdropping found throughout the play. As we have seen, eavesdroppers usually share with the audience a sense of superiority. The eavesdropping scenes of *Truculentus*, however, have quite the opposite effect. The principal eavesdroppers in this play are Diniarchus and Stratophanes, and what they observe and hear gives them not superiority, but frustration and even desperation. Their eavesdropping thus leaves the spectators feeling not superior, but implicated in the lovers' foolishness. This time the spectators find themselves learning the truth about "Phronesium's" baby along with the guilty Diniarchus.

Visual effects have been very important in this play: Phronesium's entrance surrounded by handmaids; the grand procession of Stratophanes with his attendants and gifts for Phronesium; the competing procession of Cyamus with the food and gifts from Diniarchus; and the mock battle that ensues. The most striking visual moment, however, would probably be the scene that follows. As Diniarchus watches, Callicles enters with two bound women: Phronesium's hairdresser, and one of Callicles' handmaids. The spectators learn together with Diniarchus that the women acquired for Phronesium the baby of Callicles' daughter. Several asides by Diniarchus, moving from bewilderment to comprehension, parallel the spectators' own gradual awareness that the baby is the result of Diniarchus's rape of the daughter (770–74, 785–86, 794–95, 818–20, 823–24). When his misdeed has come to light and he has arranged with Callicles that he will recover the baby and marry the girl with a reduced dowry, Diniarchus again addresses the audience, telling them he will retrieve the baby from Phronesium, but confessing that she still has power over him (850–53).

The revelation that Diniarchus is the father of the child has brought the play closer to the more familiar and, it might be thought, predictable world of typical New and Roman comedy, where young men who have raped virgins inevitably marry the girl, and a happy ending results.[24] Plautus, however, is not finished shocking his audience. Phronesium enters, again confessing her trickiness to the spectators (854–57). When she tells Diniarchus she knows exactly what he has come to ask her, Diniarchus's last aside sums up the attitude not only of Phronesium, but of almost all of the characters of *Truculentus*, who have divulged their vices to the spectators in monologue after monologue: "di immortales! ut planiloqua est!" ("Good gods, how frank she is!" 864). Then, with no struggle at all, Diniarchus allows Phronesium to use his own child for her greedy ends, and reveals that his marriage will not end his moral and financial slavery to her. One scene remains to make still clearer how ridiculous men are when they become subject to *meretrices*. Stratophanes and Strabax compete with gifts for Phronesium's attention. Both continue to speak asides (912–13, 914–16, 925–26, 944), but it is an aside by Astaphium that summarizes the situation most accurately: "stultus atque insanus damnis certant: nos salvae sumus" ("We're safe: a fool and a madman are trying to out-ruin each other," 950).[25]

We saw in the last chapter how in *Curculio* Plautus discouraged his spectators from viewing his satire as relevant only to outsiders from whom they themselves could feel a comforting distance. He prevented his audience from concluding, "These are just Greeks," by means of well-placed Roman allusions; and through monologues he encouraged the spectators to acknowledge that the satire applied to themselves as well as to bankers and pimps, two groups that most in the audience could easily consider alien. Similar techniques are at work in *Truculentus*. Roman allusions prevent the

spectators from thinking that only Greeks are being mocked, and monologues and eavesdropping associate the characters with the audience.

There remains in *Truculentus* a potential scapegoat for satire perhaps more
powerful than any other: women.[26] Satire against women pervades the Plautine corpus. Besides many jokes at the expense of individual women, the
plays include numerous generalizations about women or various classes of
women, including prostitutes.[27] Such generalizations, even when delivered
by women characters,[28] are almost inevitably negative. Although Plautus's
audience included women (*Poen.* 28–35; Ter. *Hec.* 35), characters assume
that the spectators share their own misogynistic views; women in the audience are themselves the victims of an insult in one of Plautus's prologues
(*Poen.* 32–35). Indeed, misogyny was so much a recognized part of the *palliata* that Plautus makes a self-conscious joke about it in *Cistellaria*. Halisca,
the handmaid of two *meretrices*, has lost a basket. Desperate to find it (it
contains the tokens through which her mistress will discover her parents),
Halisca begs the audience for help:

> mei homines, mei spectatores, facite indicium, si quis vidit,
> quis eam abstulerit quisve sustulerit et utrum hac an illac iter
> > institerit.
> non sum scitior, quae hos rogem aut quae fatigem,
> qui semper malo muliebri sunt lubentes. (*Cist.* 678–81)

> Dear people, dear spectators, if any of you have seen who carried
> this off or picked it up, point him out to me, and tell me whether
> he went this way or that. But what a fool I am to wear these
> people out with questions: they always take pleasure in women's
> troubles.

Halisca's plea to the audience parallels that of Euclio in *Aulularia* (see Chapter 2). Whereas Euclio responded to the spectators' laughter with a wild accusation, however, Halisca speaks the truth when she accuses the audience
of enjoying the troubles of women. Because of the misogynistic tendencies
of the *palliata*, the spectators have on countless occasions laughed not only
at individual women, but at the expense of womankind as a whole.

Given the pervasiveness of such misogynistic themes, the audience would
certainly be prepared to view *Truculentus* as just another demonstration of
the evils of women. Plautus appears at first sight to encourage such a view.
In addition to its ruthlessly conniving women characters, *Truculentus* offers
several misogynistic generalizations. The *prologus* considers Phronesium's
behavior typical of her gender as a whole:

haec huius saecli mores in se possidet:
numquam ab amatore [suo] postulat id quod datumst,
sed relicuom dat operam ne sit relicuom,
poscendo atque auferendo, ut mos est mulierum;
nam omnes id faciunt, cum se amari intellegunt. (13–17)

This woman possesses the ways of this age: she never demands
from her lover what has already been given, but she sees to it that
what's left is not left by demanding and taking, as women usually
do; for they all do that, when they realize they are loved.

During her longest monologue, Phronesium herself twice connects her actions with the vices of women in general:

                                              ut miserae
matres sollicitaeque ex animo sumus cruciamurque!
edepol commentum male, cumque eam rem in corde agito,
nimio—minus perhibemur malae quam sumus ingenio. (448–52)

How wretched we mothers are, and what troubles we have in our
souls, and how we suffer! You know, it's a wicked lie, and when
I ponder it in my heart, I think that really . . . we are considered
less bad than we really are by nature.

male quod mulier facere incepit, nisi <id> efficere perpetrat,
id illi morbo, id illi seniost, ea illi miserae miseriast;
bene si facere incepit, eius rei nimis cito odium percipit.
nimis quam paucae sunt defessae, male quae facere occeperunt,
nimisque paucae efficiunt, si quid facere occeperunt bene:
mulieri nimio male facere levius onus est quam bene. (465–70)

When a woman has set out do to something bad, if she doesn't
accomplish it, she feels sick, she feels gloomy, she feels wretched,
poor soul; but if she has set out to do something good, she immediately becomes bored with it. How few women have become
worn out when they started something bad, and how few accomplish the good things they have started to do: for a woman, doing
bad is a lot easier than doing good.

Meanwhile, Diniarchus complains that women take too long in beautifying
themselves (322–25), echoing a misogynistic complaint common both in
Plautus and throughout Roman literature.[29]

In spite of these misogynistic statements, however, Plautus does not allow his audience to dismiss this play as just another example of the evils of

women. Instead, he repeatedly reminds them that men's vices more than women's wiles create the problems presented in the play: that is, the disastrous transfer of wealth is less the responsibility of the *meretrices*, whom most members of the audience can easily dismiss as alien to themselves, than of their male lovers, who are repeatedly associated with the audience. The string of counters to the characters' misogynistic assumptions culminates in a direct contradiction of one such assumption.

Immediately following the prologue, as we have seen, is Diniarchus's tirade against voracious prostitutes: no lover's wealth, he claims, can satisfy their demands. Before he finishes, however, Diniarchus acknowledges that the real fault lies in the lovers themselves (57–63), the persons whom, as we have seen, Diniarchus associates both with the Roman world and with the spectators. During the ensuing dialogue between Diniarchus and Astaphium, the young man offers a discourse on the relative vices of male and female prostitutes. In response, Astaphium again turns the blame from seducer to seduced:

> *Astaphium*: male quae in nos vis, ea omnia tibi dicis, Diniarche,
>   et nostram et illorum vicem.
> *Diniarchus*:   qui istuc?
> *Ast.*:   rationem dicam:
>   quia qui alterum incusat probri, sumpse enitere
>   oportet.
>   tu a nobis sapiens nihil habes, nos nequam abs ted
>   habemus. (158–61)

> *Astaphium*: All the bad things you want to say against us, Diniarchus, you say against yourself, instead of against us [scil., women prostitutes] and them [scil., male prostitutes].
> *Diniarchus*: How is that?
> *Ast.*: I'll tell you the reason: it's because the one who accuses another of vice ought to be free of it himself. You, who are so wise, have nothing from us, while we worthless ones have what used to be yours.

Early on, then, Plautus's characters make clear that the siphoning of wealth to prostitutes is a product of men's profligacy more than of women's wickedness. The point becomes increasingly clear as the play progresses and each of Phronesium's victims, especially the continually confessing Diniarchus, proves himself worthless.

The inadequacy of typical misogynistic explanations is presented most emphatically when it is revealed that Diniarchus raped his former fiancée.

While Diniarchus eavesdrops, Callicles responds aside to the revelations made by the two women:

> Callicles: vide sis facinus muliebre.
> Ancilla.: magis pol haec malitia pertinet ad viros quam ad
>   mulieres:
>   vir illam, non mulier praegnatem fecit.
> Ca.:   idem ego istuc scio.
>   tu bona ei custos fuisti.
> Anc.:   plus potest qui plus valet.
>   vir erat, plus valebat: vicit, quod petebat abstulit.
>   (809–13)

Callicles: Just look at the crimes women do.
Handmaid: Goodness, this vice applies more to men than to women: a man, not a woman, made her pregnant.
Ca.: I know that. And you were a fine guardian for her.
Handmaid: The one who is stronger can do what he wants. He was a man, he was stronger: he won, and he took what he wanted.

Callicles' "Just look at the crimes women do" is almost certainly an aside to the audience: he directs at them a misogynistic interpretation of the play's events with which many would probably agree. The handmaid accurately and effectively spells out what is implied throughout the play: such interpretations are inadequate. Unusual staging underlines her message. The handmaid not only overhears Callicles' aside, but, in a movement unparalleled in Plautus, she sees and reveals to Callicles Diniarchus, who stands eavesdropping unchastised while the women are punished: "tacui adhuc: nunc <non> tacebo, quando adest nec se indicat" (I've been silent up to now: but now I will not be silent, since he is here and doesn't show himself, 817). Nowhere else in Plautus's plays does an extended eavesdropping scene end with the eavesdropper being discovered against her or his will. Then, while Diniarchus pleads with Callicles, the handmaid calls attention to the inconsistent treatment of men and women:

> Callicles, vide in quaestione ne facias iniuriam:
> reus solutus causam dicit, testis vinctos attines. (836–37)

Callicles, watch out that you don't do wrong in your investigation: the defendant is pleading his case unbound while you are keeping the witnesses tied up.

The handmaid thus brings to a climax a theme that has run throughout the play: the assumption, typical of the *palliata*, that problems such as those presented in *Truculentus* can be attributed to the wickedness of women is inaccurate.

There is no escape for the spectators. They cannot simply attribute the play's situations to the evils of women; and the hapless lovers, who receive most of the blame for what happens, are associated both with Rome and with the audience. Crowning this pointing of the satire toward the audience is Plautus's most daring epilogue, spoken by Phronesium:

> lepide ecastor aucupavi atque ex mea sententia,
> meamque ut rem video bene gestam, vostram rusum bene geram:
> rem bonam si quis[30] animatust facere, faciat ut sciam.
> Veneris causa adplaudite: eius haec in tutelast fabula.[31] (964–67)

> Well, I have done my bird-catching well, the way I wanted to; and as I see that my affairs have been taken care of well, I will take care of yours well in turn. If anyone has in mind to do well for himself, see that I find out about it. Applaud for Venus's sake: this play is under her protection.

The spectators will laugh at the implication that they, too, could become subject to the wiles of the likes of Phronesium. Yet it will be a nervous laugh, for the misfortunes of Phronesium's lovers have throughout the play been placed in the context of the audience's own Rome; and, through monologues, eavesdropping, and direct addresses, the spectators have been implicitly and even explicitly associated with those lovers.

9

HUSBANDS AND WIVES: *CASINA*

si sine uxore pati possemus, Quirites, omnes ea molestia careremus; set quoniam ita natura tradidit, ut nec cum illis satis commode, nec sine illis ullo modo vivi possit, saluti perpetuae potius quam brevi voluptati consulendum est.

If we could get on without a wife, Romans, we would all avoid that annoyance; but since nature has ordained that we can neither live very comfortably with them nor at all without them, we must take thought for our lasting well-being rather than for the pleasure of the moment.

— Q. Metellus Numidicus, censor, 102 B.C.E. (Gell. 1.6.2, Rolfe's translation; see McDonnell 1987 on attribution)

WIVES do not for the most part fare well in Plautus. Among his plays' most common jokes are second-century B.C.E. variations of Henny Youngman's "Take my wife—please." Demaenetus, for example, the *senex amator* of *Asinaria*, says he loves his wife only when she is not around (900). Callicles wishes his wife were dead (*Trin.* 42) and jokes with his friend Megaronides about whose wife is the greater evil (*Trin.* 58−65).[1] Menaechmus is thrilled that he has been able to rob his wife, whom he compares to a ravenous lioness (*Men.* 127−34, 159). Even dead wives do not escape their husbands' wit: Periphanes complains that marriage to his now-dead wife was worse than a labor of Hercules (*Epid.* 178−79; cf. *Cist.* 175).[2] Supplementing these remarks about individual wives are damning generalizations about wives in general. When, for example, the profligate Lesbonicus is made to marry at the end of *Trinummus*, his father and his father's friend debate about whether one marriage is a sufficient punishment (1184–86); and Periplec-tomenus, the old bachelor of *Miles gloriosus*, delivers a long discourse on the evils of wives (681–700; cf. *Aul.* 154–57). The wives who receive the most severe lampooning in Plautus are those who have brought their husbands large dowries: throughout Plautus's corpus, characters argue that such wives bring endless troubles to their husbands.[3]

Most of the *matronae* who appear on the Plautine stage seem to confirm the male characters' stereotypes. Two wives who are said to have brought their husbands large dowries, Artemona of *Asinaria* and the unnamed *ma-trona* of *Menaechmi*, are imperious agelasts.[4] Most of the wives presented with sympathy are comfortably and emphatically under the control of their husbands. Alcumena boasts that she considers her dowry to be her femi-nine virtues, including her obedience to her husband ("morigera tibi," *Amph.* 842). The two wives who begin *Stichus* are sympathetic precisely be-cause of their determined loyalty to their husbands, whom they refuse to leave even though they have been away for three years. Whether presented with sympathy or hostility, Plautus's *matronae* almost never bond with the audience: almost without exception, their monologues are few and short. Alcumena's long monologue on *virtus* (*Amph.* 633–53) is the exception that proves the rule: as we saw in Chapter 6, Alcumena, a male actor stuffed to look pregnant, would be the object of the audience's laughter even as she offers rhetoric with which they would agree. Throughout most of the Plautine corpus, then, *matronae* are without question placed into the cate-gory of Other. Playwright, actors (all of whom, it must be remembered, were male), and audience join together to make married women the object of their laughter.

What of the wives in the audience? They are ignored, except where Plautus extends his characters' rhetoric against wives to include them as well. The *prologus* of *Poenulus*, while giving orders to the spectators, turns a stereotype about wives against the *matronae* in the audience themselves:

> matronae tacitae spectent, tacitae rideant,
> canora hic voce sua tinnire temperent,
> domum sermones fabulandi conferant,
> ne et hic viris sint et domi molestiae. (*Poen.* 32–35)

> Wives are to watch silently and laugh silently; they should keep their melodious voices from ringing, and take their gossip home, so that they are not a pain to their husbands both here and at home.

The *prologus* assumes that wives in the audience, like wives as described by so many of Plautus's characters, are loquacious and bothersome to their husbands.[5] In *Mostellaria*, two characters joke that members of the audience are henpecked by dowered wives (279–81, 708–9).

Jokes at the expense of wives are hardly, of course, unique to Plautus. The tensions and disappointments of marriage have proved an irresistible source of laughter since the beginnings of comedy; and since most comedy until very recently has been written by men for audiences made up mostly of men, jokes about marriage have more often than not been directed against wives.[6] The virulence of comic rhetoric against wives in Plautus's plays, however, appears to reflect historical conditions as well as comic tradition.

Plautus and his audience witnessed change, controversy, and anxiety surrounding the institution of marriage. The continual warfare of Plautus's time, by removing husbands from home for long periods of time, reduced the force of traditional legal and social restrictions on wives' freedom of action. Left to manage households on their own, wives exercised prerogatives that had traditionally been granted only to their husbands or guardians.[7] Meanwhile, as wealthy Romans grew wealthier, both the inheritances and the dowries of elite women became larger. Much Roman popular wisdom held that wealthy wives with large dowries destroyed the proper power structure of a marriage. Inflated by the awareness that their husbands were dependent on them for much of their wealth, dowered wives, it was argued, henpecked their husbands and demanded luxuries.[8] Other factors may also have contributed to greater freedom and power on the part of wives and subsequent discomfort on the part of many men: divorce was becoming more common, and an increasing number of marriages were *sine manu*, in which the wife remained legally a member of her father's household, rather than the more traditional *cum manu*, in which the husband became the wife's legal guardian.[9]

Meanwhile, a group of determined wives found themselves in the middle of a cause célèbre of Plautus's day. In 215 B.C.E. the Romans had passed the Oppian Law, which forbade women from having more than one-half ounce of gold, from wearing multicolored garments, or from riding in carriages in or near the city unless they were involved in religious ritual (Livy 34.1.3). In 195, against the opposition of Cato the Elder, who was then consul, the *lex Oppia* was repealed (Livy 34.1–8.3). Livy reports that in support of the repeal, women took extraordinary action. They lined the roads to the forum, begging the men as they passed to vote to revoke the law, and they even pleaded before the magistrates and besieged the homes of the tribunes who were vetoing the law's repeal (34.1.5–7, 8.1–2).[10]

Many members of Plautus's audience, therefore, must have felt that some wives, especially those with large dowries, had grown too powerful within their marriages. The demonstrations surrounding the repeal of the *lex Oppia* would have confirmed such fears for many, as they witnessed *matronae* trying to influence the political process. Their anxieties would have made such spectators eager listeners to comic criticism of wives.

For all its asperity, however, the rhetoric of Plautus's characters against wives does not go unchallenged. Megadorus's tirade against dowered wives in *Aulularia*, Plautus's longest, actually parodies those who deliver such diatribes. *Mercator* includes both an explicit feminist statement and an implicit acknowledgment that comedy does not treat wives justly. Most significantly, *Casina* turns comic stereotypes of wives upside down and aligns the audience with a powerful wife against her husband.

The words against wives all come from the mouths of fallible characters, and their context sometimes makes them ironic. The lecherous Demaenetus, for example, has little credibility when he criticizes his wife; and when Menaechmus denounces his wife, he is himself in the dubious position of standing onstage wearing her clothing. Even the *prologus* who teases *matronae* in the audience does not speak for Plautus: he is himself a character who has already proved himself pompous and silly. The effect of characterization and context on characters' tirades against wives is most evident in the case of Megadorus, the old bachelor of *Aulularia*, who offers Plautus's longest speech against dowered wives. Megadorus boasts to the audience of his prudence in choosing for a bride the dowryless daughter of his neighbor, Euclio; and he argues that the state would be far better off if all men followed his lead (475–535). He condemns dowered wives with the greatest severity: they cause dissension, he says, their love of luxury bankrupts their husbands, and their large dowries invert the proper hierarchy in a marriage.

Megadorus's words reflect not only controversy over dowries, but also the debate over repeal of the *lex Oppia*. Livy attributes to Cato a long speech in favor of keeping the law (34.2–4). Though the historian's version of Cato's speech is his own creation,[11] Livy probably had some knowledge of the arguments made against the law's repeal. It is therefore not without significance that Cato's speech and Megadorus's harangue have some remarkable similarities. Both Cato (Livy 34.4.15; cf. 34.7.5–7) and Megadorus claim that the measures of control they favor would prevent envy among women; both Megadorus and Cato are troubled by what they see as contemporary corruption (Livy 34.4.6−11); both use a direct quotation of a hypothetical luxury-loving woman on a carriage (34.3.9); and both share a basic fear that husbands are unable to control their wives (Livy 34.2.1−4, 34.2.13−3.3, 34.4.15−18; cf. 34.7.11−13).[12]

Even if Livy's speech comes entirely from his own imagination, and the use of similar misogynistic topoi by Livy's Cato and Plautus's Megadorus is coincidental, Megadorus's speech is clearly within the context of contemporary arguments familiar to many in the audience: for he phrases his diatribe in terms reminiscent of the provisions of the Oppian Law.[13] His first evidence of the dowered wives' *luxuria* is that mules, used to pull women's carriages, are more expensive than horses (493−95); and he later claims that as things stand, the city is more full of wagons than the country (505−6). He creates a hypothetical dowered wife, who speaks as follows:

> equidem dotem ad te adtuli
> maiorem multo quam tibi erat pecunia;
> enim mihi quidem aequomst purpuram atque aurum dari,
> ancillas, mulos, muliones, pedisequos,
> salutigerulos pueros, vehicla qui vehar. (498−502)

> Well, I brought you a dowry worth much more money than you had; so it is certainly fair that I should be given purple and gold, handmaids, mules, muleteers, attendants, pages, and carriages to ride in.

Megadorus thus imagines a dowered wife who wants gold, purple clothing, and carriages, the very things forbidden by the law; and the other elements he mentions—maidservants, mules, mule-drivers, and servants to follow the carriage and greet people—would accompany the woman riding on the illicit carriage.[14] The exactness with which Megadorus cites the specific items forbidden by the Oppian Law suggests that Plautus does indeed have in mind the debate surrounding the law's repeal, in spite of the skepticism of some scholars.[15]

The passage has thus been seen by some as evidence of Plautus's Catonian conservatism, or of his desire to please a misogynistic audience.[16] Plautus's treatment of the arguments against dowries, however, is parodic rather than sympathetic; for Megadorus, whose very name ("Great Gift") suggests pomposity, gets ridiculously carried away. He begins in a calm and straightforward, even businesslike, way, reporting in short sentences that his friends approve of his choice of a bride (475−77). When he turns from the specific to the general, he begins to get more excited, and he underlines his reasons with heavy-handed polysyndeton:

> et multo fiat civitas concordior,
> et invidia nos minore utamur quam utimur,
> et illae malam rem metuant quam metuont magis,
> et nos minore sumptu simus quam sumus. (481–84)

> Our state would become much more harmonious, *and* we would experience less envy than we do now, *and* women would fear punishment more than they do now, *and* we would have less expenditure than we do now.

From here to the end of the speech, Megadorus becomes more and more impassioned. After he gives the discourse on wagon-carried wives cited above, he lists for fifteen lines tradesmen who come for payment from the husband of a dowered wife, beginning with familiar merchants (dyer, embroiderer, gold worker, and wool worker, 508), and building up through a wild mixture of Greek and Latin names for highly specialized craftsmen, until he concludes with the most obscure (hem-makers, box-makers, and dyers in saffron, 519–21). He twice suggests that he is going to finish, only to add still more specialized businessmen (517–22). Finally, he claims that the husband of a dowered wife has no money left to pay a soldier who comes requesting pay,[17] and he concludes with a fervent summation:

> haec sunt atque aliae multae in magnis dotibus
> incommoditates sumptusque intolerabiles.
> nam quae indotata est, ea in potestate est viri;
> dotatae mactant et malo et damno viros. (532–35)

> These and many other nuisances, and intolerable expenses, come with great dowries. For the woman who has no dowry is in the power of her husband; the ones with a dowry afflict their husbands with both trouble and expense.

Megadorus is another of Plautus's overly ardent moralists, so obsessed with his diatribe, so determined to convince the audience of the truth of his opinion, that he becomes ridiculous. Euclio, eavesdropping on Megadorus's monologue, finds his neighbor's arguments persuasive and impressive (496–97, 503–4, 523–24, 537). His enthusiasm, however, scarcely makes Megadorus's speech less silly; for Euclio, an absurd caricature throughout the play, has just strangled his rooster for scratching the ground in the wrong place. Rather than a serious discourse on luxury of *matronae*, then, Mega-dorus's speech is a parody of speeches made against wives in general, and probably of specific speeches contemporary with the first performance of *Aulularia*.[18]

In *Mercator*, Plautus provides a more explicit counter to the bias against wives of so many of his characters. After Eutychus learns that his mother has discovered a woman she thinks is her husband's mistress in her house, he enters the house himself, commanding his mother's old slave Syra to follow him ("sequere me," 816). The audience would expect the scene to end at this point: characters in Roman comedy who leave the stage after ordering another to accompany them are almost always followed promptly.[19] Yet Syra remains onstage. The unusual staging draws attention to the surprising monologue she speaks:

> ecastor lege dura vivont mulieres
> multoque iniquiore miserae quam viri.
> nam si vir scortum duxit clam uxorem suam,
> id si rescivit uxor, inpunest viro;
> uxor virum si clam domo egressa est foras,
> viro fit causa, exigitur matrimonio.
> utinam lex esset eadem quae uxori est viro;
> nam uxor contenta est, quae bona est, uno viro:
> qui minus vir una uxore contentus siet?
> ecastor faxim, si itidem plectantur viri,
> si quis clam uxorem duxerit scortum suam,
> ut illae exiguntur quae in se culpam commerent,
> plures viri sint vidui quam nunc mulieres. (817–29)

> By Castor, we unfortunate women live under a harsh law, much less fair than that which governs men. For if a man goes out with a whore behind his wife's back, and the wife finds out, the man goes scot-free; but if a wife goes out behind her husband's back, the man has grounds, and she is divorced. I wish husbands were subject to the same law as wives; for a wife, if she is good, is content with just her husband: why shouldn't a husband be content with just his wife? By Castor, if husbands were punished in the same way, whenever a husband took out a whore behind his wife's back, just as wives who bring blame upon themselves are divorced, I bet there would be more divorced men than there are women now.

The speech is not without its irony. The eighty-four-year-old Syra is hu-morous in her doddering antiquity,[20] and she and her mistress are mistaken about Eutychus's father (Lysimachus): the girl they have found in the house is in fact being kept for his neighbor, Demipho.[21] Nevertheless, the speech does provide a striking interjection of the wife's perspective into a theatrical genre that is more often than not antagonistic to *matronae*.[22]

This fleeting moment of feminism adds extra force to the ending of *Mercator*. A reminder by Lysimachus that Demipho will pay dearly when his wife finds out what has been going on leads to the following dialogue:

> *Demipho*: nihil opust resciscat.
> *Eutychus*:   quid istic? non resciscet, ne time.
> eamus intro, non utibilest hic locus, factis tuis,
> dum memoramus, arbitri ut sint qui praetereant per vias.
> *Demipho*: hercle qui tu recte dicis: eadem brevior fabula
> erit. eamus. (1004 – 8)

> *Demipho*: She doesn't need to find out.
> *Eutychus*: All right. She won't find out, don't worry. Let's go inside. This is not a good place for us to recount what you've done, where anybody who walks by on the street can hear us.
> *Demipho*: By Hercules, you're right: and in the same way the play will be shorter. Let's go.

The joke regarding the length of the play is patently out of place, for at 1026 lines, *Mercator* is shorter than the average Plautine play.[23] Nor do the characters really need to go inside: they have been discussing Demipho's vices in the street for over an hour. The double metatheatrical irony calls attention to the fact that Demipho's situation with respect to his wife is being ignored. The issues necessary for the resolution of the comic plot have been resolved: Charinus, Demipho's son, has acquired his girl, and Lysimachus is freed from blame. Resolution of the other potential issue, Demipho's wife, is simply avoided, although it is hard to see how she can be kept in the dark, now that Lysimachus's wife knows the truth. The joke is a conspicuous way of disregarding the problem: this is a comedy, and the concerns of wives do not require resolution. The dismissal of the wife through metatheatrical means opens the way for an epilogue that omits her. Eutychus proposes a "law" that old men, whether married or not, should neither hire prostitutes nor prevent young men from doing so. The conflict between generations, not that between husband and wife, gets the characters' attention.

Similar words about the length of the play occur near the end of *Casina*.[24] Here, the refusal to resolve the conflict between husband and wife is even more striking, for *Casina* offers Plautus's most serious challenge to the assumptions of so many of his characters concerning marriage and wives.

Elsewhere in Plautus, the struggle between husbands and wives is peripheral to the main plot. In *Casina*, however, that struggle is the plot. At the beginning of *Casina*, both Lysidamus and his son are in love with Casina, the handmaid of Lysidamus's wife, Cleostrata. Lysidamus wants his bailiff, Olympio, to marry the girl, so that he himself can have sex with her. Lysidamus's wife and son seek to win the girl for the son by marrying her to the son's armor-bearer, Chalinus. After neither slave can be persuaded to give up his claim to the girl, the opponents agree to draw lots. Olympio wins, and Lysidamus conspires with his neighbor, Alcesimus, to use the neighbor's house for his liaison with Casina. Made aware of the plan by the eavesdropping Chalinus, Cleostrata, assisted by her servant Pardalisca and Alcesimus's wife Myrrhina, plots to undo the marriage. The women first cause confusion between Alcesimus and Lysidamus, then they persuade Lysidamus that Casina rages inside with a sword, threatening to kill her would-be husband and his master. Finally, they dress Chalinus as a bride and send him in place of Casina to Alcesimus's house, where he beats and humiliates both Olympio and Lysidamus.

Scholarship on *Casina* has tended to concentrate on the character of Lysidamus. As a *senex amator* (an old man in love), Lysidamus belongs to a type seldom presented with much sympathy; and Plautus makes him even more ridiculous and lecherous than other *senes amatores*.[25] However obnoxious Lysidamus may be, though, Cleostrata's victory over him nevertheless represents a break from the rest of Plautine comedy; for she becomes aligned with the spectators in spite of her initial characterization as a stock shrewish wife. Both her characterization and her success thus undermine the assumptions made about husbands and wives elsewhere in Plautus's plays.

The play's prologue both reveals the importance of the conflict between husband and wife and suggests that that importance is to a large degree the result of Plautus's reworking of the play he adapted from the Greek playwright Diphilus.[26] The *argumentum* begins with an introduction of Lysidamus: "senex hic maritus habitat" ("a married old man lives here," 35): the unnecessary epithet *maritus* is the first hint that Lysidamus's status as husband will be important. Immediately thereafter, the *prologus* reveals that the old man also has a son, that both men are in love with *Casina*, and that each has assigned his slave as surrogate. The spectators are thus prepared for a plot similar to *Asinaria* or *Mercator*, where son and father struggle for one girl. As he continues, however, the *prologus* reveals that this plot is to have a twist:

senis uxor sensit virum amori operam dare,
propterea una consentit cum filio.
ille autem postquam filium sensit suom
eandem illam amare et esse impedimento sibi,
hinc adulescentem peregre ablegavit pater;
sciens ei mater dat operam absenti tamen.
is, ne expectetis, hodie in hac comoedia
in urbem non redibit: Plautus noluit,
pontem interrupit, qui erat ei in itinere. (58–66)

The old man's wife has figured out that her husband is after love,
so she is in agreement with her son. But after the old man real-
ized that his son was in love with the same girl and was getting
in his way, he sent the young man away. Aware of what is going
on, his mother is helping her son out while he is away. Don't
expect the son to come back to the city during this comedy
today: Plautus didn't want him to, so he destroyed the bridge
that was on his way.

The battle will be not between father and son, but between husband and
wife: the son will not even appear in the play. *Plautus noluit* ("Plautus didn't
want him to") suggests that the son did appear in Diphilus's play: Plautus
has removed him, making Cleostrata's role more central. In fact, Plautus appears to have removed from his source play not only the son, but also the
anagnorisis that revealed that the son could marry Casina legally (he merely
states in the epilogue that Casina will be discovered to be the daughter of
Lysidamus's neighbor); and he may well have added part or even all of the
deception that Cleostrata carries out on her husband in the last half of the
play.[27] He has turned a typical play of generational rivalry and anagnorisis
into a farcical triumph of *matrona* over *senex*.

Though neither *senex* nor *matrona* appears in the play's first scene, that
scene hints at a pattern that is to determine the relationship between characters and audience in what follows. Immediately after the prologue,
Olympio enters, pursued by Chalinus, and he asks in exasperation:

non mihi licere meam rem me solum, ut volo,
loqui atque cogitare, sine ted arbitro? (89–90)

Can't I talk and think about my own affairs alone, as I wish, without you as witness?

After the two have exchanged a number of insults, Olympio exits, and

Chalinus continues to follow him, saying, "hic quidem pol certo nil ages sine med arbitro" ("I tell you, you won't do *anything* here without me as witness," 143). Olympio's inability to speak without Chalinus hearing foreshadows his situation throughout the play. He will be at the bottom of the hierarchy of rapport among the play's major characters, managing only one-half of one line aside to the audience without being heard (723). Nor does the foreshadowing apply only to Olympio: Cleostrata and her allies, including Chalinus, repeatedly overhear the monologues and asides of their opponents, Lysidamus and Olympio, and this ability to eavesdrop successfully will help considerably in aligning Cleostrata's side with the spectators.

Such an alliance will scarcely seem likely, however, when Olympio and Chalinus leave the stage and Cleostrata first enters; for Cleostrata is very much the stock comic shrew.[28] She leaves the house commanding that the larder be locked up, for she refuses to obey Lysidamus's order that she have his lunch prepared; and she speaks of her husband in the most threatening and insulting terms (148–62). Aside from her tone, Cleostrata's power in the household would seem to damn her. Why is she capable of keeping her husband out of the larder? According to Plutarch, substituting keys, along with adultery and murdering children, was one of the few reasons for which Romulus allowed a husband to divorce his wife without penalty (*Rom.* 22.3). Though Romulus's law may be apocryphal, it reflects the importance early Romans placed upon a husband's access to his possessions.[29] Even though no mention is made of Cleostrata's dowry, therefore, she has the characteristics of a stereotypical *uxor dotata*, appropriating power that should be her husband's.

Myrrhina then enters, presenting what looks at first like a clear contrast between the bad woman and the good. The entrances of the two women are closely parallel in staging: both enter talking back to their servants; both explain that they are going to visit their neighbor, in case their husbands should want them; and both, presumably, proceed toward the neighbor's house, meeting in the middle.[30] The parallel staging serves to emphasize the apparent contrast between the two. Whereas Cleostrata entered with a refusal to do what the audience would see as her wifely duty, Myrrhina is in the middle of such duty: she has been spinning wool, and she asks that her distaff be brought to her as she goes to visit her neighbor.[31] The difference in tone is conspicuous as each woman tells her servants that her husband can find her at the neighbor's. Cleostrata gives a harsh command, and she implies that exasperating her husband is one reason she is leaving the house:

ego huc transeo in proxumum ad meam vicinam.
vir si quid volet me, facite hinc accersatis. (145–46)

I am going over here to my neighbor's next door. If my husband
wants anything of me, make him summon me from here.

Myrrhina is imperious to her slaves (163–65), but when she refers to her
husband, she is more accommodating, and she makes clear that she is leaving so that she can do her weaving more efficiently:

ego hic ero, vir si aut quispiam quaeret.
nam ubi domi sola sum, sopor manus calvitur. (166–67)

I will be here, if my husband or anyone looks for me. For when
I'm at home by myself, sleepiness makes my hands slow.

When Cleostrata complains to Myrrhina of her husband's behavior,
Myrrhina responds with a joke at the expense of wives, much like those
found throughout Plautus's plays. Told by Cleostrata that her husband is depriving her of her *ius* (what is rightfully hers), Myrrhina responds:

mira sunt, vera si praedicas, nam viri
ius suom ad mulieres optinere haud queunt. (191–92)

That's amazing, if you are telling the truth; for usually husbands
can't get what is rightfully theirs from their women.

Cleostrata's insistence that Casina belongs to her inspires the following
exchange:

Myrrhina: unde ea tibi est?
              nam peculi probam nil habere addecet
              clam virum, et quae habet, partum ei haud commode
                                                          est,
              quin viro aut subtrahat aut stupro invenerit.
              hoc viri censeo esse omne, quidquid tuom est.
Cleostrata: tu quidem advorsum tuam amicam omnia loqueris.
My.:   tace sis, stulta, et mi ausculta. noli sis tu illi advorsari,
              sine amet, sine quod libet id faciat, quando tibi nil
                                                domi delicuom est.
Cl.:   satin sana es? nam tu quidem advorsus tuam istaec rem
                                                loquere.

My.:   insipiens,
    semper tu huic verbo vitato abs tuo viro.
Cl.:   cui verbo?
My.:   ei foras, mulier.
                                                             (198–211)

Myrrhina: Since when is she yours? For a virtuous woman should
have no property of her own behind her husband's back, and the
one who does have her own property got it in an improper way,
stealing it from her husband or getting it through adultery. I
think whatever is yours—everything—is your husband's.
Cleostrata: Well! Everything you say you say against your friend.
My.: Oh, be quiet, silly, and listen to me. Don't oppose him,
please; let him have his love affairs, let him do what he likes, as
long as he doesn't do you wrong at home.
Cl.: Are you crazy? For really, you're speaking against your own
interests!
My.: Silly! Always avoid hearing these words from your husband . . .
Cl.: What words?
My.: "Get out of my house, woman!"[32]

Myrrhina's opinions about a wife's property reflect the most traditional Roman type of marriage: marriage *cum manu*, in which a wife and all her property are legally in the power of her husband.[33] Myrrhina's assumptions
about the duties of wives toward their husbands would no doubt be shared
by many in the audience. She is the prudent and obedient wife, whereas
Cleostrata is the troublesome shrew, who, like a stereotypical *uxor dotata*,
seeks to invert the proper power structure of her marriage. In what follows,
however, the spectators' response to Cleostrata becomes gradually more
complicated. Not only does Lysidamus become more and more outrageous,
but Plautus manipulates the hierarchy of rapport between characters and
audience, so that the spectators become aligned with Cleostrata and her
allies.

Immediately following Myrrhina's reference to the divorce formula,
Lysidamus enters, speaking the first long monologue of the play.[34] He sings
an encomium to love, which he says is superior to all things and should be
used instead of spices by cooks. He offers his own love for Casina, which
caused him to visit the perfume shops, as a demonstration of the maxim,
and he curses his wife (217–27). Lysidamus thus assumes that he can confide
in and win the sympathy of the audience. Yet his entrance is observed by

Cleostrata.[35] This monologue establishes the pattern of rapport that is to prevail throughout the play. Lysidamus speaks far more lines of monologue than any other character of the play; but his soliloquies and asides are repeatedly overheard by other characters, and from the very beginning Cleostrata knows Lysidamus's plans.[36] Lysidamus thus assumes that he has rapport with the spectators, but in fact Cleostrata and her allies attain a higher position in the hierarchy of rapport.

The dialogue that follows reinforces this hierarchy, as Cleostrata overhears her husband's asides:

> *Lysidamus:* quam ted amo!
> *Cleostrata:* nolo ames.
> *Ly.:* non potes impetrare.
> *Cl.:* enicas.
> *Ly.:* vera dicas velim.
> *Cl.:* credo ego istuc tibi.
> *Ly.:* respice, o mi lepos.
> *Cl.:* nempe ita ut tu mihi es.
> unde hic, amabo, unguenta olent?
> *Ly.:* oh perii! manufesto
> miser
> teneor. cesso caput pallio detergere.
> ut te bonu' Mercurius perdat, myropola, quia haec
> mihi dedisti.[37] (232–38)

> *Lysidamus:* How I love you!
> *Cleostrata.:* I don't want you to love me.
> *Ly.:* You can't stop me.
> *Cl.:* You're killing me.
> *Ly.* (aside): I wish I were.
> *Cl.* (aside): I believe you in that.
> *Ly.:* Look at me, my charming one.
> *Cl.:* Sure, just like you're charming to me. Tell me, please, where's that smell of perfume coming from?
> *Ly.* (aside): Oh! I'm done for! Poor me, I'm caught in the act. Quick, I'd better wipe my head with my cloak. May good Mercury destroy you, perfume salesman, for giving me this stuff.

Neither Lysidamus's use of perfume nor his aside to the audience eludes Cleostrata. There is no sign, however, that Lysidamus overhears Cleostrata's aside.

After Cleostrata exits, Lysidamus calls attention to the fact that he was unable to speak around her while she was onstage: "Hercules dique istam perdant, quod nunc liceat dicere" ("May Hercules and all the gods destroy her! I hope I can say that now," 275). He then curses Chalinus, and he is again overheard:

> *Lysidamus*.: qui illum di omnes deaeque perdant!
> *Chalinus*.: te uxor aiebat tua
> me vocare. (279–80)

> *Lysidamus*: That man! May all the gods destroy . . . !
> *Chalinus*: You, your wife said, wanted me.

The joke in Latin depends on the fact that without the delayed *me vocare*, the phrase *te uxor aiebat tua*, after the curse, means, "Your wife was saying that she wishes all the gods would destroy *you*." Another hierarchy of rapport is established, and again Lysidamus is on the bottom, for he has no idea Chalinus's words are a double entendre, and that the end of his monologue has been overheard.

In fact, Lysidamus still assumes that he has the power to guide the audience's reactions. After he fails to persuade Chalinus to give up Casina, he indulges in another monologue, beginning with a rhetorical question seeking sympathy from the audience: "sumne ego miser homo?" ("Am I not a wretched man?" 303). Fearing that Cleostrata will persuade Olympio to abandon his claim to the girl, he continues with a mournful plea for commiseration (305); and he melodramatically threatens to stab himself if he loses Casina (307–8). As Olympio enters, telling Cleostrata that he will not give up his claim to Casina, Lysidamus even manages some overhearing of his own; and he responds to what he hears with a joyful aside (312).

In the ensuing scene, Olympio and Lysidamus pepper their dialogue with insults against Cleostrata like those used to abuse wives elsewhere in Plautus: she argues continually with Lysidamus (318); she is a bitch (320); Lysidamus wishes she were dead (Olympio turns this insult into an obscene joke as well, 326–27). The familiar insults further place Cleostrata within the category of the stock *matrona*. The manipulation of rapport, however, has made it less easy for spectators simply to agree with the insults and dismiss Cleostrata as an unsympathetic character. This dissonance between Lysidamus's assumptions and the alignment of the audience continues as Lysidamus overhears Cleostrata and Chalinus entering (353–55). This is the only place in the play where Lysidamus overhears words of his opponents not intended for his ears. Not surprisingly, his brief moment of greater theatrical power leads him to another joke at the expense of Cleostrata (356).

What he learns from his eavesdropping, however, is that Chalinus and Cleostrata know something he would wish concealed, his own hostility to Cleostrata.

Given the fact that Greek dramatists almost always followed the rule of three actors, the ensuing lot scene almost certainly included only Lysidamus, Chalinus, and Olympio in Plautus's Greek original: Plautus added Cleostrata, thus continuing his emphasis on the struggle between husband and wife.[38] As he did so, he made Lysidamus's inability to hide anything from Cleostrata still more obvious; for the old man commits a chain of what we could call Freudian slips, all of them noted by Cleostrata:

> *Lysidamus*: atque ego censui aps te posse hoc me impetrare, uxor
> mea,
>   Casina ut uxor mihi daretur; et nunc etiam censeo.
> *Cleostrata*: tibi daretur illa?
> *Ly.*:   mihi enim—ah, non id volui dicere:
>   dum mihi volui, huic dixi, atque adeo mihi dum
>   cupio—perperam
>   iam dudum hercle fabulor.
> *Cl.*:   pol tu quidem, atque etiam
>   facis.
> *Ly.*:   huic—immo hercle mihi—vah, tandem redii vix
>   veram in viam.
> *Cl.*:   per pol saepe peccas.   (364–70)

Lysidamus: Nevertheless, I thought that I would be able to persuade you to do this for me, dear wife, to give Casina to me to marry; and I still think I can persuade you.
Cleostrata: To give her to *you*?
Ly.: Yes to me—ah, that's not what I wanted to say: when I wanted to say "to me" I said "to him," and since I really want her for me—now I keep on saying the wrong thing.
Cl.: You sure do, and you keep doing the wrong thing, too.
Ly.: For him—goodness no, I mean for me—ah! I still can hardly get it right.
Cl.: You really say the wrong thing a lot.

When Olympio wins the lot, all characters leave the stage except Chalinus, who delivers the longest monologue of the play thus far that is not observed by another character (excluding the prologue). In it he reveals that he, like his mistress, is suspicious of Lysidamus's motives (424–36). Before he left the stage, Lysidamus had emphasized to Olympio that he did not want to be overheard by Chalinus (423). The effect on relative rapport is thus all the greater when Lysidamus and Olympio next enter to plot strategy, and Chalinus eavesdrops on them (437–503). The audience learns along with Chalinus that Lysidamus plans to have Casina brought to the neighbor's house. The shared knowledge creates rapport between slave and spectators, and the rapport is reinforced as Chalinus comments aside repeatedly on what he hears and ends the scene with a long monologue (504–14).[39]

When Cleostrata returns to the stage, she possesses without doubt all the knowledge she needs to condemn Lysidamus, and she is indubitably in charge. She frames the next scene, during which she inspires strife between Lysidamus and Alcesimus, with monologues (531–38, 558–62). She also seems to overhear Alcesimus's monologue, either remaining onstage or listening from behind the door (558);[40] and she overhears another entrance monologue of Lysidamus. If there was some doubt as to how much of Lysidamus's previous monologue Cleostrata heard, this time Plautus makes the difference in rapport obvious. After eleven highly incriminating lines, Lysidamus finally notices his wife watching him:

> *Lysidamus*: sed uxorem ante aedis eccam. ei misero mihi,
> metuo ne non sit surda atque haec audiverit.
> *Cleostrata*: audivi ecastor cum malo magno tuo. (574–76)

> *Lysidamus*: But look! There's my wife in front of the house. Oh, poor me! I'm afraid that she's not deaf and she heard what I said.
> *Cleostrata* (aside): I heard, all right, and you'll pay for it.

Again, Lysidamus's monologue is overheard, but Cleostrata's aside is not. Finally, Cleostrata speaks a brief exit monologue, unheard by Lysidamus, even though he is onstage (589–90). The normal pattern, of course, is for exit monologues to be spoken only after the other characters have left the stage.[41]

After he has straightened out the confusion Cleostrata created with Alcesimus, Lysidamus gets to be an eavesdropper himself, but only because Pardalisca performs for him, pretending that she flees a raging Casina. This inversion of the knowledge surrounding eavesdropping places Lysidamus in a still lower position in the hierarchy of rapport. As Pardalisca then explains to her master what is allegedly happening within, she, like her mistress before her, overhears and responds to his asides (667–68, 681) and catches him in "Freudian" slips (672, 703). Pardalisca intensifies her own alliance with the spectators, established at the expense of Lysidamus, by telling them in an aside exactly what she is doing:

> ludo ego hunc facete;
> nam quae facta dixi omnia huic falsa dixi:
> era atque haec dolum ex proxumo hunc protulerunt,
> ego hunc missa sum ludere. (685–88)

I'm playing a great trick on him; for everything I told him is false. My mistress and her next-door neighbor here came up with this deception, and I have been sent to trick him.

The alliances of the play are now unmistakable: the audience is aligned with Cleostrata and her onstage allies against Lysidamus and his allies. Significantly, the "linking monologue" Lysidamus speaks between the exit of Pardalisca and the ensuing entrance of Olympio lasts for only one line (720); and his status falls still further when he reports Pardalisca's news to Olympio. Unlike his gullible master, Olympio immediately realizes that the story of the sword-bearing Casina was nothing but the women's ruse (751–52).

The audience sees the next deception entirely through Pardalisca's eyes: she reports how the cooks and the women have kept Olympio and Lysidamus from getting any supper. Pardalisca then eavesdrops on Lysidamus (780–89); and when she leaves the stage, the old man again reminds the audience that his attempts to communicate with them are being repeatedly foiled while others are onstage: "iamne abiit illaec? dicere hic quidvis licet" ("Has she gone now? Now I can say whatever I want," 794). Even now that he is alone, he only manages one line on the glories of love (795) before he sees Olympio and the *tibicen* entering, ready for the wedding.

The climax of Cleostrata's plot follows, as Chalinus, disguised as Casina, is led to Olympio's bridal chamber. Lysidamus, this time with Olympio, again overhears what the women want him to hear, as Pardalisca advises "Casina" to be a domineering and deceptive wife:

> sensim supera tolle limen pedes, mea nova nupta;
> sospes iter incipe hoc, uti viro tuo
> semper sis superstes,
> tuaque ut potior pollentia sit vincasque virum victrixque sies,
> tua vox superet tuomque imperium: vir te vestiat, tu virum
> despolies.
> noctuque et diu ut viro subdola sis,
> opsecro, memento. (815–21)

Lift your feet gently over the threshold, my new bride; make this journey safely, so that you can always stand above your husband, and so that your power will be greater, so that you will overcome your husband, and be the victor, so that your word and your command will win the day: let your husband clothe you, while you strip him. And please, be sure to remember to deceive your husband day and night.

Pardalisca parodies Roman wedding ritual and inverts Roman ideals of wifely obedience.[42] "Casina," like the stereotypical *uxor dotata*, should want power and luxuries. Plautus has now established an alliance between the spectators and those who explicitly associate themselves with the quintessential outsiders of Plautine comedy: wives who want power over their husbands.

When Olympio and Lysidamus, after receiving several blows from "Casina," have led "her" into Alcesimus's house, Myrrhina, Pardalisca, and Cleostrata enter to watch what happens. Myrrhina describes the events to come in decidedly theatrical terms:

> acceptae bene et commode eximus intus
> ludos visere huc in viam nuptialis. (855−56)

Now that we have been entertained pleasantly and well indoors, we are coming out here into the street to watch the nuptial games.

The women are now an audience, aligned with the real audience watching the discomfiture of Olympio and Lysidamus. They are also the playwrights responsible for the performance they will watch, as Myrrhina points out in the next lines:

> nec fallaciam astutiorem ullus fecit
> poeta, atque ut haec est fabre facta ab nobis. (860−61)

No poet ever made a more clever trick than this one we have crafted so skillfully.[43]

Unaware of the women's presence, Olympio enters, fleeing his bride. He addresses the spectators explicitly (879), and he delivers a long and incriminating monologue, only to learn to his chagrin that he is being observed by the women (893). He then delights both onstage and offstage spectators with an obscene report of his misadventure with "Casina": he was beaten when he tried to deflower "Casina" before Lysidamus could get to her, and what he thought was a sword was actually "Casina's" phallus.

Finally, Lysidamus enters, bruised and disheveled by his encounter with "Casina." Staging underscores the fact that Lysidamus has reached his nadir, for he is overheard now by no fewer than five eavesdroppers: Pardalisca, Chalinus, Cleostrata, Myrrhina, and his former ally, Olympio. He is in fact caught right between the eavesdroppers: when he later attempts to escape the pursuing Chalinus, he runs into his wife and her colleagues (969). This visual situation brings intense dramatic irony to Lysidamus's opening words:

> maxumo ego ardeo flagitio nec quid agam meis rebus scio,
> nec meam ut uxorem aspiciam contra oculis, ita disperii;
> <om>nia palam sunt probra,
> omnibus modis occidi miser. (937–40)

> I'm burning from the greatest shame, and I don't know what
> I should do for myself, nor how I can look my wife in the face,
> I'm so utterly ruined. All my vices are in the open, and—poor
> me!—I'm finished in every way.

Lysidamus will have to look his wife in the face sooner than he thinks, for she is watching him as he speaks: his vices are even more in the open than he realizes. Nevertheless, Lysidamus still assumes that he can confide in the audience. He even asks if any spectator will be beaten for him (949–50).[44] He also continues to assume that the spectators share his hostility to his wife: forced to choose between running back to Chalinus and running into the women, he says he chooses between wolves and bitches, his wife and her female allies being the latter (971–73). By now the inadequacy of such insults will be more than obvious.

Lysidamus's utter humiliation is further reinforced visually by the wretched state of his dress: he has lost his staff and cloak. When he tries to blame the loss on bacchants, he is rebuffed by Myrrhina:

> *Cleostrata*: quin responde, tuo quid factum est pallio?
> *Lysidamus*: Bacchae hercle, uxor—
> *Cl.*: Bacchae?
> *Ly.*: Bacchae hercle,
> uxor—
> *Myrrhina*: nugatur sciens,
> nam ecastor nunc Bacchae nullae ludunt.
> *Ly.*: oblitus fui,
> sed tamen Bacchae—

Cl.:		quid, Bacchae?
Ly.:		sin id fieri non
		potest—
Cl.:	times ecastor.	(978–82)

Cleostrata: All right now, answer me: what happened to your
cloak?
Lysidamus: By Hercules, dear wife, it was Bacchants. . . .
Cl.: Bacchants?
Ly.: By Hercules, dear wife, it was Bacchants. . . .
Myrrhina: That's nonsense and he knows it, for goodness, now
there are no bacchic revelries.
Ly.: I forgot; but just the same, Bacchants . . .
Cl.: What's that? Bacchants?
Ly.: Well, if that's not possible—
Cl.: My, but you are frightened.

With her theatrical double entendre, *ludunt*, Myrrhina reminds Lysidamus
that the women have gained power over the performance: their play, not a
performance with bacchants, is now being performed.

The reference to bacchants is also topical. Lysidamus alludes to the contemporary controversy over nocturnal rites held by worshipers of Bacchus,
rites brutally crushed after a decree of the senate in 186 B.C.E.[45] One of the
accusations made against the worshipers of Bacchus was that female revel-
ers made male participants have sex with one another: Lysidamus, caught
trying to have sex with his male slave, offers the excuse that women wor-
shiping Bacchus forced him to do it.[46] He cites an extreme example of
women's power over men, an ideal exemplum for those seeking to keep
wives and other women "in their place." Myrrhina's response reminds him
and the audience that here women's power is not a heinous aberration, but
a positive force.

Lysidamus then begs his wife for forgiveness, and Myrrhina proposes le-
niency. Cleostrata agrees:

Myrrhina: censeo ecastor veniam hanc dandam.
Cleostrata: faciam ut iubes.
propter eam rem hanc tibi nunc veniam minus gravate prospero,
hanc ex longa longiorem ne faciamus fabulam. (1004–6)

Myrrhina: I think, really, you should forgive him this time.
Cleostrata: I will do as you suggest. Here's why I'm forgiving you
more willingly now: so that we don't make this long play longer.

Cleostrata's reason for forgiving Lysidamus is not personal but theatrical: again, Lysidamus and the audience are reminded that the women control the play.[47] As in *Mercator*, the self-deprecating joke about the length of the play is ironic, for *Casina*, at 1018 lines, is even shorter than *Mercator*.[48] Behind the joke lies an additional message: the inversion of the expected roles of men and women has gone on far enough, and the real issue of the marital relationship is not to be dealt with in a comedy.[49] Not surprising, then, is Lysidamus's response to Cleostrata's mercy, using *lepidus*, with its connotations of excellent performance: "lepidiorem uxorem nemo quisquam quam ego habeo hanc habet" ("Nobody has a wife more charming than this one of mine," 1008).

Here, however, issues of husbands and wives are not as easily dismissed as they were in *Mercator*. Cleostrata's release of Lysidamus and the audience from those issues leads to the epilogue, which ostensibly returns to a narrow masculine perspective and wishes for the spectators access to a prostitute behind their wives' backs if they applaud enthusiastically. The epilogue's sudden association of the spectators with Lysidamus, as they, like him, are assumed to want sex behind their wives' backs, makes a great joke at the audience's expense. It also reminds them that in most plays, they would in fact be aligned with a man like Lysidamus against a wife like Cleostrata.[50] This play, however, has been a completely different experience.

In *Casina*, then, Plautus offered a daring plot, involving the triumph of a *matrona* who at first appears to match the characteristics of some of Plautus's least sympathetic characters. One of the ways he overcame potential resistance to this unusual plot was by establishing a clear hierarchy of rapport, with Cleostrata and her allies on the top and Lysidamus on the bottom, a hierarchy made still more powerful because through most of the play, Lysidamus thinks he is on top.

It might well be asked why Plautus chose to present such a play at all. One reason was certainly the value of novelty. Just as *Amphitruo* gave Plautus the chance to present a new variation on comic motifs, Cleostrata's triumph presents something different. An additional motive must have been the Saturnalian fun inherent in a wife overcoming her husband: the success of the usually subservient wife would bring pleasure similar to that produced by Plautus's many successful slaves. It has also been proposed that Plautus offered in Lysidamus a negative example of unbridled lust: his defeat at the hands of his wife reinforces his own worthlessness.[51] There is more at work here, however, than simply variety, topsy-turviness for its own sake, or moralizing about lust. Cleostrata's victory over Lysidamus represents a nightmare come true for those on the conservative side of contemporary debates about *matronae*. Like the worst stereotypes of women not sufficiently controlled by men—wives with big dowries, *matronae* who protested against the *lex Oppia*, women involved in Bacchanalia—Cleostrata gains complete power over her husband. Yet in spite of their initial impression of her as an unsympathetic stock *matrona*, the spectators find themselves aligned with Cleostrata against Lysidamus. The stereotype of the frightful "woman on top" has proved inadequate; and the spectators are in a position like that of Myrrhina, who begins the play on Lysidamus's side but becomes Cleostrata's ally by play's end. Plautus thus encourages the audience to view from an entirely different perspective contemporary controversies about the proper role of married women.

10

SLAVES AND MASTERS: *CAPTIVI*

IN responding to controversies about marriage and *matronae*, then, Plautus often echoed the views that were probably held by most members of his audience. Some aspects of the plays, however, subtly undermine those views; and in one play, *Casina*, he compelled his audience to view the issue from a different perspective by confounding their expectations and manipulating their relationship with characters. A similar pattern emerges in Plautus's response to questions regarding slaves and slavery. Though much of Plautus's corpus would reinforce spectators' assumptions that slaves are morally inferior to free persons, the plays also contain elements undermining those assumptions; and in one play, *Captivi*, Plautus uses metatheatrical techniques to contest the notion that slaves are inherently inferior.

I noted in earlier chapters the importance of slaves in Plautine theater, the potential discomfort caused by the outrageous behavior of slaves onstage, and how Plautus averted or overcame this discomfort through manipulation of setting and rapport. I also noted the special relevance of questions about slavery to Plautus's Rome, where slaves were becoming a more and more conspicuous presence; and to Plautine theater, where many of the actors were slaves, and slaves were present in the audience. I have not yet addressed, however, one of the most important questions raised by Plautus's portrayal of slaves: What was the playwright's response to the ideological construct of servile inferiority?

As slavery in the ancient world was not based on skin color, no physical differences distinguished slave from free; and in Rome, widespread manumission, which usually brought citizenship with it, further discouraged easy differentiation between slave and free.[1] Indeed, Roman jurists, writing some centuries after Plautus, would recognize the natural equality of slave and free, acknowledging that slavery was a product of the *ius gentium* (the law of nations), in opposition to nature (*Dig.* 1.5.4.1).[2] Nevertheless, a prejudice that slaves were not the moral equals of free persons pervaded Roman culture. A wide range of sources from all periods of Roman history reveals the common assumption that slaves were inferior to free persons in every way: uglier, less intelligent, and generally worse. This assumption was most pronounced in the area of morality. As Keith Bradley puts it, "The prevalent Roman attitude was that the downward move [scil. from freedom to slavery] was shaming, so that socially low and morally low became one and the same."[3] To most Romans, true moral worth was the domain of the free.[4]

The widespread prejudice against slaves, however, did not go unchallenged. At least from the fifth century B.C.E., some Greek philosophers had argued that there was no natural difference between masters and slaves. In spite of the opinions of Aristotle to the contrary (*Politics* 1.2.13–15), Hellenistic philosophy, especially Stoicism, brought more arguments about the lack of difference between slaves and free, so that by the first century of our era, Seneca and others could write eloquently on the shared humanity of slaves and free persons. Nor was the debate about the nature of slaves confined to the writings of philosophers. Euripides raised the question repeatedly in his tragedies, and New Comedy contained not only many sympathetically portrayed slaves, but implicit and explicit rebuttals of the assumption that slaves were by nature inferior. The "pro-slave" side of the debate never led to an abolitionist movement, or even to significant reforms in the institution of slavery. It nevertheless made problematic the automatic association between slavery and moral inferiority.[5]

There is much in Plautus that would appear to confirm the prejudice that slaves were morally inferior to free persons. Plautus's *servi callidi* revel in their trickiness, reinforcing the stereotype that slaves are by nature given to deception.[6] Other slaves, who boast about how good they are, usually make clear that they are "good slaves" only in their fawning obedience: they behave obediently not out of virtue, but because they fear punishment.[7] One of the most significant signs of the moral degradation of a character like Lysidamus is that he becomes like a slave (see Chapter 9, note 44).

Other aspects of Plautine theater, however, had the potential to undermine assumptions of servile inferiority. As we have seen, slaves in Plautus are often more intelligent, or at least more clever, than their masters and other free persons, and young masters become subservient to the clever slaves who help them win the women they love. In a few plays, slaves are also morally superior to their masters: Chalinus and Pardalisca, for example, are certainly on a higher moral plane than Lysidamus is, and Palaestrio is morally superior to Pyrgopolynices. Furthermore, the actors' performances themselves blurred the distinction between slave and free, as slave actors played the roles of free men and women, and free actors played slaves' roles.[8] Through most of Plautus's corpus, these potential threats to assumptions of servile inferiority lie discreetly in the background, or their implications are ignored. In *Captivi*, however, Plautus brings both threats and implications to the fore.

The plot of *Captivi* revolves around the failure to distinguish slaves from free persons. When the play begins, the slave Tyndarus has been captured in war, along with his master, Philocrates. Hegio purchases both captives, hoping to trade Philocrates for his son Philopolemus, also a captive. Hegio is unaware that Tyndarus is also his son, stolen as a child by a fugitive slave, Stalagmus, and sold to Philocrates' father. Tyndarus and Philocrates secretly change identities, and Philocrates returns home. The deception leads to disaster when Aristophontes, another captive who knows Philocrates, reveals that Tyndarus is a slave. Sent to the quarries by the angry Hegio, Tyndarus is rescued when Philocrates returns with Philopolemus and with Stalagmus, who reveals that Hegio is Tyndarus's father.

Philocrates, Aristophontes, and Philopolemus, as free men taken captive in war and sold, are now slaves: they are addressed and referred to as slaves (195–200, 334–35, 372, 454), and they call themselves slaves (305, 543, 621). Indeed, as captives they are in many ways the quintessential slaves. A principal bulwark of the ideology upon which ancient slavery was based was the equation of slaves with captives. By allowing themselves to be spared when defeated in battle, it was argued, slaves had both demonstrated their inferiority and relinquished all rights. Hence slavery was often defined as the result of capture, even though many were slaves because of birth, piracy, or exposure.[9] Philocrates himself echoes the connections made between slaves' inferiority and capture in war when he learns that Philopolemus was also captured: "non igitur nos soli ignavi fuimus" ("Then we weren't the only cowards," 262). Nevertheless, Philocrates and Aristophontes distinguish themselves from slaves such as Tyndarus and Hegio's henchmen, speaking as if they themselves were still free.

Still more problematic is the status of Tyndarus, not only a free person made a slave, but a slave to his own father. The *prologus* announces this extraordinary fact immediately (5), and he repeats it twice, with appropriate philosophizing (21–22, 50–51). After the prologue, verbal ironies keep

Tyndarus's double status very much in the audience's mind. Pretending to be Philocrates, Tyndarus repeatedly says things unknowingly that remind the audience of his true status: he talks about how he was previously free (305, 574–75, 628), and how he considers himself free except that he is under guard (394). Both Tyndarus and Philocrates use variations of the phrase *honore honestare* ("to honor in keeping with one's station," 247, 356, 392): the phrase, which appears only one other time in extant Latin literature,[10] is a conspicuous reminder that persons in this play are not in fact valued according to their station. Even more telling is Hegio's unintentional irony when he says to Tyndarus, "ego virtute deum et maiorum nostrum dives sum satis" ("Thanks to the virtue of the gods and our ancestors, I am rich enough," 324).[11] As the expected formula is *virtute maiorum meum* ("thanks to the virtue of *my* ancestors"),[12] Hegio unwittingly acknowledges that he and Tyndarus in fact share the same ancestors, though as a slave, Tyndarus would have no ancestors according to Roman law.[13]

The difficulty in distinguishing slave from free is further underlined as Aristophontes and Hegio fail when they think they know how free persons and slaves differ. Aristophontes nearly destroys Tyndarus because of his inability to recognize that a slave, like a free person, can be noble, honest, and unselfish. Though he begins his dialogue with Tyndarus with an acknowledgment of the truth—"tam sum servos quam tu" ("I am as much a slave as you are," 543)—he repeatedly harps upon Tyndarus's slave status (574, 577, 580, 590), and he addresses Tyndarus with insults reserved for slaves (*furcifer*, 563, 577; *mastigia*, 600). Hegio shows an equal inability to recognize that a slave can have virtue. When Tyndarus discourses nobly on his loyalty to Philocrates, Hegio can see only the tricky slave, and he refuses to rise above the level of the comic deceived master. Nor is Hegio converted: in spite of his awareness at play's end that he has punished Tyndarus unjustly, he does not express real remorse until he learns that his victim was not a slave, but his own son.[14]

Spectators could respond to all this ambiguity in two ways. By concentrating on the noble actions of Tyndarus and the fact that they know all along that he is freeborn,[15] spectators could see the play as a demonstration that in spite of appearances, the character of a freeborn person does in fact remain distinct from that of a slave. They could feel smugly superior to the characters onstage, who do not perceive that a character as admirable as Tyndarus must be freeborn. They could also, however, consider the broader implications of the plot: fortune, not character, turns people into slaves, and slaves and free persons are not nearly so easily distinguishable as some may wish to think. Plautus takes advantage of his audience's familiarity with the conventions of the *palliata* to encourage the second response. He extends the ambiguity between slave and free from the plot to the performance, ruthlessly confounding the audience's expectations regarding comic slaves. Furthermore, he draws connections between the performance onstage and the realities of Rome, thus making clear that the difficulty in distinguishing slave from free applies to life as well as to theater.[16]

The play's use of masks would in all likelihood have given the spectators their first surprise. As I noted in my introduction, evidence regarding masks in Roman comedy is meager and contradictory. What evidence there is, however, strongly suggests that characters wore masks indicative of social class, and that slave masks were very different from the masks of free persons.[17] The probability of this distinction allows some speculation about the possible combinations of masks worn by Tyndarus and Philocrates. If both actors wore free men's masks throughout the play, the audience watched those onstage take for granted that both men were slaves even as they saw the evidence that they were free. If Tyndarus wore a slave mask throughout, Hegio would accept that the man wearing the free man's mask is a slave and vice versa, and Tyndarus would still have a slave's mask even after it is revealed to all that he was born free. The latter dilemma could be avoided if Tyndarus changed masks at the end, but there is no suggestion that such changes occurred on the Roman stage. Even such a drastic measure would not solve the problem, for Tyndarus would still show characteristics generally reserved for free characters as he wore the slave's mask. It is also possible that Tyndarus and Philocrates wore masks that could not be easily identified as either slave or free, or that blended the characteristics of the two types of mask. Such masks would not relieve the sense of uncertainty for an audience accustomed to masks more emphatically determinative of social status.

Two passages describing the captives' appearance provide still more intriguing possibilities. The prologue, after explaining that Tyndarus and Philocrates have exchanged clothing and names, adds, "huius illic, hic illius hodie fert imaginem" ("That one bears this one's *imago*, and this one bears that one's *imago*," 39). *Imago* often means appearance in general, but it can also mean "mask"; and the two other uses of *fero imaginem* in Plautus suggest that the prologue speaker may well mean that each young man is wearing the other's mask.[18] In that case, the man really free but thought to be a slave wears the free man's mask, and the man known to be free (although he has just now been enslaved) wears the slave's mask. What mask, then, would each man wear in the end? Would Philocrates wear the mask that Tyndarus has worn, and Tyndarus appear in an as-yet-unseen free man's mask? Or would Tyndarus appear in his slave's mask, previously worn by Philocrates, at the moment in which he is proved to be free? To make things still more enigmatic, Philocrates' mask was topped by a head of red hair (648). Elsewhere in Plautus and Terence, red-haired men are always slaves (*Asin.* 400; *Pseud.* 1218; *Phormio* 51), and the grammarian Pollux, describing the masks of New Comedy, explicitly connects red hair with comic slaves (4.149). Whatever masks were used, there was a clear contradiction between what the audience saw and what happened onstage. This contradiction is immediately and emphatically presented to the audience in the play's unique prologue. The two captives, in an unparalleled staging, are present throughout the prologue, and the first thing the prologue does is call attention to them.[19]

Another conspicuous visual feature of the prologue is the chains the captives wear. Viewers of *palliatae* would be accustomed to hearing about chains and other forms of binding: throughout the plays, slaves joke about the danger of being bound, and masters threaten slaves with chains and manacles.[20] Almost never, however, are slaves actually bound, and when they are, they are promptly released.[21] In *Captivi*, on the other hand, Plautus repeatedly calls attention to chains and other forms of binding that appear on the slaves. The first words of Tyndarus and Philocrates are a lament that they wear chains (200a–203); Hegio makes a show of replacing the captives' large chains with small (110–13), of removing all the chains when he sends off Philocrates (354–55), and of having Tyndarus bound before he is sent to the quarry (657–59; cf. 721–22). Tyndarus returns from the quarries in large chains (997), which are to be placed on the unrepentant Stalagmus (1025–28), who himself enters wearing a collar (888–89). The visual leitmotif of chains and binding presents the audience with emphatic and unparalleled onstage reminders of the reality of slavery.[22]

Supplementing these visual surprises is unusual behavior by the play's characters, most notably Tyndarus. Tyndarus is not, of course, the only slave in Plautus discovered to be freeborn: New and Roman comedy both are full of exposed or abducted maidens freed from greedy pimps in the nick of time. Indeed, Philocrates echoes language used to describe this character type when he tells Hegio that Tyndarus was "bene pudiceque educatus" ("brought up well and chastely," 992).[23] As a male who is enslaved but should be free, however, Tyndarus is unique. Neither extant Roman comedies nor the titles or fragments of lost comedies suggest a parallel for Tyndarus's situation, and the play's prologue and epilogue claim that its plot is unusual (55, 1029–34). The audience would thus not know how to respond to Tyndarus. Plautus increases their uncertainty by sending contradictory messages regarding Tyndarus's character. Just when the spectators are prepared to respond to Tyndarus as a free person, he acts like a stock clever slave. Yet when they think they can place him easily in the category of *servus callidus*, he speaks and acts in ways incomprehensible in a comic slave.

Tyndarus's first speeches are those of a dignified freeborn person: he expresses shame that he and Philocrates are enchained (203).[24] When Tyndarus and Philocrates plot strategy, it is the latter who sounds like a scheming slave (see below); Tyndarus shows a noble willingness to help Philocrates and an understandable concern that he not be abandoned (228–35a). The audience will know what to expect of Tyndarus: he will show his freeborn nature in spite of his vicissitudes.

Just when they have become comfortable in this assumption, however, the deception of Hegio begins. As he hears Philocrates lying to Hegio, Tyndarus delivers three humorous asides, each of which recalls the words of *servi callidi* elsewhere. First he says that Hegio is in a barber's shop, for he is about to be fleeced (266–69). Palaestrio uses the same metaphor to describe the deception of Pyrgopolynices (*Mil.* 768), and the notion of "fleecing" is used of slaves' deceptions elsewhere, as victims are compared to sheep (*Bacch.* 241–42; *Epid.* 616; *Persa* 829).[25] When Philocrates philosophizes about his acceptance of slavery, Tyndarus says that he is smarter than Thales (274–76). The exaggerated mythological or historical comparison is not restricted to *servi callidi*, but it is a device of which they are particularly fond, especially when they are describing their deceptions in asides (*Aul.* 701–4; *Bacch.* 925–78, 1053–58; *Mostell.* 775–77).[26] Also typical of *servi callidi* is Tyndarus's praise of Philocrates for his "philosophical" attitude (284). Among male characters in other plays, it is only *servi callidi* who show such exultation in pure trickery as Tyndarus shows here; and Tyndarus's asides would remind the audience of other scenes in which the planner of a deception—usually a *servus callidus*—observes and comments while his assistant helps to carry out the deception.[27]

At this point, the audience would be in some doubt: is Tyndarus a *servus callidus* or a freeborn youth in distress? The next scenes would do little to answer this question. When he himself speaks with Hegio, and when he says his farewells to Philocrates, Tyndarus again sounds the way one might expect a freeborn character to speak. His philosophizing goes well beyond that of any of Plautus's slaves, as he admonishes Hegio that a god watches human actions (313–16) and praises Hegio in highly moral terms (333, 355–56, 391–92). His professions of friendship to Philocrates are filled with the abstract nouns of exalted discourse (410, 413). Hegio, moved to tears by both Tyndarus and Philocrates, praises master and slave for their "ingenium liberale" ("freeborn nature," 419). The high-flown sentiments, which show no sign of being parodic,[28] would leave the audience bewildered. Not only do they seem inconsistent with Tyndarus's earlier words, but the entire scene is a deception; so when Tyndarus sings the praises of "Tyndarus," he is in fact boasting and seeking his own freedom (see Chapter 4).

Two scenes later, Tyndarus reenters in hyperbolic desperation, elaborating in a monologue and several asides the degree to which the arrival of Aristophontes has destroyed him (516–40). The exaggerated assurance of doom would remind the audience of the almost inevitable reaction of *servi callidi* to setbacks in their plans (*Bacch.* 681; *Epid.* 81–84, 610–17; *Mil.* 180; *Mostell.* 348–65; *Pseud.* 1032); and the similarity is reinforced by verbal and stylistic features.[29] After he decides to accuse Aristophontes of insanity, Tyndarus improvises a deception just as other clever slaves do, and he colors it with a frivolous pun (578), and with the mythological allusions that are a trademark of ingenious *servi callidi* (562–63, 615). When he realizes his plan will fail, Tyndarus turns to the gruesome humor characteristic of clever slaves faced with punishment. He jokes about his racing heartbeat (636–37), and he personifies the rods that will beat him and the fetters that will bind him (650–52; cf. *Epid.* 93).

When Tyndarus's ruse does not succeed, the audience is prepared for another stock scene, the "ambush" scene, in which the master has his henchmen bind the slave who has deceived him.[30] Tyndarus, they expect, like other *servi callidi*, will blithely thumb his nose at his blustering master. Tyndarus appears to set the expected tone as he responds to Hegio's anger with a silly joke (662–63; cf. *Mostell.* 1118). After such a beginning, Tyndarus's next replies to Hegio would sound at first like the disingenuous protestations of innocence familiar from other *servi callidi*:[31]

> decet innocentem servom atque innoxium
> confidentem esse, suom apud erum potissimum. (665–66)

A good and innocent slave should be self-assured, especially in the presence of his master.

> fateor, omnia
> facta esse ita ut <tu> dicis, et fallaciis
> abiisse eum abs te mea opera atque astutia;
> an, obsecro hercle te, id nunc suscenses mihi? (677–80; cf. 669)

I confess, everything was done just as you say, and he escaped from you through trickery, thanks to my industry and cleverness; but goodness, are you really angry at me for that?

Then, however, Tyndarus reveals that in fact he is completely serious, and he has moved the discourse to a new level:

> dum ne ob male facta, peream, parvi aestumo.
> si ego hic peribo, ast ille ut dixit non redit,
> at erit mi hoc factum mortuo memorabile,
> <me> meum erum captum ex servitute atque hostibus
> reducem fecisse liberum in patriam ad patrem,
> meumque potius me caput periculo
> praeoptavisse, quam is periret, ponere. (682–88)

> So long as it is not on account of evil deeds, let me perish, I do not care. If I perish here, and Philocrates does not return as he said he would, at least this deed of mine will be remembered when I am dead: that I allowed my captured master to return home to his fatherland and his father, free from slavery and his enemies, and I preferred to endanger my own life rather than let him perish.

Tyndarus has suddenly abandoned the world of the *servus callidus*, leaving the audience aware that their expectations have deceived them. His next words are a powerful *sententia*, far removed from the ironic *sententiae* of *servi callidi*: "qui per virtutem, periit, at non interit" ("He who perishes through virtue does not really die," 690). He remains on a high moral level for most of the rest of the scene, responding to Hegio's accusations with protestations of loyalty to Philocrates (705–20) and philosophical reflections on the brevity of life (739–43). Before he leaves for the quarries, Tyndarus turns from noble sentiments to bitter acceptance of his fate (744–46). To disorient the spectators even further, however, Tyndarus returns to his *servus callidus* persona as he leaves, joking about being pushed and pulled at the same time (750).

Even more perplexing to the audience than what Tyndarus says would be what he suffers. The prologue speaker had revealed how the play would end:

> et hic hodie expediet hanc docte fallaciam,
> et suom erum faciet libertatis compotem,
> eodemque pacto fratrem servabit suom
> reducemque faciet liberum in patriam ad patrem. (40–43)

> And this fellow [scil., Tyndarus] will carry out this deception cleverly today, and he will get his master his freedom, and in the

same way he will save his brother and will enable him to return a free man to his fatherland and his father.

The prologue speaker thus establishes that the ruse of Tyndarus and Philocrates will succeed, and he later assures his hearers that the play is a comedy (61). The audience will expect a typical Plautine deception play: Tyndarus, like all other clever slaves, will escape punishment for his disobedience.

The expectation will only get stronger through the scenes leading up to Tyndarus's final confrontation with Hegio. The great fun of the despair of *servi callidi* is that the audience knows it is unfounded: the slave will, either through cleverness, luck, or stage convention, escape any real suffering. Tyndarus's "despair speeches" and his farcical attempt to persuade Hegio that Aristophontes is insane give every sign that he will have equal good fortune. Just as they would know how Tyndarus will behave in the "ambush" scene, so they would know what he will experience: something like what happens in the "ambush" scenes of *Epidicus*, where Periphanes binds Epidicus but then must beg him to let him release him; or *Mostellaria*, where Tranio is rescued by Callidamates; or *Bacchides*, where Nicobulus, determined to get vengeance on Chrysalus, ends up seduced by the Bacchis sisters. As the scene begins, Hegio adds to the sense that this is a typical ambush scene. He had shown the gullibility of the stock *senex*, believing the most outrageous things Tyndarus said; now he uses language very similar to that used by other stock *senes* when they realize they have been duped (641– 42, 651, 653–57, 660–61, 670–77, 681).[32] Visually as well, the scene has all the trappings of the stock "ambush" scene, as the *lorarii* ("henchmen") come on and bind the recalcitrant slave. One *lorarius* even contributes to the anticipation of amusement with a joke (658).

The first clue that something is not right is aural: the musical accompaniment stops when Hegio orders that Tyndarus be bound. The sudden silence from the *tibia* player in mid-scene hints that the ensuing ambush scene may not be as amusing as the audience expects.[33] Gradually, the metrical omen is fulfilled. Unlike all other clever slaves, Tyndarus's fears of being carried off in chains actually come true. At this point, some spectators would recall that although the prologue speaker assured them that Tyndarus would succeed in making the exchange between Philocrates and Philopolemus (40–43), he did not mention the fate of Tyndarus himself: their assumption that he would avoid all real trouble has led them astray, and they have no way of knowing for sure that Philocrates will return in time to save Tyndarus.

Philocrates does, of course, return, but the play's denouement offers no resolution to the audience's perplexity. When Tyndarus first reappears, he is slavelike again, even though his true identity has now been revealed to the other characters: he makes a wild mythological allusion and a pun about the pickax he is carrying (998-1004). As Tyndarus himself learns his identity, the frivolity is replaced not with the joy an audience would expect in a comic anagnorisis, but with bitterness. When Hegio calls Tyndarus *gnate* ("son"), Tyndarus responds with a sardonic joke (1006–8), and his greeting to Philocrates is hardly enthusiastic: "et tu, quoius causa hanc aerumnam exigo" ("And you, for whose sake I suffer these troubles," 1009).

Equally disrupting to comic stereotypes is the behavior of Philocrates. It is made clear throughout Roman comedy that deception, especially when it involves the pretense of being someone else, is suitable for slaves and for members of the lowest classes, such as parasites and *meretrices*.[34] The *adulescens* Pleusicles is exceedingly uncomfortable with the disguise he dons in *Miles* (1284–89), as is the freeborn maiden of *Persa* (337–89). Lovers almost inevitably get their slaves or a parasite to do their deceptions for them. When Megaronides and Callicles plan a deception in *Trinummus*, they hire an actor, and in *Casina*, Cleostrata and Myrrhina use the slaves Pardalisca and Charinus to carry out the core of their deception. Philocrates, however, takes on the role of the deceiving slave with enthusiasm, and he often sounds more like a stock *servus callidus* than does Tyndarus. When the two captives talk between themselves, Philocrates takes charge, inverting the usual form of Plautine planning scenes, where slaves give orders to their masters. Like the clever slaves Palaestrio (*Mil.* 596–609) and Tranio (*Mostell.* 472–74), Philocrates elaborates on the need to avoid eavesdroppers (219–28); and he uses the stock language of slave planners, describing the plan as *fallacia* (221) and *doli* (222), and admonishing Tyndarus to act *docte* (226).[35] Philocrates thus acts like a *servus callidus* even before it is necessary for him to play the slave.[36] When he speaks with Hegio, Philocrates shows that he has taken on the slave's role completely. He had earlier told Hegio's henchmen, when they suggested that he and Tyndarus would flee if their chains were removed, that he would certainly never imitate fugitive slaves (209–10). Now he contradicts his previous words and echoes the henchmen, saying that he and his companion should not be blamed, if they try to flee (259–60). Like so many Plautine slave tricksters, Philocrates exaggerates wildly, giving his father a long Greek name (Thensaurochrysonicochrysides) and attributing extreme greed to him (285–92). When Hegio later asks him to accomplish the exchange between "Philocrates" and Philopolemus, Philocrates remains the comic slave, joking that Hegio can use him as a wheel, turning him however he wishes (368 – 70).[37]

In many ways, the antics of the parasite Ergasilus provide a welcome relief from the disconcerting actions of the main plot. He embodies the spirit of escapist comedy: the serious dilemmas of the play proper become for him mere obstacles to dinner, and when Hegio wants to talk about his plan to get his son back, Ergasilus changes the subject (172 – 73). Yet even Ergasilus blurs the distinction between slave and free, calling attention in his own comic way to the questions that pervade the main plot. When he offers to sell himself to Hegio in return for dinner, he recalls ironically the sale of human beings going on in the play proper (179 – 81). The most conspicuously metatheatrical moment of the play comes when Ergasilus enters as a running slave:

> nunc certa res est, eodem pacto ut comici servi solent
> coniciam in collum pallium. (778 – 79)

> Now I have made up my mind; I will put my cloak over my shoulder in the same way comic slaves do.

This is not the only time in Plautus a character calls attention to the fact that he is doing the "running slave" routine (cf. *Amph.* 984 – 89; *Epid.* 194 – 95), nor is it the only time a parasite plays "running slave" (cf. *Curc.* 280 – 98). Here, however, the self-consciousness has special significance, for it continues in a humorous vein the confusion over what makes a comic slave. It is as if Ergasilus is saying, "No one is doing the slave parts right, so I will have to." Finally, just as Ergasilus tried to make himself Hegio's slave at his first appearance, in his moment of triumph he tries to make Hegio his slave, ordering the old man about until Hegio finally says, "tu mi igitur erus es" ("So then, you are my master," 857).[38]

The play's unusual *lorarii* ("henchmen") also call attention to the paradoxes of slavery.[39] Elsewhere in Plautus, *lorarii* are mere oafs who say practically nothing.[40] In *Captivi* they have dialogues with both Hegio and the captives, in which they provide realistic correctives to the opinions of the main characters regarding slavery and freedom. Their unparalleled eloquence confounds yet another set of expectations about comic slaves.

Hegio first enters accompanied by a *lorarius*. He admonishes the slave to watch the captives carefully, for a *liber captivos* ("free captive" or "captive free person": the expression itself is an oxymoron indicative of the rampant ambiguities here) is like a bird, who flies away if given the chance. The *lorarius* responds:

> *Lorarius*: omnes profecto liberi lubentius
>   sumus quam servimus.
> *Hegio*:   non videre ita tu quidem.
> *Lo.*:   si non est quod dem, mene vis dem ipse—in pedes?
> *He.*:   si dederis, erit extemplo mihi quod dem tibi.   (119–22)

> *Lorarius*: All of us of course are much happier to be free than
> slaves.
> *Hegio*: That doesn't seem true of you at least.
> *Lo.*: If I don't have anything to give [scil., money to buy my free-
> dom with], do you want me to give myself—to flight?
> *He.*: If you do that, I'll have something to give you right away
> [scil., punishment].

The banter between *lorarius* and master is unparalleled in Roman comedy. The first thing the audience sees, after the introductory words of the prologue and Ergasilus, is a philosophical discourse from a slave character of a type usually mute or nearly so. The uniqueness of his speech will cause the *lorarius* to get the audience's attention as he reveals the great blind spot of Hegio: Hegio cannot see the perspective of a slave, but naively assumes that his own slave does not wish to be free. *Lorarii* likewise accompany the first entrance of Philocrates and Tyndarus, and again they provide a realistic perspective. The *lorarii*[41] admonish the new arrivals that slavery must be endured: "indigna digna habenda sunt, erus quae facit" ("Whatever your master does you must consider deserved, even if it is undeserved," 200). When Philocrates shows disdain for slaves who flee (hypocritically, as he is concurrently planning his own escape), the *lorarii* again are more realistic: they say they would recommend that the captives do flee, if given the chance (210).

To some, perhaps, Stalagmus would provide a solution to the problems presented by the play. He, they could argue, is the real slave, showing the baseness that Tyndarus, a free man by birth, lacks. Hence Stalagmus is to receive Tyndarus's chains at play's end.[42] Yet Stalagmus, too, is problematic to anyone familiar with the *palliata*. No less than Tyndarus and the *lorarii*, he is unique and unexpected. Like Tyndarus, he echoes the language of *servi callidi* but fails to meet the expectations of that language. As he boasts that he was never good (956), openly confesses what he has done (961), reminds Hegio that he is no stranger to blows (963–64), and jokes about the fact that he will receive Tyndarus's heavy chains (1028), he sounds very much like slaves of other comedies who revel in their badness.[43] Yet the same kind of confession that in the mouth of Stasimus or Tranio creates comic fun is from Stalagmus bitter cynicism, for the audience realizes that Stalagmus is not merely *malus* in the comic sense of tricky, but is truly an evil man; and whereas other comic slaves only talk about fleeing, Stalagmus has actually been a fugitive. Thus, though Stalagmus provides the audience some comfort as a scapegoat, this sinister variation of the *servus callidus* raises yet another question about the nature of the comic slave; and, like the articulate *lorarii* and Tyndarus's punishment, he provides a reminder of the reality that lies behind the fantasy of comic slavery.

Plautus thus extends the uncertainty regarding the distinction between slave and free from the plot of *Captivi* to its performance. The audience sees not only that Tyndarus, though he is freeborn, is treated as a slave, but that their own expectations regarding the portrayal of slaves and free persons on the comic stage are inadequate. The theatrical confusion encourages them to recognize that more is at stake here than a simple case of a free person unjustly enslaved: basic assumptions about the distinctions between slaves and free are called into question. Plautus further encourages his audience to consider the plot's broader implications by drawing connections between the performance and the world of the audience.

Even as he provides a comic escape from the difficult questions of the main plot, Ergasilus connects that plot with the audience by repeatedly crossing the geographical line between the play's setting in Aetolia and the audience's Roman milieu. Each of Ergasilus's three appearances includes conspicuous Roman allusions (90, 156–64, 489, 492–94, 813–22,[44] 881–85). In his final Roman allusion, Ergasilus connects the themes of slavery and captivity with contemporary Rome, as he describes Stalagmus, whom Philopolemus and Philocrates lead home with a collar around his neck:

> *Ergasilus*: sed Stalagmus quoius erat tunc nationis, cum hinc abit?
> *Hegio*: Siculus.
> *Erg.*:   at nunc Siculus non est, Boius est, Boiam terit:
> liberorum quaerundorum causa ei, credo, uxor datast. (887–89)

> *Ergasilus*: But what nationality was Stalagmus, when he left here?
> *Hegio*: A Sicilian.
> *Erg.*: Well, now he is not a Sicilian, but a Boian, for he's rubbing against a Boian woman [or "a collar"]: I suppose a wife was given to him for the sake of producing children.

The Latin includes a double pun. *Tero*, meaning "to rub," can be a euphemism for sexual intercourse, and *boia* is a word for either a collar or a Boian woman. The Boians, a Gallic tribe of northern Italy, had recently been defeated by the Romans, and many of them were enslaved.[45]

Most of the play's conspicuous Roman allusions are reserved for the Ergasilus scenes. The one obvious Roman reference made by Tyndarus, however, is significant. Returning from the quarries, Tyndarus jokes that he was given a pickax just as *patricii pueri* ("patrician boys") are given toys (1002). This is the moment when the slave-free ambiguity is at its most intense: Tyndarus, now recognized to be free, enters wearing the chains of a slave. Verbal ambiguity reinforces the visual effect, for the word *puer*, like "boy" in the antebellum South, could mean either a male child or a slave. The reference to the Roman upper class at such a moment encourages the audience to acknowledge the relevance of the question to their own Rome.[46]

The Roman allusions could perhaps be dismissed as mere jokes. Less easy to ignore would be an association between the characters, the actors, and members of the audience made in the play's prologue. The *prologus* not only points out Tyndarus and Philocrates in chains; he also connects them with some of the spectators:

> hos quos videtis stare hic captivos duos,
> illi quia astant, hi stant ambo, non sedent;[47]
> hoc vos mihi testes estis me verum loqui. (1–3)

> Both these two captives whom you see standing here, are standing, not sitting, because those folks are standing; you are witnesses that I am telling the truth.

Lindsay proposed that *illi* ("those folks") are latecomers who have not found a seat.[48] Other Plautine passages, however, suggest that social status rather than time of arrival determined who got seats in the early Roman theater: those standing are not latecomers, but slaves, and perhaps some members of the poorest classes.[49] The line is thus not only a joke, but also an explicit connection between both the characters and actors onstage and those who stand in the back of the theater. The two captives, like many if not all of the standing spectators, are slaves; and the actors, like those forced to stand, are either slaves or others of the lowest classes. By calling upon the sitting spectators (*vos*), whom he later equates with the Roman propertied classes,[50] to witness the connection, the speaker makes a rare acknowledgment of the slaves and other standees who are usually ignored.

This awareness of slaves onstage and in the audience helps explain the odd sentence with which the prologue speaker ends his *argumentum*: "haec res agetur nobis, vobis fabula" ("This matter will be acted as reality for us, as a play for you," 52). The line is an amusing pleasantry relying on the double meaning of both *res* ("matter" and "reality") and *fabula* ("play" and "fiction").[51] Like so many jokes in Plautine prologues, it reminds the audience that dramatic performance is simultaneously real and false. It has additional significance, however, in the context of the previous references to slaves on and off the stage. First, it reminds the audience that onstage, slave and free really are interchangeable, as slave actors pretend to be free, and free men pretend to be slaves. More important, it associates the slaves onstage and in the audience with the plight of Tyndarus. The *prologus* has repeated several times the fact that Tyndarus is a slave to his own master, and he has connected Tyndarus's predicament with the human condition (21–22, 50–51). Now he reminds the free spectators that in their presence are persons who know all too well the significance of Tyndarus's situation and of the *argumentum* as a whole. "To you free spectators," he says, "this is only a fiction, but we (the slave actors and the previously-mentioned slave spectators) know the reality of slavery."

It would be unwise to exaggerate the subversiveness of *Captivi*; the play is no more an abolitionist tract than are any of the other ancient arguments on the humanity of slaves.[52] Nevertheless, by choosing a play in which distinctions between slave and free were blurred, then presenting that play in a manner that confounded expectations regarding slaves in comedy, and then drawing a connection between the enslaved characters and slaves in the presence of the audience, Plautus produced one of antiquity's most powerful challenges to comforting assumptions regarding the inferiority of slaves.

CONCLUSION

IT is time to return to the question posed in the introduction: What did Plautus accomplish through his manipulation of the actor-audience relationship? I hope I have demonstrated in the preceding chapters that that relationship is central to Plautus's humor, that it involved a great sense of fun in the awareness of theater itself, that it was a vital part of how Plautus won over his audiences, and that it reflects sophisticated and varied responses to the social milieu of the plays' performances.

In the all-too-serious pursuit of scholarship, it is easy to forget the most conspicuous strength of Plautine theater: "Plautus made them laugh."[1] Humor is an inevitable product of almost all the ways Plautus shapes the actor-audience relationship. In spite of their nonillusory tendencies, Plautus's plays offer enough pretense of being "real" that sudden blatant reminders of the fact of performance would inspire laughter in the audience. Most of the metatheatrical techniques examined above involve an intensification of this comic effect. Passages where actors express their need for the audience's approval become humorously transparent attempts at manipulation. The failure of some characters to gain rapport with the audience in spite of their most earnest attempts is itself comical, and the principal emotion shared between the audience and those who have rapport is laughter at the expense of those who do not. Allusions to place produce juxtaposition jokes shared by actors and audience. The inadequacies of theatrical moralizing are a source of amusement throughout the plays; and satire like that found in *Truculentus* and *Curculio* is always funny, even when it is most harsh. Much of the challenge to spectators' assumptions offered in plays like *Casina* and *Captivi* is accomplished through unexpected sources of laughter.

Closely related to humor is the enchantment with which Plautus's audience responded to the phenomenon of theater itself. Previous studies of Plautine metatheater have rightly emphasized Plautus's own fascination with theater. Plautus's highly metatheatrical plays, however, would not have succeeded if many members of his audience had not shared the same fascination. Theater, at least as a part of official festivals, was still relatively new in Rome. Many in Plautus's audience therefore found the very existence of theatrical pretense enchanting, and they liked to be reminded that what they viewed onstage was both real and imaginary. Like humor, this fascination with theater is evident in each of the areas studied above. Desire for approval, teasing, and concern with rapport are the attitudes simultaneously of both characters and actors and thus are a reminder of the ambiguous nature of performance. A principal effect of Plautus's play with his setting is to remind the audience that it watches not real events in Greece, but a play in Rome. Plautus's self-conscious responses to the theatrical conventions surrounding moralizing, misogyny, and slaves depend for their effect upon the audience's awareness of those conventions. Awareness of the play as play lies at the heart of both the flattery of the spectators that pervades *Pseudolus* and *Amphitruo* and the challenges presented in *Casina* and *Captivi*. Many of Plautus's most pointedly satirical moments, such as the speech of the *choragus* in *Curculio* and Stratophanes' entrance in *Truculentus*, would inspire delight because of their extreme metatheatricality even if they did not include critical allusions to contemporary Rome.

Inspiring laughter and playing with the nature of theater are two of the ways Plautus used the relationship between actors and audience to maintain the spectators' goodwill. There are others. Even as they teased and criticized, actors never let the spectators forget that they aimed to please them and were dependent on their approval. Characters' desire for rapport likewise made the spectators feel important and superior. The rejection of didacticism brings with it an emphasis on the spectators' pleasure as the end of performance. The importance of the actor-audience relationship in winning over spectators is most conspicuous in plays like *Pseudolus*, which Plautus wanted to make special, and plays like *Amphitruo* and *Casina*, which presented special challenges.

Even plays as metatheatrical as Plautus's, however, are not only about theater, or even about pleasing the audience. How he manipulated the relationship between his actors and their audience was also a large part of the way Plautus responded to the social context in which his plays were performed. Now is therefore an appropriate time to evaluate in general terms Plautus's response to his social surroundings.

By this point, my sympathies with the approach to Plautus of Erich Segal will be evident. Many details of Segal's book have been justly criticized: he exaggerated the difference between Plautine and New Comedy, the extent to which legitimate authority figures are undone in Plautus's plays, and the separation between comic theater and reality; and he presented an oversimplified view of Roman society in the second century B.C.E.[2] Segal's theory nevertheless explains much of the effect of Plautine comedy. The escape from everyday taboos is one of the essential elements of comedy in general,[3] and that element is especially important in Plautus. Much of Plautus's manipulation of the actor-audience relationship contributed to this Saturnalian effect. Plautus encouraged a bond between actors and audience, even though most of the former were of the lowest social classes; and he granted his actors the license to tease and satirize the audience itself, and sometimes even the magistrates in charge of the production. He arranged monologues, eavesdropping, and other elements so that the audience would feel the greatest rapport with the characters who overturn social hierarchies most effectively: the *servi callidi* and other deceivers. His self-conscious play with setting reinforced the audience's awareness that his "Greece" was an imaginary land where Roman moral restrictions could be flouted; and his rejection of theatrical moralizing emphasized the removal from everyday morality still further.

Saturnalian inversion, however, is only part of the story. Even comedy that provides its audience with the most topsy-turvy escape from everyday reality nevertheless participates in social discourse.[4] As much as he may have given his spectators an escape from their society, Plautus nevertheless responded to that society in each play. The changes mentioned in earlier chapters with respect to religion, wives, prostitutes, banking and money-lending, and slaves were only a part of the sea change affecting Rome during Plautus's career, as Romans responded to their new wealth and power and to the ever-increasing influence of Greek culture. Scholars have differed radically in their views of how Plautus responded to these changes. To some, Plautus was a conservative, aligned with Cato the Censor in opposition to "newfangled" features of Roman life such as Greek philosophy and culture, luxury, and greater freedom for women.[5] Others find in Plautus's plays a progressive philhellenist's alternative to traditional Roman mores.[6] Erich Gruen sees in Plautus a less partisan observer who mocks various extremes on all sides of contemporary controversies.[7] Gruen is closest to the truth. Only tendentious picking and choosing of evidence can make Plautus consistently either conservative or subversive: he mocks reactionary views, but his responses to Hellenic culture and the vast changes in his society were ambivalent at best. Both Greeks and Romans, reactionaries and philhellenists, are the victims of Plautus's humor.

Yet Plautus did not merely laugh from a distance at the controversies of the day. By its very nature, theater offers perspectives different from those found in everyday life; and theater like Plautus's, which inverts social norms, always has the potential to subvert those norms.[8] By the way they approach their plays, playwrights can reduce or increase the degree to which their new perspectives and their carnivalesque inversion challenge their audience.

Plautus had strong motivation to rein in the potentially subversive elements of his theater. The Roman audience was very conservative, as was the theatrical tradition to which Plautus belonged; and ultimate control over theatrical production was in the hands of magistrates and other members of the ruling class whose interests would not be served by challenges to existing authority. It is not surprising, therefore, that in our examination of Plautus's approach to the actor-audience relationship, we have often found the playwright using techniques that restricted potentially subversive elements in his plays. Actors repeatedly show deference to the audience, in keeping with their low social status. Rapport with slaves who behave unacceptably is delayed, so that it is kept more clearly within the fantasy world of the play; and slaves' forbidden behavior is placed emphatically in Greece. Plautus consistently elevates the audience's pleasure over any messages the plays may send them. In *Amphitruo*, this emphasis on pleasing the audience, along with insistent theatricalization, eliminates any threat to the religious status quo. In *Pseudolus*, Plautus may even have given extra emphasis to the audience's pleasure in response to desires of those who sponsored the production. In his portrayal of women and of slaves, Plautus usually confirms his audience's stereotypes, and much of his satire is directed at "out-groups" from whom most of the spectators could easily dissociate themselves: extreme misers, pimps, bankers, foreigners, prostitutes. Perhaps most importantly, Plautus's emphasis on the theatrical, his insistence that his audience remain aware of the play as play, encourages spectators to dissociate potentially subversive action onstage from the world outside of the theater.

This very awareness of theater, however, along with the actors' close relationship with the spectators, could also be used to make the plays more challenging. For all their obsequiousness, actors teased the audience, and this teasing sometimes went beyond Saturnalian license to social criticism. Rapport with clever slaves was delayed, but it existed nonetheless, subtly challenging the assumed distance between slaves and free; and juxtaposition jokes undermined the geographical alienation from the audience of unacceptable activity by slaves and others. Plautus's rejection of theater that sends messages ironically sends a message of its own, questioning the traditional Roman penchant for moralizing. Through Roman allusions and addresses to the audience, Plautus implicates the spectators in the deception found in *Curculio* and in the depravity that pervades *Truculentus*. The clearest challenges come in *Captivi* and *Casina*, where Plautus molds the actor-audience relationship in such a way that the spectators are encouraged to reconsider their preconceptions about wives and slaves.

Plautus was without a doubt first and foremost an entertainer. Even the most determined entertainer, however, can have something to say. Plautus rejected overt didacticism, and he made sure his audience knew that he and his fellow performers were working to amuse them. Yet within that context of diversion and even escapism, Plautus offered some scathing satire, and on more than one occasion he challenged the preconceptions of many specta-tors. Plautus molded the relationship between his actors and their audience in such a way as to create an atmosphere of goodwill between stage and au-dience. Relying on that atmosphere of goodwill, Plautus used those same techniques of shaping the actor-audience relationship not only to entertain, but also to provoke and challenge his audience.

NOTES

INTRODUCTION

1. For what can be recovered about the logistics of performance in Plautus's day, see especially Duckworth 1952, 73–138; Loitold 1957; Bieber 1961, 147–89; Beare 1964, 159–232, 241–63, 267–309, 335–39; Csapo and Slater 1995, 207–20, 275–85, 306–17, and passim. See also, on the evidence from vases, Trendall 1967 and Taplin 1993; on Pompeian paintings, Beacham 1992, 56–85; on the Terence manuscripts, Weston 1903, 37–54; Jones and Morey 1930–31; on later Roman theaters, Beacham 1992, 157–83; on stages, Tanner 1969; Rosivach 1970; Wiles 1991, 55–62; on acting styles, Taladoire 1951; Garton 1972, 169–88; Wiles 1991, 192–208; on blocking, Steidle 1975; on costumes, Saunders 1909; and on props, Ketterer 1986a, 1986b, 1986c.

2. Beare (1964, 303–9) made what I consider a convincing case that Plautus's actors wore masks, and that the late antique grammarian Diomedes is wrong when he claims that masks were not worn until well after Plautus's death (Keil 1:489). Many, however, remain unconvinced. See, in favor of the use of masks, Duckworth 1952, 92–94; Gratwick 1982, 83–84; Wiles 1991, 132–33; against the use of masks, Maurach 1964, 578; Della Corte 1975; Kinsey 1980; Dupont 1985, 80–81.

3. A twenty-first play, *Vidularia*, is hopelessly fragmentary. Also invaluable are the six plays of Plautus's successor, Terence, and the fragments of a number of other Roman comic playwrights.

4. See, for example, Ubersfeld 1982, 22–23; Beckerman 1990, 186–87; Bennett 1990, 161; De Marinis 1993, 15–30.

5. Cf. Beckerman 1970, 133–34; Ubersfeld 1981, 311–18.

6. Cf. Lucas 1968, 258–72; Rau 1970, 91–92; Flashar 1974.

7. Ingarden 1971, 536; Beckerman 1970, 14–17. Cf. Elam 1980, 90–92; De Marinis 1993, 48–51. Beckerman later refined his views of theatricalism versus realism and direct versus indirect presentation (1990, 38, 110–11).

8. See, for example, Crahay and Delcourt 1952; Langer 1953, 306–25; Koestler 1964, 301–10. On the problems inherent in the concept of "dramatic illusion," see Sifakis 1971, 7–14; Bain 1977, 3–7.

9. Brecht 1964, 22–24, 33–42, 57–61, 191–97, and passim; 1967, 263–65, 683–84, and passim. Cf. Pfister 1988, 69–84.

10. Brecht 1964, 224; 1967, 305, 310–11, 362–64, 680. Cf. Witzmann 1964, 19–22, 39–40, 75–123, and passim; Görler 1973; Warning 1976, 313–15; Lada 1996.

11. On performance criticism and its history, see Styan 1977; Thompson and Thompson 1989, 13–23; Slater 1993a, 3–11. On nonillusory theater, see Styan 1975, 180–223.

12. See especially Nelson 1958; Righter 1962; Abel 1963; Calderwood 1971; Hornby 1986.

13. E.g., Evanthius *De fabula* 3.8; Norwood 1932, 15–99; Blancké 1918, 51–69 (somewhat more favorable).

14. Collections of passages: Knapp 1919; Terzaghi 1930; Kraus 1934; Duckworth 1952, 132–36. Chronology: Hough 1940a.

15. See especially Leo 1908, 46–89; Fraenkel 1960, 135–221 and passim; Gaiser 1972, 1047–50, 1088–93; Slater 1985c. Note also the recent efforts by Eckard Lefèvre and his school of Neo-Analysts to prove, in part by pointing out the

metatheatrical nature of Plautine theater, that Plautus was more dependent on the Italian farcical tradition than has previously been assumed (Stärk 1989; Lefèvre, Stärk, and Vogt-Spira 1991; Benz, Stärk, and Vogt-Spira 1995; Lefèvre 1995; cf. Slater 1993b). On the other hand, metatheatrical elements have also been observed in the remains of Greek New Comedy (Leo 1908, 79–89; 1960, 3–9; Bain 1977, 105–34, 185–222; Blundell 1980, passim; Dedoussi 1995; and Otto Zwierlein has proposed that many of the metatheatrical passages in our texts are the work of later interpolators 1991a, 228–35 and passim; see also Zwierlein 1990, 1991b, and 1992). For an excellent concise history of the "originality question," see Lowe 1992, 152–57.

16. Barchiesi 1969; Schiappa de Azevedo 1975–76; Chiarini 1979; Blänsdorf 1982, 131–35, 141–44; Petrone 1983, 5–98, 153–209; Slater 1985b; Muecke 1986.

CHAPTER 1

1. Cf. Goldman 1975, 6–7; Beckerman 1990, 40–41; Bennett 1990, 162–63.

2. On Plautus's mimicry of improvisation, see especially Slater 1985b, 16–18 and passim; 1993b; Benz, Stärk, and Vogt-Spira 1995, passim.

3. Bickford 1922, 60. For convenience I call any speech in which a character is clearly not addressing another character a monologue. My term "monologue" thus includes what many would describe as "soliloquies" (usually used of speeches spoken while a character is alone onstage) and "asides" (speeches that are made while another character is onstage but that are not intended to be heard by the other character). It also includes what some call "monodies": passages not addressed to other characters that were accompanied and may have been sung. On the various functions of monologues in New Comedy and Roman comedy, see especially Leo 1908, 38–89; Bickford 1922; Prescott 1939; Duckworth 1952, 103–9; Denzler 1968; Swoboda 1971, 63–76; Bain 1977, 105–84; Blundell 1980; Slater 1985b, 155–60; Frost 1988.

4. Fraenkel (1967) argued correctly that second-person verbs need not be addressed to anyone in particular. In Plautus, however, where the presence of the spectators is so readily acknowledged, it seems most likely that second-person-plural verb forms not addressed to others onstage are in fact directed to the audience. Second-person-singular verb forms need not be directed explicitly at the audience, which is, of course, plural. Actors who use second-person-singular verbs conceivably could have spoken the lines as if they were merely thinking aloud, as when modern speakers of English mutter things like, "You would think he would know better," "Imagine that!" or, "You can't take it with you." Cf. Barsby 1986, 108. The second-person verbs, however, especially when they cluster together, create an intimate, conversational tone, and therefore would encourage actors to acknowledge that they intend their words for the audience. Actors may also have addressed individual members of the audience when they used second-person-singular verbs. In two passages, such addresses to individuals are made explicit in the text (*Aul.* 719–20; *Stich.* 224).

5. See Cèbe 1960; Chalmers 1965, 43–47; Wright 1974, 190–92; Handley 1975. MacMullen, however, exaggerates the extent to which Plautus's spectators were members of the upper classes (1991, 421–22).

6. Gruen (1992, 210–15) argues that the two prologues of *Hecyra* describe imagined rather than real events. Though Gruen does well to point out some of the problems in the prologues (as does Goldberg [1995, 40–43]), he does not to my

mind provide sufficient evidence to overturn the logical assumption that Terence, even if he does exaggerate somewhat, describes actual events. Cf. Gilula 1981; Vogt-Spira 1995, 236 n. 28.

7. Parker (1996, 592–601) makes a persuasive case that those who disrupted the first two performances of *Hecyra* were not actual members of the audience, but others who entered the theater from outside. Regardless of who the persons creating the disturbances were, the basic difficulties of performance and the vulnerability of the actors remain.

8. For the severity of later Roman audiences in judging actors' performances, see Cic. *Q Rosc.* 30 (a comic actor is driven off the stage with hisses and insults), *Paradoxa Stoicorum* 3.26 (actors who make minor errors are hissed and driven off the stage).

9. On seating, see Moore 1994.

10. Some of the disdain for actors expressed by writers in the late Republic and empire may postdate Plautus (so Gruen 1990, 89–90; Goldberg 1995, 30–31), but it is unlikely that professional actors as a group were respected at any time in Roman history. On the social class of actors, see Rawson 1985, 112; Dumont 1987, 517–24. On the legal disabilities of freeborn actors (*infamia*), see Green 1933; Dupont 1985, 95–98; Ducos 1990; Jory 1995, 139–45. On attitudes toward actors in general, see Edwards 1993, 123–31; Csapo and Slater 1995, 276–79.

11. On the susceptibility of actors to beatings, see Cic. *Planc.* 30–31; Suet. *Aug.* 45; Tac. *Ann.* 1.77; Naudet 1830, 241; Edwards 1993, 124.

12. Cf. Naudet 1830, 648.

13. Cf. Muecke 1985.

14. On the *advocati* and their status as actors, see Petrone 1983, 16–33.

15. Portions of Plautus's prologues may be later interpolations (part of the *Casina* prologue certainly is). Most of the prologues, however, are probably Plautine. See Abel 1955, 105–6 and passim. For the role of *prologi* in providing induction into the world of the play, see Slater 1985b, 149–52.

16. *Asin.* 1, 14; *Capt.* 6; *Cas.* 21–22, 29; *Cist.* 154–55; *Men.* 4–5; *Merc.* 14–15; *Mil.* 79–80, 98; *Poen.* 3, 58, 123; *Trin.* 4–5, 22.

17. Cf. *Merc.* 14–15; *Mil.* 79–80; *Trin.* 20–21; *Truc.* 1–8.

18. On the sense of this passage, see Maurach 1988, 55. When used in a prologue, *argumentum* is the summary of background information leading up to the situation at the beginning of the play, and sometimes contains some prediction of what will happen in the plot itself.

19. *Asin.* 15; *Capt.* 67–68; *Cas.* 87–88; *Cist.* 197–202; *Rud.* 82.

20. E.g., *Asin.* 6–7; *Aul.* 1; *Cist.* 155; *Men.* 23, 47, 50; *Mil.* 150; *Poen.* 47, 116; *Trin.* 4–7.

21. Cf. Bain 1977, 153, on Plautus's (and to a lesser extent Terence's) "almost Homeric delight in certain more or less fixed formulae" of explanation in monologues.

22. Cf. *Poen.* 920–22, 1224; *Pseud.* 387–89, 720–21; Petrone 1983, 25–27.

23. Such an extended series of jokes is more likely to be the creation of Plautus than of Philemon, whose play Plautus adapted. Cf. Fraenkel 1960, 215; Lefèvre 1995, 22–24.

24. E.g., *Asin.* 307; *Epid.* 376, 665; *Men.* 760; *Merc.* 31–38, 608; *Persa* 167; *Pseud.* 573, 687; *Trin.* 806.

25. Wright 1974.

26. Some other examples of characters reminding the audience that they them-

selves or other characters are fulfilling the expectations of their stock character: *Bacch.* 772; *Cist.* 120–23, 150; *Curc.* 65–66; *Mil.* 213; *Persa* 118–26, 280a, 291; *Poen.* 328, 613, 861; *Rud.* 47–48, 341.

27. E.g., *Aul.* 1; *Cas.* 64–66; *Cist.* 782–83; *Pseud.* 1234; *Stich.* 446; *Trin.* 16; *Truc.* 482. Cf. Ter. *An.* 980; *Ad.* 22.

28. Cf. *Asin.* 256–57; *Capt.* 55; *Pseud.* 1239–41; Ter. *An.* 582–84; *Hec.* 866–67.

29. Cf. *Asin.* 1–3, 14–15.

30. Hellegouarc'h 1972, 215–16; Moore 1989, 98–100.

31. On the *Poenulus* prologue, see Jocelyn 1969a; Slater 1992a. Slater is right, I believe, to defend the prologue's authenticity against Jocelyn's criticisms.

32. Cf. Gargola 1995, 46–47.

33. So Pius and Lambinus, cited by Maurach (1988, 61). Scaliger and others, also cited by Maurach, have suggested that the *prologus* alludes to a children's game involving a rope.

34. Contemporary triumphs: Ritschl 1845, 423–27; Barsby 1986, 181; Gruen 1990, 137. Comic slaves: Fraenkel 1960, 227; Wright 1974, 105. This seems to me a case where the allusion is both topical and metatheatrical.

35. See especially Wright 1974, 127–51; Goldberg 1986, 209–19.

36. Of Plautus's nineteen extant epilogues, fourteen are in the form of imperatives. On Plautus's epilogues, see Monaco 1970.

37. On the importance of *mos maiorum* in Roman society, see Barrow 1949, 14–26.

38. On Plautine chronology, see Schutter 1952.

39. Cf., for example, the epilogues of Shakespeare's *Twelfth Night, Midsummer Night's Dream, Tempest, All's Well That Ends Well,* and, especially, *As You Like It* and *Troilus and Cressida*; and the prologues and epilogues of Restoration and eighteenth-century British plays, on which see Knapp 1961.

40. For the mixture of blandishment and teasing, note especially the addresses to the judges by the choruses of Clouds (*Clouds* 1115–30) and Birds (*Birds* 1101–17), promising rewards if they grant their play the prize, but threatening them if they do not. For abuse, note, e.g., *Clouds* 607–26, 1096–1101; *Lys.* 1219–20; *Thesm.* 814–45; *Frogs* 276; *Eccl.* 439–40, 888–89. On Aristophanes' audience addresses, see Stow 1936, 22–56; Schmid and Stählin 1946, 47; Chapman 1983, 3; Russo 1984, 85; Hubbard 1991.

41. Surviving examples: Menander *Dys.* 965–69; *Misoumenos* 993–96; *Sam.* 733–37; *Sikyonios* 420–23.

42. Requests for approval: Menander *Dys.* 45–46; *Pk.* 170–71; *Sikyonios* 23–24; Philemon *PCG* 50 (cf. Aristophanes *Knights* 37–39). Flattery: Menander, fr. 13 Koerte; fr. 396 Koerte (cf. *CGF* 252, 9–10). Desire to be understood: Menander *Aspis* 113–14, 146–47; *Pk.* 127–28; *Sam.* 5–6; *Phasma* 19–20 (cf. Aristophanes *Knights* 36–37; *Wasps* 54–55; Heniochus *PCG* 5.5). On audience address in the prologues of New Comedy, see Bain 1977, 186–89. Cf. Hubbard 1991, 1 n. 1.

43. Bain 1977, 188–89.

44. Cf. ibid., 142, 179, and passim.

45. An exception: Hegesippus *PCG* 1.29–30. Given the exceedingly fragmentary state of Middle and New Comedy, we must not exclude the possibility that there was a good deal more blandishment and teasing in lost comedies, especially those of playwrights other than Menander. We can be confident, however, that neither flattery nor teasing ever reached the levels found in Aristophanes or Plautus.

46. *An.* 8, 24–27; *Haut.* 12, 25–30, 35; *Eun.* 44–45; *Phorm.* 29–34; *Hec.* 8–57; *Ad.* 4–5, 24–25.

47. Turpio suggests (*Haut.* 1–3) that it was unusual for the lead actor to speak the prologue. On Terence's prologues, see Gelhaus 1972; Arnott 1985; Goldberg 1986, 31–60; Slater 1992b, 86–98.

48. E.g., *An.* 215–27, 231–32; *Eun.* 670, 919; *Hec.* 361–414, 799–806; *Ad.* 26–80, 83, 548.

49. See Haffter 1953, 85–100; Posani 1962, 68; Denzler 1968, 152–54; and *contra*, Ludwig 1968, 178.

50. On Plautus's Saturnalian plots, see especially Segal 1987.

CHAPTER 2

1. The practice goes back to Greek tragedy. Fraenkel (1960, 166) proposed that the phenomenon reflects a general Greek tendency. Cf. Leo 1908, 75–78; Williams 1968, 581–82; Swoboda 1971, 64.

2. Contrast Plaut. *Persa* 449–58, where a similar *sententia* receives considerably more attention.

3. Fraenkel 1960, 154–59. Note also that Plautus's successor Caecilius added a generalizing *sententia* to the beginning of his adaptation of a monologue from Menander's *Plocion* (Menander fr. 333 Sandbach; Caecilius *CRF* 142–43). On the fondness of Roman playwrights in general for *sententiae* introducing speeches, see Jocelyn 1972, 1004 n. 163.

4. Cf. Leo 1908, 75–78; Fraenkel 1960, 150.

5. Fraenkel 1960, 136.

6. Leo's brackets around these three lines are unnecessary.

7. On the significance of Philolaches' monologue for *Mostellaria* as a whole, see Leach 1969a.

8. Both Philolaches' simile and Menaechmus's lament show clear signs of Plautine workmanship. On Philolaches' monologue, see Fraenkel 1960, 160–69; Leach 1969a, 319. On Menaechmus's speech, see Fraenkel 1960, 152–54; Stärk 1989, 90. Some other examples of rhetorical monologues: *Bacch.* 385–403 (Mnesilochus works to convince the audience of the value of a good friend); *Men.* 127–34 (Menaechmus wants the audience to appreciate the heroism of his theft of his wife's cloak), 446–61 (Peniculus argues that people who have luncheon invitations should not be expected to attend political meetings); *Merc.* 544–54 (Demipho argues that old men rather than young should be lovers); *Mil.* 21–24 (Artotrogus on the boastfulness of Pyrgopolynices); *Poen.* 823–44 (Syncerastus on the depravity of his master's household); *Truc.* 209–45 (Astaphium defends the greedy behavior of prostitutes).

9. Ergasilus refers to the custom of calling out the name of one's beloved for good luck while throwing dice (cf. *Asin.* 780; *Curc.* 356).

10. Cf. *Persa* 64, 474–75; *Stich.* 294.

11. Cf. *Bacch.* 615a, 623; *Cas.* 303; *Merc.* 588; *Truc.* 635–36.

12. Cf. *Amph.* 507; *Asin.* 149; *Aul.* 46–47; *Bacch.* 137; *Cas.* 246; *Curc.* 188; *Men.* 472; *Merc.* 169; *Mil.* 200; *Mostell.* 887; *Persa* 788; *Pseud.* 152, 892, 1288; *Stich.* 270, 310; *Trin.* 847; *Truc.* 353, 601, 809; Terence *An.* 231; *Eun.* 265, 670, 919; *Ad.* 228.

13. Cf. Terence *An.* 217.

14. Cf. *Merc.* 431–37, where similar assumptions of "buyers" are made during an auction conducted in dialogue (see below). Also in this category may be the

places where characters call upon *cives* or *populares* ("fellow citizens") for help, if the actor addresses such lines to the audience (*Amph.* 376; *Aul.* 406–7; *Men.* 1000; *Rud.* 615–26; Terence *Ad.* 155).

15. Lefèvre (1995, 21–31) makes a strong case that most of these scenes are additions by Plautus to his Greek original.

16. Nixon's translation.

17. On the monologue as a unifier of actor and audience, cf. Styan 1975, 153–56; 1989, 198–200; Berry 1989.

18. Cf. Slater 1985b, 162–63.

19. Hiatt 1946, 4–7. Cf. Loitold 1957, 177.

20. Cf. Slater 1985b, 164. For examples, see Chapters 6 (Mercury in *Amphitruo*) and 9 (Pardalisca in *Casina*).

21. Cf. Wieand 1920, 9–15; Petrone 1983, 5–98.

22. Cf. Petrone 1983, 53–56.

23. Pistoclerus and Mnesilochus observe Chrysalus's entrance, but they show no sign of hearing any of his triumph monologue.

24. Nicobulus is evidently onstage reading Mnesilochus's letter throughout this scene. Cf. Barsby 1986, 169.

25. On Chrysalus's aside at 772, see Slater 1983.

26. "Nam ego illud argentum tam paratum filio / scio esse quam me hunc scipionem contui" ("For I am as sure that money is ready for my son as I am that I see this staff," 123–24). If a Scipio was the magistrate in charge at the games where *Asinaria* was first produced, the line would be a particularly pleasing allusion. Radermacher (1903) proposed from this line that *Asinaria* was first performed in 212, when P. Cornelius Scipio was curule aedile. Cf. Schutter 1952, 14–20.

27. The first author to use *servus callidus* explicitly of a stock comic character is Quintilian (*Inst.* 11.3.178). His and Apuleius's (*Flor.* 16) use of the term in lists of stock characters, however, suggests that the name had become a standard description long before their day. Cf. *Amph.* 268; Ter. *Haut.* 886–87; *Eun.* 1011.

28. He also addresses the imaginary birds who give him a sign (261).

29. For some intriguing speculation on how this scene might have been played, see Slater 1985b, 23–24.

30. I follow Leo in deleting line 398. If the line is authentic (Lindsay does not bracket it), Pseudolus may begin addressing the audience in that line, when he says, "neque nunc quid faciam scio" ("Nor do I know what to do now").

31. On the first scene, cf. Wright 1974, 1–10; Mariotti 1992.

32. Contrast *Cas.* 949–50, where a similar request by Lysidamus fails to win him rapport because it is overheard.

33. Indeed, Anderson 1983 has argued that Chalinus is not a stock *servus callidus*. Cf. Slater 1985b, 82–83.

34. Chalinus may also address the audience at 814, as he enters in drag, but the attribution of the line is not certain. See MacCary and Willcock 1976, 186–87; O'Bryhim 1989, 93–95.

35. Fraenkel 1960, 223–41. Cf. Spranger 1984, 98; Anderson 1993, 88–106.

36. Segal 1987, 99–136. Cf. Lefèvre 1988. Dingel (1981), Dumont (1987, 446–58), and Anderson (1993, 147–50) have argued that the Saturnalian element of slaves' deception is limited, for most victims of the slaves' deceptions are themselves unsympathetic and immoral characters. Though it is true that many of those deceived in Plautus are unworthy of the audience's sympathy, the deceivers are nevertheless slaves, so their successful deception would remain unacceptable outside the theater.

37. Slaves in the audience: *Poen.* 23 (cf. Moore 1994, 116–17). Arrival of new slaves: cf. Westermann 1955, 60–62; Brunt 1971, 17–19; Harris 1979, 80–85. Parker (1989, 242–46) has suggested that many members of the audience would on an unconscious level actually identify with the slaves. Because of Rome's strict rules of *patria potestas*, audience members with living fathers would be legally subject to a father figure, just as slaves are subject to their masters: many in the audience would therefore see an unconscious wish-fulfillment in the slaves' successes. If Parker is right, the delay in rapport would also help to resolve the tension between spectators' wish-fulfillment and guilt.

38. As Segal (1987, 137–62) and Parker (1989, 238) point out, the many allusions clever slaves make to potential punishment serve a similar function, reminding the spectators that the slaves' ability to get away with such outrageous behavior is limited to the stage.

39. Cf. Harsh 1944, 362.

40. Chrysalus enters at line 170 of the extant play, and at least two scenes are lost at the play's beginning. On the lost opening of *Bacchides*, see Law 1929; Bader 1970; Barsby 1986, 93–97; Zwierlein 1992, 122–27.

41. Cf. *Aul.* 587–607; *Mostell.* 858–84; *Persa* 7–12; *Pseud.* 1103–23; *Rud.* 906–37; Fraenkel 1960, 234–36; Hunter 1985, 145–47.

42. Hunter (1985, 145–46) is too hard on Messenio when he suggests that the speech is undermined by the fact that in the next scene, Messenio rescues his master's brother rather than his master. The rescue is admirable and beneficial, even if Messenio is mistaken about whom he is rescuing.

43. Because the name of Lyconides' slave is uncertain, I have followed Lindsay in keeping him anonymous. Leo accepts the name given in the manuscripts, Strobilus. Cf. Ludwig 1961, 255–57; Stockert 1983, 16–18.

44. Cf. Molière's adaptation of this dialogue in *L'Avare* 5.3.

45. On the play's lost ending, see Stockert 1983, 6–8. For a plausible and elegant reconstruction of the ending, see the translation of Watling (1965, 42–49).

46. On Euclio's isolation, see Konstan 1983, 33–46. Konstan argues that Euclio's fixation with his gold causes him to exile himself from the community to which he belongs.

47. Hiatt 1946, 13–15. The unusual pattern and other features of these scenes suggest extensive Plautine reworking in this part of the play, on which see Hunter 1981, 37–41.

48. The order of the lines is uncertain. The order in the manuscripts—718, 719, 717—cannot be made to make sense. Most modern editors besides Leo write 719, 717, 718. This order provides less coherence than Leo's, but it may be right, given Euclio's hysterical state. Cf. Stockert 1983, 186–87.

49. Cf. Moore 1994, 121–22.

50. Leo reads *eo* ("in this") as equivalent to *auro* ("gold"), and assumes that the others are those who have stolen the gold. Because *laetificantur* is plural, however, and Euclio has just referred to the laughter of the audience, it seems more likely that *eo* is Euclio's situation in general, and *alii* are the spectators.

51. Note that Molière's approach in his adaptation of *Aulularia* is quite different. Although Molière wrote a close adaptation of the accusation speech (*L'Avare* 4.7), Harpagon, Molière's miser, never attains rapport with the audience, nor does he experience a conversion. On the differences between Euclio and Harpagon, cf. Konstan 1995, 153–64.

52. See Berry 1989.

53. *Dis exapaton* and *Bacchides*: see Lefèvre 1978; Barsby 1986, 170 (with bibli-

ography); Lowe 1989, 390–91; Owens 1994, 381–98. *Aspis*: cf. Bain 1977, 106–8; Goldberg 1980, 29–43; Blänsdorf 1982, 137–41. On deception in New Comedy, cf. Petrone 1983, 144–51.

54. According to Bickford (1922, 60–62), 17% of Plautus's corpus is made up of monologues, 12% of Terence's.

CHAPTER 3

1. Gruen 1990, 157. Cf. Momigliano 1975, 49.

2. Note also the self-conscious play with place in the remains of a prologue by Heniochus (*PCG* 5), and a reference to Athenians in a play by Macho, set in Athens but performed in Alexandria (*PCG* 1).

3. Terence, however, avoids both incongruous allusions to Rome and emphatic references to Greek locales and institutions. Cf. Haffter 1953, 80–84; Williams 1968, 290–95.

4. On Shakespeare's self-conscious use of the Italian setting, see especially Levith 1989; McPherson 1990; Marrapodi et al. 1993. On play with setting in *Mikado*, see Williamson 1953, 143; Hayter 1987, 45–46, 59–60.

5. Not ridiculing Romans: Perna 1955, 225; Chalmers 1965, 24. Escape: Petrone 1977, 66–67; Segal 1987, 31–39. Hellenophobia: Della Corte 1952, 92–93; Owens 1986; Anderson 1993, 133–51. Mockery of Greek and Roman life: Chalmers 1965, 25; Gruen 1990, 156–57. Lists: Middelmann 1938; Duckworth 1952, 136. Originality: Westaway 1917, 16–70; Fraenkel 1960, 378, passim; Gaiser 1972, 1079–93. Chronology: see especially Buck 1940, passim; Hough 1940a; Schutter 1952, passim; and the cautions of Harvey 1986. Metatheater: Chiarini 1979, 24; Petrone 1983, 31–37; Gilula 1989, 103–6. Cf. Williams 1968, 285–89; Rawson 1989, 438.

6. Watson 1967, 157–58.

7. Cf. Colin 1905, 143–47; Seaman 1954, 115–16; Chalmers 1965, 30–45; Perna 1955, 226; Blänsdorf 1978, 106–7; Gruen 1992, 232.

8. Cf. Hengel 1977, 51.

9. *Pace* Parker (1989, 239–40).

10. On the importance of Roman allusions in making plays familiar, cf. Chalmers 1965, 28.

11. There is no evidence for foreign visitors in Plautus's audience, but some may have been present.

12. Deschamps 1980–81, 151.

13. *LSJ* 306.

14. See Pociña 1976, 425–32; Leeman 1983, 350–52; Petrone 1983, 31–37; Dumont 1987, 580–83; Gilula 1989, 104–5; and cf. Hoenselaars 1993, 36–38, on allusions to England by Shakespeare's Italian characters.

15. Ergasilus refers to the practice whereby a magistrate brought a prosecution before the *comitia tributa*. See Hallidie 1891, 144.

16. As the context of the Pacuvius passage has not survived, it is possible that the use of *Graii* here had some intended effect, or that the lines were spoken by a non-Greek, but Cicero's comments suggest otherwise ("quasi vero non Graius hoc dicat!" "As if it were not a Greek who says this!"). A similar passage occurs in Seneca's *Thyestes* 396, where the chorus of Argive elders refers to *Quirites* (Romans).

17. E.g., Duckworth 1952, 136; Fraenkel 1960, 378.

18. Leo unnecessarily brackets Tedigniloquides Nugides Palponides.

19. Williams 1968, 289–90.

20. See McPherson 1990, 40–42, 91–116; Lombardo 1993; Mullini 1993.

21. Cf. Petrochilos 1974, 43–45; Segal 1987, 37–38.

22. See Jory 1970, 229–30; Gruen 1990, 87–88.

23. For various opinions on the significance of this passage, see Segal 1987, 37; Gilula 1989, 102–3; Gruen 1990, 156; Anderson 1993, 137–38.

24. Gratwick 1993, 134. Note also, as Kenneth Reckford has pointed out to me in private correspondence, that *ubi factum dicitur* ("where it is said to have happened") "takes away with one hand what it gives with the other": the location remains the product of hearsay.

25. The two Menaechmus brothers were born in Sicily, but the abduction that sets the *argumentum* in motion occurs in Tarentum, and the play is set in Epidamnus.

26. Cf. Hor. *Epist.* 2.1.58. Stärk (1989, 56) proposes that Plautus is making a programmatic statement here: his play will not have a traditional Attic New Comedy plot, but will draw on the Italian farcical tradition.

27. Lindsay's text. There is no need to follow Watling (1965, 104) and Gratwick (1993, 134) in moving these lines to a place earlier in the prologue. The prologue speaker is an incorrigible rambler, and he is obsessed with the falseness of the play's location. He therefore does not establish the setting firmly until the *argumentum* is completed, and he rambles on about the false setting after references to place are unnecessary. Cf. Groton 1995, 616.

28. Because of its proximity to *parasitus*, and because kings, unlike the other characters mentioned in these two lines, have no role in *palliatae*, I have read *rex* as a rich man, who would be the patron of a parasite, a common meaning of the word (cf. *Asin.* 919; *Capt.* 92; *Men.* 902; *Stich.* 455; Ter. *Phorm.* 70).

29. So, for example, Williams 1968, 288.

30. On the identity of Pseudolus's *satis poti viri* as bankers, see Willcock 1987, 109. Arcellaschi (1978, 139) argues unconvincingly that the *satis poti viri* are priests.

31. Gruen 1992, 262–63.

32. Cf. Easterling 1985, 9, on Euripides' use of anachronism to encourage his spectators to "look closely at the disturbing implications" of events within the heroic world of tragedy.

33. Cf. Owens 1986, 163–93.

34. Shipp 1953; Chalmers 1965, 39–42; Gruen 1990, 156.

35. Cf. Hofmann 1992, 151–58; Maltby 1995.

36. References to the senate need not necessarily have struck Plautus's audience as incongruous in a Greek setting, for *senatus* could be used of an assembly in a Greek city (*Rud.* 713). Combined with the other Roman allusions, however, the allusion to the senate reinforces Epidicus's Romanness.

37. Cf. Dumont 1987, 498.

38. Cf. Gowers 1993, 53–54.

39. On the identification of the *poeta barbarus* as Naevius, see Marmorale 1953, 112–16; Jocelyn 1969b, 34–37; Gaiser 1972, 1091; Frangoulidis 1994, 72–73. For more skeptical views, see Gruen 1990, 104; Goldberg 1995, 33–36.

40. Aside from *Capt.* 1002, on which see Chapter 10, the *TLL* (10.1.748.41; cf. 10.1.746.20) cites no other uses of *patricius* applied to non-Romans before Seneca.

41. Lindsay's text. Leo's crux here is unnecessary.

42. On *basilicus* and *basilice*, cf. Harsh 1936, 65; Fraenkel 1960, 183–86.

43. Cf. Owens 1986, 190–92; Segal 1987, 32–33.

44. Bradley 1987, 28–29.

CHAPTER 4

1. See, for example, Oppermann 1962 and 1967; Earl 1967; Otis 1967, 197–203; Williams 1968, 578–633. On the extent to which notions of the Roman obsession with morality have been exaggerated, see Momigliano 1975, 16; Bondanella 1987, 8–18 and passim.

2. See Duckworth 1952, 272–304; Rawson 1987. There was also a strong tradition of moral didacticism in Greek comedy, although the countless moral precepts gathered from the plays of Menander and others are often ironic within their original context. See, on Aristophanes, McLeish 1980, 59–61; Reckford 1987, 285–311 and passim; Hubbard 1991, passim; MacDowell 1995, 3–6; and, on New Comedy, Webster 1970, 135–41, 159, 171–72; 1974, 43–55; Sandbach 1977, 101–2; Hunter 1985, 137–47; Zagagi 1994, 33–38; Easterling 1995, 155–60.

3. The *virgo* as a speaking part is most likely a creation of Plautus himself. See Lowe 1989.

4. Cf. Chiarini 1979, 35–178; Slater 1985b, 41–50; Gerdes 1995, 125–28.

5. *Haud indocte*, echoing Toxilus's *docte* from earlier in the scene (551), also implies that the *virgo* has learned her part well. Cf. Chiarini 1979, 147.

6. Other moralizing by deceivers: *Amph.* 938–43; *Curc.* 494–515; *Epid.* 225–35; *Mil.* 477, 563–65, 1292–95; *Poen.* 633–36; *Pseud.* 460–61, 492–93; *Trin.* 924, 946–47.

7. Cf. Segal 1987, 195.

8. These words refer to the situation in other comedies (e.g., *Truculentus*) in which a prostitute pretends that she is the mother of someone else's infant. Cf. Ter. *Eun.* 39.

9. Segal 1987, 211.

10. Lindsay's text.

11. Plautus probably added both the *Curculio* passage and the *Truculentus* passage to his Greek originals. See Fraenkel 1960, 157–60.

12. Cf. Crahay and Delcourt 1952, 88.

13. Schaaf 1977, 120–24, 149, 192–97. Cf. Webster 1970, 175.

14. The most common explanation of this apparent incongruity is that Plautus felt that Palaestrio's step out of character was necessary for the audience to follow the plot (Gaiser 1972, 1050). In fact, these lines are more likely to confuse than to clarify; for in spite of his *ne erretis* ("so that you do not misunderstand"), there is no clarity in Palaestrio's reference to one woman as two, for which the audience has no context. Williams (1958a, 101) suggests that Plautus, anxious to keep his audience's attention, could not resist the temptation to tell the audience "something of the treat in store for them." Cf. Frangoulidis 1996.

15. Cf. Fantham 1973, 199.

16. On Plautus's *servi callidi* as playwrights, see Petrone 1983, 7 and passim; Slater 1985b, 172–77 and passim.

17. Palaestrio is putting his chin on his hand, like Rodin's "Thinker." On the allusion to Naevius, see Chapter 3, note 39. On Periplectomenus's obscure *os columnatum*, which may have a metaphorical rather than a physical meaning, see Allen 1896; Killeen 1973; Jocelyn 1987; Gruen 1990, 104.

18. Knapp 1919, 39–41.

19. Cf. Gerdes 1995, 165–66. Gerdes points out that Periplectomenus even does some acting in this scene, mimicking the speeches of hypothetical wives (687–98).

20. E.g., Pind. *Ol.* 6.1–4; *Pyth.* 7.3; Ar. *Peace* 749–50; Hor. *Carm.* 3.30.1; Ov. *Met.* 15.871. Cf. Taillardat 1965, 438–49; Steiner 1986, 55.

21. Hammond, Mack, and Moskalew 1963, 154; Forehand 1973b, 9; Schaaf 1977, 302.

22. On the role of the *choragus*, see Fredershausen 1906, 68; Saunders 1909, 17–19. It is even possible that the actor playing Periplectomenus was the actual *choragus* of the play, given that the *choragus* appears onstage in *Curculio* (462–86; see Chapter 7). Cf. *Persa* 159; *Trin.* 858.

23. On the importance of instruction in Plautine metatheater, see Petrone 1983, 37–42 and passim.

24. On *ludi* in Plautus as a reference to games featuring theatrical performances, see Knapp 1919, 45. Cf. Plautus *Cornicula*, frag. 1.

25. *Asin.* 69 implies that dressing up as a ship's captain in order to get a girl may have been a comic topos. The use of a *nauclericus ornatus* would thus further reinforce the image of actors performing a play.

26. Cf. Slater 1985b, 49 n. 12.

27. This bit of staging will be especially effective if, as some editors suggest, the *servus* of the last scene is Sceledrus, the other major spectator of a deception play.

28. On the significance of the play-within-the-play in modern drama, see the works cited at Introduction, note 12. Plautus's original must also have included some playacting, but even conservative judges of Plautine originality would agree that much of the metatheater in the *Miles* is original to Plautus. The reference to a *poeta barbarus* that establishes Palaestrio as a playwright is obviously Roman; and the other passages most important in reinforcing the notion of a comic troupe— Periplectomenus's long description of himself (cf. Lefèvre 1984, 43–46), Acroteleutium's elaborate metaphor of shipbuilding (cf. Shipp 1955, 151; Pomey 1973, 502–3; Schaaf 1977, 302), and the three long instruction scenes (cf. Fraenkel 1960, 61–62; Lefèvre 1984, 37–38)—all show clear signs of Plautine workmanship. Several of the metatheatrical references depend for their effect on Latin puns or wordplay (293, 324–25, 590–91, 991, 1066, 1073). Cf. Frangoulidis 1994.

29. The word *lepidus* occurs thirty-five times in *Miles*, far more often than in any other Plautine play. Even accounting for the fact that *Miles* is Plautus's longest play, the frequency is remarkable. The thirty-five occurrences mean that the word appears almost once every forty-one lines. In *Poenulus*, where the word is next most frequent, it appears approximately once every seventy-one lines. On the association between *lepidus* and performance, see Chiarini 1979, 76 n. 80, 124.

30. On the varying moral tone of *Stichus*, cf. Arnott 1972; Petrone 1977, 30–71.

31. Cf. Garzya 1969. For two elegant interpretations of the play's moral messages, see Leach 1974; Konstan 1983, 73–95.

32. *Cum lusi* is the reading of the manuscripts. Some editors, including Leo, have considered the words a crux, and Lindsay proposed the hapax *conlusim*. As Petrone (1983, 201) points out, however, *cum lusi* makes sense if we consider the possibility of a metatheatrical reading. Cf. Marx 1928, 213.

33. Cf. Marx 1928, 211.

34. On Gripus's speech, cf. Hunter 1985, 140–41; Slater 1991, 22. For a more serious reading of the scene, see Konstan 1983, 83–85. Riemer (1996, 159–61) presents a cogent argument that the entire role of Gripus is an addition by Plautus to his Greek original.

35. The dialogue-prologue is almost certainly original to Plautus, as Luxuria says that Plautus gave her and Inopia their names (8–9). Cf. Abel 1955, 24; Lefèvre 1995, 86–87, 120; and *contra*, Hunter 1980, 226.

36. Cf. Stein 1970, 7.

37. On the similarities between Cato and Megaronides, see Benz 1990; Lefèvre 1993, 181–88; 1995, 139–45.

38. Livy's Lucretia, for example, kills herself even though she is innocent of wrongdoing because she does not want other unchaste women to live with her as an example (1.58.10). Caesar divorced his wife even though she was probably not guilty of the sexual crime for which she was charged, saying that his wife must be above suspicion (Plut. *Caes.* 10.6).

39. On plays performed in the forum, just below the Capitoline, see Chapter 7.

40. E.g., *Mil.* 575: "*Sceledrus*: numquid nunc aliud me vis? *Periplectomenus*: ne me noveris" ("*Sceledrus*: You don't want anything else of me, do you? *Periplectomenus*: Yes, that you don't know me"). Cf. Hough 1945, 283–84.

41. On the Plautine nature of this passage, see Fraenkel 1960, 177–80. On the loiterers (Latin *scurrae*), see Corbett 1986, 27–43.

42. On the degree to which Plautus has altered the Greek original of Lysiteles' speech, see Fraenkel 1960, 133; Anderson 1979, 336–39; Zagagi 1980, 90–104; Lefèvre 1995, 94–95.

43. Asyndeton combined with inconcinnity (*rapax avarus invidus* joined with plural verbs, 286; *rape trahe, fuge late*, with no grammatical connection to the surrounding words, 291).

44. Philto also jokes that the Capuans, always known for their effete way of life, are passive homosexuals: *patientia* can mean both "ability or willingness to endure" and "submission to sexual intercourse" (*OLD*, s.v.).

45. The theatrical reference is probably Plautine rather than an importation from Philemon. Cf. Slater 1985a. On the metatheatrical effect of this scene, cf. Lefèvre 1995, 103–4.

46. Cf. Anderson 1979, 343.

47. *Scitum consilium* (764, cf. *Amph.* 506; *Bacch.* 209; *Pseud.* 748), *graphice* (767, cf. *Persa* 306, 464, 843), *sycophanta* (815, cf. *Amph.* 506; *Asin.* 546; *Bacch.* 764; *Persa* 325; *Poen.* 376, 425, 654; *Pseud.* 527, 572, 672).

48. On Charmides, see Anderson 1979, 339–40; Muecke 1985, 184.

49. Cf. Stein 1970, 11.

50. Cf. *Persa* 75–76: "sed sumne ego stultus, qui rem curo publicam, / ubi sint magistratus, quos curare oporteat?" ("But isn't it foolish for me to worry about public affairs, when there are magistrates whose job is to worry about such things?"). On Plautus's expansion of Stasimus's speech, see Fraenkel 1960, 146–50; Hunter 1980, 227–30.

51. *Veteres mores* (Stasimus, 1028; Megaronides, [*antiqui mores*], 73–74; Philto, [*mores maiorum*], 295, [*mores antiqui*], 297), *mores mali* (Stasimus, 1029, 1040; Megaronides, 30, 33; Philto, 286, 531), *mores* (Stasimus, 1032, 1037, 1044; Megaronides, 28; Philto, 284, 299), *publicus* (Stasimus, 1046, 1057; Megaronides, 38, 220; Philto, 287, 331, 548), *fides* (Stasimus, 1048; Megaronides, 27, 117, 128, 153), *frugi* (Stasimus, 1018; Megaronides, 118; Philto, 320, 321).

52. Rose (1924, 156) proposed that Stasimus could not have had access to a full Athenian talent, and that he means the much less valuable Sicilian or South Italian talent. Given what Stasimus said earlier about his pilfering of Lesbonicus's coffers, however (413), it seems quite likely that Stasimus did have that much money at his disposal. The rest of Rose's argument, that *talentum* alone in Plautus means a South Italian rather than an Athenian talent unless the context makes clear that an Athenian talent is meant, is not convincing. Cf. Lefèvre 1995, 79.

53. Slater 1987, 268.

54. If Gratwick (1981), followed by Slater (1987), is correct, Charmides compares Stasimus to the title character of Plautus's own *Curculio* (Gratwick reads *Curculio* for the manuscripts' *gurgulio* in line 1016). The echo does not imply, however, that Charmides gives an endorsement of Stasimus's words (*pace* Slater).

55. Cf. *Poen.* 845–46, where Milphio responds aside to Syncerastus, who complains about the evil goings-on in the pimp's house: "proinde habet orationem, quasi ipse sit frugi bonae, / qui ipsus hercle ignaviorem potis est facere Ignaviam" ("You know, he speaks as if he himself were worth something, but by Hercules he himself could make Sloth herself more slothful").

56. Though as Stein (1970, 8) and Lefèvre (1995, 93) point out, Callicles does break his promise to Charmides when he tells Megaronides about the hidden treasure.

57. Lefèvre (1995, 61–123) makes a strong case that the roles of Megaronides and Philto are additions by Plautus to his Greek original. Riemer (1996, 28–132) is inclined to attribute Philto and Megaronides (in a much smaller role) to Philemon's play, but he makes an even stronger case that the entire Sycophant scene is Plautine. The other passages cited in my argument—the prologue, Lysiteles' speech, Stasimus's framing of the debate between Lesbonicus and Lysiteles, and Stasimus's moralizing monologue—are creations original to Plautus or vast expansions of passages in Philemon's *Thesauros*. For less ironic readings of *Trinummus*, see Wright 1982, 519–20; Segal 1987, 214–26.

CHAPTER 5

1. See especially Taladoire 1956, 138–41; Barchiesi 1969, 127–29; Wright 1975; Petrone 1983, 5–6, 64–74; Slater 1985b, 118–46; Barsby 1995; Sharrock 1996.

2. On the importance of the bets in *Pseudolus*, and the likelihood that Plautus added them to his Greek original, see Görler 1983; Lefèvre 1997, 23–27. Cf. Lefèvre 1977.

3. Cf. Petrone 1983, 69.

4. E.g., by Freté 1929–30, 289; and Primmer 1984, 18–19.

5. See especially Conrad 1915; Duckworth 1952, 98–101; Paratore 1959; Beare 1964, 212–13; Questa 1970, 210–13.

6. *Luc.* 20. Cf. Donat. *De comoedia* 8.11; Wille 1967, 22.

7. On the monologues, cf. Petrone 1983, 64–74.

8. Petrone 1981, 113.

9. Cf. Fraenkel 1960, 142, 414.

10. Cic. *Q Rosc.* 7.20. Cf. Garton 1972, 169–88.

11. Cf. Dohm 1964, 139–54, and Lowe 1985, on the extent to which Plautus probably expanded the cook scene he found in his Greek original. Lefèvre (1997, 69–76) has argued that the Greek original of *Pseudolus* had no cook. Gowers (1993, 93–107) and Hallett (1993) propose that the cook, like Pseudolus, is a metaphor for Plautus himself.

12. Thus when Pseudolus first hears Callipho speak, he exclaims, "lepidum senem" 435. Cf. Sharrock 1996, 164.

13. For parallel sets of friends, cf. *Bacch.*, *Epid.*, *Merc.*, *Mostell.*, and *Trin.*

14. On the *puer* scene, cf. Kwintner 1992.

15. On Simia as performer, cf. Slater 1985b, 136–40.

16. Cf. *Epid.* 666–74; *Mostell.* 1064–1115.

17. Cf. *Asin.* 727; *Truc.* 219; Pacuvius *TRF* 366–75.

18. On *magnificus* as a word describing performance, see Slater 1985b, 122–23. Slater is wrong, I think, to suggest that the word implies a criticism.

19. See Usener 1913, 377–80; Kelly 1966, 21–23; Lintott 1968, 8–10.

20. *Cantores* is a reference both to the chantlike nature of *flagitatio* or *occentatio* and to the chanting or singing of actors. On the connection between *probitas* ("excellence") and *officium* ("duty"), see Hellegouarc'h 1972, 286.

21. Leo unnecessarily brackets these lines.

22. For *poeta* in Plautus meaning "playwright," cf. *Capt.* 1033; *Cas.* 18, 861; *Curc.* 591; *Men.* 7.

23. Cf. Petrone 1981, 114.

24. The Latin has a pun dependent on the word *ballista*: "missile" (cf. Jocelyn 1990, 5–6).

25. Cf. Slater 1985b, 132 n. 20. Leo unnecessarily brackets the line.

26. Cf. Morel 1964, 377–81; Dunn 1984, 58–59.

27. Elsewhere Plautus uses the phrases *de capite comitia* (*Aul.* 700) and *capiti comitia* (*Truc.* 819), but there the phrases are merely metaphors for important decisions about the speakers to be made on or off the stage. Ballio's addition of *centuriata* to *comitia* makes much stronger the allusion to a specific Roman assembly that decided cases. Cf. Mommsen 1886, 357–58; Taylor 1966, 2–3.

28. Lindsay's text.

29. Ritschl (1845, 296) proposed plausibly that Pseudolus invites the audience to a performance on the next day. Note the contrast with the similar passage at the end of *Rudens*. There Daemones says that he will invite the spectators to dinner if they come back in sixteen years, emphasizing the promise's impossibility rather than suggesting a possibility.

30. The date is revealed by the play's didascalia, or list of production information, one of only two that survive from Plautus's plays (the other is from *Stichus*, produced in 200). The date given for the dedication is April 191; but as the Roman calendar was four months out of sync at this time, the actual date would have been in late 192 (Drury 1982, 808).

31. Veyne 1976, 419–21; Morgan 1990, 27–29; Gruen 1992, 188–97. It is not clear what role theatrical presentations usually played at privately sponsored *ludi* such as votive games, triumphal games, and funeral games (see Gruen 1992, 195–97).

32. As they do in the annalistic notices preserved in Livy (e.g., 27.6.19, 31.50.2, 32.7.14).

33. Cf. Millar 1984, 12; Gold 1987, 41.

34. Gruen (1992, 194) argues that the *conductores* are "contractors or subcontractors, such as the *choragi*, who had responsibility for the particulars of the production." Gruen's argument, that "the proposition that aediles who presided over the event were placed last in the roster and given a vague designation strains credulity," is not convincing. The *conductores* are in fact at the end of a crescendo of importance. After the generic "me and you" (cf. *Men.* 2), the speaker begins again with the company, then builds to the leaders of the company (though, as Gruen suggests, these need not be masters of slaves, the name *dominus* does suggest a position of authority; cf. *TLL* 5.1.1915; Jory 1966, 103; Dumont 1987, 520–22), then to the magistrates who hired the company and its leaders. The name will be clear enough. Note also the possible allusion later in *Asinaria* (124) to a Scipio presiding over the games at which that play was performed (see Chapter 2, note 26).

35. Within this context, Plautus's several parodic allusions to *senatus* in the plays would all be taken in good fun. Cf. Hoffmann 1987. On senatorial domination of the theatrical *ludi*, see Gruen 1992, 221–22.

36. Gruen 1990, 69–72.

37. Cf. Briscoe 1981, 275. As Briscoe points out, Scipio's colleague in the consulship, Manius Acilius, if he was still in Rome (Livy's text contradicts itself regarding the date of his departure for Asia), would also have a claim to dedicate the temple: he was about to lead an army to Asia against Antiochus, and the Magna Mater had come from Asia. Briscoe suggests that Iunius may have been chosen as a compromise between the two consuls' claims.

38. This scenario does not require that we accept H. H. Scullard's theory of a competition between a Scipionic faction and other groups running throughout the first decades of the second century (1973, 75–189). If, however, there is some truth in Scullard's proposal, it is probably not without significance that according to Scullard, M. Iunius finds himself elsewhere aligned with the anti-Scipionic faction (ibid., 184).

39. For the political autonomy of poets in Plautus's day, see Gruen 1990, 79–123; Goldberg 1995, 31–33, 111–34.

40. On the importance of the Magna Mater, see Gruen 1990, 5–33; Burton 1996. On the temple, and performances there, see Hanson 1959b, 13–16; Richardson 1992, 242.

CHAPTER 6

1. Middle Comedy: Reinhardt 1974; Hunter 1987. South Italian farce: Stewart 1958; Chiarini 1980. Tragedy: Lefèvre 1982; Slater 1990. Steidle 1979 suggests that Plautus added the report of Heracles' birth to a play of New Comedy.

2. Cf. Niebergall 1937, 25. Caecilius's *Aetherio* or *Aethrio* (*CRF* 4) may have included gods, but it was almost certainly written after the death of Plautus.

3. E.g., *Ariadne, Armorum Iudicium, Marsya, Sisyphus*. Cf. *CRF*, pp. 391–92; Frassinetti 1967, 9, 13.

4. Höttemann 1993, 93–96.

5. Cf. Costa 1965, 91; Wright 1974, 130, n. 9. Segal (1987, 171–91) argues that the play offers a Saturnalian inversion of the important Roman ideal of feminine chastity.

6. Cf. Cèbe 1966, 67–69; Jocelyn 1966, 101; Liebeschuetz 1979, 1–4; Tatum 1993, 13–14.

7. Cf. Gulick 1896; Tolliver 1952; Hanson 1959a; Cèbe 1966, 70–71.

8. Early influence of Greek mythology: see especially Wissowa 1912, 47–52; Altheim 1938, 247–55; Latte 1960, 213–31, 264–65; Dumézil 1970, 2:441–56; Radke 1987, 31–57; Wiseman 1989, 131–36. Explanations: *Aul.* 555–57, 559 (Euclio explains allusions to Argus and Pirene), *Poen.* 443–44 (Milphio explains an allusion to Oedipus), *Pseud.* 199–201 (Ballio explains the fate of Dirce). Brooks (1981, 2–3, 76–82) argues that most of Plautus's mythological allusions were drawn from contemporary tragedy. Cf. Latte 1960, 265 n. 1.

9. Auxilium, for example, is put out that the *lena* who spoke before him has revealed part of the plot (*Cist.* 149–53). Cf. the gently humorous portrayal of Pan in the prologue of Menander's *Dyscolos*.

10. Cf. Bailey 1932, 130; Niebergall 1937, 33; Tolliver 1952, 54–55 (though she exaggerates the impiety here and elsewhere in Plautus); Dumézil 1970, 2:492.

11. Compare the insistent theatricality of medieval religious drama, on which see Kolve 1966, 8–32; Goldman 1975, 77–80.

12. Cf. Fantham 1973, 198.

13. E.g., *Asin.* 316, 474; *Bacch.* 147, 463; *Cas.* 411; *Men.* 249, 977; *Mil.* 547, 584; *Mostell.* 858, 860; *Persa* 361; *Truc.* 814.

14. On the analogous situation in *Captivi* of a slave playing a free man playing a slave, cf. Segal 1987, 212.

15. *Mil.* 901, 902, 915, 919, 1139; *Poen.* 1110; cf. Slater 1990, 106.

16. Cf. Apollo in Ennius 316–18 Jocelyn (*pace* Ribbeck 1875, 148).

17. The manuscript reading *tragicocomoedia*, abandoned by almost all editors, is defended by Ussing (1875–92, 1:239–40) and Seidensticker (1982, 21).

18. On tragicomedy as it has developed since Giambattista Guarini's *Compendio della poesia tragicomica* (1601), see especially Guthke 1966; Hirst 1984; Dutton 1986; Shawcross 1987.

19. Cf. Stewart 1958, 360–61.

20. "Nunc de Alcumena ut rem teneatis rectius" ("Now so that you may understand better about Alcumena," 110); "nunc ne hunc ornatum vos meum admiremini" ("Now don't be surprised at this costume I am wearing," 116).

21. The meaning of *torulus*, literally a "little knot," is not clear here. Cf. *OLD*, s.v.

22. On the accompanied and unaccompanied scenes of *Amphitruo*, cf. Dupont 1987.

23. This scene is largely, if not completely, original to Plautus (Milch 1957, 168–69; Fraenkel 1960, 21, 98, 171–72; Lefèvre 1982, 8–13).

24. Slater 1990, 109.

25. Cf. Ennius 8 Jocelyn (patriotism); Ennius 9, 153–54, 165, 381 Jocelyn (battle reports); Fraenkel 1912, 38–39; 1960, 333–35; Leo 1912, 134; Herrmann 1948, 319–21; Galinsky 1966, 204–6; Slater 1990, 109 n. 18. As Slater points out, the speech has a "tragic" effect, whether or not Sosia's words also parody the language of inscriptions (Marouzeau 1932, 272), requests for triumphs (Halkin 1948; cf. Cugusi 1991, 298–302), or epic (Lelièvre 1958; Oniga 1985), or recall a specific recent battle or campaign (Janne 1933; Traina 1954; Galinsky 1966, 223–25).

26. Cf. Hunter 1987, 293.

27. Cf. Ennius 188–91 Jocelyn; Accius *TRF* 100, 566–67, 691.

28. Cf. Naevius *TRF* 45 (from *Lycurgus*): "ut videam Volcani opera haec flammis flora fieri."

29. Cf. Naevius *TRF* 46–47 (also from *Lycurgus*): "proinde huc Dryante regem prognatum patre, / Lycurgum cette!" The two reminiscences of *Lycurgus* so close together may reflect deliberate parody of that play in this scene.

30. For the joke of a slave speaking of his parents or his ancestors, cf. *Cas.* 418; *Mil.* 373. See also Chapter 10.

31. For tragic praise of *virtus*, cf. Ennius 254–57 Jocelyn.

32. Cf. Chiarini 1980, 120–21; Perelli 1983; Phillips 1985; Slater 1990, 113. A modern analogy for this scene is the scene in *Funny Girl* where Fanny Brice sings her tender bridal song with a pillow tucked under her dress.

33. 700–701, 707, 718–19, 723–24, 738–40, 775–76, 784–86, 801, 814, 825–29, 843, 845–46, 855–56.

34. On the force of *ne transigam* here, see García-Hernández 1984.

35. On Jupiter's status as an actor here, see Dupont 1976, 135–36. Dupont even proposes that *in superiore . . . habito cenaculo* refers to the actor's own upstairs room in a Roman apartment building.

36. Cf. Lefèvre 1982, 25; Slater 1990, 114.

37. For the ubiquity and predictability of the *servus currens*, cf. Terence *Haut.* 37; Duckworth 1936, 93; 1952, 106–7; Petrone 1983, 166–70.

38. Cf. Dupont 1987, 52.

39. Note that "Jupiter" is again associated with the class *homines*, human beings.

40. Elsewhere in Plautus, parasites deliver their own versions of the *servus currens* speech (*Capt.* 778–835; *Curc.* 280–304), and one of the frequent tasks of parasites in New and Roman comedy is to assist lovers (cf. Damon 1997, 31–32). Mercury had earlier made an unsuccessful attempt at playing the parasite's role (515–21). On Mercury as parasite, see Guilbert 1963.

41. Reference is made to a roof on the house of Periplectomenus (*Mil.* 173), but there is no suggestion that the roof appears onstage; nor need we assume that the roof is visible when Sceparnio refers to roof tiles lost to the storm in *Rudens* (83–88). Characters may have appeared in a second-story window or balcony of Thais's house in Terence's *Eunuch* 783. Cf. Loitold 1957, 71, 209 n. 255; Stewart 1958, 370–71. At least one tragedy from during or shortly after Plautus's lifetime whose title has survived almost certainly ended with an appearance on the roof: Ennius's *Medea* (cf. the end of Euripides' *Medea*).

42. Line 1006, and the next two lines, in which Mercury explains what he will do, switch unexpectedly back to unaccompanied iambic senarii. As the lines are redundant, they may be an interpolation (so Ussing 1875–92, 1:327). The switch to iambic senarii, however, is effective, for it encourages a close link between Mercury and the audience before he performs the dousing of Amphitruo for them.

43. For a plausible reconstruction of the lost scenes, see Fantham 1973.

44. Aesch. *Sept.* 422–36; Soph. *Ant.* 127–37; *OC* 1318–19; Eur. *Supp.* 496–99; *Phoen.* 1172–86. For Jupiter's thunderbolt in tragedy contemporary with Plautus, cf. Naevius *TRF* 10, 12 (from *Danae*, where it is quite possible that Jupiter himself also appeared; cf. Ribbeck 1875, 55).

45. Cf. Fraenkel 1912, 39, 65; 1960, 335; Lefèvre 1982, 36–37; Deuling 1994, 16–21.

46. Nixon's translation.

47. Cf. Tiresias's role in Sophocles' *Antigone* and *Oedipus Tyrannos*, and Euripides' *Bacchae* and *Phoenissae*.

CHAPTER 7

1. Cf. Lefèvre, Stärk, and Vogt-Spira 1991, 77–79.

2. E.g., *Persa* 745 and passim (cf. Scafuro 1993); *Poen.* passim (on the similarities between *Curculio* and *Poenulus*, see Zwierlein 1990, 272–80); *Rud.* 866–67, 1281–85; *Truc.* 761–63.

3. On the absence of a prologue, cf. Fantham 1965, 85.

4. Cf. Zwierlein 1990, 261.

5. On the play's Roman allusions, cf. Deschamps 1980–81, 151–77.

6. 30–32 (a pun on *testis* ["witness" and "testicle"]), 35–38 (reference to laws on sexual morality), 47–48 (metaphor drawn from legal language of lending and borrowing [*mutuom facere*]), 162–64 (metaphor drawn from appearance in court on security [*vadimonium*]), 174 (metaphor drawn from legal transfer of ownership [*abalienare*]), 212 (manumission [*vindictam parare*]).

7. Cf. Ussing 1875–92, 2:317, 539; Warnecke 1927; Petrone 1983, 37 n. 23.

8. Cf. Wiles 1991, 59–60.

9. Leo 1913, 146; Zwierlein 1990, 242–43.

10. Corbett 1986, 27–43. Petrone (1983, 170–75) proposes that the *Graeci palliati* and the slaves of the *scurrae* are actors, and that Curculio's threat to force from the *Graeci palliati* a *crepitus polentarius* ("barley-meal fart") is an allusion to the Roman practice of eating porridge. The effect on the audience would be the same whether Plautus created the passage himself from scratch (Fraenkel 1960, 123–27) or derived most of it from his Greek original (Csapo 1989, 150–54).

11. On Plautus's use of *trapezita* and *argentarius*, see Shipp 1955, 139–41; Andreau 1968, 468–77, 488–89; Giangrieco Pessi 1981, 51–97.

12. There is no need to follow Leo in deleting lines 377–79.

13. F. Coarelli in Steinby 1993, 310–11. Cf. Milphio's description of the *advocati* hired by Agorastocles as *comitiales meri* (*Poen.* 584), and Agorastocles' request that these same *advocati* meet him *in comitio* (*Poen.* 807).

14. Cf. N. Purcell in Steinby 1995, 332: "The *forum Romanum* was synonymous with legal justice."

15. Nixon's translation.

16. Cf. Schutter 1952, 63–64. The connection between Curculio's *rogitationes* and the laws of 193 was first made by Teuffel (1889, 325). Even if, as Schutter suggests, the reference to *rogitationes* is insufficient to date *Curculio* to 193 B.C.E., Curculio's words almost certainly refer to contemporary Roman controversies. Livy records that in 192, the curule aediles gained enough money from fines levied against moneylenders to place gilded four-horse chariots and twelve gilded shields on the Capitolium (35.41.9–10). André (1983) connects the concern over moneylending in *Curculio* and other plays with a shortage of credit in the early second century. Cf. Billeter 1898, 153–54; Gruen 1990, 146–48; Lefèvre, Stärk, and Vogt-Spira 1991, 102–3.

17. On the speech, see Moore 1991a, and the bibliography cited there. Cf. also Dumont 1987, 501–2, 585.

18. On the authenticity of this line, unjustifiably placed in brackets by Leo, see Moore 1991a, 354–55. The *choragus* interrupts himself at the end of line 484 before he reaches the verb on which depend *pistorem, lanium, haruspicem*, and the assumed antecedents of the two *quis*. I have altered the punctuation accordingly.

19. This line has been justifiably excised by almost all editors. See Moore 1991a, 358.

20. The meaning of *halapanta* is not certain. Cf. Owens 1986, 172; Moore 1991a, 361 n. 61.

21. Cf. *Capt.* 57; *Pseud.* 1081–83; Ter. *Ad.* 188–89.

22. Cf. Ussing 1875–92, 2:565; Bosscher 1903, 76.

23. Cf. *Capt.* 58; *Curc.* 633; *Mil.* 87; Ter. *Eun.* 31, 38; Cic. *Amic.* 98.

24. See Moore 1991a, 348. Cf. Hill 1989, 11.

25. Cf. *Bacch.* 117; *Epid.* 319; *Pseud.* 415; *Truc.* 63, 82; Ter. *Haut.* 1034; Ussing 1875–92, 2:565.

26. Nearly all commentators and translators have assumed that the *scorta* here are female, but the *TLL* (5.2.1543, lines 11–12) suggests that *scorta exoleta*, like *exoleti* elsewhere in Latin literature, are male. That the *TLL* is correct is confirmed by *Poen.* 17, where the *prologus* modifies *scortum exoletum* with a masculine adjective. Cf. Abel 1955, 146 n. 559; Adams 1983, 322. On male prostitutes elsewhere in Plautus, see Lilja 1983, 30.

27. Cf. *Cist.* 375; Jordan 1880, 130; Amatucci 1904, 331.

28. *Dig.* 45.1; de Zulueta 1953, 149. Cf. Kaser 1968, 37–38.

29. Coarelli 1985, 149–50; Andreau 1987a, 159. Richardson (1979, 210–11) suggests that when *Curculio* was first performed, the *tabernae argentariae* ("bankers'

shops") on the north side of the forum had not yet been rebuilt after the fire of 210 (Livy 26.27.2–4), and temporary *tabernae* were in the basilica itself. Cf. Gros 1983, 65 n. 13. On the identity of the basilica, see Gaggiotti 1985.

30. So Bosscher 1903, 84. Andreau's objection (1987a, 161) that the *choragus* would not refer to a professional class such as *argentarii* in such a vague way is unconvincing, given the vagueness of references throughout the passage.

31. E.g., *Cas.* 490–503, 719; *Men.* 208–13; *Merc.* 754; *Mostell.* 66–67; *Truc.* 740; Ter. *Ad.* 117, 964–65; Naevius *CRF* 50; Caecilius *CRF* 180.

32. See Chapter 3. Epidicus also jokes about *symbolae* prepared for his shoulder blades when he fears a beating (*Epid.* 125).

33. Cf. *Phormio* 339. That dinners provided with *symbolae* were not considered ordinary events in Rome even much later is evident in *Biblia Vulgata*, Proverbs 23.21, where *dantes symbola* is used for the Hebrew *zolel*, which means a frivolous squanderer or glutton.

34. On the identification of the *forum infimum*, see Ussing 1875–92, 2:566.

35. Cf. Richardson 1992, 68; H. Bauer in Steinby 1993, 226.

36. Paulus's Festus 40 L: "canalicolae forenses homines pauperes dicti, quod circa canales fori consisterent" ("Poor men who hang about the forum are called gutter dwellers, because they stand around the gutters of the forum").

37. Friedrich 1891, 711; Bosscher 1903, 86; Corbett 1986, 31.

38. *Asin.* 489; *Bacch.* 267; *Men.* 520; *Pseud.* 1173; *Truc.* 299.

39. Huelsen 1909, 149–53; Johnson 1927, 48–53; Gioffredi 1943, 268–71; Welin 1953, 75–96; Richardson 1973, 223–24; Small 1982, 79–82. For the history of the debate regarding the location of the praetors' courts, see Moore 1991a, 352 n. 27.

40. Andreau (1968, 481 n. 1; 1987a, 161; 1987b, 335 n. 14) has suggested that those lending money here are not *argentarii* like Lyco, but moneylenders like the *danistae* of *Epidicus* and *Mostellaria*. Though Andreau is correct that Plautus distinguishes between moneylenders and *argentarii*, and he usually presents the *argentarii* as keeping money on deposit rather than lending money (Andreau, 1987a, 157–59; cf. Barlow 1978, 68–72), Plautus ignores the distinction in *Curculio*, where Curculio accuses Lyco and all *argentarii* of destroying people with *faenus* ("interest," 508; *argentarii* are also clearly lenders of money at *Cas.* 25). Nor is it likely that the *tabernae veteres*, which were also called *tabernae argentariae* (Coarelli 1985, 142), lacked *argentarii*. Cf. Frank 1933, 206.

41. That *quibus credas male* are *argentarii* seems more likely than that they are slave-dealers (*pace* Harris 1980, 138 n. 90; Spranger 1984, 62).

42. De Robertis (1963, 57 n. 25) argues that *sese venditant* is a scornful reference to manual workers. In *Miles gloriosus*, however, after Sceledrus sees Philocomasium in the arms of Pleusicles, he complains: "non ego possum quae ipsa sese venditat tutarier" ("I can't guard her when she sells herself," 312). The direct parallel, and a reference in a later writer to prostitutes on the *vicus Tuscus* (pseudo-Acro ad Hor. *Sat.* 2.3.228), suggests that Plautus speaks not of workers here, but of prostitutes.

43. Cf. Lilja 1983, 30.

44. For the Romanness of *lanii* in particular, see Fraenkel 1960, 124–25, 408–13. *Haruspices* are of Etruscan origin and therefore would be a Roman rather than a Greek phenomenon. Pliny's assertion (*HN* 18.107) that professional bakers did not work in Rome until the time of the Third Macedonian War (171–168 B.C.E.) is probably wrong. If it is correct, the *pistor* here is a miller rather than a baker. Cf. Moore 1991a, 355 n. 37.

45. *Pistores: Asin.* 200, 709; *Bacch.* 781; *Capt.* 160–61; *Epid.* 121; *Mostell.* 17;

Pseud. 494; *Trin.* 407; Naevius *CRF* 114; Ter. *An.* 199; *Haut.* 530; *Phorm.* 249.

Lanii: *Capt.* 818, 905; *Epid.* 199; *Pseud.* 197, 327; *Trin.* 407; Ter. *Eun.* 257.

Haruspices: *Amph.* 1132; *Mil.* 693; *Poen.* 463, 746, 791, 1206, 1209; Naevius *CRF* 20–24; Ter. *Phorm.* 709.

46. On the textual and interpretive problems in this line, see Moore 1991a, 356–58.

47. Ibid., 357 n. 50; Richardson 1992, 406.

48. Cf. *Capt.* 489, where Ergasilus refers to a dishonest cartel of oil merchants on the Velabrum.

49. Cf. Gaggiotti 1985, 60.

50. Saunders 1913, 93–95. Cf. Staccioli 1961; N. Purcell in Steinby 1995, 332.

51. Ussing 1875–92, 2:565; Huelsen 1909, 14; Duckworth 1955, 59.

52. Possible exceptions are the fish market, which may have been obscured from view by the basilica, the area behind the temple of Castor and Pollux (though the audience would have been able to see the temple itself), and the Velabrum, which may have been hidden behind the *tabernae veteres*. Also visible to many of the spectators over the back of the stage would be the Capitolium, referred to earlier (269).

53. Huelsen 1909, 5; Saunders 1913, 95.

54. On the balconies, called *Maeniana*, see Coarelli 1985, 146; Gaggiotti 1985, 60; Richardson 1992, 375–76.

55. Cf. *Trin.* 858, where the Sycophant says of Megaronides, who hired him: "ipse ornamenta a chorago haec sumpsit suo periculo" ("He himself took this costume from the *choragus* at his own risk").

56. Cf. Slater 1991, 3–8.

57. See especially Freyburger 1986, 103–225; Nörr 1989, 102–3; Owens 1994, 399–401.

CHAPTER 8

1. On the satirical nature of *Truculentus*, cf. Della Corte 1952, 280–88; Enk 1964; Grimal 1970, 95–97; 1971–74, 540–43; Dessen 1977; Konstan 1983, 142–64; Lefèvre, Stärk, and Vogt-Spira 1991, 189–99; and *contra*, Broccia 1982, 157–60.

2. Lefèvre, however, proposes that the play may be modeled not on a Greek play, but on an Italian farce (Lefèvre, Stärk, and Vogt-Spira 1991, 178).

3. Cf. Fantham 1975, 50–52, 63–66; Henry 1985; Brown 1990.

4. Schuhmann 1975, 213–19; 1978, 101; Bradley 1987, 147; Evans 1991, 139–42, 144.

5. Galinsky 1969.

6. So Leo 1913, 144; and Fraenkel 1960, 144–45. On the semantic distinction between *meretrix* and *scortum*, see Adams 1983, 321–27. Note, however, that *scortum* can be used of any prostitute, regardless of her pretensions, if the speaker wants to produce a more pejorative effect.

7. Comic influence: Scafuro 1989, and bibliography cited there. Historicity of Hispala: Tierney 1947, 116; Pailler 1988, 369; Gruen 1990, 64–65.

8. Cf. the descriptions of the houses of the pimps Lycus (*Poen.* 831–44) and Ballio (*Pseud.* 173–229).

9. According to Bickford (1922, 60), *Truculentus* is 28% soliloquy. Only *Mercator* has a higher percentage of lines of soliloquy (31%), and the figure for that play includes Charinus's long prologue.

10. So Dessen 1977, 148.

11. Lindsay's text. Leo reads † *mulier*.

12. Schutter 1952, 149; Enk 1953, 1:28–29. Cf. Tatum 1983, 209 n. 2.

13. Enk's text.

14. Tatum's translation.

15. Cf. Lefèvre, Stärk, and Vogt-Spira 1991, 182.

16. Cf. Schutter 1952, 150–51; Gruen 1990, 129–33; Goldberg 1995, 111. Because he is associated syntactically with *milites*, I am inclined to identify Stratophanes' Homeronides as a *miles gloriosus* from a lost comedy. Frank (1939, 86–87) proposed that Plautus makes a topical allusion to Ennius, who described the exploits of Marcus Fulvius Nobilior, and who claimed to be a reincarnation of Homer (Lucr. 1.120–26). Richard Thomas, in responding to an earlier version of my argument, proposed that Homeronides may be Livius Andronicus, the first writer of Roman comedy (hence the first Roman to produce braggart soldiers) and, as a translator of the *Odyssey*, metaphorically a descendant of Homer. On the possible identities of Homeronides, cf. Enk 1953, 2:117–18.

17. On the Roman qualities of Plautus's *milites gloriosi* in general, see Hanson 1965, 52–61; and *contra*, Maurach 1966, 677–78.

18. Phronesium recognizes at the end of the monologue that Stratophanes has been speaking, but she does not recognize who he is; and neither she nor Astaphium appears to understand what he says.

19. Frayn 1984, 168.

20. Cf. Dessen 1977, 152: "All of Rome's income from business ventures in the city, rural wealth, and the spoils of war is being dissipated in the same unprofitable manner."

21. On the importance of *parsimonia* in the traditional Roman value system, see Moore 1989, 133–34.

22. Cf. Ramage 1960, 68–70; 1973, 29, 33–34.

23. Schutter 1952, 151–52; Enk 1953, 1:30, 2:173.

24. E.g., *Aul.*; Men. *Sam.*; Ter. *Ad.* Cf. Men. *Epit.* and Ter. *Hec.*

25. The last scene may also contain yet another conspicuous allusion to Italy, if we accept Schoell's emendation of line 942, which includes a reference to a Campanian. Cf. Enk 1953, 2:211.

26. On Plautus's portrayal of women, see Leffingwell 1918, 39–56; Grimal 1970; Schuhmann 1975 and 1978; Petrone 1989; Pérez Gómez 1990; Gerdes 1995. Cf. Richlin 1984, on the importance of women as an "out-group" in Roman satire.

27. Some examples for individual women: *Asin.* 16–24, 43, 87, 893–95, 900–901; *Cas.* 227, 353–54; *Cist.* 175; *Epid.* 173–80; *Men.* 127–34, 1160; *Merc.* 760–61; *Rud.* 895–96, 1203–4; *Trin.* 42, 58–65. Women in general: *Amph.* 836; *Mil.* 185–94, 456, 464–65; *Poen.* 875–76, 1145; *Rud.* 1114. Prostitutes: *Asin.* 220–25; *Bacch.* 40; *Mostell.* 190; cf. Ter. *Eun.* 931–33; *Hec.* 756–57, 834. On Plautus's portrayals of wives, see Chapter 9.

28. E.g., *Aul.* 123–26, 138–40; *Epid.* 546; *Mil.* 887–90; *Poen.* 210–31, 240–47, 1201–4; *Rud.* 685–86. Cf. Petrone 1977, 76–77.

29. See especially *Mil.* 1292–95; *Poen.* 210–15; *Stich.* 744–47; Livy 34.7.7–10. Cf. Wyke 1994, 136.

30. *Rem bonam* is a plausible suggestion of Buecheler for the manuscripts' hopelessly corrupt *romabo*. Schoell, who provided the correction of the manuscripts' *quid* to *quis* and *faciam* to *faciat*, made the intriguing suggestion of *Romae habeo*—"I live in Rome"—for *romabo*. The emendation has not won support (Enk proposes "si quis quid ob amorem animust facere"; both Leo and Lindsay keep the crux), and indeed, it seems unlikely that even Plautus would be quite so audacious about re-

moving the pretense of a Greek setting. Still, Schoell's proposal is in keeping with the spirit of *Truculentus*, for if Phronesium herself does not live at Rome, the play suggests that she and all the play's other characters have their equivalents in Rome, and that men like her lovers can be found among the spectators themselves.

31. The redundancy of an additional line, "spectatores, bene valete, plaudite atque exurgite" (968), suggests that it is an alternate ending used in productions after Plautus's death (Enk 1953, 2:216).

CHAPTER 9

1. See Anderson 1979, 334–35; and Riemer 1992, 53 n. 16, on the probability that Plautus added these words against wives to his Greek original.

2. Cf. Caecilius *CRF* 163. Other statements made by Plautine characters against individual wives: *Asin.* 19–24, 43, 87, 893–95, 900–901; *Men.* 1160; *Merc.* 760–61; *Rud.* 895–96, 1203–4.

3. E.g., *Aul.* 167–69; *Epid.* 180; *Mil.* 679–81; *Mostell.* 703–10. Cf. Caecilius *CRF* 144–46.

4. Cf. Segal 1987, 23–29.

5. Cf. *Cas.* 497–98; *Merc.* 556–57; *Rud.* 905.

6. See Rogers 1966, 266 and passim. For Aristophanes, cf. Taafe 1993, 54–55, 89, and passim. For Greek New Comedy, cf. Hunter 1985, 91. For twentieth-century American and British situation comedies, cf. Gray 1994, 46–57 and passim. Nor is mockery of wives a phenomenon only of Western comedy: it is, for example, a central theme in a number of Japanese Kyogen plays (e.g., Kenny 1989, 49–52, 58–69).

7. Pomeroy 1975, 180–81; Evans 1991, 26–33.

8. See Cato *ORF* 158; Schuhmann 1975, 90–124, 200–208; 1976, 32; 1977; Evans 1991, 50–100; Treggiari 1991, 329–31. Stärk (1990) argues that Plautus's *uxores dotatae* reflect not historical conditions, but the influence of popular farce.

9. Cf. Pomeroy 1975, 155; Hallett 1984, 91–95; Dixon 1985; 1992, 71–79; Wiles 1989, 41; Evans 1991, 17–20, 50–100. It has also been suggested (Veyne 1978, 48; Hallett 1984, 211–43) that marriages in the Roman Republic tended to involve less mutual affection than is expected in most modern marriages. Cf. Bradley 1991, 6–8; and *contra*, Treggiari 1991, 243–61; Dixon 1992, 83–90.

10. On the events surrounding the repeal, see especially Pomeroy 1975, 180; Culham 1982; Hallett 1984, 229–30; Evans 1991, 16, 63–64.

11. See Scullard 1973, 257; Astin 1978, 25–26; Johnston 1980, 147; Briscoe 1981, 39–40. Kienast (1954, 20–22), however, argues that Livy wrote the speech with Cato's speech before him. Cato later delivered a speech *de vestitu et vehiculis* (*ORF* 93). Cf. Wagner 1864, 15–16; Evans 1991, 63.

12. Cato in a later speech expressed similar concerns about husbands unable to control wives with dowries (*ORF* 158).

13. Cf. Schutter 1952, 21–22; Stockert 1983, 136.

14. Cf. Culham 1982, 790.

15. E.g., Harvey 1986, 300–301; Gruen 1990, 144–45. Megadorus also refers to dowered wives' carriages and purple earlier in the play, when he objects to his sister's suggestion that he marry a woman with a large dowry (168–69). The echoes of the debate would have the same effect whether the *Aulularia* was first produced shortly before or shortly after the law's repeal.

16. Catonian: Schuhmann 1975, 208; Cugusi 1991, 291–92. Included to please misogynists: Perelli 1978, 309. Cf. Evans 1991, 64.

17. On the mysterious reference to the *miles impransus* (the soldier left without his lunch), see Fraenkel 1960, 130–31; Gabba 1979, 410–11; Rosivach 1989.

18. Cf. Johnston 1980, 148–49; Gruen 1990, 146.

19. Of the numerous passages in Plautus and Terence where a speaker says *sequere* ("follow me") to his interlocutor and then leaves the stage (e.g., *Merc.* 542; *Persa* 328; *Poen.* 808), there are only three other places where the person ordered to follow speaks a monologue after the interlocutor has left. Two of these monologues are very short and would provide little delay (*Capt.* 766–67; Ter. *Hec.* 879–80); before the third monologue, Epidicus warns Periphanes that he will not follow him yet (*Epid.* 305). Cf. Hough 1940b, 46; Frost 1988, 14.

20. In fact, Syra does not necessarily disobey Eutychus's order to follow: as her entrance revealed (672–75), she is remarkably slow, so that it may just take her the time it takes to say her monologue to get in the door! Cf. Leo 1912, 120–21.

21. Cf. Hunter 1985, 86–87.

22. For a far different perspective on the double standard roughly contemporary with Plautus, see Cato *ORF* 222.

23. The average length of Plautus's extant plays is approximately 1058 lines (I have not counted the *alter exitus* of *Poenulus*). Unless Otto Zwierlein's extreme view regarding the amount of interpolation in the extant plays is correct (see Zwierlein 1990, 1991a; 1991b; 1992), the original average must have been considerably higher, as *Amphitruo*, *Aulularia*, *Bacchides*, and *Cistellaria* are all missing large portions.

24. On the similarities between *Casina* and *Mercator*, cf. O'Bryhim 1989, 85–87.

25. Cf. Forehand 1973a, 240; Cody 1976, 454–61; Chiarini 1978, 119–20; Slater 1985b, 82–84, 93; O'Bryhim 1989, 96–102; Beacham 1992, 232 n. 20; Sutton 1993, 104–6. Tatum, however, argues that even as they laugh at Lysidamus, the spectators feel a "wry affection for him" (1983, 89). For possible connections between Lysidamus and contemporaries of Plautus, see Hallett 1996.

26. While a portion of the prologue must postdate Plautus, as it refers explicitly to a revival, most of the prologue is probably authentic. See Leo 1912, 207 n. 2; Abel 1955, 55–61; MacCary and Willcock 1976, 97; and *contra*, Slater 1985b, 70–74.

27. See Cody 1976, 461–76; Lefèvre 1979; O'Bryhim 1989.

28. On the similarity between Cleostrata and other stock *matronae* such as Artemona in *Asinaria* or the *matrona* in *Menaechmi*, see Schuhmann 1975, 90–110; Gerdes 1995, 49–52.

29. Cf. Treggiari 1991, 441.

30. Cf. Beacham 1992, 94. Beacham's chapter on *Casina* (86–116) is a useful guide to staging throughout the play.

31. On the importance of wool-working in the life of an ideal Roman matron, see Pomeroy 1975, 199–200; Treggiari 1991, 243–44.

32. *Ei foras* ("Get out of my house!") is a Roman formula for divorce. Cf. Rosenmeyer 1995, 206–7, 212–13. For similar sentiments, see *Men.* 120–22, 784–802; and the debate between Adriana and Luciana in Shakespeare's *Comedy of Errors* 2.1.

33. Cf. Treggiari 1991, 29.

34. Slater argues that lines 151–62 are a monologue, and that they allow Cleostrata to "bring her case for sympathy directly to the audience" (1985b, 157). It seems more likely, however, that Cleostrata addresses most, if not all, of those lines to Pardalisca, who follows her out of the house, and whom she addresses explicitly in 148.

35. It is not clear how much of Lysidamus's monologue Cleostrata actually hears: she does not react explicitly to anything he says (cf. the similar situation at *Men.* 562–603). Since she announces his entrance before he begins speaking (213), however, she is clearly onstage watching through his entire monologue.

36. While Cleostrata only learns the details of Lysidamus's plot several scenes later, she knows from the play's beginning that Lysidamus wants Casina for himself (58, 150, 196, 243, 266, 276–78). On the role of this extra knowledge in drawing the audience's sympathies toward Cleostrata, cf. Slater 1985b, 74–75.

37. Lindsay's text.

38. Cf. Lefèvre 1979, 327; Anderson 1993, 55–58.

39. On the progress of Chalinus's rapport, see Chapter 2.

40. See Hiatt 1946, 65. For a character overhearing another character's monologue from offstage, cf. *Mercator* 477.

41. Cf. Duckworth 1952, 107.

42. Williams 1958b, 17–19; O'Bryhim 1989, 89–90. Williams proposes that the lines here are spoken not by Pardalisca, but by Cleostrata herself.

43. Cf. Petrone 1983, 11–12; Slater 1985b, 88.

44. The request makes Lysidamus seem like a slave who fears punishment (cf. *Mostell.* 354–61). He goes on to suggest that he should imitate a fugitive slave, and to fear for his shoulder blades, as slaves often do (cf. *Asin.* 315; *Epid.* 125; *Persa* 32; *Poen.* 153; *Trin.* 1009). He then follows the formula with which clever slaves end other comedies: he seeks forgiveness using an advocate (Myrrhina), and he promises that he will be subject to punishment if he does wrong again (cf. the end of *Mostellaria*). Cf. Forehand 1973a, 249; Slater 1985b, 89–90.

45. Cf. Schutter 1952, 49–50; MacCary and Willcock 1976, 207; Slater 1985b, 91–92. The effects of the allusion proposed here would be the same whether, as most scholars have argued, Myrrhina's *nunc Bacchae nullae ludunt* means that the rites have already been suppressed, or, as Gruen proposes (1990, 151 n. 145), she means only that the rites are not onstage at this moment.

46. MacCary 1975.

47. Cf. Hallett 1989, 69.

48. The tattered state of the manuscript between lines 899 and 989 does not appear to have affected the number of lines significantly.

49. Cf. Forehand 1973a, 251.

50. Compare the epilogue of *Truculentus*, which capped an alliance between lovers and spectators that had pervaded the play. Here, the original alliance between spectators and Lysidamus has eroded in the course of the play, only to be ironically assumed at play's end.

51. So Forehand 1973a, 254. Cf. Slater 1985b, 93.

CHAPTER 10

1. Lack of physical distinction: cf. Snowden 1983, 70–71; Thompson 1989, 12–20. Manumission: cf. Hopkins 1978, 115–18; Finley 1980, 97–98.

2. Cf. Buckland 1908, 1–3; Watson 1987, 7–8.

3. Bradley 1994, 27.

4. The evidence is collected by Bradley (1994, 122–24, 142–45, and passim). See also Westermann 1955, 77; Freyburger 1977; Finley 1980, 117–20; Wiedemann 1981, 61–77; Patterson 1982, 89–92 and passim.

5. Philosophy: see especially Davis 1966, 62–63, 66–82; Guthrie 1969, 155–60; Vogt 1975, 14; Cambiano 1987; Brunt 1993, 351–56; Garnsey 1996, 64–72 and

passim. Euripides and New Comedy: see especially Dumont 1987, 524–75 (for a different view of slaves in New Comedy, see Wiles 1988a). Lack of abolitionist movement or serious reform: see especially Treggiari 1969, 241–43; Yavetz 1988, 115–18; Bradley 1994, 134–40; Garnsey 1996, 237–40 and passim.

6. Cf. Vogt 1975, 129; Bradley 1987, 28–29.

7. Cf. Bradley 1987, 38–39.

8. Cf. Garton 1972, 171–72; Dumont 1987, 523–24.

9. See especially *Dig.* 1.5.4.2. Cf. Watson 1987, 8; Bradley 1994, 25–26.

10. Sall. *Cat.* 35.3. *Honestare* is used with the plural *honoribus* at *Pan. Lat.* 3.1.3 and 3.25.5.

11. Leo's deletion of this line is unnecessary.

12. *Persa* 390; *Pseud.* 581. Cf. *Trin.* 346. Plautus uses *virtute deum et maiorum nostrum* elsewhere only at *Aul.* 166, where Megadorus is addressing his sister, Eunomia.

13. Note Aristophontes' response when Hegio speaks of Tyndarus's father: "quem patrem, qui servos est?" ("What do you mean, 'father'? He's a slave!" 574). Cf. Dumont 1987, 415–16. On the importance of "natal alienation" in defining the slave, see Patterson 1982, 35–76.

14. Cf. Konstan 1983, 70; Dumont 1987, 592.

15. Had Tyndarus been a Roman, he would not legally be a slave, having been kidnapped. Cf. Watson 1987, 20–21.

16. The author of the Greek original of *Captivi* was clearly also interested in the question of slavery (Grimal 1969; Kraus 1977; Konstan 1983, 57–72), but much of the metatheatrical manipulation of slave roles is probably original to Plautus.

17. See Bieber 1961, 155–56; Questa 1982; Wiles 1991, 133–40, 150–87.

18. *Amph.* 141; *Mil.* 151. Cf. Fantham 1973, 199.

19. Lowe (1991, 35–36) makes a strong case that Philocrates and Tyndarus did not appear onstage at the beginning of Plautus's Greek original.

20. E.g., *Amph.* 280; *Asin.* 301, 342, 549–50; *Mostell.* 1065. Cf. *Aul.* 347; *Persa* 21–22; *Rud.* 476–77.

21. *Bacch.* 862; *Epid.* 722–31; *Truc.* 838. Cf. Ketterer 1986b, 101–2, 107–8.

22. On the significance of the chains, cf. Ketterer 1986b, 113–18; Dumont 1987, 390–92.

23. Cf. *Cist.* 172–73; *Curc.* 518, 698.

24. Spranger 1984, 29 (though Spranger is wrong to suggest that Tyndarus never acts like a slave [27]).

25. See Brotherton 1926, 50–51.

26. Cf. Fraenkel 1960, 7–20.

27. Cf. *Mil.* 386, 464–68; *Persa* 622–35; *Poen.* 647–84; *Pseud.* 969–1037; Petrone 1983, 86.

28. On Tyndarus's seriousness here, see Franko 1995, 160–66.

29. Lists of abstract qualities that have abandoned him (517–23, 529; cf. *Mostell.* 350–51); clauses beginning with *nisi* (529–30, 539; cf. *Epid.* 81–84); deliberative questions (531, 535–36; cf. *Asin.* 258; *Epid.* 98; *Pseud.* 395–96); military imagery (534; cf. *Asin.* 106; *Persa* 753–56; *Pseud.* 580–83, 1027; Fraenkel 1960, 223–26); a curse (537–38; cf. *Mostell.* 655–56). On Tyndarus's similarity to a stock *servus callidus* here, cf. Pasquali 1927; Muecke 1986, 229.

30. That such ambush scenes were very familiar is obvious from Simo's claim that he will ambush Pseudolus in a different manner from masters in other comedies (*Pseud.* 1239–41).

31. Cf., e.g., *Mostell.* 1116; *Pseud.* 460–61.

32. Cf. Leach 1969b, 285; Segal 1987, 205.

33. Terence achieves a similar effect in *Andria*: the meter changes to iambic senarius as Simo has his slave Davos dragged off the stage (866). Cf. Bruder 1970, 44.

34. Cf. Petrone 1983, 42.

35. *Fallacia*: cf. *Asin.* 250, 266; *Poen.* 195; *Pseud.* 672, 705a, 765; Brotherton 1926, 8–9. *Doli*: cf. *Asin.* 312; *Bacch.* 643, 950, 952, 1070; *Epid.* 88, 375; *Mil.* 147, 198, 773, 1154; *Mostell.* 716; *Persa* 480; *Poen.* 1110; *Pseud.* 580, 614, 672, 705a, 927, 932; Brotherton 1926, 14–15. *Docte*: cf. *Epid.* 373; *Mil.* 466, 1087; *Persa* 148, 551; *Pseud.* 765.

36. Cf. Segal 1987, 199.

37. I do not mean to suggest that free *adulescentes* in Plautus do not make jokes: indeed, some of them are quite ridiculous. Pure unmotivated silliness like Philocrates', however, is more typical of slaves.

38. On Ergasilus, cf. Leach 1969b.

39. On the *lorarii* here as a Plautine innovation, see Lowe 1991, 33–38. On the sentiments of the *lorarii*, cf. Spranger 1984, 21–22; Dumont 1987, 391, 472–77.

40. *Lorarii* speak only a few words in *Pseudolus* (159) and *Rudens* (764, 826–36, 879–80), and they cry out when they are driven off by Messenio in *Menaechmi* (1015–16). Elsewhere they are mute.

41. Or one of the *lorarii*: it is not clear whether they speak individually or as a group.

42. Cf. Konstan 1983, 70–71; Dumont 1987, 464–65.

43. E.g., *Asin.* 310–16; *Bacch.* 649–61; *Epid.* 10; *Mostell.* 1178–79; *Persa* 21–22; *Pseud.* 932–33; *Trin.* 413.

44. Cf. Moore 1991b.

45. See Lindsay 1900, 320; Schutter 1952, 29, 47–48; Wellesley 1955, 298–99; Franko 1995, 169.

46. On *patricius*, see Chapter 3, note 40.

47. Lindsay's text. The manuscripts read "illi qui astant, hi [or i] stant ambo, non sedent." Even for a Plautine prologue, this makes an exceptionally insipid joke, and it requires that *illi* and *i* or *hi* refer to the same persons, a very unusual usage. Lindsay's addition of a single *a* gives the line a much more reasonable sense and removes the need for more radical emendation.

48. Lindsay 1900, 117.

49. Moore 1994.

50. "Vos qui potestis ope vestra censerier" ("You who can be counted among the propertied classes in the census," 15).

51. Cf. Hallidie 1891, 86.

52. Cf. Spranger 1984, 6, 109, 118; Anderson 1993, 141. Dumont (1974; 1987, 588–93) likewise assumes too much when he concludes that *Captivi* is an antiwar play.

This chapter was in press before I obtained Thalmann 1996. Thalmann proposes that *Captivi* combines the "suspicious" model of slavery, according to which slaves (e.g., Stalagmus) are by nature inferior, and the "benevolent" model, which acknowledges the possibility of the "good slave" (scil. Tyndarus) and assimilates the master-slave relationship to kinship. Through this juxtaposition of models, Thalmann argues, "*Captivi* negotiates anxieties surrounding slavery and the master-slave relation in order finally to exorcise them" (116). A number of Thalmann's arguments parallel my own, but to my mind his reading of the play does not account for Tyndarus's characterization as a *servus callidus* or for the play's other metatheatrical ironies.

CONCLUSION

1. Segal 1987, 7.

2. Plautus and New Comedy: Fantham 1977, 27 n. 13. Authority figures: see Chapter 2, note 36. Separation of theater and reality: Sutton 1993, 64. Second-century society: Wiles 1988b, 263–65; Anderson 1993, 143–44.

3. On the importance of the rejection of everyday morality and authority in both ancient and modern comedy, see especially Barber 1959; Bakhtin 1968, 1–58; Donaldson 1970; Carrière 1979, 29–32; Rösler 1986, 36–39; Halliwell 1991, 294–96.

4. On the extent to which Saturnalian inversion does not preclude social commentary, see especially Rayner 1987, 5–23; Lada 1996, 100–102.

5. E.g., Della Corte 1952, 81–93; Petrone 1977, 20–24; Dingel 1981; Cugusi 1991; Hoffmann 1991, 186. On Cato's views, which are not as one-sided as has often been thought, see Astin 1978, 91–103, 157–81, and passim; Gruen 1992, 52–83. Anderson (1993, 133–51) argues that Plautus joins with his audience in their anti-Hellenic bias.

6. E.g., Mommsen 1907, 894–97; Perelli 1978; Gizewski 1989, 91–93; Sutton 1993, 55–108.

7. Gruen 1990, 157.

8. Different perspectives: cf. Styan 1975, 239–41. Potential for subversion: Davis 1975, 97–151; Bristol 1985, 26–39 and passim.

WORKS CITED

ABBREVIATIONS

Abbreviations of ancient works are those in *The Oxford Classical Dictionary*, 3d ed., edited by Simon Hornblower and Antony Spawforth (Oxford: Oxford University Press, 1996).

CGF	*Comicorum Graecorum fragmenta in papyris reperta*. Ed. Colin Austin. Berlin: de Gruyter, 1973.
CIL	*Corpus inscriptionum Latinarum*. Berlin: Reimer, de Gruyter, 1863 –.
CRF	*Comicorum Romanorum fragmenta*. Ed. Otto Ribbeck. 3d ed. Leipzig: Teubner, 1898.
Jocelyn	*The Tragedies of Ennius: The Fragments*. Ed. H. D. Jocelyn. Cambridge: Cambridge University Press, 1967.
Keil	*Grammatici Latini*. Ed. Heinrich Keil. 8 vols. Leipzig: Teubner, 1855 – 78.
Koerte	*Menandri quae supersunt*. Ed. Alfred Koerte. Part 2, revised by Andreas Thierfelder. Leipzig: Teubner, 1959.
Lindsay	*T. Macci Plauti comoediae*. Ed. Wallace M. Lindsay. 2 vols. Oxford: Clarendon, 1904 – 5.
LSJ	*A Greek-English Lexicon*. Compiled by Henry George Liddell and Robert Scott, revised by Henry Stuart Jones. Oxford: Clarendon, 1968.
Nixon	*Plautus*. Trans. Paul Nixon. 5 vols. Cambridge, Mass.: Harvard University Press, 1916 – 38.
OLD	*Oxford Latin Dictionary*. Ed. P.G.W. Glare. Oxford: Clarendon, 1968 – 82.
ORF	*Oratorum Romanorum fragmenta liberae rei publicae*. 2d ed. Ed. Enrica Malcovati. Turin: I. B. Paravia, 1955.
PCG	*Poetae comici Graeci*. Ed. R. Kassel and C. Austin. Berlin: de Gruyter, 1983 –.
Sandbach	*Menandri reliquiae selectae*. Ed. F. H. Sandbach. Oxford: Clarendon, 1990.
TLL	*Thesaurus Linguae Latinae*. Leipzig: Teubner, 1900 –.
TRF	*Tragicorum Romanorum fragmenta*. Ed. Otto Ribbeck. 3d ed. Leipzig: Teubner, 1897.
Warmington	*Remains of Old Latin*. Trans. E. H. Warmington. 4 vols. Cambridge, Mass.: Harvard University Press, 1935 – 40.

Abel, Karlhans. 1955. *Die Plautusprologe*. Mülheim (Ruhr)-Saarn: Carl Fabri.

Abel, Lionel. 1963. *Metatheatre: A New View of Dramatic Form*. New York: Hill and Wang.

Adams, J. N. 1983. "Words for 'Prostitute' in Latin." *Rheinisches Museum für Philologie* 126: 321 – 58.

Allen, F. D. 1896. "On '*os columnatum*' (Plautus M.G. 211) and Ancient Instruments of Confinement." *Harvard Studies in Classical Philology* 7: 37 – 64.

Altheim, Franz. 1938. *A History of Roman Religion*. Trans. Harold Mattingly. London: Methuen.

Amatucci, Aurelio-Giuseppe. 1904. Review of Hermann Bosscher, *De Plauti Curculione disputatio*. *Rivista di Filologia e d'Istruzione Classica* 32: 329–32.

Anderson, William S. 1979. "Plautus' *Trinummus*: The Absurdity of Officious Morality." *Traditio* 35: 333–45.

———. 1983. "Chalinus *armiger* in Plautus' *Casina*." *Illinois Classical Studies* 8: 11–21.

———. 1993. *Barbarian Play: Plautus' Roman Comedy*. Toronto: University of Toronto Press.

André, Jean-Marie. 1983. "L'Argent chez Plaute: Autour du *Curculio*." *Vichiana* 12: 15–35.

Andreau, Jean. 1968. "Banque grecque et banque romaine dans le théâtre de Plaute et de Térence." *Mélanges d'Archéologie et d'Histoire de l'École Française de Rome* 80: 461–526.

———. 1987a. "L'Espace de la vie financière à Rome." In *L'Urbs: Espace urbain et histoire (Ier siècle av. J. C.–IIIe siècle ap. J. C.)*, pp. 157–74. Rome: École Française de Rome.

———. 1987b. *La Vie financière dans le monde romain: Les Métiers de manieurs d'argent (IVe siècle av. J.C.–IIIe siècle ap. J. C.)*. Rome: École Française de Rome.

Arcellaschi, André. 1978. "Politique et religion dans le *Pseudolus*." *Revue des Études Latines* 56: 115–41.

Arnott, W. Geoffrey. 1972. "Targets, Techniques, and Tradition in Plautus' *Stichus*." *Bulletin of the Institute of Classical Studies of the University of London* 19: 54–79.

———. 1985. "Terence's Prologues." *Papers of the Liverpool Latin Seminar* 5: 1–7.

Astin, Alan E. 1978. *Cato the Censor*. Oxford: Clarendon.

Bader, Bernd. 1970. "Der verlorene Anfang der plautinischen 'Bacchides'." *Rheinisches Museum für Philologie* 113: 304–23.

Bailey, Cyril. 1932. *Phases in the Religion of Ancient Rome*. Berkeley: University of California Press.

Bain, David. 1977. *Actors and Audience: A Study of Asides and Related Conventions in Greek Drama*. Oxford: Oxford University Press.

Bakhtin, Mikhail. 1968. *Rabelais and His World*. Translated by Helene Iswolsky. Cambridge, Mass.: MIT Press.

Barber, C. L. 1959. *Shakespeare's Festive Comedy: A Study of Dramatic Form and Its Relation to Social Custom*. Princeton: Princeton University Press.

Barchiesi, Marino. 1969. "Plauto e il 'metateatro' antico." *Il Verri* 31: 113–30.

Barlow, Charles T. 1978. "Bankers, Moneylenders, and Interest Rates in the Roman Republic." Ph.D. diss., University of North Carolina, Chapel Hill.

Barrow, R. H. 1949. *The Romans*. Harmondsworth: Penguin.

Barsby, John, ed. and trans. 1986. *Plautus: Bacchides*. Oak Park, Ill.: Bolchazy-Carducci.

———. 1995. "Plautus' *Pseudolus* as Improvisatory Drama." In Benz, Stärk, and Vogt-Spira 1995, 55–70.

Beacham, Richard C. 1992. *The Roman Theatre and Its Audience*. Cambridge, Mass.: Harvard University Press.

Beare, William. 1964. *The Roman Stage: A Short History of Latin Drama in the Time of the Republic*. 3d ed. London: Methuen.

Beckerman, Bernard. 1970. *Dynamics of Drama: Theory and Method of Analysis.* New York: Alfred A. Knopf.

———. 1990. *Theatrical Presentation: Performer, Audience and Act.* Edited by Gloria Brim Beckerman and William Coco. New York: Routledge.

Bennett, Susan. 1990. *Theatre Audiences: A Theory of Production and Reception.* London: Routledge.

Benz, Lore. 1990. "Megaronides Censorius—Eine anticatonische Konzeption im plautinischen Trinummus?" In *Theater und Gesellschaft im Imperium Romanum,* ed. Jürgen Blänsdorf, pp. 55–68. Tübingen: Francke Verlag.

Benz, Lore, Ekkehard Stärk, and **Gregor Vogt-Spira**, eds. 1995. *Plautus und die Tradition des Stegreifspiels.* Tübingen: Gunter Narr.

Berry, Ralph. 1989. "Hamlet and the Audience: The Dynamics of a Relationship." In *Shakespeare and the Sense of Performance: Essays in the Tradition of Performance Criticism in Honor of Bernard Beckerman,* ed. Marvin and Ruth Thompson, pp. 24–28. Newark: University of Delaware Press.

Bickford, John Dean. 1922. *Soliloquy in Ancient Comedy.* Princeton: John Dean Bickford.

Bieber, Margarete. 1961. *The History of the Greek and Roman Theater.* 2d ed. Princeton: Princeton University Press.

Billeter, Gustav. 1898. *Geschichte des Zinsfusses im griechisch-römischen Altertum bis auf Justinian.* Leipzig: Teubner.

Blancké, Wilton Wallace. 1918. *The Dramatic Values in Plautus.* New York: Humphrey.

Blänsdorf, Jürgen. 1978. "Voraussetzungen und Entstehung der römischen Komödie." In *Das römische Drama,* ed. Eckard Lefèvre, pp. 91–134. Darmstadt: Wissenschaftliche Buchgesellschaft.

———. 1982. "Die Komödienintrige als Spiel im Spiel." *Antike und Abendland* 28: 131–54.

Blundell, John. 1980. *Menander and the Monologue.* Göttingen: Vandenhoeck und Ruprecht.

Bondanella, Peter. 1987. *The Eternal City: Roman Images in the Modern World.* Chapel Hill: University of North Carolina Press.

Bosscher, Hermann. 1903. *De Plauti Curculione Disputatio.* Leiden: Brill.

Bradley, Keith R. 1987. *Slaves and Masters in the Roman Empire: A Study in Social Control.* New York: Oxford University Press.

———. 1991. *Discovering the Roman Family: Studies in Roman Social History.* New York: Oxford University Press.

———. 1994. *Slavery and Society at Rome.* Cambridge: Cambridge University Press.

Brecht, Bertolt. 1964. *Brecht on Theatre: The Development of an Aesthetic.* Edited and translated by John Willett. New York: Hill and Wang.

———. 1967. *Gesammelte Werke in acht Bänden: VII: Schriften I: Zum Theater.* Frankfurt: Suhrkamp.

Briscoe, John. 1981. *A Commentary on Livy Books XXXIV–XXXVII.* Oxford: Clarendon.

Bristol, Michael D. 1985. *Carnival and Theater: Plebeian Culture and the Structure of Authority in Renaissance England.* New York: Methuen.

Broccia, Giuseppe. 1982. "Appunti sull'ultimo Plauto: Per l'interpretazione del Truculentus." *Wiener Studien* 95: 149–64.

Brooks, Robert A. 1981. *Ennius and Roman Tragedy.* New York: Arno.

Brotherton, Blanche. 1926. *The Vocabulary of Intrigue in Roman Comedy.* Menasha, Wis.: George Banta.

Brown, P. G. McC. 1990. "Plots and Prostitutes in Greek New Comedy." *Papers of the Leeds International Latin Seminar* 6: 241–66.

Bruder, Hans Werner. 1970. *Bedeutung und Funktion des Verswechsels bei Terenz.* Zürich: Juris.

Brunt, P. A. 1971. *Social Conflicts in the Roman Republic.* New York: W. W. Norton.

———. 1993. *Studies in Greek History and Thought.* Oxford: Clarendon.

Buck, Charles Henry, Jr. 1940. *A Chronology of the Plays of Plautus.* Baltimore.

Buckland, W. W. 1908. *The Roman Law of Slavery: The Condition of the Slave in Private Law from Augustus to Justinian.* Cambridge: Cambridge University Press.

Burton, Paul J. 1996. "The Summoning of the Magna Mater to Rome (205 B.C.)." *Historia* 45: 36–63.

Calderwood, James L. 1971. *Shakespearean Metadrama.* Minneapolis: University of Minnesota Press.

Cambiano, Giuseppe. 1987. "Aristotle and the Anonymous Opponents of Slavery." In *Classical Slavery*, ed. M. I. Finley, pp. 22–41. London: Frank Cass.

Carrière, Jean Claude. 1979. *Le Carnaval et la politique: Une Introduction à la comédie grecque suivie d'un choix de fragments.* Paris: Les Belles Lettres.

Cèbe, Jean-Pierre. 1960. "Le Niveau culturel du public plautinien." *Revue des Études Latines* 38: 101–6.

———. 1966. *La Caricature et la parodie dans le monde romain antique des origines à Juvenal.* Paris: E. de Boccard.

Chalmers, Walter R. 1965. "Plautus and His Audience." In *Roman Drama*, ed. T. A. Dorey and Donald R. Dudley, pp. 21–50. London: Routledge and Kegan Paul.

Chapman, G.A.H. 1983. "Some Notes on Dramatic Illusion in Aristophanes." *American Journal of Philology* 104: 1–23.

Chiarini, Gioachino. 1978. "Casina o della metamorfosi." *Latomus* 37: 105–20.

———. 1979. *La recita: Plauto, la farsa, la festa.* Bologna: Pàtron.

———. 1980. "Compresenza e conflittualità dei generi nel teatro latino arcaico (per una rilettura dell'*Amphitruo*)." *Materiali e Discussioni per l'analisi dei testi classici* 5: 87–124.

Coarelli, Filippo. 1985. *Il foro Romano II: Periodo repubblicano e augusteo.* Rome: Quasar.

Cody, Jane M. 1976. "The *senex amator* in Plautus' *Casina.*" *Hermes* 104: 453–76.

Colin, G. 1905. *Rome et la Grèce de 200 à 146 avant Jésus-Christ.* Paris: Albert Fontemoing.

Conrad, Clinton C. 1915. *The Technique of Continuous Action in Roman Comedy.* Menasha, Wis.: George Banta.

Corbett, Philip. 1986. *The Scurra.* Edinburgh: Scottish Academic Press.

Costa, C.D.N. 1965. "The Amphitryo Theme." In *Roman Drama*, ed. T. A. Dorey and Donald R. Dudley, pp. 87–122. London: Routledge and Kegan Paul.

Crahay, R., and **M. Delcourt.** 1952. "Les ruptures d'illusion dans les comédies antiques." *Annuaire de l'Institut de Philologie et d'Histoire Orientales et Slaves de l'Université Libre de Bruxelles* 12: 83–92.

Csapo, Eric. 1989. "Plautine Elements in the Running-Slave Entrance Monologues?" *Classical Quarterly* 39: 148–63.

Csapo, Eric, and William J. Slater. 1995. *The Context of Ancient Drama*. Ann Arbor: University of Michigan Press.

Cugusi, Paolo. 1991. "Plauto e Catone." *Bollettino di Studi Latini* 21: 291–305.

Culham, Phyllis. 1982. "The *Lex Oppia*." *Latomus* 41: 786–93.

Damon, Cynthia. 1997. *The Mask of the Parasite: A Pathology of Roman Patronage*. Ann Arbor: University of Michigan Press.

Davis, David Brion. 1966. *The Problem of Slavery in Western Culture*. Ithaca, N.Y.: Cornell University Press.

Davis, Natalie Zemon. 1975. *Society and Culture in Early Modern France*. Stanford, Calif.: Stanford University Press.

Dedoussi, Christina. 1995. "Greek Drama and Its Spectators: Conventions and Relationships." In *Stage Directions: Essays in Ancient Drama in Honour of E. W. Handley*, ed. Alan Griffiths, pp. 123–32. London: Institute of Classical Studies, University of London.

Della Corte, Francesco. 1952. *Da Sarsina a Roma: Ricerche Plautine*. Genoa: Istituto Universitario di Magistero.

———. 1975. "Maschere e personaggi in Plauto." *Dioniso* 46: 163–93.

De Marinis, Marco. 1993. *The Semiotics of Performance*. Translated by Áine O'Healy. Bloomington: Indiana University Press.

Denzler, Bruno. 1968. *Der Monolog bei Terenz*. Zürich: P. G. Keller.

Deschamps, Lucienne. 1980–81. "Épidaure ou Rome? A propos du *Curculio* de Plaute." *Platon* 32–33: 144–77.

Dessen, Cynthia S. 1977. "Plautus' Satiric Comedy: The *Truculentus*." *Philological Quarterly* 56: 145–68.

Deuling, Judy. 1994. "Canticum Bromiae (et al.)—*Amphitruo* 1053–1130." *Prudentia* 26, 2: 15–25.

Dingel, J. 1981. "Herren und Sklaven bei Plautus." *Gymnasium* 88: 489–504.

Dixon, Suzanne. 1985. "Polybius on Roman Women and Property." *American Journal of Philology* 106: 147–70.

———. 1992. *The Roman Family*. Baltimore, Md.: The Johns Hopkins University Press.

Dohm, Hans. 1964. *Mageiros: Die Rolle des Kochs in der griechisch-römischen Komödie*. Munich: Beck.

Donaldson, Ian. 1970. *The World Upside-Down: Comedy from Jonson to Fielding*. Oxford: Clarendon.

Drury, Martin. 1982. "Appendix of Authors and Works." In *The Cambridge History of Classical Literature II: Latin Literature*, ed. E. J. Kenney and W. V. Clausen, pp. 799–935. Cambridge: Cambridge University Press.

Duckworth, George E. 1936. "The Dramatic Function of the *servus currens* in Roman Comedy." In *Classical Studies Presented to Edward Capps on His Seventieth Birthday*, pp. 93–102. Princeton: Princeton University Press.

———. 1952. *The Nature of Roman Comedy: A Study in Popular Entertainment*. Princeton: Princeton University Press.

———. 1955. "Plautus and the Basilica Aemilia." In *Ut pictura poesis: Studia latina Petro Iohanni Enk septuagenario oblata*, ed. P. de Jonge et al., pp. 58–65. Leiden: Brill.

Ducos, Michèle. 1990. "La Conditions des acteurs à Rome: Données juridiques et sociales." In *Theater und Gesellschaft im Imperium Romanum*, ed. Jürgen Blänsdorf, pp. 19–33. Tübingen: Francke Verlag.

Dumézil, Georges. 1970. *Archaic Roman Religion*. Translated by Philip Krapp. 2 vols. Chicago: University of Chicago Press.

Dumont, Jean Christian. 1974. "Guerre, paix et servitude dans les *Captifs*." *Latomus* 33: 505–22.

———. 1987. *Servus: Rome et l'esclavage sous la république*. Rome: École Française de Rome.

Dunn, William Richard. 1984. "Formal Language in Plautus." Ph.D. diss., Harvard University, Cambridge, Mass.

Dupont, Florence. 1976. "Signification théâtrale du double dans l'*Amphitryon* de Plaute." *Revue des Études Latines* 54: 129–41.

———. 1985. *L'Acteur-roi, ou, Le Théâtre dans la Rome antique*. Paris: Les Belles Lettres.

———. 1987. "*Cantica* et *diverbia* dans l'*Amphitryon* de Plaute." In *Filologia e forme letterarie: Studi offerti a Francesco Della Corte* 2: 45–56. Urbino: Università degli Studi di Urbino.

Dutton, Richard. 1986. *Modern Tragicomedy and the British Tradition*. Norman: University of Oklahoma Press.

Earl, Donald C. 1967. *The Moral and Political Tradition of Rome*. Ithaca, N.Y.: Cornell University Press.

Easterling, Pat E. 1985. "Anachronism in Greek Tragedy." *Journal of Hellenic Studies* 105: 1–10.

———. 1995. "Menander: Loss and Survival." In *Stage Directions: Essays in Ancient Drama in Honour of E. W. Handley*, ed. Alan Griffiths, pp. 153–60. London: Institute of Classical Studies, University of London.

Edwards, Catharine. 1993. *The Politics of Immorality in Ancient Rome*. Cambridge: Cambridge University Press.

Elam, Keir. 1980. *The Semiotics of Theatre and Drama*. London: Methuen.

Enk, P. J. 1953. *Plauti Truculentus*. 2 vols. Leiden: A. W. Sijthoff.

———. 1964. "Plautus' *Truculentus*." In *Classical, Mediaeval and Renaissance Studies in Honor of Berthold Luis Ullman*, vol. 1, ed. Charles Henderson, Jr., pp. 49–65. Rome: Edizioni di Storia e Letteratura.

Evans, John K. 1991. *War, Women and Children in Ancient Rome*. London: Routledge.

Fantham, Elaine. 1965. "The *Curculio* of Plautus: An Illustration of Plautine Methods in Adaptation." *Classical Quarterly* 15: 84–100.

———. 1973. "Towards a Dramatic Reconstruction of the Fourth Act of Plautus' *Amphitruo*." *Philologus* 117: 197–214.

———. 1975. "Sex, Status, and Survival in Hellenistic Athens: A Study of Women in New Comedy." *Phoenix* 29: 44–74.

———. 1977. "Adaptation and Survival: A Genre Study of Roman Comedy in Relation to Its Greek Sources." In *Versions of Medieval Comedy*, ed. Paul G. Ruggiers, pp. 19–49. Norman: University of Oklahoma Press.

Finley, Moses I. 1980. *Ancient Slavery and Modern Ideology*. New York: Viking.

Flashar, Hellmut. 1974. "Aristoteles und Brecht." *Poetica* 6: 17–37.

Forehand, Walter E. 1973a. "Plautus' *Casina*: An Explication." *Arethusa* 6: 233–56.

———. 1973b. "The Use of Imagery in Plautus' *Miles Gloriosus*." *Rivista di Studi Classici* 21: 5–16.

Fraenkel, Eduard. 1912. *De media et nova comoedia quaestiones selectae*. Göttingen: Officina Academica Dieterichiana.

————. 1960. *Elementi Plautini in Plauto*. Translated by Franco Munari. Florence: La Nuova Italia.

————. 1967. "Anreden an nur gedachte Zuhörer." *Museum Helveticum* 24: 190–93.

Frangoulidis, Stavros A. 1994. "Palaestrio as Playwright: Plautus, *Miles Gloriosus* 209–212." In *Studies in Latin Literature and Roman History VII*, ed. Carl Deroux, pp. 72–86. Collection Latomus 227. Brussels: Latomus.

————. 1996. "A Prologue-within-a-Prologue: Plautus, *Miles Gloriosus* 145–153." *Latomus* 55: 568–70.

Frank, Tenney. 1933. *An Economic Survey of Ancient Rome*. Vol. 1, *Rome and Italy of the Republic*. Baltimore: The Johns Hopkins University Press.

————. 1939. "Plautus Comments on Anatolian Affairs." In *Anatolian Studies Presented to William Hepburn Buckler*, ed. W. M. Calder and Josef Keil, pp. 85–88. Manchester: Manchester University Press.

Franko, George Fredric. 1995. "*Fides*, Aetolia, and Plautus' *Captivi*." *Transactions of the American Philological Association* 125: 155–76.

Frassinetti, Paolo, ed. 1967. *Atellanae fabulae*. Rome: Ateneo.

Frayn, Joan M. 1984. *Sheep-Rearing and the Wool Trade in Italy During the Roman Period*. Liverpool: Francis Cairns.

Fredershausen, Otto. 1906. *De iure Plautino et Terentiano*. Göttingen: Goldschmidt und Hubert.

Freté, A. 1929–30. "Essai sur la structure dramatique des comédies de Plaute." *Revue des Études Latines* 7: 282–94, and 8: 36–81.

Freyburger, Gérard. 1977. "La Morale et la *fides* chez l'esclave de la comédie." *Revue des Études Latines* 55: 113–27.

————. 1986. *Fides: Étude sémantique et religieuse depuis les origines jusqu'à l'époque augustéene*. Paris: Les Belles Lettres.

Friedrich, Gustav. 1891. "Die Parabase im *Curculio* des Plautus." *Jahrbücher für classische Philologie* 37: 708–12.

Frost, K. B. 1988. *Exits and Entrances in Menander*. Oxford: Clarendon.

Gabba, Emilio. 1979. "Sul miles inpransus dell'*Aulularia* di Plauto." *Rendiconti dell' Istituto Lombardo, Classe di Lettere, Scienze Morali e Storiche* 113: 408–14.

Gaggiotti, Marcello. 1985. "Atrium regium-basilica (Aemilia): Una insospettata continuità storica e una chiave ideologica per la soluzione del problema dell'origine della basilica." *Analecta Romana Instituti Danici* 14: 53–80.

Gaiser, Konrad. 1972. "Zur Eigenart der römischen Komödie: Plautus und Terenz gegenüber ihren griechischen Vorbildern." *Aufstieg und Niedergang der römischen Welt* 1, 2: 1027–1113.

Galinsky, G. Karl. 1966. "Scipionic Themes in Plautus' *Amphitruo*." *Transactions of the American Philological Association* 97: 203–35.

————. 1969. "Plautus' *Poenulus* and the Cult of Venus Erycina." In *Hommages à Marcel Renard*, ed. Jacqueline Bibauw, 1: 358–64. Brussels: Latomus.

García-Hernández, Benjamín. 1984. "Plaut. *Amph.* 867–868: Solución semántica de una cuestión de traducción y de crítica textual." *Habis* 15: 117–24.

Gargola, Daniel J. 1995. *Lands, Laws, and Gods: Magistrates and Ceremony in the Regulation of Public Lands in Republican Rome*. Chapel Hill: University of North Carolina Press.

Garnsey, Peter. 1996. *Ideas of Slavery from Aristotle to Augustine*. Cambridge: Cambridge University Press.

Garton, Charles. 1972. *Personal Aspects of the Roman Theatre*. Toronto: Hakkert.

Garzya, Antonio. 1969. "À propos de l'interprétation du *Rudens* de Plaute." In *Hommages à Marcel Renard*, ed. Jacqueline Bibauw, 1: 365–73. Brussels: Latomus.

Gelhaus, Hermann. 1972. *Die Prologe des Terenz: Eine Erklärung nach den Lehren von der inventio und dispositio*. Heidelberg: Carl Winter.

Gerdes, Mary Womble. 1995. "Women in Performance in Plautus." Ph.D. diss., University of North Carolina, Chapel Hill.

Giangrieco Pessi, Maria Vittoria. 1981. "Argentarii e trapeziti nel teatro di Plauto." *Archivio Giuridico* 201: 39–106.

Gilula, Dwora. 1981. "Who's Afraid of Rope-Walkers and Gladiators? (Ter. Hec. 1–57)." *Athenaeum* 59: 29–37.

———. 1989. "Greek Drama in Rome: Some Aspects of Cultural Transposition." In *The Play Out of Context: Transferring Plays from Culture to Culture*, ed. Hanna Scolnicov and Peter Holland, pp. 99–109. Cambridge: Cambridge University Press.

Gioffredi, Carlo. 1943. "I tribunali del Foro." *Studia et Documenta Historiae et Iuris* 9, 2: 227–82.

Gizewski, Christian. 1989. "Mores maiorum, regimen morum, licentia: Zur Koexistenz catonischer und plautinischer Sittlichkeitsvorstellungen." In *Festschrift Robert Werner zu seinem 65. Geburtstag*, ed. Werner Dahlheim et al., pp. 81–105. Konstanz: Universitätsverlag Konstanz.

Gold, Barbara K. 1987. *Literary Patronage in Greece and Rome*. Chapel Hill: University of North Carolina Press.

Goldberg, Sander M. 1980. *The Making of Menander's Comedy*. Berkeley: University of California Press.

———. 1986. *Understanding Terence*. Princeton: Princeton University Press.

———. 1995. *Epic in Republican Rome*. New York: Oxford University Press.

Goldman, Michael. 1975. *The Actor's Freedom: Toward a Theory of Drama*. New York: Viking.

Görler, Woldemar. 1973. "Über die Illusion in der antiken Komödie." *Antike und Abendland* 18: 41–57.

———. 1983. "Plautinisches im Pseudolus." *Würzburger Jahrbücher für die Altertumswissenschaft* 9: 89–107.

Gowers, Emily. 1993. *The Loaded Table: Representations of Food in Roman Literature*. Oxford: Clarendon.

Gratwick, Adrian S. 1981. "Curculio's Last Bow: Plautus, *Trinummus* IV.3." *Mnemosyne* 34: 331–50.

———. 1982. "Drama." In *The Cambridge History of Classical Literature II: Latin Literature*, ed. E. J. Kenney and W. V. Clausen, pp. 77–137. Cambridge: Cambridge University Press.

———, ed. 1993. *Plautus: Menaechmi*. Cambridge: Cambridge University Press.

Gray, Frances. 1994. *Women and Laughter*. Basingstoke: Macmillan.

Green, William M. 1933. "The Status of Actors at Rome." *Classical Philology* 28: 301–4.

Grimal, Pierre. 1969. "Le Modèle et la date des *Captivi* de Plaute." In *Hommages à Marcel Renard*, ed. Jacqueline Bibauw, 1: 394–414. Brussels: Latomus.

———. 1970. "A propos du *Truculentus*: L'Antiféminisme de Plaute." In *Mélanges Marcel Durry* (= *Revue des Études Latines* 47 bis, 1969: 85–98). Paris: Les Belles Lettres.

————. 1971–74. "Le 'Truculentus' de Plaute et l'esthétique de la 'palliata.'" *Dioniso* 45: 532–48.

Gros, Pierre. 1983. "La Basilique de Forum selon Vitruve: La Norme et l'expérimentation." In *Bauplanung und Bautheorie der Antike*, pp. 49–69. Berlin: Deutsches Archäologisches Institut.

Groton, Anne H. 1995. Review of A. S. Gratwick, ed., *Plautus: Menaechmi*. *Bryn Mawr Classical Review* 6: 613–16.

Gruen, Erich S. 1990. *Studies in Greek Culture and Roman Policy*. Leiden: Brill.

————. 1992. *Culture and National Identity in Republican Rome*. Ithaca, N.Y.: Cornell University Press.

Guilbert, D. 1963. "Mercure-Sosie dans l'*Amphitryon* de Plaute: Un Rôle de parasite de comédie." *Les Études Classiques* 31: 52–63.

Gulick, Charles Burton. 1896. "Omens and Augury in Plautus." *Harvard Studies in Classical Philology* 7: 235–47.

Guthke, Karl S. 1966. *Modern Tragicomedy: An Investigation into the Nature of the Genre*. New York: Random House.

Guthrie, W.K.C. 1969. *A History of Greek Philosophy*. Vol. 3: *The Fifth-Century Enlightenment*. Cambridge: Cambridge University Press.

Haffter, Heinz. 1953. "Terenz und seine künstlerische Eigenart." *Museum Helveticum* 10: 1–20, 73–102.

Halkin, Léon. 1948. "La Parodie d'une demande de triomphe dans l'*Amphitryon* de Plaute." *L'Antiquité Classique* 17: 297–304.

Hallett, Judith P. 1984. *Fathers and Daughters in Roman Society: Women and the Elite Family*. Princeton: Princeton University Press.

————. 1989. "Women as *Same* and *Other* in Classical Roman Elite." *Helios* 16: 59–78.

————. 1993. "Plautine Ingredients in the Performance of the *Pseudolus*." *Classical World* 87: 21–26.

————. 1996. "The Political Backdrop of Plautus's *Casina*." In *Transitions to Empire: Essays in Greco-Roman History, 360–146 B.C., in Honor of E. Badian*, ed. Robert W. Wallace and Edward M. Harris, pp. 409–38. Norman: University of Oklahoma Press.

Hallidie, Archibald R. S., ed. 1891. *The Captivi of T. Maccius Plautus*. London: Macmillan.

Halliwell, Stephen. 1991. "The Uses of Laughter in Greek Culture." *Classical Quarterly* 41: 279–96.

Hammond, Mason, Arthur M. Mack, and **Walter Moskalew**, eds. 1963. *T. Macci Plauti Miles Gloriosus*. Cambridge, Mass.: Harvard University Press.

Handley, Eric Walter. 1975. "Plautus and His Public: Some Thoughts on New Comedy in Latin." *Dioniso* 46: 117–32.

Hanson, John Arthur. 1959a. "Plautus as a Source Book for Roman Religion." *Transactions of the American Philological Association* 90: 48–101.

————. 1959b. *Roman Theater-Temples*. Princeton: Princeton University Press.

————. 1965. "The Glorious Military." In *Roman Drama*, ed. T. A. Dorey and Donald R. Dudley, pp. 51–85. London: Routledge and Kegan Paul.

Harris, William V. 1979. *War and Imperialism in Republican Rome 327–70 B.C.* Oxford: Clarendon.

————. 1980. "Towards a Study of the Roman Slave Trade." In *The Seaborne Commerce of Ancient Rome: Studies in Archaeology and History*, ed. J. H. D'Arms and E. C. Kopff. Rome: American Academy in Rome. (= *Memoirs of the American Academy in Rome* 36: 117–40.)

Harsh, Philip Whaley. 1936. "Possible Greek Background for the Word *rex* as Used in Plautus." *Classical Philology* 31: 62–68.

———. 1944. *A Handbook of Classical Drama*. Stanford, Calif.: Stanford University Press.

Harvey, Paul B., Jr. 1986. "Historical Topicality in Plautus." *Classical World* 79: 297–304.

Hayter, Charles. 1987. *Gilbert and Sullivan*. New York: St. Martin's.

Hellegouarc'h, J. 1972. *Le Vocabulaire latin des relations et des partis politiques sous la République*. 2d ed. Paris: Les Belles Lettres.

Hengel, Martin. 1977. *Crucifixion in the Ancient World and the Folly of the Message of the Cross*. Philadelphia: Fortress Press.

Henry, Madeleine Mary. 1985. *Menander's Courtesans and the Greek Comic Tradition*. Frankfurt: Peter Lang.

Herrmann, Léon. 1948. "L'Actualité dans l'*Amphitryon* de Plaute." *L'Antiquité Classique* 17: 317–22.

Hiatt, Vergil Emery. 1946. "Eavesdropping in Roman Comedy." Ph.D. diss., University of Chicago.

Hill, Philip V. 1989. *The Monuments of Ancient Rome as Coin Types*. London: B. A. Seaby.

Hirst, David L. 1984. *Tragicomedy*. London: Methuen.

Hoenselaars, A. J. 1993. "Italy Staged in English Renaissance Drama." In Marrapodi et al., 1993, 30–48.

Hoffmann, Zsuzsanna. 1987. "Der Senat bei Plautus." *Acta Classica Universitatis Scientiarum Debreceniensis* 23: 27–29.

———. 1991. "Die *nova flagitia* bei Plautus." *Gymnasium* 98: 180–86.

Hofmann, Walter. 1992. "Zur Funktion der Fremdsprachen bei Plautus." In *Zum Umgang mit fremden Sprachen in der griechisch-römischen Antike*, ed. Carl Werner Müller, Kurt Sier, and Jürgen Werner, pp. 143–58. Stuttgart: Franz Steiner.

Hopkins, Keith. 1978. *Conquerors and Slaves*. Cambridge: Cambridge University Press.

Hornby, Richard. 1986. *Drama, Metadrama and Perception*. Lewisburg, Pa.: Bucknell University Press.

Höttemann, Barbara. 1993. "Phylakenposse und Atellana." In *Beiträge zur mündlichen Kultur der Römer*, ed. Gregor Vogt-Spira, pp. 89–112. Tübingen: Gunter Narr.

Hough, John N. 1940a. "Miscellanea Plautina: Vulgarity, Extra-Dramatic Speeches, Roman Allusions." *Transactions of the American Philological Association* 71: 186–98.

———. 1940b. "Plautine Technique in Delayed Exits." *Classical Philology* 35: 39–48.

———. 1945. "The *numquid vis* Formula in Roman Comedy." *American Journal of Philology* 66: 282–302.

Hubbard, Thomas K. 1991. *The Mask of Comedy: Aristophanes and the Intertextual Parabasis*. Ithaca, N.Y.: Cornell University Press.

Huelsen, Christian. 1909. *The Roman Forum: Its History and Its Monuments*. Translated by Jesse Benedict Carter. New York: G. E. Stechert.

Hunter, Richard L. 1980. "Philemon, Plautus and the *Trinummus*." *Museum Helveticum* 37: 216–30.

———. 1981. "The 'Aulularia' of Plautus and Its Greek Original." *Proceedings of the Cambridge Philological Society* 27: 37–49.

————. 1985. *The New Comedy of Greece and Rome*. Cambridge: Cambridge University Press.

————. 1987. "Middle Comedy and the *Amphitruo* of Plautus." *Dioniso* 57: 281–98.

Ingarden, Roman. 1971. "Les Fonctions du langage au théâtre." Translated by Hélène Roussel. *Poetique* 8: 531–38.

Janne, Henri. 1933. "L'Amphitryon de Plaute et M. Fulvius Nobilior." *Revue Belge de Philologie et d'Histoire* 12: 515–31.

Jocelyn, Henry David. 1966. "The Roman Nobility and the Religion of the Republican State." *Journal of Religious History* 4: 89–104.

————. 1969a. "*Imperator histricus.*" *Yale Classical Studies* 21: 95–123.

————. 1969b. "The Poet Cn. Naevius, P. Cornelius Scipio and Q. Caecilius Metellus." *Antichthon* 3: 32–47.

————. 1972. "The Poems of Quintus Ennius." *Aufstieg und Niedergang der römischen Welt* 1, 2: 987-1026.

————. 1987. "Plautus, *Miles Gloriosus* 209–212." *Sileno* 13: 17–20.

————. 1990. "Plautus, *Poenulus* 200–202 and the *ballistarium.*" *Liverpool Classical Monthly* 15: 5–8.

Johnson, Harriet Dale. 1927. "The Roman Tribunal." Ph.D. diss., The Johns Hopkins University, Baltimore.

Johnston, Patricia A. 1980. "*Poenulus* I,2 and Roman Women." *Transactions of the American Philological Association* 110: 143–59.

Jones, Leslie Webber, and **C. R. Morey**. 1930–31. *The Miniatures of the Manuscripts of Terence Prior to the Thirteenth Century*. 2 vols. Princeton: Princeton University Press.

Jordan, H. 1880. "Die Parabase im Curculio des Plautus." *Hermes* 15: 116–36.

Jory, E. J. 1966. "*Dominus gregis?*" *Classical Philology* 61: 102–5.

————. 1970. "Associations of Actors in Rome." *Hermes* 98: 224–53.

————. 1995. "Ars ludicra and the ludus talarius." In *Stage Directions: Essays in Ancient Drama in Honour of E. W. Handley*, ed. Alan Griffiths, pp. 139–52. London: Institute of Classical Studies, University of London.

Kaser, Max. 1968. *Römisches Privatrecht: Ein Studienbuch*. 6th ed. Munich: Beck.

Kelly, J. M. 1966. *Roman Litigation*. Oxford: Clarendon.

Kenny, Don. 1989. *The Kyogen Book: An Anthology of Japanese Classical Comedies*. Tokyo: Japan Times.

Ketterer, Robert C. 1986a. "Stage Properties in Plautine Comedy I." *Semiotica* 58: 193–216.

————. 1986b. "Stage Properties in Plautine Comedy II." *Semiotica* 59: 93–135.

————. 1986c. "Stage Properties in Plautine Comedy III." *Semiotica* 60: 29–72.

Kienast, Dietmar. 1954. *Cato der Zensor: Seine Persönlichkeit und seine Zeit*. Heidelberg: Quelle und Meyer.

Killeen, J. F. 1973. "Plautus *Miles Gloriosus* 211." *Classical Philology* 68: 53–54.

Kinsey, T. E. 1980. "Masks on the Roman Stage." *Revue Belge de Philologie et d'Histoire* 58: 53–55.

Knapp, Charles. 1919. "References in Plautus and Terence to Plays, Players, and Playwrights." *Classical Philology* 14: 35–55.

Knapp, Mary Etta. 1961. *Prologues and Epilogues of the Eighteenth Century*. New Haven, Ct.: Yale University Press.

Koestler, Arthur. 1964. *The Act of Creation*. New York: Macmillan.

Kolve, V. A. 1966. *The Play Called Corpus Christi*. Stanford, Calif.: Stanford University Press.

Konstan, David. 1983. *Roman Comedy.* Ithaca, N.Y.: Cornell University Press.

———. 1995. *Greek Comedy and Ideology.* New York: Oxford University Press.

Kraus, Walther. 1934. "'Ad spectatores' in der römischen Komödie." *Wiener Studien* 52: 66–83.

———. 1977. "Die Captivi im neuen Lichte Menanders." In *Latinität und Alte Kirche: Festschrift für Rudolf Hanslik zum 70. Geburtstag,* pp. 159–70. Vienna: Hermann Böhlau.

Kwintner, M. 1992. "Plautus *Pseudolus* 782: A Fullonius Assault." *Classical Philology* 87: 232–33.

Lada, Ismene. 1996. "'Weeping for Hecuba': Is It a 'Brechtian' Act?" *Arethusa* 29: 87–124.

Langer, Susanne K. 1953. *Feeling and Form: A Theory of Art Developed From Philosophy in a New Key.* New York: Charles Scribner's Sons.

Latte, Kurt. 1960. *Römische Religionsgeschichte.* Munich: Beck.

Law, Helen. 1929. "The Metrical Arrangement of the Fragments of the *Bacchides.*" *Classical Philology* 24: 197–201.

Leach, Eleanor Winsor. 1969a. "De exemplo meo ipse aedificato: An Organizing Idea in the *Mostellaria.*" *Hermes* 97: 318–32.

———. 1969b. "Ergasilus and the Ironies of the *Captivi.*" *Classica et Mediaevalia* 30: 263–96.

———. 1974. "Plautus' *Rudens*: Venus Born from a Shell." *Texas Studies in Literature and Language* 15: 915–31.

Leeman, A. D. 1983. "L'Hyperbole et l'ironie chez les Romains en tant que méchanismes de défense et d'assimilation à l'égard de la culture Grecque." In *Hommages à Robert Schilling,* ed. Hubert Zehnacker and Gustave Hentz, pp. 347–55. Paris: Les Belles Lettres.

Lefèvre, Eckard. 1977. "Plautus-Studien I: Der doppelte Geldkreislauf im Pseudolus." *Hermes* 105: 441–54.

———. 1978. "Plautus-Studien II: Die Brief-Intrige in Menanders *Dis exapaton* und ihre Verdoppelung in den Bacchides." *Hermes* 106: 518–38.

———. 1979. "Plautus-Studien III: Von der Tyche-Herrschaft in Diphilos' Klerumenoi zum Triummatronat der Casina." *Hermes* 107: 311–39.

———. 1982. *Maccus vortit barbare: Vom tragischen Amphitryon zum tragikomischen Amphitruo.* Wiesbaden: Franz Steiner.

———. 1984. "Plautus-Studien IV: Die Umformung des Ἀλαζών zu der Doppel-Komödie des 'Miles Gloriosus.'" *Hermes* 112: 30–53.

———. 1988. "Saturnalia und palliata." *Poetica* 20: 32–46.

———. 1993. "Politics and Society in Plautus' *Trinummus.*" In *Theater and Society in the Classical World,* ed. Ruth Scodel, pp. 177–90. Ann Arbor: University of Michigan Press.

———. 1995. *Plautus und Philemon.* Tübingen: Gunter Narr.

———. 1997. *Plautus' Pseudolus.* Tübingen: Gunter Narr.

Lefèvre, Eckard, Ekkehard Stärk, and **Gregor Vogt-Spira.** 1991. *Plautus barbarus: Sechs Kapitel zur Originalität des Plautus.* Tübingen: Gunter Narr.

Leffingwell, Georgia Williams. 1918. *Social and Private Life at Rome in the Time of Plautus and Terence.* Columbia University Studies in History, Economics, and Public Law 81.1. New York: Columbia University.

Lelièvre, F. J. 1958. "Sosia and Roman Epic." *Phoenix* 12: 117–24.

Leo, Friedrich. 1908. *Der Monolog im Drama, Ein Beitrag zur griechisch-römischen Poetik.* Göttingen: Gesellschaft der Wissenschaft.

————. 1912. *Plautinische Forschungen: Zur Kritik und Geschichte der Komödie.* 2d ed. Berlin: Weidmann.

————. 1913. *Geschichte der römischen Literatur.* Vol. 1, *Die archaische Literatur.* Berlin: Weidmann.

————. 1960. *Ausgewählte kleine Schriften.* Edited by Eduard Fraenkel. Rome: Edizioni di Storia e Letteratura.

Levith, Murray J. 1989. *Shakespeare's Italian Settings and Plays.* New York: St. Martin's.

Liebeschuetz, J.H.W.G. 1979. *Continuity and Change in Roman Religion.* Oxford: Clarendon.

Lilja, Saara. 1983. *Homosexuality in Republican and Augustan Rome.* Societas Scientiarum Fennica, Commentationes Humanarum Litterarum 74. Ekenäs: Ekenäs Tryckeri.

Lindsay, Wallace M., ed. 1900. *The Captivi of Plautus.* London: Methuen.

Lintott, A. W. 1968. *Violence in Republican Rome.* Oxford: Clarendon.

Lodge, Gonzalez. 1904–33. *Lexicon Plautinum.* Leipzig: Teubner.

Loitold, Elfriede. 1957. "Untersuchungen zur Spieltechnik der Plautinischen Komödie." Ph.D. diss., Vienna.

Lombardo, Agostino. 1993. "The Veneto, Metatheatre, and Shakespeare." In Marrapodi et al. 1993, 143–57.

Lowe, J.C.B. 1985. "The Cook Scene in Plautus' *Pseudolus.*" *Classical Quarterly* 35: 411–16.

————. 1989. "The *virgo callida* of Plautus, *Persa.*" *Classical Quarterly* 39: 390–99.

————. 1991. "Prisoners, Guards, and Chains in Plautus, *Captivi.*" *American Journal of Philology* 112: 29–44.

————. 1992. "Aspects of Plautus' Originality in the *Asinaria.*" *Classical Quarterly* 42: 152–75.

Lucas, Donald William. 1968. *Aristotle: Poetics.* Oxford: Clarendon.

Ludwig, Walther. 1961. "Aulularia-Probleme." *Philologus* 105: 44–71 and 247–62.

————. 1968. "The Originality of Terence and His Greek Models." *Greek, Roman and Byzantine Studies* 9: 169–82.

MacCary, W. Thomas. 1975. "The Bacchae in Plautus' *Casina.*" *Hermes* 103: 459–63.

MacCary, W. Thomas, and M. M. Willcock, eds. 1976. *Plautus: Casina.* Cambridge: Cambridge University Press.

McDonnell, Myles. 1987. "The Speech of Numidicus at Gellius, *N.A.* 1.6." *American Journal of Philology* 108: 81–94.

MacDowell, Douglas M. 1995. *Aristophanes and Athens: An Introduction to the Plays.* New York: Oxford University Press.

McLeish, Kenneth. 1980. *The Theatre of Aristophanes.* London: Thames and Hudson.

MacMullen, Ramsay. 1991. "Hellenizing the Romans (2nd Century B.C.)." *Historia* 40: 419–38.

McPherson, David C. 1990. *Shakespeare, Jonson, and the Myth of Venice.* Newark: University of Delaware Press.

Maltby, R. 1995. "The Distribution of Greek Loan-Words in Plautus." *Papers of the Leeds International Latin Seminar* 8: 31–69.

Mariotti, Italo. 1992. "La prima scena della Mostellaria di Plauto." *Museum Helveticum* 49: 105–23.

Marmorale, Enzo V. 1953. *Naevius Poeta.* Florence: La Nuova Italia.

Marouzeau, J. 1932. Review of A. Stein, *Römische Inschriften in der antiken Literatur. Revue des Études Latines* 10: 271–72.

Marrapodi, Michele, A. J. Hoenselaars, Marcello Cappuzzo, and **L. Falzon Santucci,** eds. 1993. *Shakespeare's Italy: Functions of Italian Locations in Renaissance Drama.* Manchester: Manchester University Press.

Marx, Friedrich, ed. 1928. *Plautus Rudens.* Leipzig: Hirzel. Repr. Amsterdam: Hakkert, 1959.

Maurach, Gregor. 1964. Review of Mason Hammond, Arthur W. Mack, and Walter Moskalew, eds., *T. Macci Plauti Miles Gloriosus. Gnomon* 36: 577–80.

———. 1966. Review of T. A. Dorey and Donald R. Dudley, eds., *Roman Drama. Gnomon* 38: 676–79.

———. 1988. *Der Poenulus des Plautus.* Heidelberg: Carl Winter.

Middelmann, Franz. 1938. "Griechische Welt und Sprache in Plautus' Komödien." Ph.D. diss., Münster.

Milch, Wilhelm. 1957. "Zum Kapitel 'Plautinische Zwischenreden.'" *Hermes* 85: 159–69.

Millar, Fergus. 1984. "The Political Character of the Roman Republic, 200–151 B.C." *Journal of Roman Studies* 74: 1–19.

Momigliano, Arnaldo. 1975. *Alien Wisdom: The Limits of Hellenization.* Cambridge: Cambridge University Press.

Mommsen, Theodor. 1886. *Römisches Staatsrecht.* Vol. 3, part 1. Leipzig. Repr. Graz: Akademische Druck- und Verlagsanstalt, 1952.

———. 1907. *Römische Geschichte.* Vol. 1: *Bis zur Schlacht von Pydna.* 10th ed. Berlin: Weidmann.

Monaco, Giusto. 1970. "Spectatores, plaudite." In *Studia Florentina Alexandro Ronconi sexagenario oblata,* pp. 255–73. Rome: Ateneo.

Moore, Timothy J. 1989. *Artistry and Ideology: Livy's Vocabulary of Virtue.* Frankfurt: Athenäum.

———. 1991a. "*Palliata togata:* Plautus, *Curculio* 462–86." *American Journal of Philology* 112: 343–62.

———. 1991b. "Plautus, *Captivi,* 818–822." *Latomus* 50: 349–51.

———. 1994. "Seats and Social Status in the Plautine Theatre." *Classical Journal* 90: 113–23.

Morel, J.-P. 1964. "'Pube praesenti in contione, omni poplo' (Plaute, *Pseudolus,* v. 126): *Pubes* et *contio* d'après Plaute et Tite-Live." *Revue des Études Latines* 42: 375–88.

Morgan, M. Gwyn. 1990. "Politics, Religion and the Games in Rome, 200–150 B.C." *Philologus* 134: 14–36.

Muecke, Frances. 1985. "Names and Players: The Sycophant Scene of the *Trinummus (Trin.* 4.2)." *Transactions of the American Philological Association* 115: 167–86.

———. 1986. "Plautus and the Theatre of Disguise." *Classical Antiquity* 5: 216–29.

Mullini, Roberta. 1993. "Streets, Squares and Courts: Venice as a Stage in Shakespeare and Ben Jonson." In Marrapodi et al. 1993, 158–70.

Naudet, J., ed. 1830. *M. Accii Plauti Comoediae.* Vol. 1. Paris: Nicolaus Eligius Lemaire.

Nelson, Robert J. 1958. *Play Within a Play: The Dramatist's Conception of His Art: Shakespeare to Anouilh.* New Haven, Ct.: Yale University Press.

Niebergall, Volker. 1937. "Griechische Religion und Mythologie in der ältesten Literatur der Römer." Ph.D. diss., Giessen.

Nörr, Dieter. 1989. *Aspekte des römischen Völkerrechts: Die Bronzetafel von Alcántara*. Munich: Verlag der Bayerischen Akademie der Wissenschaften.

Norwood, Gilbert. 1932. *Plautus and Terence*. New York: Longmans, Green.

O'Bryhim, Shawn. 1989. "The Originality of Plautus' *Casina*." *American Journal of Philology* 110: 81–103.

Oniga, Renato. 1985. "Il canticum di Sosia: Forme stilistiche e modelli culturali." *Materiali e Discussioni per l'Analisi dei Testi Classici* 14: 113–208.

Oppermann, Hans, ed. 1962. *Römertum: Ausgewählte Aufsätze und Arbeiten aus den Jahren 1921 bis 1961*. Darmstadt: Wissenschaftliche Buchgesellschaft.

———, ed. 1967. *Römische Wertbegriffe*. Darmstadt: Wissenschaftliche Buchgesellschaft.

Otis, Brooks. 1967. "The Uniqueness of Latin Literature." *Arion* 6: 185–206.

Owens, William Martin. 1986. "Ethnic Characterization in Plautus." Ph.D. diss., Yale University, New Haven, Ct.

———. 1994. "The Third Deception in *Bacchides*: Fides and Plautus' Originality." *American Journal of Philology* 115: 381–407.

Pailler, Jean-Marie. 1988. *Bacchanalia: La Répression de 186 av. J.-C. à Rome et en Italie: Vestiges, images, tradition*. Rome: École Française de Rome.

Paratore, Ettore. 1959. "Il flautista nel Δύσκολος e nello *Pseudolus*." *Rivista di Cultura Classica e Medioevale* 1: 310–25.

Parker, Holt. 1989. "Crucially Funny or Tranio on the Couch: The *Servus Callidus* and Jokes about Torture." *Transactions of the American Philological Association* 119: 233–46.

———. 1996. "Plautus vs. Terence: Audience and Popularity Re-examined." *American Journal of Philology* 117: 585–617.

Pasquali, Giorgio. 1927. "Un monologo dei *Captivi*." *Rivista di Filologia* 55: 24–30.

Paton, W. R., trans. 1923. *Polybius: The Histories*. Vol. 3. Cambridge, Mass.: Harvard University Press.

Patterson, Orlando. 1982. *Slavery and Social Death: A Comparative Study*. Cambridge, Mass.: Harvard University Press.

Perelli, Luciano. 1978. "Società romana e problematica sociale nel teatro plautino." *Studi Romani* 26: 307–27.

———. 1983. "L'Alcmena plautina: Personaggio serio o parodico?" *Civiltà Classica e Cristiana* 4: 383–94.

Pérez Gómez, Leonor. 1990. "Roles sociales y conflictos de sexo en la comedia de Plauto." In *La mujer en el mundo mediterránneo antiguo*, ed. Aurora López, Cándida Martínez, and Andrés Pociña, pp.137–67. Granada: Servicio de Publicaciones de la Universidad de Granada.

Perna, Raffaele. 1955. *L'Originalità di Plauto*. Bari: "Leonardo da Vinci."

Petrochilos, Nicholas. 1974. *Roman Attitudes to the Greeks*. Athens: S. Saripolos.

Petrone, Gianna. 1977. *Morale e antimorale nelle commedie di Plauto: Ricerche sullo Stichus*. Palermo: Palumbo.

———. 1981. "Iuppiter lenonius: A proposito di *Pseud*. 335–339." *Pan* 7: 113–18.

———. 1983. *Teatro antico e inganno: Finzioni plautine*. Palermo: Palumbo.

———. 1989. "Ridere in silenzio: Tradizione misogina e trionfo dell'intelligenza femminile nella commedia plautina." In *Atti del II convegno nazionale di studi su la donna nel mondo antico, Torino 18–19–20 Aprile 1988*, ed. Renato

Uglione, pp. 87–103. Turin: Associazione Italiana di Cultura Classica, Delegazione di Torino: Regione Piemonte, Assessorato alla Cultura.

Pfister, Manfred. 1988. *The Theory and Analysis of Drama.* Translated by John Halliday. Cambridge: Cambridge University Press.

Phillips, Jane E. 1985. "Alcumena in the *Amphitruo* of Plautus: A Pregnant Lady Joke." *Classical Journal* 80: 121–26.

Pociña, Andrés. 1976. "El barbarus en Plauto: ¿Crítica social?" *Helmantica* 27: 425–32.

Pomeroy, Sarah B. 1975. *Goddesses, Whores, Wives, and Slaves: Women in Classical Antiquity.* New York: Schocken.

Pomey, Patrice. 1973. "Plaute et Ovide architectes navals!" *Mélanges de l'École Française de Rome: Antiquité* 85: 483–515.

Posani, Maria Rosa. 1962. "Aspetti del comico in Terenzio." *Atene e Roma* 7: 65–76.

Prescott, Henry W. 1939. "Link Monologues in Roman Comedy." *Classical Philology* 34: 116–26.

Primmer, Adolf. 1984. *Handlungsgliederung in Nea und Palliata: Dis Exapaton und Bacchides.* Vienna: Verlag der Österreichischen Akademie der Wissenschaften.

Questa, Cesare. 1970. "Alcune strutture sceniche di Plauto e Menandro." In *Ménandre*, ed. Eric G. Turner, pp. 183–215. Fondation Hardt Entretiens 16. Geneva: Fondation Hardt.

———. 1982. "Maschere e funzioni nelle commedie di Plauto." *Materiali e Discussioni per l'analisi dei testi classici* 8: 9–64.

Radermacher, L. 1903. "Die Zeit der Asinaria." *Rheinisches Museum für Philologie* 58: 636–38.

Radke, Gerhard. 1987. *Zur Entwicklung der Gottesvorstellung und der Gottesverehrung in Rom.* Darmstadt: Wissenschaftliche Buchgesellschaft.

Ramage, Edwin S. 1960. "Early Roman Urbanity." *American Journal of Philology* 81: 65–72.

———. 1973. *Urbanitas: Ancient Sophistication and Refinement.* Norman, OK: University of Oklahoma Press.

Rau, Peter. 1970. Review of Eberhard Rechenberg, *Beobachtungen über das Verhältnis der Alten attischen Komödie zu ihrem Publikum. Gnomon* 42: 91–92.

Rawson, Elizabeth. 1985. "Theatrical Life in Republican Rome and Italy." *Papers of the British School at Rome* 53: 97–113.

———. 1987. "Speciosa locis morataque recte." In *Homo viator: Classical Essays for John Bramble*, ed. Michael Whitby, Philip Hardie, and Mary Whitby, pp. 79–88. Oak Park, Ill.: Bolchazy-Carducci.

———. 1989. "Roman Tradition and the Greek World." In *The Cambridge Ancient History*, Vol. 8: *Rome and the Mediterranean to 133 B.C.*, ed. A. E. Astin et al., 2d ed., pp. 422–76. Cambridge: Cambridge University Press.

Rayner, Alice. 1987. *Comic Persuasion: Moral Structure in British Comedy from Shakespeare to Stoppard.* Berkeley: University of California Press.

Reckford, Kenneth J. 1987. *Aristophanes' Old-and-New Comedy.* Vol. 1: *Six Essays in Perspective.* Chapel Hill: University of North Carolina Press.

Reinhardt, Udo. 1974. "Amphitryon und Amphitruo." In *Musa iocosa: Arbeiten über Humor und Witz, Komik und Komödie der Antike: Andreas Thierfelder zum siebzigsten Geburtstag am 15 Juni 1973*, edd. Udo Reinhardt and Klaus Sallmann, with Karl Heinz Chelius, pp. 95–130. Hildesheim: Georg Olms.

Ribbeck, Otto. 1875. *Die Römische Tragödie im Zeitalter der Republik.* Leipzig: Teubner.

Richardson, Lawrence, Jr. 1973. "The Tribunals of the Praetors of Rome." *Mitteilungen des Deutschen Archäologischen Instituts, Römische Abteilung* 80: 219–33.

———. 1979. "Basilica Fulvia, modo Aemilia." In *Studies in Classical Art and Archaeology: A Tribute to Peter Heinrich von Blanckenhagen*, ed. Günter Kopcke and Mary B. Moore., pp. 209–15. Locust Valley, N.Y.: J. J. Augustin.

———. 1992. *A New Topographical Dictionary of Ancient Rome.* Baltimore: The Johns Hopkins University Press.

Richlin, Amy. 1984. "Invective Against Women in Roman Satire." *Arethusa* 17: 67–80.

Riemer, Peter. 1992. "Plautus *Trinummus* 48–67." *Prometheus* 18: 49–57.

———. 1996. *Das Spiel im Spiel: Studien zum plautinischen Agon in "Trinummus" und "Rudens."* Stuttgart: Teubner.

Righter, Anne. 1962. *Shakespeare and the Idea of the Play.* London: Chatto and Windus.

Ritschl, Friedrich. 1845. *Parerga zu Plautus und Terenz.* Vol. 1. Berlin. Repr. Amsterdam: Hakkert, 1965.

Robertis, Francesco Maria de. 1963. *Lavoro e lavoratori nel mondo romano.* Bari: Adriatica.

Rogers, Katharine M. 1966. *The Troublesome Helpmate: A History of Misogyny in Literature.* Seattle: University of Washington Press.

Rolfe, John C., trans. 1946. *The Attic Nights of Aulus Gellius.* Vol. 1. Rev. ed. Cambridge, Mass.: Harvard University Press.

Rose, H. J. 1924. "De talento Plautino." *Classical Review* 38: 155–57.

Rosenmeyer, Patricia A. 1995. "Enacting the Law: Plautus' Use of the Divorce Formula on Stage." *Phoenix* 49: 201–17.

Rosivach, Vincent J. 1970. "Plautine Stage Settings (*Asin., Aul., Men., Trin.*)." *Transactions of the American Philological Association* 101: 445–61.

———. 1989. "The *miles impransus* of Plaut. *Aul.* 528." *Latomus* 48: 344–45.

Rösler, Wolfgang. 1986. "Michail Bachtin und die Karnevalskultur im antiken Griechenland." *Quaderni Urbinati di Cultura Classica*, n.s. 23, 2: 25–44.

Russo, Carlo Ferdinando. 1984. *Aristofane autore di teatro.* 2d ed. Florence: Sansoni.

Sandbach, F. H. 1977. *The Comic Theatre of Greece and Rome.* New York: Norton.

Saunders, Catharine. 1909. *Costume in Roman Comedy.* New York: Columbia University Press.

———. 1913. "The Site of Dramatic Performances at Rome in the Times of Plautus and Terence." *Transactions of the American Philological Association* 44: 87–97.

Scafuro, Adele C. 1989. "Livy's Comic Narrative of the Bacchanalia." *Helios* 16: 119–42.

———. 1993. "Staging Entrapment: On the Boundaries of the Law in Plautus' *Persa*." In *Intertextualität in der griechisch-römischen Komödie*, ed. Niall W. Slater and Bernhard Zimmermann (= *Drama* 2: 55–77). Stuttgart: M und P Verlag für Wissenschaft und Forschung.

Schaaf, Lothar. 1977. *Der Miles Gloriosus des Plautus und sein griechisches Original: Ein Beitrag zur Kontaminationsfrage.* Munich: Wilhelm Fink.

Schiappa de Azevedo, Maria Teresa. 1975–76. "Um momento Plautino: 'sed quasi poeta . . .'." *Humanitas* 27–28: 95–130.

Schmid, Wilhelm, and **Otto Stählin**. 1946. *Geschichte der griechischen Literatur, I: Die klassische Periode, 4*. Munich: Beck.

Schuhmann, Elisabeth. 1975. "Die soziale Stellung der Frau in den Komödien des Plautus." Ph.D. diss., Leipzig.

———. 1976. "Ehescheidungen in den Komödien des Plautus." *Zeitschrift der Savigny-Stiftung für Rechtsgeschichte* 93: 19–32.

———. 1977. "Der Typ der *uxor dotata* in den Komödien des Plautus." *Philologus* 121: 45–65.

———. 1978. "Zur sozialen Stellung der Frau in den Komödien des Plautus." *Altertum* 24: 97–105.

Schutter, Klaas Herman Eltjo. 1952. *Quibus annis comoediae Plautinae primum actae sint quaeritur*. Groningen: Dewaal.

Scullard, H. H. 1973. *Roman Politics, 220–150 B.C.* 2d ed. Oxford: Clarendon.

Seaman, William M. 1954. "The Understanding of Greek by Plautus' Audience." *Classical Journal* 50: 115–19.

Segal, Erich. 1987. *Roman Laughter: The Comedy of Plautus*. 2d ed. New York: Oxford University Press.

Seidensticker, Bernd. 1982. *Palintonos Harmonia: Studien zu komischen Elementen in der griechischen Tragödie*. Göttingen: Vandenhoeck und Ruprecht.

Sharrock, A. R. 1996. "The Art of Deceit: Pseudolus and the Nature of Reading." *Classical Quarterly* 46: 152–74.

Shawcross, John T. 1987. "Tragicomedy as Genre, Past and Present." In *Renaissance Tragicomedy: Explorations in Genre and Politics*, ed. Nancy Klein Maguire, pp. 13–32. New York: AMS Press.

Shipp, G. B. 1953. "Greek in Plautus." *Wiener Studien* 66: 105–12.

———. 1955. "Plautine Terms for Greek and Roman Things." *Glotta* 34: 139–52.

Sifakis, G. M. 1971. *Parabasis and Animal Choruses: A Contribution to the History of Attic Comedy*. London: Athlone.

Slater, Niall W. 1983. "A Note on Plautus' *Bacchides* 772." *Classical World* 77: 20–21.

———. 1985a. "A Note on Plautus' *Trinummus* 705–707." *Classical World* 79: 33–34.

———. 1985b. *Plautus in Performance: The Theatre of the Mind*. Princeton: Princeton University Press.

———. 1985c. "Play and Playwright References in Middle and New Comedy." *Liverpool Classical Monthly* 10: 103–5.

———. 1987. "The Date of Plautus' *Curculio* and *Trinummus* Reconsidered." *American Journal of Philology* 108: 264–69.

———. 1990. "*Amphitruo, Bacchae*, and Metatheatre." *Lexis* 5–6: 101–25.

———. 1991. "The Market in Sooth: Supernatural Discourse in Plautus." Unpublished manuscript.

———. 1992a. "Plautine Negotiations: The *Poenulus* Prologue Unpacked." *Yale Classical Studies* 29: 131–46.

———. 1992b. "Two Republican Poets on Drama: Terence and Accius." In *Antike Dramentheorien und ihre Rezeption*, ed. Bernhard Zimmermann (= *Drama* 1: 85–103). Stuttgart: M und P Verlag für Wissenschaft und Forschung.

———. 1993a. "From Ancient Performance to New Historicism." In *Intertextualität in der griechisch-römischen Komödie*, ed. Niall W. Slater and Bernhard

Zimmermann (= *Drama* 2: 1–13). Stuttgart: M und P Verlag für Wissenschaft und Forschung.

———. 1993b. "Improvisation in Plautus." In *Beiträge zur mündlichen Kultur der Römer*, ed. Gregor Vogt-Spira, pp. 113–24. Tübingen: Gunter Narr.

Small, Jocelyn Penny. 1982. *Cacus and Marsyas in Etrusco-Roman Legend.* Princeton: Princeton University Press.

Snowden, Frank M., Jr. 1983. *Before Color Prejudice: The Ancient View of Blacks.* Cambridge, Mass.: Harvard University Press.

Spranger, Peter P. 1984. *Historische Untersuchungen zu den Sklavenfiguren des Plautus und Terenz.* 2d ed. Stuttgart: Franz Steiner.

Staccioli, Romolo A. 1961. "Spettacoli antichi e moderni al Foro Romano." *Capitolium* 36: 18–22.

Stärk, Ekkehard. 1989. *Die Menaechmi des Plautus und kein griechisches Original.* Tübingen: Gunter Narr.

———. 1990. "Plautus' uxores dotatae im Spannungsfeld literarischer Fiktion und gesellschaftlicher Realität." In *Theater und Gesellschaft im Imperium Romanum*, ed. Jürgen Blänsdorf, pp. 69–79. Tübingen: Francke Verlag.

Steidle, Wulf. 1975. "Probleme des Bühnenspiels in der Neuen Komödie." *Grazer Beiträge* 3: 341–86.

———. 1979. "Plautus' *Amphitruo* und sein griechisches Original." *Rheinisches Museum für Philologie* 122: 34–48.

Stein, J. Peter. 1970. "Morality in Plautus' *Trinummus*." *Classical Bulletin* 47: 7–13.

Steinby, Eva Margareta, ed. 1993. *Lexicon Topographicum Urbis Romae. I: A–C.* Rome: Quasar.

———, ed. 1995. *Lexicon Topographicum Urbis Romae, II: D–G.* Rome: Quasar.

Steiner, Deborah. 1986. *The Crown of Song: Metaphor in Pindar.* London: Duckworth.

Stewart, Zeph. 1958. "The *Amphitruo* of Plautus and Euripides' *Bacchae*." *Transactions of the American Philological Association* 89: 348–73.

Stockert, Walter, ed. 1983. *T. Maccius Plautus Aulularia.* Stuttgart: Teubner.

Stow, Harry Lloyd. 1936. "The Violation of the Dramatic Illusion in the Comedies of Aristophanes." Ph.D. diss., Chicago.

Styan, J. L. 1975. *Drama, Stage, and Audience.* New York: Cambridge University Press.

———. 1977. *The Shakespeare Revolution: Criticism and Performance in the Twentieth Century.* Cambridge: Cambridge University Press.

———. 1989. "Stage Space and the Shakespeare Experience." In Thompson and Thompson, 1989, 195–209.

Sutton, Dana F. 1993. *Ancient Comedy: The War of the Generations.* New York: Twayne.

Swoboda, Michael. 1971. "De soliloquiorum in antiquo drammate ab Aeschyli temporibus usque ad Terentium adhibitorum munere scaenico." *Eos* 59: 57–76.

Taafe, Lauren K. 1993. *Aristophanes and Women.* London: Routledge.

Taillardat, Jean. 1965. *Les images d'Aristophane: Études de langue et de style.* Paris: Les Belles Lettres.

Taladoire, Barthélémy-A. 1951. *Commentaires sur la mimique et l'expression corporelle du comédien romain.* Montpellier: Ch. Déhan.

———. 1956. *Essai sur le comique de Plaute.* Monte Carlo: Imprimerie Nationale de Monaco.

Tanner R. G. 1969. "Problems in Plautus." *Proceedings of the Cambridge Philological Society* 15: 95–105.

Taplin, Oliver. 1993. *Comic Angels and Other Approaches to Greek Drama through Vase-Paintings*. Oxford: Clarendon.

Tatum, James, trans. 1983. *Plautus: The Darker Comedies: Bacchides, Casina, and Truculentus*. Baltimore: The Johns Hopkins University Press.

Tatum, W. Jeffrey. 1993. "Ritual and Personal Morality in Roman Religion." *Syllecta Classica* 4: 13–20.

Taylor, Lily Ross. 1966. *Roman Voting Assemblies from the Hannibalic War to the Dictatorship of Caesar*. Ann Arbor: University of Michigan Press.

Terzaghi, N. 1930. "Plauto, Terenzio, il pubblico." *Atti della Società Italiana per il Progresso delle Scienze* 18, 1: 749–81.

Teuffel, W. S. 1889. *Studien und Charakteristiken zur griechischen und römischen Literaturgeschichte*. Leipzig: Teubner.

Thalmann, William G. 1996. "Versions of Slavery in the *Captivi* of Plautus." *Ramus* 25: 112–45.

Thompson, Lloyd A. 1989. *Romans and Blacks*. Norman: University of Oklahoma Press.

Thompson, Marvin, and **Ruth Thompson**. 1989. "Performance Criticism: From Granville-Barker to Bernard Beckerman and Beyond." In *Shakespeare and the Sense of Performance: Essays in the Tradition of Performance Criticism in Honor of Bernard Beckerman*, ed. Marvin Thompson and Ruth Thompson, pp. 13–23. Newark: University of Delaware Press.

Tierney, J. J. 1947. "The Senatus Consultum de Bacchanalibus." *Proceedings of the Royal Irish Academy* 51, sec. C, no. 5: 89–117.

Tolliver, Hazel M. 1952. "Plautus and the State Gods of Rome." *Classical Journal* 48: 49–57.

Traina, Alfonso. 1954. "De primo Amphitruonis cantico." *Latinitas* 2: 127–32.

Treggiari, Susan. 1969. *Roman Freedmen During the Late Republic*. Oxford: Clarendon.

———. 1991. *Roman Marriage: Iusti Coniuges from the Time of Cicero to the Time of Ulpian*. Oxford: Clarendon.

Trendall, A. D. 1967. *Phylax Vases*. 2d ed. London: Institute of Classical Studies, University of London.

Ubersfeld, Anne. 1981. *L'École du spectateur: Lire le théâtre 2*. Paris: Éditions Sociales.

———. 1982. *Lire le théâtre*. 4th ed., with addenda. Paris: Éditions Sociales.

Usener, Hermann. 1913. *Kleine Schriften*. Vol. 4: *Arbeiten zur Religionsgeschichte*. Leipzig: Teubner.

Ussing, Johan Louis. 1875–92. *Commentarius in Plauti Comoedias*. Copenhagen. Repr. with addenda by Andreas Thierfelder, Hildesheim: Georg Olms, 1972.

Veyne, Paul. 1976. *Le Pain et le cirque: Sociologie historique d'un pluralisme politique*. Paris: Seuil.

———. 1978. "Le Famille et l'amour sous le haut-empire romain." *Annales: Économies, Sociétés, Civilisations* 33: 35–63.

Vogt, Joseph. 1975. *Ancient Slavery and the Ideal of Man*. Translated by Thomas Wiedemann. Cambridge, Mass.: Harvard University Press.

Vogt-Spira, Gregor. 1995. "Plautus und die Überwindung des Stegreifspiels." In Benz, Stärk, and Vogt-Spira 1995, 229–39.

Wagner, Wilhelm. 1864. *De Plauti Aulularia*. Bonn: apud A. Marcum.

Warnecke, B. 1927. "*Ludii barbari.*" *Rheinisches Museum für Philologie* 76: 220–21.

Warning, Rainer. 1976. "Elemente einer Pragmasemiotik der Komödie." In *Das Komische*, ed. Wolfgang Preisendanz and Rainer Warning, pp. 279–333. Munich: Wilhelm Fink.

Watling, E. F., trans. 1965. *Plautus: The Pot of Gold, The Prisoners, The Brothers Menaechmus, The Swaggering Soldier, Pseudolus.* London: Penguin.

Watson, Alan. 1967. *The Law of Persons in the Later Roman Republic.* Oxford: Clarendon.

———. 1987. *Roman Slave Law.* Baltimore: The Johns Hopkins University Press.

Webster, T.B.L. 1970. *Studies in Later Greek Comedy.* 2d ed. New York: Barnes and Noble.

———. 1974. *An Introduction to Menander.* New York: Barnes and Noble.

Welin, Erik. 1953. *Studien zur Topographie des Forum Romanum.* Lund: C.W.K. Gleerup.

Wellesley, K. 1955. "The Production Date of Plautus' *Captivi.*" *American Journal of Philology* 76: 298–305.

Westaway, Katharine Mary. 1917. *The Original Element in Plautus.* Cambridge: Cambridge University Press.

Westermann, William L. 1955. *The Slave Systems of Greek and Roman Antiquity.* Philadelphia: American Philosophical Society.

Weston, Karl E. 1903. "The Illustrated Terence Manuscripts." *Harvard Studies in Classical Philology* 14: 37–54.

Wieand, Helen E. 1920. *Deception in Plautus.* Boston: Richard G. Badger.

Wiedemann, Thomas. 1981. *Greek and Roman Slavery.* Baltimore: The Johns Hopkins University Press.

Wiles, David. 1988a. "Greek Theatre and the Legitimation of Slavery." In *Slavery and Other Forms of Unfree Labour*, ed. Léonie J. Archer, pp. 53–67. London: Routledge.

———. 1988b. "Taking Farce Seriously: Recent Critical Approaches to Plautus." In *Themes in Drama*, vol. 10: *Farce*, ed. James Redmond, pp. 261–71. Cambridge: Cambridge University Press.

———. 1989. "Marriage and Prostitution in Classical New Comedy." In *Themes in Drama*, vol. 11: *Women in Theatre*, ed. James Redmond, pp. 31–48. Cambridge: Cambridge University Press.

———. 1991. *The Masks of Menander: Sign and Meaning in Greek and Roman Performance.* Cambridge: Cambridge University Press.

Willcock, M. M., ed. 1987. *Plautus: Pseudolus.* Oak Park, Ill.: Bolchazy-Carducci.

Wille, Günther. 1967. *Musica Romana: Die Bedeutung der Musik im Leben der Römer.* Amsterdam: Verlag P. Schippers.

Williams, Gordon. 1958a. "Evidence for Plautus' Workmanship in the *Miles Gloriosus.*" *Hermes* 86: 79–105.

———. 1958b. "Some Aspects of Roman Marriage Ceremonies and Ideals." *Journal of Roman Studies* 48: 16–29.

———. 1968. *Tradition and Originality in Roman Poetry.* Oxford: Clarendon.

Williamson, Audrey. 1953. *Gilbert and Sullivan Opera: A New Assessment.* London: Rockliff.

Wiseman, T. P. 1989. "Roman Legend and Oral Tradition." *Journal of Roman Studies* 79: 129–37.

Wissowa, Georg. 1912. *Religion und Kultus der Römer.* Munich: Beck.

Witzmann, Peter. 1964. *Antike Tradition im Werk Bertolt Brechts*. Berlin: Akademie-Verlag.

Wright, John. 1974. *Dancing in Chains: The Stylistic Unity of the Comoedia Palliata*. Rome: American Academy in Rome.

———. 1975. "The Transformations of Pseudolus." *Transactions of the American Philological Association* 105: 403–16.

———. 1982. "Plautus." In *Ancient Writers: Greece and Rome*, vol. 1: *Homer to Caesar*, ed. T. James Luce, pp. 501–23. New York: Charles Scribner's Sons.

Wyke, Maria. 1994. "Woman in the Mirror: The Rhetoric of Adornment in the Roman World." In *Women in Ancient Societies: An Illusion of the Night*, ed. Léonie J. Archer, Susan Fischler and Maria Wyke, pp. 134–51. New York: Macmillan.

Yavetz, Zvi. 1988. *Slaves and Slavery in Ancient Rome*. New Brunswick, N.J.: Transaction Books.

Zagagi, Netta. 1980. *Tradition and Originality in Plautus: Studies of the Amatory Motifs in Plautine Comedy*. Göttingen: Vandenhoeck und Ruprecht.

———. 1994. *The Comedy of Menander: Convention, Variation and Originality*. London: Duckworth.

Zulueta, Francis de. 1953. *The Institutes of Gaius*. Part 2: *Commentary*. Oxford: Clarendon.

Zwierlein, Otto. 1990. *Zur Kritik und Exegese des Plautus I: Poenulus und Curculio*. Stuttgart: Franz Steiner.

———. 1991a. *Zur Kritik und Exegese des Plautus II: Miles gloriosus*. Stuttgart: Franz Steiner.

———. 1991b. *Zur Kritik und Exegese des Plautus III: Pseudolus*. Stuttgart: Franz Steiner.

———. 1992. *Zur Kritik und Exegese des Plautus IV: Bacchides*. Stuttgart: Franz Steiner.

INDEX OF PASSAGES CITED

517–539, 227n.29; 574, 227n.13; 766–
767, 225n.19; 778–779, 14; 778–835,
219n.40; 793–833, 88; 811, 89; 818,
221–222n.45; 863, 109; 888–889, 70;
905, 221–222n.45; 905–956, 966, 70;
1002, 195, 211n.40; 1033, 216n.22;
1029–1036, 70–71; 1034–1036, 18

Cas., 62–64, 165–180; 1–2, 16; 18,
216n.22; 21–22, 205n.16; 25, 221n.40;
25–28, 59, 127; 29, 205n.16; 58,
226n.36; 64–66, 206n.27; 67–78, 20;
71–78, 62–63; 84–86, 141; 87–88,
205n.19; 148, 225n.34; 150–278,
226n.36; 151–162, 225n.34; 227,
223n.27; 246, 207n.12; 303, 207n.11;
323–337, 109; 353–354, 223n.27; 411,
218n.13; 418, 218n.30; 424–436, 39;
490–503, 221n.31; 497–498, 224n.5;
504–514, 39; 652–762, 63–64; 719,
221n.31; 788, 13; 814, 208n.34; 861,
216n.22; 878–902, 29–30, 71; 949–
950, 11, 30, 208n.32; 1006, 14; 1015–
1018, 19–20, 141

Cist., 120–123, 205–206n.26; 145–146,
35; 149–153, 217n.9; 149–202, 109;
150, 205–206n.26; 154–155, 205n.16;
155, 205n.20; 172–173, 227n.23; 175,
158, 223n.27; 188–189, 13; 194, 71;
197–202, 205n.19; 229, 29; 366, 13;
375, 220n.27; 678–681, 30, 153; 782–
783, 206n.27; 782–785, 10; 786–787, 18

Cornicula, frag. 1, 213n.24

Curc., 77, 126–139; 30–48, 219n.6; 65–
66, 205–206n.26; 73–74, 20; 162–212,
219n.6; 188, 207n.12; 269, 222n.52;
280–281, 14; 280–298, 192; 280–304,
219n.40; 301, 30; 356, 207n.9; 462–
486, 131–139, 213n.22; 473, 141; 482,
141; 494–515, 212n.6; 506–511, 59;
508, 221n.40; 518, 227n.23; 590, 30;
591, 216n.22; 591–592, 72, 212n.11;
633, 220n.23; 698, 227n.23

Epid., 37–38, 60–62; 10, 228n.43; 25–
28, 61–62; 59, 61; 81–84, 8, 188,
227n.29; 81–195, 37–38; 88, 228n.35;
93, 188; 98, 227n.29; 121, 221n.45; 125,
221n.32, 226n.44; 173–180, 223n.27;
178–179, 158; 180, 224n.3; 182, 61,
109; 188, 61; 194, 14; 194–195, 192;
199, 221–222n.45; 225–235, 212n.6;
305, 225n.19; 306–307, 60; 319,

220n.25; 343, 61; 373, 228n.35; 375,
228n.35; 376, 205n.24; 398, 208n.30;
501–502, 60–61; 546, 223n.28; 610–
617, 188; 616, 187; 620–647, 127; 665,
205n.24; 666–674, 215n.16; 678, 61;
722–731, 227n.21

Men., 42–43, 1–76, 56–58, 142–143; 2,
216n.34; 3, 21; 4–5, 205n.16; 7,
216n.22; 10, 211n.24; 23, 205n.20; 47,
205n.20; 50, 205n.20; 51–55, 20; 120–
122, 225n.32; 127–134, 158, 207n.8,
223n.27; 128, 20; 159, 158; 208–213,
221n.31; 249, 218n.13; 250–253, 42;
267, 54; 441–444, 42; 446–461, 207n.8;
472, 207n.12; 520, 221n.38; 562–603,
226n.35; 571–589, 27–28, 207n.8; 760,
205n.24; 784–802, 225n.32; 879–881,
30; 902, 211n.28; 977, 218n.13; 1000,
207–208n.14; 1015–1016, 228n.40;
1031–1032, 11, 30; 1160, 223n.27,
224n.2

Merc., 30–35, 164–165; 3–8, 15; 14–15,
205nn.16,17; 31–38, 205n.24; 160,
14; 169, 207n.12; 431–437, 207n.14;
477, 226n.40; 525, 59; 542, 225n.19;
544–554, 207n.8; 556–557, 224n.5;
588, 207n.11; 608, 205n.24; 664, 62;
672–675, 225n.20; 754, 221n.31; 760–
761, 223n.27, 224n.2; 816–829, 164–
165; 851, 13; 985, 118; 1004–1008, 14,
165; 1015–1026, 19; 1017–1024, 141;
1018, 118

Mil., 41, 62, 72–77; 21–24, 207n.8; 79–
80, 16, 205nn.16,17; 81–82, 10, 16; 87,
220n.23; 98, 205n.16; 147, 228n.35;
150, 205n.20; 151, 227n.18; 173,
219n.41; 180, 188; 185–194, 223n.27;
198, 228n.35; 200, 207n.12; 209–213,
73–74; 213, 86, 205–206n.26; 293,
213n.28; 310, 53; 312, 221n.42; 324–
325, 213n.28; 372, 53; 373, 218n.30;
386, 227n.27; 456, 223n.27; 464–465,
223n.27; 464–468, 227n.27; 466,
228n.35; 477, 212n.6; 547, 218n.13;
563–565, 212n.6; 575, 214n.40; 584,
218n.13; 590–591, 213n.28; 596–609,
191; 679–681, 224n.3; 681–700, 159;
693, 221–222n.45; 768, 187; 773,
228n.35; 862, 30; 887–890, 223n.28;
901–919, 218n.15; 991, 1066, 1073,
213n.28; 1087, 228n.35; 1130–1131, 13;

INDEX

Abel, Lionel, 3

actors: as actors, 8–23 (see also license; obsequiousness); as characters, 49, 73 (see also rapport); Greeks as, 10, 56; low status of, 10–12, 18, 22; males as, 120; punishment of, 10–12, 111, 114; slaves as, 10–11, 40, 183, 195–196; three-actor rule, 173; vulnerability of, 9–13, 16, 18, 20, 21, 24, 49, 114

addresses to audience (see also aside; monologues), 8, 23, 33, 36–39, 41, 43–47, 101–103, 117, 119, 142, 145–147, 149–152, 176

adulescens, 29, 30–31, 41, 95–97, 122, 135, 191

adultery, 11, 76–77, 109, 117, 168

age (old vs. young), 19, 33, 165, 167

ambitio, 88, 105

"ambush" scene, 97, 104, 188, 190

anachronism, 52, 53, 211n.32

ancilla, 39, 63, 124, 145–147, 150–151, 153, 155–157, 174–176

applause, request for, 11, 18–19, 71; in Menander, 21

architectus, 75, 112

argentarius, as character, 127, 129, 130–131, 139

argumentum, 205n.18

Aristophanes, 21, 48, 50, 89, 109, 212n.2, 224n.6

aside, 33–44, 47, 85, 88, 102, 115–121, 146–147, 149–150, 152, 156, 168, 172, 174, 187, 204n.3; in Terence, 48

assemblies, Roman, 64, 102–104

Atellan farce, 109

attention: actors' desire for, 12, 16, 20; characters' desire for, 29–32, 49, 56; in Terence, 22

audience: as judges, 13, 16, 103–104; nature of, 9–10, 40–41, 52, 53, 109, 120, 141, 153, 161, 170, 197, 199; power of, over actors, 21, 22, 102, 110, 111; seduction of, 40–41, 49, 77; Terence and, 9–10, 22

augury, language of, 61

Bacchanalian Conspiracy, 142, 177–180

bakers, 136

bankers: as characters (see argentarius); in Rome, 58, 129, 131, 134–136, 138, 139, 144

barbarus, 54, 55, 62, 63–64, 128

basilica, 134, 138

basilicus, 64, 89

battle reports, 115–116

beating. See punishment

Beaumarchais, 50–51

Beckerman, Bernard, 2

binding, of slaves on stage, 186, 188, 190–191, 193, 195

boni homines, 135

Bradley, Keith, 182

Brecht, Bertolt, 2, 3

brevity, importance of, 13–14, 17, 100–101, 165, 179; in Aristophanes, 21

butchers, 136, 139

Caecilius Statius, 9, 207n.3, 217n.2

canalis, 135, 138

Capua, 85, 223n.25

Cato the Elder, 82, 135, 140, 160–162, 199

census, Roman, 13, 228n.50

chains. See binding

challenge to audience's assumptions, 139, 153–157, 166, 179–180, 196, 199–200

characters (see also rapport): as actors, 68–69, 73–76, 86, 87, 97, 98, 100, 215n.15, 218n.35; gods as, 12, 108–125; neediness of, 24; as playwrights, 38, 73, 75–76, 92, 98–99, 121, 176; as spectators, 68–69, 73, 76, 85–86, 142, 146, 151, 176

choragus, 12, 69, 75, 76, 105, 131–139

chronology, Plautine, 21, 51, 105, 224n.15

claques, 10, 114

colony, Roman, 61

comitium, 129, 130, 133, 134, 137

conductor, 87, 105–106

conservatism: in Plautus, 199; in Rome, 82, 88, 162, 180, 199

contumelia, 136

cook, 94, 95, 100, 149

costumes, 1, 3, 12, 69, 75, 76, 95, 100, 110, 114–116, 121, 133, 138, 148, 177, 191

crucifixion, 30, 39, 53

wrights); *currens*, 14, 31, 38, 88, 122, 128, 139, 192

setting, theatricality of, 50, 56–58, 143

severitas, 83

Shakespeare, William, 47, 50–51, 56, 206n.39, 210n.14

shipbuilding metaphor, 75, 213n.28

situation comedies, television, 224n.6

slaves (*see also* actors, slaves as), 40, 66, 118, 129, 141, 181–196; assumed inferiority of, 181–183; in audience, 11, 40, 195–196; as characters (*see ancilla; servus*); clever (*see servus, callidus*); good (*see servus, bonus*); marriages of, 63; running (*see servus, currens*)

social commentary, 22–23, 28, 90, 157, 179–180, 196, 199–201, 229n.4

soldiers: as characters (*see miles gloriosus*); in Rome, 134, 149

soliloquy (*see also* monologue), 204n.3

spectatores, 8, 10, 13, 14, 17, 18, 33, 36, 70, 101, 104, 105, 123, 145–146, 147, 153, 224n.31

spectators. *See* audience

staging/visual effects, 44, 76, 95, 102, 120, 122, 129, 151–152, 164, 168, 177, 186, 195, 208n.29

stock characters (*see also names of character types*), 14, 28, 96–98, 134, 168, 187

subversive elements, 199–200

symbolae, 135

sympathy. *See* rapport

tabernae argentariae, 134, 144

tabernae veteres, 136, 138

Tarentum, 150

teasing, of audience, 15–21, 49, 113, 137–138, 141, 143, 146, 179; in Aristophanes, 21; in New Comedy, 22; in Terence, 22

Temple: Capitoline, 83, 128, 222n.52; of

Castor and Pollux, 136, 137, 222n.52; of Magna Mater, 105–107; (shrine) of Venus Cloacina, 134, 135, 138

Terence, 9–10, 18, 22, 48–49, 205n.21, 210n.3, 228n.33

text, and performance, 1–2

third person, use of, 47, 101, 144

tibicen, 93–94, 99, 175, 190

togata, fabula, 40, 60

topical allusions, 18, 52, 58–59, 130–131, 144, 148–149, 151, 161–162, 178, 194, 208n.26

tragedy, 15, 55, 67, 69, 72, 94, 108–109, 116, 120, 122–124, 182, 207n.1, 211n.32, 217n.8; language of, 80, 97, 116–118, 120, 123–124

tragicomoedia, 113–114

trapezita, 129

triumphs, 17–18, 148–149

triumph speeches, 17–18, 35, 36, 94, 102, 103

Turpio, Lucius Ambivius, 9, 22

uxor dotata, 159–163, 168, 170, 176, 180

vaudeville, 2

Velabrum, 136, 137, 222n.52

Vicus Tuscus, 136

wedding, Roman, 176

Wilde, Oscar, 47

wives: as characters (*see matrona*); in Rome, 159–162, 164

women (*see also* misogyny; prostitutes; wives): in Plautus, 153–157, 158–166, 177–180; in Rome, 83, 141–142, 160–161, 217n.5

Wright, John, 14

youth. *See adulescens*